Development of
British Monetary Orthodoxy

Development of British Monetary Orthodoxy

1797-1875

Frank Whitson Fetter

HARVARD UNIVERSITY PRESS

Cambridge, Massachusetts

1 9 6 5

Distributed in Great Britain by Oxford University Press, London

Publication of this volume has been aided by a grant
from the Ford Foundation

Library of Congress Catalog Card Number 65–11589
Printed in the United States of America

To the Memory of Two Great Teachers

Robert Clarkson Brooks
Swarthmore

Frederick Jackson Turner
Harvard

PREFACE

IN 1797 the Bank of England suspended specie payments and touched off one of the world's historic monetary controversies. Payments were resumed in 1821, but argument continued. From 1797 until 1875, the date of the last Parliamentary investigation of English monetary and banking problems before the First World War, there was an almost continuous discussion of theory and policy. In these years the British debated and decided the main features of pre-1914 orthodoxy: the gold standard; a central bank nominally independent of government, with a virtual monopoly of the note issue, holding a major part of the nation's gold reserve, and prepared to act as a lender of last resort in time of crisis; and other banks, although stripped of the right of issue, virtually unmolested in the creation of deposit currency.

The primary purpose of this book is to explain the interplay of forces in these controversies and in the decisions that were reached. It is not a conventional history of theory, of legislation, or of monetary and banking institutions, although it has much of the material that would be included in such studies. It is written on the assumption that in the growth of monetary orthodoxy there was no simple causation, but that principles were translated into policy within a framework of political and economic institutions and beliefs, and that legislation was the product of a combination of analysis, economic and political climate of opinion, and the influence of personality.

For aid in the research that went into this book, and in its writing, I am indebted to many institutions and persons. A fellowship of the John Simon Guggenheim Memorial Foundation enabled me to spend ten months in England in 1937–38. Haverford College, where I was then teaching, gave me leave to accept the fellowship, and in 1941 a sabbatical to do further research and to write up some of the results. Northwestern University gave me leave in 1954–55 to spend a year in England, and has aided me with grants from the Committee on Research Funds of its graduate school. A grant from the American Philosophical Society assisted me during this second period in England. The Ford Foundation made possible a quarter of leave from my teaching in the spring of 1958, devoted to writing based on earlier research.

A large part of the research was done in the two great economic libraries assembled by Professor Herbert S. Foxwell—the Goldsmiths' Library at the University of London and the Kress Library at the Harvard Graduate School of Business Administration. The courtesies of the staff of these libraries went far beyond what a visitor had any right to expect. The Henry L. Wagner Collection at Yale University was particularly valuable in its many provincial pamphlets, not elsewhere available, which helped to give a feeling of attitudes outside of London on monetary and banking problems. Books, periodicals, and manuscript material at the John Rylands Library in Manchester, the Birmingham Public Libraries, the Liverpool Reference Library, the Newberry Library in Chicago, and the libraries of the Royal Irish Academy in Dublin, the London School of Economics, the University of Birmingham, Harvard University, Northwestern University, the University of Pennsylvania, the University of Chicago, the Hollander Collection at the University of Illinois, and the Seligman Collection at Columbia University helped to fill in the picture, as did manuscript material in the British Museum and in the Public Record Office of Northern Ireland.

To Miss Doris Coates, head of the National Register of Archives in London, I am indebted for putting me in touch with manuscript collections. Some were in libraries, but through the help of Miss Coates I was able to secure permission to consult a number in private hands. I am indebted to Major Quintin E. Gurney, of Bawdeswell Hall, Norfolk, for permission to examine the papers of Hudson Gurney and to quote from his diary; to Mr. David Holland for making available papers of Spencer Perceval; to Mr. Dudley Perceval for permission to consult papers of Spencer Perceval on deposit at the National Register of Archives; to Lt. Col. A. H. Spottiswoode for permission to consult papers of John Charles Herries on deposit at the National Register of Archives; to Major Simon Whitbread of Southill, Bedford, for permission to consult the papers of Samuel Whitbread; and to Lord Congleton for bringing to the National Register of Archives, and allowing me to examine there, papers of Sir Henry Parnell, later first Lord Congleton. The courtesy of Mr. E. M. Forster in making available to me the papers of his great-grandfather Henry Thornton, made a visit to his rooms at King's College, Cambridge, a delightful personal experience as well as an informative research journey. Lady Eleanor Langman, the grandniece of Francis Horner, gave me access to his papers, which have since been deposited at the London School of Economics. The Manchester Chamber of Commerce and the Bank of

Ireland permitted me to examine manuscript material, and the Edinburgh Chamber of Commerce and Manufactures and the Glasgow Chamber of Commerce furnished me with copies of their minutes relating to the Bank Acts of 1844 and 1845. The opportunity to examine the records of the Bank of England for the years 1791–1832 added much to an understanding of the events of those years. To these persons, and to the officials of these institutions, I am grateful.

I am indebted to the Royal Economic Society and to Mr. Piero Sraffa for permission to quote from *The Works and Correspondence of David Ricardo* (Cambridge, 1951–1955); to George Allen & Unwin, Ltd., for permission to quote from Henry Thornton's *Enquiry into the Nature and Effects of the Paper Credit of Great Britain*, edited by F. A. Hayek (London, 1939); and to Macmillan and Co., Ltd., for permission to quote from *The Journal of Mrs. Arbuthnot: 1820–1832*, edited by Francis Bamford and the Duke of Wellington (London, 1950).

Professor Arthur H. Cole, formerly librarian of the Baker Library of the Harvard Graduate School of Business Administration, has helped me as friend, adviser, and librarian. Professor Jacob Viner has given me wise counsel and the benefit of his wide knowledge of English economics. Mr. Piero Sraffa, editor of Ricardo's *Works*, has answered many inquiries about the Ricardian period. My colleagues at Northwestern University, Professor Harold F. Williamson and Professor Franklin S. Scott, read an earlier draft of this book, and I have benefited from their comments. To Mr. J. Keith Horsefield of the International Monetary Fund, and to Professor R. S. Sayers of the London School of Economics, I am indebted for stimulating suggestions that have developed out of our exchanges of ideas, and for painstaking and searching criticism of earlier drafts.

F. W. F.

Northwestern University
July 1964

CONTENTS

Development of
British Monetary Orthodoxy

ABBREVIATIONS

C.B.   Court Book, Bank of England
C.T.   Committee of the Treasury, Minute Book, Bank of England
P.P.   Parliamentary Papers

I

THE MONETARY AND BANKING WORLD
OF 1797

IN 1797 there was in England no generally accepted theory of a monetary
and banking system. There were only laws and institutions, inadequate
and in some cases inconsistent. The two decades before 1797, despite
the economic growth of the country and the expansion of banking, had
been almost devoid of any fundamental analysis of the monetary standard,
of banking theory, or of the position of the Bank of England. The suspension of specie payments by the Bank of England on February 27, 1797, and
similar action by the Bank of Ireland a few days later, precipitated a controversy that continued for over three quarters of a century. Out of this
controversy developed most of the principles of monetary and banking
orthodoxy, not only of England but of virtually the entire Western world
in the forty years before 1914.

Gold or Silver Standard

Previous to 1666 the Mint had coined both gold and silver for the public,
but at frequently changing ratios, and subject to the payment of Mint
charges. Under legislation of 1666 "for encouraging of coinage" [1] all such
charges were abolished, thus in effect establishing free and unlimited
coinage of gold and silver. Silver was used more than gold up to the end
of the seventeenth century. John Locke and William Lowndes in their
debate in 1695 over recoinage agreed that silver was generally considered
to be the monetary standard; but gold, particularly after the bad state of the
silver coinage during the Protectorate, had come increasingly to be used for
larger payments. The widespread use of gold dates from the coinage of
guineas in 1663, which by the proclamation of that year were to pass at
20 shillings. Guineas, by the custom of merchants, soon were generally
accepted at a higher rate, corresponding roughly to the current market

[1] 18 Car. II, c. 5.

price of gold in terms of underweight silver coin. By 1694 the guinea passed current at around 22s. and for a brief period in 1695 at 30s.[2]

Following the provisions in 1696 for coinage of new silver to replace clipped and worn coin,[3] Parliament fixed the maximum price of the guinea at 22s.[4] Later administrative orders set 21s.6d. as the maximum price at which guineas would be received in payment of taxes, and they were generally accepted in private transactions at the same rate. Gold came to be used increasingly in payments, and within a few years after 1696 England was close to a *de facto* gold standard. The price consequences of using gold rather than silver as the standard were virtually nil, however, in view of the narrow range of fluctuations of the gold-silver ratio. After Sir Isaac Newton's recommendations of 1717, made in response to a request from The Lords Commissioners of His Majesty's Revenue as to "what method may be best for preventing the melting down of the silver coyn," a proclamation set the maximum price of the guinea at 21s. The intention of Newton's recommendation was to preserve silver, along with gold, as a standard at a time when the official rating of gold in relation to silver, together with a public preference for the more convenient gold coins, was keeping silver out of circulation.[5] The effect, however, was to ensure a *de facto* gold standard.

The slight overvaluation of gold at the 21s. rate became greater within a few years as a consequence of a rise in the market value of silver in relation to gold. Not only was little silver brought to the Mint, but soon all but badly worn silver coins went out of circulation. Throughout the eighteenth century the shortage of silver coin and the condition of the existing circulation were a subject of continual complaint. Yet no author, to my knowledge, came out before 1797 with a specific recommendation to demonetize silver. This situation may have reflected a failure of organized thought to keep up with monetary changes that had in fact been accepted by business practice, but it is also possible that it was the result of the

---

[2] J. Keith Horsefield, *British Monetary Experiments: 1650–1710* (London, 1960), discusses this situation in chapters 7 and 8, and gives the quotation of the guinea in 1694–1696 in table C, pp. 254–255.

[3] A detailed analysis of the controversy over the recoinage is given in Horsefield, chs. 3–6; a shorter account is in A. E. Feavearyear, *The Pound Sterling: A History of English Money*, 2d ed. (London, 1963), ch. 6.

[4] 7 & 8 Will. III, c. 19.

[5] For fuller discussion of Newton's relation to the currency question see G. Findley Shirras and J. H. Craig, "Sir Isaac Newton and the Currency," *Economic Journal*, LV, 217–241 (June–September 1945); Sir John Craig, *Newton at the Mint* (Cambridge, 1946); Sir John Craig, *The Mint: A History of the London Mint from A.D. 287 to 1948* (Cambridge, 1953), ch. 12.

public attitude toward fiduciary silver coins. Debasement of coins by government had for centuries been such an abuse that any idea of fiduciary silver coins undoubtedly would have aroused widespread opposition on the ground that it was a form of debasement. The closest approach to a proposal for fiduciary silver came from Adam Smith, who suggested a reduction in the specie content of silver coins as a remedy for the "inconveniency" of the melting of silver coin as a result of the undervaluation of silver.[6] However, the tentative nature of Smith's suggestion, and the lack of any contemporary support of what seems so reasonable in the light of later monetary theory and history, point to the strength of the prevailing conviction that all silver coins should be full weight.

I find practically no mention in any literature of the century before 1797 of the idea that figured in discussions for a few years before and after the resumption of 1821, and was so prominent in the bimetallic controversy in the last quarter of the nineteenth century: that one metal would give more stable prices than would the other, or that the use of two metals as a standard would give greater price stability than would a single gold standard or silver standard. This failure to consider the possible deflationary effects of a monometallic standard is surprising, in view of the discussion by many writers of the seventeenth and eighteenth centuries as to England's supply of the precious metals. Apparently writers with mercantilist leanings were so concerned with the narrower problem of securing gold and silver from other nations that they rarely asked the more fundamental question of the world-wide adequacy of gold or silver to serve as a monetary standard. Locke's remark, "Riches do not consist in having more gold and silver, but in having more in proportion than the rest of the world, or than our neighbours,"[7] illustrates this, but others, both before and after, expressed essentially the same idea.

On the other hand, one might have expected that philosophers like Hume and Smith, with their emphasis on economic growth and freedom from the mercantilist bias about precious metals, would have shown concern about the adequacy of the world supply of gold and silver. That they did not is possibly due to the same situation that appears to explain the mercantilists' lack of concern. Hume and Smith concentrated their attention on attempting to show that the supply needed for monetary purposes

---

[6] *An Inquiry into the Nature and the Causes of the Wealth of Nations,* ed. Edwin Cannan (London. 1904), I, 46.

[7] *Considerations of the Consequences of the Lowering of Interest, and Raising the Value of Money* (London, 1692), reprinted in *The Works of John Locke* (London, 1823), V, 13.

would come in the ordinary course of trade, as opposed to the mercantilist view that special action was necessary to that end.

Specie Movements and Exchange Rates

The mercantilist controversy over government policy toward the outflow of the precious metals had led, in the middle of the seventeenth century, to a working compromise that goes far to explain the futility of many of the debates over monetary and banking policy during the Restriction period after 1797. Legislation of 1663[8] had permitted the export of foreign gold and silver coin and bullion, but did not change the prohibitions on the melting of full-weight British coin and on the export of British coin or of any bullion melted from such coin. Thomas Mun, in *England's Treasure by Forraign Trade*—written around 1630 but not published until 1664—had suggested some relation between the monetary supply, prices, and the state of the foreign exchanges. The first extended analysis of the process of international adjustment came from Isaac Gervaise in *The System or Theory of the Trade of the World* (London, 1720),[9] in which he considered the effects both of income changes and of price changes. David Hume's presentation in 1752[10] of a self-adjusting international balance through price changes, brought about by changes in the monetary supply, lacked the sophistication of Gervaise's presentation, but reached a much larger audience, both of contemporaries and of succeeding generations. However, even Hume's forceful statement of the idea that the forces of the market, and not regulation, were the means by which a country's monetary supply was protected brought no change in existing legislation.

The British monetary system in the eighteenth century, despite the restrictions on melting and export, behaved in a way suggestive of the gold standard as the late nineteenth and the early twentieth century knew it, with exchange rates with other countries on a metallic standard stabilized within narrow limits. This was due partly to the existence in England of substantial stocks of foreign coin and bullion, but probably even more to smuggling, or to regarding lightly a false oath, when the exchanges turned against England. The result was the inconsistency of legislation

[8] 15 Car. II, c. 7.

[9] Gervaise's publication of 1720 has been reprinted with an Introduction by J. M. Letiche and a Foreword by Jacob Viner (Baltimore, 1954). J. M. Letiche discusses Gervaise's analysis in "Isaac Gervaise on the International Mechanism of Adjustment," *Journal of Political Economy*, LX, 34–43 (February 1952).

[10] "Of the Balance of Trade," in *Political Discourses* (Edinburgh, 1752), reprinted in *Early Economic Thought*, ed. A. E. Monroe (Cambridge, 1930), pp. 323–338.

which if strictly enforced placed virtually no limit on the depreciation of the pound in terms of foreign currencies at the same time that there was a general acceptance by bankers and merchants of London of the idea that in practice British gold was exported when the exchanges were unfavorable, and that hence there were "normal" limits on the depreciation of the pound on the foreign exchanges.

The legal facts are clear, but the economic significance is not. In the years before 1797 many criticisms of the prohibition on the melting and export of coin leave the reader in doubt as to whether the argument was simply that the law was arbitrary and that hence it was to be expected that it would be evaded; whether it was that the law was so generally evaded that the result for the exchanges and for credit policy was practically the same as if there were free export of specie; or whether it was that the law was evaded when the profit was sufficiently great.

Some critics, like Hume[11] and Adam Smith,[12] who were concerned primarily with policy, and particularly with the removal of the restraints of the mercantile system, stressed the evasion of the law, without, however, stating that the law had no effect. Those more concerned with the details of trade gave greater attention to the effect of the prohibition. William Petyt in 1680 said that "upon the going out of an *East-India Fleet*" the price of silver rose from 5*s*. to 5*s*.4*d*., which "must cause our weighty Coin to be melted into Bullion, and so exported as it hath been noted. And upon like occasions 'tis observable, that Guinnies rise to 22*s*. apiece, & broad Gold to 24*s*. apiece, which does evince, that those who use that Trade do not confine themselves to Bullion."[13] Many others, including John Locke,[14] Sir Isaac Newton,[15] and the author of the article "Ballance of Trade" in Malachy Postlethwayt's *Universal Dictionary of Trade and Commerce*,[16] developed the same idea, that coin went to the melting pot or was illegally exported when it reached a sufficient premium, and that this premium varied, depending on the supplies of legally exportable coin and bullion and on the vigilance of law enforcement.

[11] "Of the Balance of Trade," p. 323: "These prohibitions serve to no other purpose, than to raise the exchange against them, and produce a still greater exportation."

[12] *Wealth of Nations*, I, 322: "But having no employment at home, it [money] will, in spite of all laws and prohibitions, be sent abroad."

[13] *Britannia Languens* (London, 1680), p. 149.

[14] *Further Considerations concerning raising the Value of Money* (London, 1695), reprinted in *Works*, V, 183–184.

[15] "Report of 1717 on State of the Gold and Silver Coin," reprinted in William A. Shaw, *Select Tracts and Documents Illustrative of English Monetary History, 1626–1730* (London, 1896); reprint of 1934, pp. 166–171.

[16] Second ed. (London, 1757), pp. 187–188.

There thus existed before 1797 a real but unresolved conflict between the law and economic realities, and the economic realities did not conform to any neat and clear-cut logic. This situation goes far to explain the futility of much of the debate after 1797 as to whether the British pound was depreciated. By the tests of the gold standard, as the world knew it in 1914, the pound was depreciated; but both law and experience were on the side of those who defended the Bank Restriction on the ground that it had never been British law to permit the export of gold or silver coin to bolster the exchanges, and that even violations of the law had not made the exchanges behave as they would have had there been no restrictions on melting and export.

Banking Organization

The Bank of England, which had been established in 1694 primarily as an agency of government finance, in 1797 enjoyed a monopoly of joint-stock banking in England. Banks with six partners or less operated both in London and the provinces. As a matter of practice the London private banks had by 1797 ceased to issue notes, but outside of the immediate neighborhood of London notes of private country banks made up almost the entire paper circulation. In Scotland the three chartered banks—the Bank of Scotland, the Royal Bank of Scotland, and the British Linen Bank—and private banks, in addition to carrying on a deposit business, issued notes whose circulation was limited to Scotland. The Bank of Ireland was the only joint-stock bank in Ireland, but private banks, both in Dublin and the interior, issued notes and carried on a deposit business, and the notes of these private banks also had some circulation in Dublin. All banks were required to redeem their notes in coin.

Bank Credit and the Monetary Supply

Until the Bank Restriction, with the exception of a few pamphlets in the 1790's, there was no organized discussion of the relation of bank credit to the total money supply, or of the national problems raised by the growth of banking. As is true with so many economic institutions, banking as a creator of money supply, as distinguished from banking as a middleman between lenders and borrowers, developed well in advance of any theory of the nature and effects of bank credit. In their origins the English private banks were not monetary institutions, but were institutions for the safeguard of specie and the bringing together of borrowers and lenders. The evolution of banking from the early goldsmiths' receipt of deposits and issue of notes against which a 100 per cent reserve was held, to the mid-nineteenth century situation of England, in which an overwhelming proportion of total payments was made by the transfer of bank liabilities, either bank notes or deposit currency, equal to many times the country's specie supply, emerged out of the convenience of business and the desire of banks to make profits. The explanation of what was taking place, and the changes in public opinion and in law necessary to regulate these private banking institutions in a larger public interest, came later. The Bank of England had been organized to meet the financial needs of government rather than to carry out the functions of a modern central bank.

The little discussion of banking theory before Adam Smith was largely incidental to a treatment of other issues.[17] There was no integrated and accepted banking theory, and views ranged all the way from the idea that bankers were legalized counterfeiters to embryonic versions of the "real bills" doctrine that as long as banks confined their lending to "sound security" they could not overissue or cause a price inflation.

John Law and the Theory of Banking

The closest approach to a theory of banking before Adam Smith's discussion is found in John Law.[18] He claimed that notes could not be overissued as long as they did not exceed the money value of their collateral. His emphasis was on land as collateral, but the basic theoretical point was not the land basis of the currency; it was the relation of the note issue to the market price of a productive asset. The essence of Law's banking theory is given in this omnibus passage:

What I shall propose, is to make Money of Land equal to its Value; and that Money to be equal in Value to Silver Money, and not liable to fall in Value as Silver Money falls . . . This Paper Money will keep its Value, and there will always be as much Money as there is Occasion or Imployment for, and no more . . . Since it is very practicable to make Land Money, it would be contrary to Reason to limit the Industry of the People, by making it depend on a Species

[17] A treatment of the fragments of banking theory before Adam Smith is in Lloyd W. Mints, *A History of Banking Theory in Great Britain and the United States* (Chicago, 1945), chs. 2 and 3. Horsefield, *British Monetary Experiments,* ch. 19, deals with the banking ideas of the 1690's.

[18] Law's works have been edited, with an Introduction, by Professor Paul Harsin of the University of Liége: *John Law. Oeuvres Complètes,* 3 vols. (Paris, 1934). Most of Law's writings were in French, but his most famous publication, and the one that gives the fullest statement of his monetary theory, was *Money and Trade Considered; with a Proposal for Supplying the Nation with Money* (Edinburgh, 1705). All page references are to the second edition of 1720.

is not in our Power, but in the Power of our Enemies; when we have a Species of our own every way more qualified.[19]

Law had some penetrating analysis, well ahead of his time, of the effect of monetary expansion in a single country, or the demonetization of silver, which he assumed to be the monetary standard, upon the purchasing power of silver.

Suppose Silver to be no more us'd as Money in *Europe,* its Quantity would be the same, and the Demand for it much lesser, which might lower it two Thirds or more; for besides that the Demand would be less, its Uses as Plate, *&c.* are not near as necessary, as that of Money. . . .

If *England* set up a Money of another kind, Silver will not fall to one Third, because used in other places as Money; but the lesser Demand besides the ordinary Fall from the greater Quantity coming into *Europe,* would occasion an extraordinary Fall perhaps of 10 *per Cent.* If the new Money then in *England* did not encrease beyond the Demand for it, it would keep its Value, and be equal to so much more Silver at home or abroad than it was coin'd for; as Silver would be of less Value, from the ordinary and extraordinary Fall.[20]

Banking Theory between John Law and Adam Smith

Between John Law and Adam Smith there were many references to banking. However, with the exception of some passages in Richard Cantillon's essay on the nature of commerce of 1755, no organized discussion attempted to interpret the significance of banking in expanding the monetary supply to keep pace with the expansion of production, analyze the inflationary potential in banking, or consider the effect of bank credit in a single country upon the world-wide level of prices. Cantillon appears to have been the first to expound an idea, which figured prominently in English discussion between 1793 and 1844, that the issue of notes by financially weak banks led to occasional violent contractions of the note issues because of loss of public faith in money issued by individual banks.[21]

Sir James Steuart's long discussion of banking was largely descriptive. He spoke in glowing terms of the accomplishments of Law's bank, although he gave little analysis of the economic significance of bank operations.[22] Steuart's favorable attitude toward Law is the exception. In general the collapse of Law's ambitious projects put a shadow of suspicion over all banks, and probably explains the lukewarm attitude toward banking in England throughout most of the eighteenth century. Hume, with all his

---

[19] *Money and Trade,* pp. 68, 72, 95.

[20] *Money and Trade,* pp. 59–60.

[21] *Essai sur la nature du commerce en général* (London, 1755), ed. Henry Higgs (London, 1931), p. 311.

[22] *An Inquiry into the Principles of Political Economy* (London, 1767), bk. IV, pt. ii.

sympathy for the rising industrialism and his interest in economic growth, was critical of banks on the ground that they raised prices and drove specie out of the country. His position symbolizes a conflict, which appears in a number of isolated passages from 1700 to 1797, between the idea that banking simply increases prices—the Irving Fisher effect—and the view that it only increases production and employment—the Keynes effect. Hume, after discussing the relation of prices to the ability to sell abroad, said: "This had made me entertain a doubt concerning the benefit of *banks* and *paper-credit,* which are so generally esteemed advantageous to every nation. . . . And in this view, it must be allowed, that no bank could be more advantageous, than such a one as locked up all the money it received, and never augmented the circulating coin, as is usual, by returning part of its treasure into commerce."[23]

Yet shortly after this discussion, which apparently attached only price effects to an expansion of bank money, came this oft-quoted passage: "Accordingly we find, that, in every kingdom, into which money begins to flow in greater abundance than formerly every thing takes a new face: labour and industry gain life; the merchant becomes more enterprising, the manufacturer more diligent and skilful, and even the farmer follows his plow with greater alacrity and attention."[24]

Adam Smith and the Theory of Commercial Banking

Adam Smith gave the first organized analysis of banking since John Law, but showed a greater familiarity with its details, and an underlying conservatism that was lacking in Law's work. It is possible that much of what Smith wrote was novel only in its formal exposition, and that from his association with the merchants and bankers of Glasgow he had absorbed an oral tradition that had never been presented in written form.[25] His discussion of banking was marked by three main points relevant to the English monetary and banking controversy after 1797: (1) development of the "real bills" doctrine, with emphasis on short-term paper as the basis of bank credit, but all within the limits of specie convertibility; (2) assumption that banking operations in a single country with a convertible currency have no effect on prices in other countries; and (3) failure to assign to the Bank of England any special significance as the holder of reserves of other banks.

[23] "Of Money" (1752), reprinted in *David Hume: Writings on Economics,* ed. Eugene Rotwein (London, 1955), pp. 35–36.

[24] "Of Money," p. 37.

[25] Smith's discussion of banking is in *Wealth of Nations,* I, 276–312.

It is curious that Smith, whose interest in economics centered on growth, had a static theory of banking. He discussed inconvertible paper only as something to be avoided. He disapproved of the paper money issues of the American colonies, in contrast to his generally sympathetic view toward their economic aspirations. With the sternness of a Scottish covenanter he spoke of the colonial actions as "a scheme of fraudulent debtors to cheat their creditors." [26] Smith was never specific on the point, later so prominent in the bullion controversy and in the debate between the currency school and the banking school, whether, if a bank followed the "real bills" test of bank credit, it could ever cause an overexpansion of the means of payment. Smith's analysis was all within the framework of convertibility, so that the question whether occasional misjudgment might lead to temporary overexpansion of a convertible money supply was really of little significance, in contrast with inconvertibility, where the "real bills" test rests on the assumption that there can never be overexpansion of the monetary supply from bank advances of the proper type.

In the light of modern banking theory, particularly as influenced by Keynesian thought, which stresses the importance of banks in expanding the money supply to keep pace with—or to make possible—expansion of the physical volume of business without a deflation of prices, there is a temptation to read into Smith's picture of the benefits of banking more than is really there. Smith was forward-looking in most of his treatment of economic problems, but in his analysis and defense of banking he took a narrow view that looked to the past. In Smith's presentation bank notes did not increase the total money supply, they simply permitted the substitution of paper for coin. Basically his defense of banking had no relation to the monetary supply; it was essentially the argument of the twentieth century advocates of the gold-exchange standard for a country of limited resources—it could turn part of its specie supply to the acquisition of products from abroad, and hence tie up less national capital in the monetary system. Smith, unlike John Law, did not consider the possibility that export of specie, as a result of bank expansion in England, might raise prices in other countries and thus lead to an increase of English prices even though the country remained on the specie standard. He referred to the Bank of England as "the greatest Bank of circulation in Europe," but made no mention of it as a holder of the reserves of other banks or as a lender of last resort. His emphasis was on the Bank's financial operations for the government, and he described it as "a great engine of state."

[26] *Wealth of Nations*, I, 309.

Smith also hinted at the idea, which has appeared recurrently in monetary literature ever since, of the inherent dangers in any system of fractional reserve banking: "The commerce and industry of the country, however, it must be acknowledged, though they may be somewhat augmented, cannot be altogether so secure, when they are thus, as it were, suspended upon the Daedalian wings of paper money, as when they travel about upon the solid ground of gold and silver. Over and above the accidents to which they are exposed from the unskillfulness of the conductors of this paper money, they are liable to several others, from which no prudence or skill of those conductors can guard them."[27] On balance, however, Smith approved the principle of fractional reserve banking, however much he might criticize the excesses of individual banks.

New Problems in a Wartime Setting

From the publication of *The Wealth of Nations* in 1776 until the commercial crisis of 1793, which followed close on the outbreak of war with France, monetary and banking controversy were placed in the background by the problems of the American Revolution, the French Revolution, the slave trade, and the growing agitation for Parliamentary reform. In the decade before 1793 there was a great increase in the number of country banks—probably at least a doubling[28]—but there was virtually no discussion of the significance of this growth in the sources of the money supply. There was no great bank failure like that of the Ayr Bank in 1772, which undoubtedly had colored what Adam Smith wrote on banking; there were no significant price changes; and there were no fluctuations in the ratio of gold and silver sufficient to cause a re-examination of the monetary standard. The condition of the silver coin was already so bad that there does not seem to have been public concern as it became even worse. What little was written, or said in Parliament, on monetary and banking questions was in large part incidental to discussion of the public debt. There were a few criticisms of private banking, with recurrence of such phrases as "paper mint" and "private coinage of paper,"[29] which writers of the

---

[27] *Wealth of Nations,* I, 304.

[28] L. S. Pressnell, *Country Banking in the Industrial Revolution* (Oxford, 1956), pp. 6–11, summarizes the evidence on the growth of country banking in this period. Sir Francis Baring, *Observations on the Establishment of the Bank of England* (London, 1797), pp. 15–19, discussed the increase in country banks between the failure of the Ayr Bank and the crisis of 1793.

[29] John Gray, *An Essay Concerning the Establishment of a National Bank in Ireland* (Dublin, 1779), pp. 17, 55; Thomas Paine, *Prospects on the War and Paper Currency* (London, 1793), p. 50. Paine's work was first published in 1787 with the title *Prospects on the Rubicon.*

next half century were to re-echo. A rumor that the Bank of Scotland and the Royal Bank of Scotland were to come under common ownership produced two Edinburgh pamphlets in 1778; at least one pamphlet was written in 1781 on the renewal of the Bank of England's charter; and agitation that led to the establishment of the Bank of Ireland in 1783 was the occasion for several pamphlets. The Bank's problems of 1782 and 1783, although they sound impressive when written up by a historian with access to Bank records,[30] did not stimulate either pamphleteering or Parliamentary discussion.

The political and social issues of the French Revolution so dominated English interest in events across the Channel that the economic aspects of the assignats seem to have been virtually unnoticed, although Parliament in 1792 prohibited their circulation in England.[31] The outbreak of war with France in February 1793 found the British public unprepared, either from first-hand experience or from discussion, to appraise the problems of wartime monetary expansion, inconvertible paper money, and disordered exchanges. The long period of virtual demonetization of the historic silver standard, and the loosely enforced but still economically significant prohibition on the melting and export of British coin, had created a *de facto* monetary situation that did not fit into a neat pattern. It is small wonder that in the next quarter century there was room for honest difference of opinion as to what the standard had been before the Restriction, or what respect for tradition, made even more dear to the governing classes by the events of the French Revolution, called for in monetary law and practice.

The outbreak of war was followed within a month by one of the worst financial and commercial crises that England had experienced up to that time. The bankruptcies included a number of banks and substantial commercial houses,[32] but the crisis, if we accept Thomas Tooke's judgment—and the available evidence seems to bear him out—had its origin in a situation existing before the outbreak of war.[33] There was no suspension of specie payments by the Bank, and no evidence of loss of confidence in its notes as compared with gold. Its circulation increased from barely £11.5 million in the latter part of February to over £13 million in late March and early April, but by June was again down to less than £11.2 million.[34] There are no data on the changes in the Bank's outstanding

---

[30] Sir John Clapham, *The Bank of England: A History* (Cambridge, 1945), I, 252–256.

[31] 32 Geo. III, c. 61.

[32] Pressnell gives in app. 28, pp. 546–547, Henry Thornton's partial estimate as of March 7, 1793, of the bankruptcies. The original is in the Chatham Papers, Public Record Office/30/8/183.

[33] *A History of Prices* (London, 1838), I, 176–177.

[34] See "Note on Bank of England Statistics and Records to 1832," at the end of this chapter.

credit or in its bullion in the weeks between February 28, before the crisis broke, and August 31, after it was over, but in that half year bullion increased from £4,010,680 to £5,322,010, and total credit fell from £16,005,250 to £14,809,680. The exchanges were bringing in specie from abroad. Insofar as the public turned to the Bank for gold, this seems to have been to supply the place of the notes of closed banks, to furnish gold to those who preferred it to country bank notes, or to increase the specie reserve of country banks as a protection against threatened runs.

The events of 1793 raised no problems of price movements and the exchanges, but they did provide a trial run on a related problem that loomed large in nineteenth century debate: the responsibility of the Bank of England in time of crisis. The widespread bankruptcies involved a director of the Bank of England, and almost engulfed Sir James Sanderson, a member of Parliament and Lord Mayor of London, to whom the Bank made a loan because of "the mischief and alarm that must ensue if Sir James Sanderson in the present station he filled of Lord Mayor of London should stop payment." [35]

The Bank's records, despite what they reveal on individual credits, are silent as to its policy in the early weeks of the crisis. They do not tell to what extent it regarded the crisis as something in which it had no responsibility, other than maintaining its own solvency and perhaps strengthening its relative position by inaction while its more irresponsible rivals reaped the harvest of their folly, and to what extent it acted as a lender of last resort. Certain facts are clear, however. The Bank's credits in March 1793 may have saved individual merchants, but the crisis continued. On April 22 a delegation from the City of London met with Pitt, the Prime Minister, who suggested an issue of Exchequer bills. The following day an *ad hoc* committee of eleven leaders in the City, of whom the chairman was the Lord Mayor, so recently saved from failure by the Bank, and four others were Bank directors, urged "that an issue of Exchequer Bills, under certain regulations and stipulations, was the best practicable remedy." [36] The House of Commons then appointed a Select Committee on the Present State of Commercial Credit. The committee held hearings, and on April 29 recommended an issue, by a board of

---

[35] C.T., 1, March 21 and 25, 1793; Clapham, I, 259–265, gives an account of the crisis and some of the houses and persons involved. However, as a result of misreading the Bank's record, his account underplays the seriousness of the Lord Mayor's plight. Clapham says that the Lord Mayor "was promised £6000 on 21 March, and more on the quarter-day," whereas the original discount was £60,000, and the "further assistance of a discount" on March 25, 1793, was £57,000.

[36] *Committee on Commercial Credit*, 1793, p. 5. The report was also printed in *The Parliamentary History of England*, XXX, 739–755, April 29, 1793.

commissioners, of Exchequer bills not in excess of 50 per cent of the value of "goods" or "such personal securities of a given number of persons as shall be satisfactory to the Commissioners." It said in support of its recommendation:

If the present distress were confined in its effects to individuals, however they might regret the extent of private calamity, they should not consider the case as justifying an extraordinary public interposition; much less should they recommend such a measure, if the pressure had been felt only by houses of doubtful credit, or who had suffered from the consequences of rash and unwarrantable speculations; but it appears to Your Committee, that the embarrassments arising from the want of credit, have already affected houses of undoubted solidity and sufficient ultimate resources; and that there is too much reason to apprehend that these embarrassments may extend in a degree which no individual exertions can counteract, with sufficient expedition and certainty, to prevent consequences of the most serious national importance.[37]

Clapham's suggestion that, although we do not know whose the plan was, "It sounds like a Bank plan," is plausible.[38] Neither in the committee's summary of the evidence nor in its report is there a mention of the Bank, but in several contemporary pamphlets[39] and in both Houses of Parliament the Bank was criticized for its failure to act in support of the market. The most outspoken of the critics said: "Trustees of a great trading company, instituted not less for the public good than for private emolument, it might have been expected that they would have stept into the breach, and have given the weak and wounded individual time to escape, at least with life . . . Instead . . . the directors pusillanimously led the way in the general discomfiture, or were active only in enriching themselves from the spoils of those who had fallen in the struggle."[40]

In the Commons debate that followed immediately upon the report of the Parliamentary committee, Charles James Fox, leader of the Whig opposition, said that "he would wish to know, why the Bank of England should not do what is now proposed by them? It was their interest to use their money to advantage; and he had no doubt it would be their wish to support general credit."[41] In the Lords critics were equally vocal, but no

---

[37] *Committee on Commercial Credit*, 1793, p. 7.

[38] *Bank of England*, I, 263.

[39] *Thoughts upon the Commercial Bill* (London, 1793), pp. 14–18; *Reflections on the Causes which have Produced the Present Distress in Commercial Credit* (London, 1793), pp. 10–11; [William Roscoe], *Thoughts on the Causes of the Present Failures* (London, 1793), p. 20; Colbert, Jr. (pseud.), *The Age of Paper*, 2d ed. (London, 1793).

[40] [Roscoe], *Thoughts on the Causes of the Present Failures*, p. 20.

[41] *Parliamentary Register*, XXXV, 319, April 29, 1793. Similar suggestions were made by Charles Grey (p. 321), and two days later by William Adam (p. 344).

more successful than in the Commons. That perennial Cassandra of the economic situation of England, the eighth Earl of Lauderdale, and Lord Rawdon raised the same objection as had Fox, that the Bank and not the Government should support the market in time of crisis.[42] Questions and criticism came largely from opposition members, who were in a mood to oppose any proposals of Government, but their queries were pertinent and their criticism valid in the light of subsequent ideas as to what a central bank should do in such a situation. Samuel Thornton, a Bank director and a member of the committee of eleven that had proposed the Exchequer bills, in supporting the legislation in Parliament defended the Bank against the charge that it and not the Government should have come to the support of the market, on the narrow ground that the Bank was not accustomed to making the type of advances needed in the crisis.[43] The legislation was passed on May 8, 1793.[44]

In addition to the emergency circulating medium provided by Exchequer bills, the crisis was also eased by an action, unique in British monetary history, of the issue of circulating notes by the Corporation of Liverpool.[45] The crisis was particularly severe in this second port of the British Isles. Following a meeting of March 20, called by the mayor after a petition from local merchants, a delegation went to London and requested, without success, a loan from the Bank on the pledge of the Corporation. The Liverpool spokesmen then petitioned Parliament for the right to issue negotiable notes. On May 10, three days after authorization of the Exchequer bills, legislation was passed to permit an issue by Liverpool of notes up to £300,000.[46]

The sequence of events suggests legislative jockeying and a close connection between the Liverpool issues, the issue of Exchequer bills, and the policy of the Bank of England, and a story that may be revealed in full by some private papers as yet unworked by economists. The maximum issue of Liverpool bills was £68,510, and of Exchequer bills £2,202,000— both sums well below the Parliamentary authorization. The operations

---

[42] Parliamentary Register, XXXVI, 205–208, May 7, 1793.

[43] Parliamentary Register, XXXV, 322, April 29, 1793. Thornton had previously said much the same thing in connection with the petition from Liverpool for an expansion of credit (pp. 209–210, April 11, 1793).

[44] 33 Geo. III, c. 29.

[45] For this account of the Liverpool issue I have drawn on, in addition to the Parliamentary record, C. K. Gonner, "Municipal Bank Notes in Liverpool, 1793–5," Economic Journal, VI, 484–487 (September 1896), and Francis E. Hyde, Bradbury B. Parkinson, and Sheila Marriner, "The Port of Liverpool and the Crisis of 1793," Economica, n.s., XVIII, 363–378 (November 1951). These accounts made use of Liverpool municipal records.

[46] 33 Geo. III, c. 31.

were eventually liquidated without loss to either the Corporation of Liverpool or the Exchequer.

During and after the crisis of 1793 several pamphleteers drew a moral from the recent events. They pointed out the danger of having so much of the currency in the form of notes of small and weak banks; and the idea of the inherent instability of any banking system that combined fractional reserves and demand liabilities was specifically stated or was implicit in several discussions.[47] Edward King anticipated the principle on which Peel was to base his legislation of 1844 and 1845 on bank notes: "The issuing out of *any notes for general circulation* ought to be as sacred to Government . . . as the issuing out of gold and silver coin is sacred to Government; and to the *Mint at the tower*." [48] The insight of these pamphlets, and their suggestions of policy to come, were lost in the political and military concern of the early years of the war and had no immediate results. Furthermore the crisis of 1793, by wiping out many weaker banks, although it inspired criticism of the banking situation, at the same time eliminated temporarily some of the basis for the criticism.

Foreign War Expenditures

The outbreak of war, in addition to the need for Bank advances to Government, soon involved large foreign expenditures. On other issues raised by the Restriction the preceding half century may not have led to any organized and generally accepted analysis, but it had at least produced incidents that provided a starting point for analysis of the new problems. But on the question of international unilateral transfers there was virtually nothing to turn to. As early as Thomas Mun unilateral transfers had been mentioned, but simply as one of the constituent items in the balance. In the discussions before Adam Smith such transfers generally were not treated any differently from payments for commodity imports. The Irish absentee remittances had been a political and economic issue for over a century, but the emphasis had been on what the remittances did to the people of Ireland, and not on what they did to the exchanges.

Adam Smith had devoted several pages to overseas expenditures in war, but slanted the discussion toward undermining mercantilist views

---

[47] Colbert, Jr., *The Age of Paper,* p. 22; *Thoughts upon the Commercial Bill,* p. 6; [Joseph Smith], *An Inquiry into the Causes of the Present Derangement of Public Credit in Great Britain* (London, 1793), pp. 11, 38; *Reflections on the Causes which have Produced the Present Distress in Commercial Credit,* pp. 16–18.

[48] *Considerations on the Utility of the National Debt* (London, 1793), pp. 37, 44.

on the importance of gold and silver. He argued that limited payments could be made by substituting paper for specie, that "fewer goods are circulated there [in the country], and less money becomes necessary to circulate them . . . All this, however, could afford but a poor resource for maintaining a foreign war, of great expence and several years duration." His statement: "The enormous expence of the late [Seven Years'] war, therefore, must have been chiefly defrayed, not by the exportation of gold and silver, but by that of British commodities of some kind or other," was true. But the question as to why this should be true, and whether it would be true if foreign expenses increased abruptly and formed a substantial part of total foreign payments, or if the necessity of making increased foreign payments coincided with new obstacles to export, was left untouched. Smith, assuming a body of alert profit-seeking merchants and manufacturers and appropriate elasticities of demand, clinched his appeal to history by this rough and ready theoretical analysis: "When the government, or those who acted under them, contracted with a merchant for a remittance to some foreign country, he would naturally endeavour to pay his foreign correspondent, upon whom he had granted a bill, by sending abroad rather commodities than gold and silver." [49]

This was a useful historical survey and sage judgment from economics' great practitioner of the long view. It contributed little, however, to an analysis of the day to day and year to year problems that England, for over two decades after 1793, faced with the loans and subsidies to its allies and the meeting of its own military and naval expenditures abroad. This discussion has much in common with the controversies of 1914–1918 and 1939–1945 over war finance and inflation, but the comparison can be misleading, because the emphasis of England's experience in the Napoleonic period was on the problem of foreign transfers rather than upon the consequences of war finances as such.

In the first three and a half years of war hardly a line appeared in print on the economic issues involved in foreign war expenditures, although in June 1794 the Bank sold £300,000 of silver to the government to pay the Prussian subsidy. [50] Beginning in January 1795 the Bank repeatedly expressed concern over the government's demands for credits and for specie to make foreign payments. [51] However, any conclusion that either the

[49] *Wealth of Nations,* I, 407–409.
[50] C.T., 1, June 4, 1794.
[51] *Commons Committee,* 1797, app. 9.

Bank advances or the government's foreign expenditures[52] were the "cause" of the fall in reserves and the suspension of payments must be viewed with great reservation.

Following the crisis of 1793 the Bank's specie increased, and in February 1794 was nearly £7 million, the highest since August 1791, and almost £3 million above a year earlier at the outbreak of war and before the crisis broke. This increase was probably due in part, although the evidence is not conclusive, to the export of gold from France in the wake of the depreciating assignats. Beginning in the latter part of 1794 specie holdings had a downward trend, but in June 1795 they were still over £6 million. They declined sharply for the next ten months, and in April 1796 were £2,236,000, and then fell almost steadily to less than £1 million when specie payments were suspended in February 1797.

This dangerous fall in reserves came in a period of comparatively little change either in total Bank credit or in Bank credit to government. At the end of February 1793 the Bank's total credit was £16 million, of which £9.5 million was public and £6.5 million private. Credits to government showed little change in the first two years of the war, and as late as August 1795 were only £8,863,048, less than at any semiannual date since February 1790. These public credits started up in late 1794 and by August 1795 were over £13 million, but a decline in private credits left total credits less than £1 million in excess of the total of February 1793. Government credits declined in the next two years, and at the end of February 1797, the day after the suspension of specie payments, were down to £11,714,431. Total credits, which had been £16,005,250 on February 28, 1793, were only £16, 837,750 on February 28, 1797. The Bank's note circulation, as well as its deposits, were less on February 28, 1797, than they had been four years earlier.

"Expences Abroad . . . since the beginning of the War . . . including the Imperial Loan, and the Advances made to the Emperor," were £36,439,269 in 1793–1796. Of this total £5,570,000 represented the privately

---

[52] Logically the two developments were distinct. An expansion of Bank credit to government could turn the exchanges against London and lead to an export of specie, even in the absence of foreign loans or foreign war expenditure. Similarly, in the absence of Bank expansion or even with Bank contraction, large foreign payments might lead to substantial specie exports, either with or without convertibility. However, in discussions around 1810 the problems of credits to government and foreign payments were frequently treated as practically synonymous, and in much of N. J. Silberling's treatment of the problem over a century later, "Financial and Monetary Policy of Great Britain during the Napoleonic Wars," *Quarterly Journal of Economics*, XXXVIII, 214–233 (February 1924), there is a tacit identification of the two problems of advances to government and foreign payments.

placed loan to the Austrian emperor guaranteed by the British Government; £5,714,413 subsidies and payments to foreign emigrant corps; and the balance general war expenditures.[53] The relation between these foreign expenses and the Bank's loss of reserves is at best tenuous. Foreign expenses of nearly £9 million in 1794 were accompanied by virtually no loss of reserves; and in 1795, when foreign expenses were over £15 million, reserves fell by about £2.7 million. In 1796, when foreign expenses were over £10 million, reserves fell more than another £1 million, but this was the result of an internal drain. Exchange was above the specie export point for much of the year, and in the closing months of the year and early in 1797, when the drain on reserves was greatest, the exchange made profitable the import of specie.[54]

Internal Drain on the Bank's Reserves

Developments other than the Bank's advances to Government or foreign war expenditures were the main causes of the drain on the Bank's reserves. The collapse of the assignats, which began early in 1795, led to an increase in the use of a metallic currency in France, and substantial amounts of gold and silver probably found their way from the vaults of the Bank into the monetary system of England's enemy.[55] The impact of the return to a metallic currency in France seems to have spent itself by early 1796, but in late 1796 and early 1797 an internal drain—including a drain to Ireland—precipitated the crisis that forced the suspension of payments in February 1797.

Substantial amounts of gold moved to Ireland in 1795, 1796, and early 1797. In 1794 and 1795 Ireland, then under a separate Parliament, had raised loans of £500,000 and £1 million in England. Testimony before the Commons Committee of 1797 was that gold exports to Ireland, about £300,000 in earlier years, were around £600,000 in 1794 and over £1 mil-

---

[53] *Lords Committee,* 1797, Papers and Accounts, no. 23. No. 24 presents the same information as a consolidated figure covering the four years, and with some adjustments, the major ones being a deduction of a figure equal to military and naval expenditures in the years 1789–1792. This estimate of additional foreign expenses due to the war was £33,510,779.

[54] *Lords Committee,* 1797, p. 262; Third Report, *Commons Committee,* 1797, p. 7.

[55] In this connection I have drawn on the account of Sir Ralph Hawtrey, *Currency and Credit,* 3d ed. (London, 1928), chs. 17 and 18, in particular pp. 327–328. Hawtrey appears to have been the first economist to point out the connection between French monetary policy of the period and the Bank's reserves. I have not come across any evidence of the period to call in question Clapham's statement: "What no contemporary in England appreciated, so far as the records go, was the connection of the unfavourable exchanges and the drain with the return to a metallic currency in France, after the disastrous inflation of the revolutionary assignats" (*Bank of England,* I, 267).

lion in 1795.[56] How much of this gold remained in Ireland is not clear. Gold was constantly coming back to England, in particular in payment for coals, and the net loss for the years may have been much less. In any case, there is no evidence in the Accounts and Papers or in the correspondence between Pitt and the Bank submitted to the committees of 1797 that the Bank was at the time concerned about these Irish loans of 1794 and 1795, although in February 1797 the Bank protested to Pitt against a proposed Irish loan.[57] Recorded shipments of gold to Ireland in 1796 were only £208,115, but there may have been unrecorded shipments to meet hoarding demands.[58] In December the distrust of Irish banks and the desire to hold specie became critical. Following the appearance of a French fleet off Bantry Bay, the Cork banks, acting on a recommendation of a meeting of citizens "not to make any payments during the present alarm, but such as would be sufficient to discharge the Wages of the Artificers and Labourers," suspended specie payments for some weeks.[59] In Dublin a similar proposal for a voluntary suspension of specie payments was made at a public meeting on December 28, but was turned down.[60] In the days immediately following "very considerable sums" were withdrawn from the Dublin banks and the Irish demand for gold was felt by the Bank of England.[61] Daniel Giles, the Governor of the Bank of England, told the Commons Committee of 1797: "I do not believe that any [specie] has gone out to Foreign Countries since the Beginning of the present Year," but in response to the question, "Has any gone to Ireland?" replied: "I believe a great deal" (p. 9). Samuel Bosanquet (p. 25) and Godfrey Thornton (p. 79), who were Bank di-

---

[56] John Puget, of the firm of Puget and Bainbridge, the London agents for the Bank of Ireland, believed that except for a shipment by Robert Shaw in 1794 in connection with the Irish loan, his firm had handled all important shipments of gold to Ireland, and the figures above are based on his statement about the shipments that his firm and Shaw had made (*Commons Committee*, 1797, pp. 38–40). Appendix 2 of the 1797 report gives details of his firm's specie shipments to Ireland in 1794–1797.

[57] *Lords Committee*, 1797, Accounts and Papers, no. 5, items 27, 28.

[58] A Dublin dispatch of January 26, 1797, from Lord Camden, the Lord Lieutenant, to Pitt, reported that since summer "a gradual and regular drain of specie took place and has continued to the present Day." Lord Camden spoke of a recent withdrawal of £400,000 in specie from the Bank of Ireland by "Bankers and Merchants of the North of Ireland," and said that with the recent threats of invasion "a great many persons began making up purses of Guineas with a view probably of securing their removal to England in case of confusion here" (British Museum, Add. MS. 33,103, fol. 85).

[59] The account of the action is in the *Hibernian Chronicle* of Cork, December 29, 1796. The report of "The City of Cork Committee" in the same journal of February 6, 1797, indicated that the local crisis had passed.

[60] *Dublin Evening Post*, December 29, 1796.

[61] *Times*, January 11; *ibid.*, January 16, reporting an item in the *Dublin Evening Post* of January 12.

rectors, also spoke of large shipments of gold to Ireland in late 1796 and early 1797.

There is no evidence of a comparable crisis in England or Scotland before February 1797. However, it is probable that these countries were experiencing what in the United States in the early 1930's was known as a "dry run." In view of the state of the exchanges in late 1796 and early 1797 it is difficult to explain the decline in the Bank's specie during the months except on the basis of a strengthening of the specie reserves of the banks of Scotland and England and of hoarding of gold by individuals. Sir Richard Carr Glynn, a London banker with extensive connections with Scottish and English country banks, told the Commons Committee of 1797 that in late December and January he had supplied more cash than usual to banks, particularly in Northumberland and the west of Scotland (p. 67). Thomas Thompson, a banker in Hull, asked when the "unusual demand" had started in Hull, replied: "I think about a month preceding that Period [the Restriction] when the Farmers and others first began to talk of an Invasion. In consequence of that Rumour, they got down Specie as fast as they could" (pp. 97–98).

The crisis that forced the Restriction broke in Newcastle on Saturday, February 18, when following a rumor of invasion farmers brought their livestock and produce into town and on receiving payment went to the banks and converted their notes into specie.[62] The following Monday the Newcastle banks suspended payments, as did the Durham and Sunderland banks.[63] Bank runs followed in other towns, the demand on the Bank for specie increased, and the report reaching London on February 25 that the French had landed 1200 men at Fishguard, in Wales, increased the alarm. The bullion of the Bank was falling sharply; on February 24 the governor had an interview with Pitt; on February 26 the King issued an Order in Council forbidding the Bank to make payments in specie when it opened for business on February 27.

Responsibility of the Bank of England

On the last day of 1795, following the increase in subsidy and loan payments to the Continent, the Bank had passed a resolution calling for a rationing of discounts "without regard to the Respectability of the Party . . . sending in the same, or the Solidity of the Bills themselves." In the situation of the moment this action appears to have been directed

[62] This follows closely the account given by Rowland Burndon, a Newcastle banker, before the Commons Committee of 1797 (p. 71).

[63] An account of the suspension is in the *Newcastle Chronicle* and the *Newcastle Courant* of February 25, 1797.

against an external drain. The Bank continued to lose specie after this action, but as suggested earlier it is probable that a large part of the specie went to Ireland, into bank reserves, or into internal hoards. The drain to the Continent had slackened by the spring of 1796, and by late in the year specie was flowing in. But the Bank continued its restrictive discount policy right up to the date of the Restriction. Although there were grumblings in 1796 about the Bank's policy, this does not seem to have been based on any distinction between the problems of an internal drain and an external drain. Sir John Sinclair had written to the Bank directors in September 1796 urging a larger issue, but this represented Sir John's feeling, expressed repeatedly over some forty years, that more money was the answer to all economic problems, and not any nice distinction between appropriate credit policy when the Bank was losing specie by an internal drain and a foreign drain.[64]

When Henry Thornton, a London banker and member of Parliament, appeared before the Parliamentary committees a few weeks after the Restriction, he gave a classic statement of the dependence of the entire British banking structure on the Bank of England, of the Bank's responsibility in time of crisis, and of the need for the Bank to ease credit in the face of an internal run. After pointing out that the Bank was "universally considered as the repository for Cash, on which every individual in the country, who is in want of Guineas, has a right to Draw," and that a private bank was not in this situation, he drew this conclusion:

I conceive, therefore, that the Bank of England can find no safety for themselves, except by seeking it in the safety of the commercial world, in the general support of Government credit, and of the general prosperity of the Nation. It follows, therefore, that if any great suppression of their Notes is injurious to general credit, it must be injurious also to the Bank of England itself; and that the Bank of England, in respect to the issuing of Notes, does not stand on the same footing as an Individual Country Banker. . . . I think that an increased Quantity of Notes, proportioned to the increased Occasion for them, must tend to prevent a Demand for Guineas rather than to promote it.[65]

Sir Francis Baring, close on the heels of the Restriction, preached much the same message as Thornton,[66] and said that in time of crisis the Bank

---

[64] These letters were later published by Sinclair in *Letters Written to the Governor and Directors of the Bank of England, in September, 1796* (London, 1797).

[65] References to Thornton's evidence are to the modern edition of his *Enquiry into the Nature and Effects of the Paper Credit of Great Britain*, ed. F. A. Hayek (London, 1939), pp. 288, 298. This work was originally published in London in 1802.

[66] *Observations on the Establishment of the Bank of England; and Further Observations on the Establishment of the Bank of England* (London, 1797).

was "the *dernier resort.*" The report of the Lords Committee of 1797 also recognized the unique position of the Bank of England: "The Bank of England is at the Head of all Circulation. It is the great Repository of the spare cash of the Nation, and alone carries the Bullion to the Mint to be coined. It is subject, on that Account, to be called on for Cash, directly or indirectly, by those who are in Want of it, and necessarily sensible of every material Failure or Distress, which arises from any Deficiency or Want of Coin, in every part of this Kingdom or Ireland" (p. 250).[67]

The Emerging Controversy

The negotiations between the Bank and the Government between 1793 and 1797 brought into sharper relief the issue, latent from the very foundation of the Bank, of the relative role of the Bank and the Government and the relation of these two institutions to private banks. Strictly speaking, this was a problem of sovereignty, and falls within the field of political science rather than economics. But politics and economics never can be completely separate in practice, and they never were even when the English in the age of Victoria were confidently proclaiming their separation. Any understanding of the great issues of monetary and banking policy involves considerations that transcend the jurisdictional limitations that economists sometimes impose on themselves. There are often larger objectives of policy not subject to analysis in any terms the economist, narrowly defined, is accustomed to handle. Even with agreement on group objectives and on cause and effect relations, there is ample room for disagreement as to where responsibility for carrying out policy shall rest: in government in the formal sense, in a central bank, or in private banks.

The Bank of England was not established in 1694 to perform "central banking functions" any more than the goldsmiths, when earlier in the century their evidences of deposits came to be accepted as a more convenient substitute for specie, planned to perform "commercial banking functions." That fixing the standard and minting of coin was a royal prerogative was unchallenged in England in the early seventeenth century. The expansion of the goldsmiths' operations into more formalized banking, the development of the note issues of the Bank of England into an important part of the total currency supply, and the use of their notes and deposits as the form in which other banks held reserves took place

---

[67] Much the same idea is in the Third Report, *Commons Committee*, 1797, p. 9.

so surely, but so gradually, that by 1797 institutional realities no longer squared with legal provisions or expressed beliefs. The events of 1793 and 1797 had made clear that banks were supplying a large part of the circulating medium; that the failure of a bank had a far greater economic significance than a failure of an ordinary business; and that with a system of fractional reserve banking some agency—either the Bank or the Government—must assume responsibility in time of crisis.

Between the publication of *The Wealth of Nations* and the Bank Restriction far-reaching changes had taken place, both in the economic significance of the private banks and of the Bank of England and in the emergence of the latent political issue of the relation of government to the Bank and to the other banks. Events had run far ahead of public recognition of the significance of these events. Hence the Restriction of 1797 not only brought into open debate the immediate issues that it raised, but it brought to the surface longer-run problems that had been accumulating unanswered in those years of domestic and international political tension. This situation, when added to the many changes in the economic situation of England during the Napoleonic wars and the years immediately following, produced twenty-four years of almost uninterrupted controversy on monetary and banking problems in Parliament, in pamphlets, and in the press.

Note on Bank of England Statistics to 1832

Figures on the Bank of England's total credits, divided between private securities and public securities, are available for the last day of February and of August 1778–1832 (*Bank Charter Committee,* 1832, app. 5). Before 1832 there is no continuous series giving total credits at more frequent intervals, but figures for special types of credits for limited periods were published at various times between 1797 and 1832 in Parliamentary Papers and committee reports. The only continuous credit series before 1832 is for the private category "Bills and Notes Discounted" and the public category "Exchequer Bills and Exchequer Bills Purchased," which on a semimonthly basis for 1794–1830 N. J. Siberling secured, together with a cash figure, from the Bank of England records in 1919. Siberling, in "British Prices and Business Cycles, 1779–1850," *The Review of Economics and Statistics,* volume V, supplement 2 (October 1923), published a quarterly average of this total credit and of the public credit. Arthur D. Gayer, W. W. Rostow, and Anna Jacobson Schwartz, in the microfilm appendix of *The Growth and Fluctuation of the British Economy, 1790–1850,* give a monthly average of these figures, which were brought up through 1832 from data furnished to the authors by the Bank. Through the courtesy of Mrs. Schwartz I was able to consult the tables, now in the records of the National Bureau of Economic Research, of semimonthly figures originally collected by Silberling and Gayer and associates. These semimonthly figures, although used by both Silberling and Gayer and his associates as if they were practically synonymous with total private and public credits of the Bank, for many comparable dates are well below the published semiannual "Private Securities" and "Public Securities," and some cases are less than half the published figures. I have made no use of the Silberling figures except where so indicated.

Bank of England circulation is given weekly for January 7, 1792 through August 4, 1832, in *Bank Charter Committee,* 1832, appendix 83; Bank of England deposits for the last day of February and August are given in *Bank Charter Committee,* 1832, appendix 5.

The only continuous figures on the Bank's specie before 1832 are also in *Bank Charter Committee,* 1832, appendix 5, given for the last day of February and of August; figures for 1814–1832 are in appendix 28, and those for 1816–1832 in appendix 88. The unpublished Silberling figures, beginning in 1794, give semimonthly figures for "Cash," and a comparison of these figures with the published semimonthly February and August bullion figures indicates that Silberling's "Cash" is practically identical in coverage with the bullion figures. In the absence of published figures I have occasionally used these Silberling figures.

II

THE RESTRICTION PERIOD, 1797–1815

THE RELATIONS between money, prices, and exchange rates during the Restriction have been repeatedly examined by economists. After Jacob Viner's comprehensive treatment of the entire period over a quarter of a century ago in *Studies in the Theory of International Trade,* and later discussion of selected aspects of the Restriction by Hayek in his Introduction to the reprint of Thornton's *Paper Credit of Great Britain,* by R. S. Sayers in his examination of Ricardo's monetary theory,[1] and by Will E. Mason in three articles on transfer theory,[2] there is little to add to the theoretical analysis. But this theory was born of a controversy that involved much more than technical monetary and banking relations. A full understanding of the significance of these theoretical issues and of their bearing on later events involves a consideration of them in the broader economic and political setting of the controversy.

Meaning of the Bullion Controversy

The term "bullion controversy" is by convention a catchall description of the conflict of opinions during the Restriction, but it can be misleading in its suggestion of a clearly defined controversy over a single economic issue. The controversy until after Waterloo fell into five main periods, which can be distinguished both in the nature of the monetary problem under discussion, and in the theoretical analysis that emerged:

1. From 1797 until late in 1800, during which time there was only a small premium on gold, little depreciation of the exchanges—either of the Dublin exchange in relation to London or of the London exchange in

---

[1] "Ricardo's Views on Monetary Questions," *Quarterly Journal of Economics,* LXVII, 30–49 (February 1953), reprinted in T. S. Ashton and R. S. Sayers, *Papers in English Monetary History* (Oxford, 1953), pp. 76–95.

[2] "Some Neglected Contributions to the Theory of International Transfers," *Journal of Political Economy,* LXIII, 529–535 (December 1955); "The Stereotypes of Classical Transfer Theory," *ibid.,* LXIV, 492–506 (December 1956); "Ricardo's Transfer-Mechanism Theory," *Quarterly Journal of Economics,* LXXI, 107–115 (February 1957).

relation to the Continent—and some political controversy but virtually no theoretical writing about the problems of inconvertible paper money.

2. A few months late in 1800 and early 1801, when a discount of the English currency in terms of the Hamburg exchanges provoked an intensive but short-lived discussion of the causes of exchange rate fluctuations.

3. The closing months of 1803 and 1804, when a depreciation of the Irish pound in relation to the English pound produced Parliamentary debate, a Parliamentary investigation and report, and a large pamphlet literature.

4. A period of two years beginning late in 1809, marked by a sharp depreciation of the British pound in relation to Hamburg and by an increase in the price of gold and silver. This led to Ricardo's first writing on economics, to an outpouring of pamphlet literature, to the report of the Bullion Committee, and to extended Parliamentary debate.

5. From the closing months of 1811 until after Waterloo, when, although the English pound was still at a substantial discount in terms of Hamburg exchange, and gold and silver at a premium, there was only limited discussion of monetary policy and of monetary theory.

It is impossible to make a hard and fast classification of the dominant issues of the controversy, because they frequently overlapped and because their relative importance at different times during the Restriction, and in the minds of different persons at any given time, was not always the same. However, the more important issues were (1) causes of the rise in the price of bullion, of Hamburg exchange, and to a lesser degree, of the rise in commodity prices; (2) the role of the Bank of England, including the influence of its credit policy and its relations to other banks; (3) London banks and country banks as independent factors in inflation and deflation; (4) the nature of the English monetary standard, both what it was in 1797 and what it should be; and (5) appropriate criteria for bank credit, particularly in the absence of a metallic standard.

Price of Bullion and of Foreign Exchange

Before 1797 the British coinage price of standard gold bullion was £3.17.10½ an ounce. As long as the Bank redeemed in gold, the market price, in coin or Bank notes, of gold eligible for export had rarely risen above this parity price and then only by a small percentage. The principal foreign exchange operations were with Hamburg, which was on the silver standard, and fluctuations in the London-Hamburg rate were linked to changes in the gold-silver ratio in Hamburg. In contemporary debate the prices in London of gold, silver, and Hamburg exchange were generally used interchangeably. Although these tests gave different quantitative measures of "appreciation" or "depreciation" of the Bank of England note, changes in the gold-silver ratio in Hamburg were generally so small as compared with movements of the price of gold and silver in London, or of the London-Hamburg exchange rate, that the nature and force of any argument as to depreciation of the Bank of England note was practically the same, no matter what test was applied.[3] However, the market price in Hamburg of silver in terms of gold between 1798 and 1816 was almost continuously lower than it had been in 1797. Hence any figures based on the Hamburg exchange or on the price of silver in London understated the depreciation of the Bank of England note in terms of gold, as Ricardo pointed out with an impressive parade of statistics.[4]

The term "bullionist" came to be applied to those who found the major explanation of the rise in the price of gold and silver, and of the depreciation of the pound on the foreign exchanges, in monetary expansion, and particularly expansion by the Bank of England. The antibullionists attributed the rise in bullion prices and in foreign exchange primarily to the wartime disruption of trade and to foreign war expenditures by the British government; and they rejected or minimized any monetary explanation of these movements of prices and of exchange rates.

Inconvertivility without Depreciation, 1797–1800

There was relative calm during the first three years of inconvertibility. The Bank of England's circulation at the end of February 1799, despite the fact that nearly £1.5 million of its notes were of denominations under £5, which it had not issued before the Restriction and which in large part replaced guineas, was under £13 million. It is true that this was an increase of about 30 per cent over the circulation in August 1796 and February 1797, but these had been the lowest figures since February 1788, and the circulation of February 1799 was less than that of February 1795.

---

[3] Weekly figures on exchange rates and specie prices for the period January 29, 1790, to February 23, 1819, are in *Commons Committee*, 1819, app. 14. N. J. Silberling, "British Financial Experience of 1790–1830," *The Review of Economics and Statistics*, preliminary vol. I, 282–297 (July 1919), calculates the annual fluctuations in the London-Hamburg rates, with allowance for changes in the gold-silver ratio. Unless otherwise indicated, all references to exchange rates and specie prices in the Restriction period are based on these sources. Hawtrey, *Currency and Credit*, p. 335, has assembled much of this information on a percentage basis.

[4] *Reply to Mr. Bosanquet's Practical Observations on the Report of the Bullion Committee*, reprinted in *The Works and Correspondence of David Ricardo*, ed. Piero Sraffa (Cambridge, 1951–1955), III, 163–175, 195–201.

The fluctuations in exchange rates and specie prices were little greater than might have been expected under convertibility. Hence there was no problem of explaining depreciation, however depreciation might be measured. There was simply a question of defending or attacking what had been done, or of prophesying what might happen if the Bank were to expand its issues.

In these three years the pamphlet literature, with one notable exception, and the Parliamentary debates made virtually no contribution to the theoretical issues raised by the suspension of payments. Edward Long Fox's *Cursory Reflections on the Causes, and some of the Consequences, of the Stoppage of the Bank of England* (Bristol, 1797), was an attack on Pitt, the Restriction, and proposals to make Bank notes legal tender. Sir John Sinclair, in his "Conclusion" in *Letters Written to the Governor and Directors of the Bank of England* (London, 1797), went off in all directions at once, as he so often did: he wanted a large note issue, was concerned about the "coinage of paper money," and urged a speedy resumption of specie payments.

Only one pamphleteer, Sir Francis Baring, displayed any economic statesmanship or independence of view. Baring, in addition to his analysis, mentioned in Chapter I, of the central position of the Bank of England and the dependence of other banks upon it in time of crisis, showed a remarkable insight into the essentials of inconvertible paper money and a sensing of the problems likely to arise out of the long continuance of the Restriction. He supported the Restriction as a necessary war measure, but his warning against the dangers of monetary expansion and his statement that "any paper, whether Bank or Government, if issued in excess will depreciate" were at variance with the distinction that Pitt and his supporters drew between the evils of government paper money, like the assignats, and the benefits of paper money issued by a private institution like the Bank of England. Baring wished to take away the right of note issue from country banks and to make Bank notes legal tender. He called the existing situation of not making the notes legal tender but practically forcing the public to accept them "a miserable subterfuge." [5] The volume went through two editions and was followed in the same year by *Further Observations,* in which he said that many persons did not agree with his views on legal tender, and then restated his position. These restrained warnings from one of the leading figures

[5] *Observations on the Establishment of the Bank of England* (London, 1797), pp. 79, 66–67.

in the City may have had a moderating influence on the Government and the Bank in holding down Bank credit, although there is no direct evidence on this point.

In Parliament Charles James Fox combined a demand that the Bank limit its discounts and resume payments no matter what the consequences, with a criticism of the Government for not having made peace proposals to France.[6] Richard Brinsley Sheridan, playwright turned Whig politician, prophesied: "We were doomed to all the horrors of a paper circulation."[7] William Pitt, facing opposition taunts that the Restriction was simply an imitation of French monetary policy, opposed making Bank notes legal tender,[8] but supported legislation that for all practical purposes gave the ordinary man no choice but to accept them unless he wished to face a fruitless lawsuit.

Soon the Whig prophecies that the Bank of England notes would go the way of the assignats seemed foolish political outbursts, and in 1798 and 1799 no one, either in or out of Parliament, was interested in debating the Restriction. The price of food rose sharply in 1799, but short crops and the difficulty of imports seemed so obvious an explanation that of many pamphlets of 1799 and 1800 on the high price of foodstuffs, only a small minority, including Malthus', mentioned a possible monetary cause. And Malthus said that he "should be inclined to consider" an increase of paper money "rather as the effect than the cause of the high price of provisions."[9] In the debate in the Commons in March 1800 on the renewal of the Bank's charter[10] no mention was made of the exchange situation; and the reports of the Commons Select Committee on the High Price of Provisions, presented in December 1800, made no reference to possible monetary causes of high prices.

Exchange Depreciation of 1800–1801

In 1800 the situation deteriorated: in May the exchange on Hamburg was well below the specie export point under convertibility, and gold bullion sold at £4.5.0 an ounce, or 9 per cent above the Mint price. The problems of the French war and of the Union with Ireland, finally carried through in 1800, took most of the public's attention, but early in 1801

---

[6] *Parliamentary History*, XXXIII, 40–48, March 9, 1797.

[7] *Parliamentary History*, XXXIII, 76, March 10, 1797.

[8] *Parliamentary History*, XXXIII, 354–355, March 27, 1797.

[9] *An Investigation of the Cause of the Present High Price of Provisions* (London, 1800), p. 14.

[10] *Parliamentary History*, XXXV, 12, March 21, 1800.

a debate was touched off by the publication of Walter Boyd's *Letter to the Right Honourable William Pitt, on the Influence of the Stoppage of Issues in Specie at the Bank of England; on the Prices of Provisions, and other Commodities.* [11] Boyd was a controversial figure in English finance around the turn of the century, and some of the literature provoked by his pamphlet suggests that it was Boyd, as much as the policy of the Bank of England or the country banks, who was the center of the argument.[12] He was a partner in the banking firm that had floated the loan of 1794 to the Austrian Emperor, and he was elected to Parliament in 1796. The same year he had been a leader in the protest against the restriction of credit by the Bank of England. Boyd was a witness before the Lords and Commons committees of 1797, where he furnished details on the transfer of the Austrian loan in 1794 and 1795, and also gave a forceful and well-reasoned argument that Bank credit should not have been tightened, but loosened, in the fourteen months before the Restriction.[13] Boyd's firm failed in 1800, following the denial of further credit from the Bank and Pitt's refusal to allow them to be a contractor for the loan of 1799.

Boyd was not an unprejudiced observer of monetary policy, but there is no denying the force of the argument in his *Letter*. It combined an insight into basic economic issues with a stretching of the argument for more than it was worth in the circumstances, the whole discussion being overlaid with an animus against the Bank of England. Boyd's thesis was a simple one: the suspension of specie payments had permitted the Bank to issue more notes than would have been possible under convertibility, and this was responsible for the rise in the price of commodities and of foreign exchange. However, in his debating zeal he practically assimilated the price of foodstuffs and the price of foreign exchange, largely ignoring the fact that the increase in the price of food had been much greater than

---

[11] The *Letter* was dated November 11, 1800, with the Preface December 31, 1800. A few months later Boyd published a second edition with an expansion of the title: *With Additional Notes; and a Preface, Containing Remarks on the Publication of Sir Francis Baring, Bart.* The "Preface" of 50 pages, although brilliant controversial writing, added practically nothing to the economic analysis in the original edition. As the second edition is a comparatively scarce volume, all citations in Arabic numerals are to the first edition, but the citations in Roman numerals are to the preface of the second edition.

[12] A sketch of Boyd is in the *Dictionary of National Biography.* I am indebted to Mr. S. R. Cope, now with the International Bank for Reconstruction and Development, for making available to me his unpublished dissertation of 1947 at the London School of Economics, "The History of Boyd, Benfield and Co." Clapham, *Bank of England*, II, 16–18, also gives details on Boyd's financial operations.

[13] *Lords Committee*, 1797, pp. 106–117; *Commons Committee*, 1797, pp. 49–58.

the increase in the price of bullion and of foreign exchange. He took the categorical position that country banks could not be a cause of monetary expansion, inasmuch as they were compelled to redeem their notes in specie or Bank of England notes.

Boyd recognized that unusual foreign expenditures could have an unfavorable effect on the exchanges (*Letter,* pp. 28–35), but when he warmed up to his argument that the Bank of England had expanded unduly its note issues the consideration of such payments as an influence on the exchanges fell by the wayside. However, out of the recognition in principle that the foreign exchanges might depreciate from causes other than internal inflation he developed an important theoretical point, suggestive of modern discussions of the bearing of elasticities of supply and demand upon exports following exchange depreciation: "If the increase of prices in the home-market should fortunately not keep pace with the depression of the exchange, all our articles of exportation must feel the effects of the increased demand in the foreign markets, in consequence of the diminished value of British money abroad; and although, in many of these articles, no increase in demand can add to the quantity to be exported, in many others, this increased demand may, and I trust, will, add to the means of supplying it" (p. 37).

Boyd's pamphlet attracted widespread attention that must have been embarrassing both to the Bank and the Government, and Boyd probably was right in his suggestion that some of the replies came from subsidized writers (*Letter,* p. xvii). The most effective answer, however, was that of Sir Francis Baring, in his *Observations on the Publication of Walter Boyd* (London, 1801). He certainly was no hack writer, and his words had more the ring of counsel of an elder statesman of finance than of special pleading for either the Government or the Bank.

Boyd, probably because the public was more concerned about the price of provisions than about Hamburg exchange, in his indictment of the Bank laid the emphasis upon commodity prices and particularly the prices of food. Baring, in turn, concentrated his criticism of Boyd on the commodity price argument. By contrasting the relatively small rise in the price of Hamburg exchange and the absence of any premium on guineas (*Observations,* pp. 21–23) with the sharp rise in commodity prices, he exposed the weakness of Boyd's argument of taking specie convertibility as the proper basis for monetary circulation and then citing the rise in food prices as evidence of excessive issues. Boyd made a feeble reply by stating that bank note expansion raised all prices, including prices in terms of specie (*Letter,* p. x), but without in any way showing how the policy of the Bank of England could affect the purchasing power of the precious metals.

Baring went beyond the relatively solid ground of the effect of exchange depreciation upon the price of imported products to the slippery field of the relation between exchange depreciation and the price of domestically produced products. He argued that depreciation of the exchange could have no effect on prices of domestic products. His claim that "neither the Exchange on Hamburg nor foreign Exchanges in general, can ever operate so as to produce any material advance in the price of provisions, grown and consumed in Great Britain" (*Observations*, p. 31), was in large part based on theoretical analysis, although to bolster this analysis he pointed out that a rise of 7 per cent in the exchanges in a twenty-eight-day period in January 1801, had not had the "slightest effect . . . in lowering the price of provisions" (p. 21).

The controversy had important theoretical implications that neither Boyd nor Baring really developed. It would be possible for domestic prices to be virtually unaffected by short-run exchange rate movements if (1) the domestic product were neither exported nor imported; (2) the product were imported, but the foreign supply were small in relation to the domestic supply; or (3) the domestic product were exported, but exports were a large proportion of the supply in foreign markets.

The third case was not involved, but it is not clear whether Boyd and Baring thought they were discussing the first or second case, although illustrations in their argument seemed to point to the second case. In reply to Baring's contention that fluctuations of exchange rates had no effect upon domestic prices, Boyd denied that he had ever argued "that the low exchange with Hamburg occasions the high price of Essex-wheat" (*Letter,* p. xxxi). This was quite consistent with his emphasis on the effect of Bank expansion on commodity prices: if the depreciated exchange were simply a reflection of domestic inflation, then the exchange depreciation could not be the explanation of the prior price inflation that had caused it. Baring, on the other hand, never admitted any prior domestic price inflation resulting from Bank expansion. As a consequence the argument, so suggestive in its implications as to the effect of exchange fluctuations upon prices, was inconclusive.

Relations between the Bank of England and the Country Banks

The Boyd-Baring skirmish also raised, but did little to clarify, an issue that was to be prominent in the battles of the bullion controversy, and in the later setting of convertibility was to reverberate until the 1860's: the relative responsibility of the Bank of England and of the country banks for changes in the monetary supply. Modern central banking theory, with its emphasis on the significance of central bank credit as a cause of changes in commercial bank reserves, is likely to make the historical problem of the relation between central banks and other money-creating banks appear simpler than it really was. An understanding of the Boyd-Baring controversy on the relation of the Bank of England and country banks, and of subsequent controversies, makes desirable a sketch of the prevailing reserve practice of British and Irish banks:

1. London private banks held their reserves largely in notes of the Bank of England.

2. English country banks kept their reserves principally in deposits with London private banks, and in Exchequer bills and private bills, which could be converted into Bank notes as needed; and to a limited degree in Bank of England notes.

3. Scottish private banks held most of their reserves in notes and deposits of the chartered banks of Scotland.

4. The three chartered banks of Scotland kept their reserves largely in deposits with the Bank of England.

5. The Bank of Ireland, which like the Bank of England was free of any obligation to redeem its notes in anything, apparently kept its reserves largely in gold. It carried no account with the Bank of England until 1821, but the London firm of Puget and Bainbridge, whose senior partner, John Puget, was a director of the Bank of England from 1790 to 1805, was its London agent. He probably provided more contact between the two banks than the formal records would indicate.

6. Dublin private banks and Irish country banks presumably kept the larger part of their reserves in gold, and in Bank of Ireland notes, in which by common consent their notes were redeemable, although little specific information is available on their reserve practices.

These facts are reasonably clear, but neither to contemporaries nor to later students of the bullion controversy has it been clear what inflationary or deflationary action banks could in practice take, independent of action by the Bank of England or by the Bank of Ireland. A survey of the theoretical problem involved may help to clarify the probable significance of the institutional relations in the particular setting of the Restriction.

As soon as the promises of private parties to pay, whether these promises be circulating notes or deposits subject to check, come to be generally accepted as a means of payment, the question arises as to the relative responsibilities of the various creators of money in changing the total monetary supply. The inflationary or deflationary power of any group of banks is a combined result of legal relations and of institutional practices. Even in the simplest situation of one bank, redeeming in exportable specie, it would be possible for the bank temporarily to inflate or deflate the monetary supply in a way that would not be possible with a purely metallic currency.[14] As soon as a second bank is brought into the picture the situation becomes more complex. The ability of one of the banks to inflate or deflate is affected not only by international gold flows, and by internal hoarding or dishoarding of gold, but also by a change in public preference as between notes of the two banks.

The situation is complicated when the various money-creating banks are no longer parallel in their actions, as when they operate in different geographic areas or with different economic groups, when the denominations of their notes are different, or when one has its liabilities largely or exclusively in deposits that are both subject to check and have a transactions velocity different from that of circulating notes. In such a situation an expansion in the notes of a particular bank may represent nothing more than a geographic shift in industry, a seasonal pickup in retail trade, or a rise in the price of individual commodities, whose increased prices, fixed by forces outside the area, are the basis for an increased money supply in all areas where these commodities are produced.

The situation is further complicated when the liabilities of one or more of the banks, in addition to serving as a means of payment, serve as reserves of other banks. But no one can say with assurance in what way it will be different, or how much credit control one bank can exercise over other banks, particularly if reserve practices are not crystallized by custom or law. This relation of a *de facto* central bank to other banks becomes doubly elusive when the central bank is no longer required to redeem in specie, but the other banks are required to redeem in central bank obligations. This was the situation during the English and the Irish Bank Restriction. The limitation on commercial bank credit from external drain, or from an internal drain to hoard specie, was no longer there. If the areas of circulation of Bank of England notes and country bank notes were mutually exclusive, then an expansion of country bank notes, no matter how high the credit rating of the country bank, faced a limit

[14] In outlining the problem I ignore any possible effect of banking policy in a single country upon the international purchasing power of the precious metals. I have couched the discussion in terms of gold, but the analysis would be the same with a silver standard, bimetallism, or a dollar or sterling exchange standard.

in the form of a demand for redemption in Bank notes that would be comparable, both in its causes and effects on credit within the area, to an external drain of gold in a country on the gold standard. An expansion of Bank of England notes, on the other hand, faced no such limitation comparable to an external drain.

The question of how far the country banks during the Restriction expanded credit independently of the Bank of England, or in Ireland independently of the Bank of Ireland, had two aspects. There was the possibility, which was a reality in Ireland, of country banks and Dublin private banks poaching on the areas that the Bank of Ireland considered its own, and thus having an inflationary effect independent of Bank of Ireland action. The Bank of Ireland and the Bank of England were by law excused from honoring their legal promises, and the other banks, even though by law still required to redeem in specie, were in fact not required to do so, and this situation probably encouraged lax banking standards. As early as 1799, George Rose, Secretary to the Treasury of Ireland, recognized the probable existence of such a situation in Ireland: "It may have happened that bankers and others may have lately issued more notes than usual, from the necessity of keeping gold to answer them being lessened, from the general understanding that no man's credit can be hurt by his not being able to pay in cash." [15] Many comments on country banks, in pamphlet literature and in evidence before the Bullion Committee, suggest a similar laxity in England.

Boyd did not let any niceties of analysis interfere with his argument that the Bank of England was entirely responsible for any monetary expansion. On the relation between the Bank of England and the country banks he was emphatic and dogmatic: the obligation of country banks to redeem in Bank of England notes made their credit operations subject to a limitation comparable to, if not identical with, the limitation that the obligation to redeem in specie had placed on the Bank of England. Baring did not discuss specifically Boyd's views on the relation of expansion by the Bank of England and expansion by country banks, but his emphasis on the pivotal role of the Bank made his view close to Boyd's. Baring disagreed with Boyd's claim that the Bank had overexpanded, and hence his defense of the Bank was not weakened by agreement with Boyd's

---

[15] Letter of March 21, 1799, to Viscount Castlereagh, then Chief Secretary of the Civil Department for Ireland, *Memoirs and Correspondence of Viscount Castlereagh* (London, 1848), II, 219.

view on the relation of Bank of England credit and country bank expansion.

Revival of Controversy in 1803

Just before Boyd's pamphlet appeared the Commons had turned down, 32 to 16, a motion for a committee on the state of the gold coin.[16] Except for an abortive motion in the Lords in March 1801 for a committee to investigate the note issue of country banks "in order to ascertain what effect it may have had on the High Price of Provisions," [17] there was no further Parliamentary discussion until April 1802, when a brief debate took place on a bill to continue the Restriction until 1803.[18] Henry Thornton's judicious *Paper Credit of Great Britain,* as Professor Hayek suggests in his Introduction, may have been "intended partly as a reply to Boyd" (p. 45). But when it appeared public interest in the issues raised by Boyd had pretty well died down, and Thornton's book was not the occasion for reopening the controversy. However, in 1803, when the Irish exchange, whose parity was £108.33 Irish to £100 English, became unfavorable to an unprecedented degree of over 10 per cent, discussion broke out, both in Parliament and in pamphlets, on the relation of money, prices, and exchange rates. Lord King started the new phase of the controversy in the debate on extension of the Bank Restriction Act in February 1803,[19] and continued it in the discussion in May 1803 on the Irish Bank Restriction Bill.[20] He followed this with a pamphlet, *Thoughts on the Restriction of Payments in Specie at the Banks of England and Ireland* (London, 1803), which came out in an enlarged second edition in 1804 as *Thoughts on the Effects of the Bank Restrictions.*

King avoided the argument over the absolute level of English commodity prices with which Boyd had befuddled his analysis, and based his criticism of the Bank of England and the Bank of Ireland on the proposition that "the market price of bullion and the state of foreign exchanges have been selected, as furnishing in conjunction the most accurate criterion of the pure or depreciated state of a currency" (*Effects,* p. 13). He did not deny that there were fluctuations in the purchasing power of gold and silver, but as a disciple of the Enlightenment he took

---

[16] *Parliamentary History,* XXXV, 713–719, December 5, 1800.
[17] *Parliamentary History,* XXXV, 1264–1269, March 30, 1801.
[18] *Parliamentary History,* XXXVI, 540–548, April 9, 1802.
[19] *Parliamentary History,* XXXVI, 1156–1157, February 22, 1803.
[20] *Parliamentary History,* XXXVI, 1247, May 3, 1803.

the view that it was better not to interfere with these "natural" fluctuations. He stated specifically what seems to have been assumed implicitly by so many Victorian defenders of the gold standard: "A paper circulation which cannot be converted into specie, is deprived of this natural standard, and is incapable of admitting any other. The persons to whom the duty of regulating such a circulation is entrusted are in danger, with the very best intentions, of committing perpetual mistakes. The greatest possible degree of skill and integrity can only protect them against gross errors. They will probably in no one instance be exactly right" (*Effects*, p. 28).

King argued that the increase in the note issues of the Bank of England and the Bank of Ireland had made prices higher than they would have been under specie payments, and that this had been the major cause of the rise in the price of specie and of foreign exchange, but he had no mechanistic theory of the relation between money, prices, and the exchanges. He recognized, in an analysis that is modern in its suggestions of "liquidity preference" and "income velocity of circulation," that absolute figures of circulation were almost meaningless as a test of the adequacy of the monetary supply: "It is manifest for these reasons that the proportion of circulating medium required in any given state of wealth and industry is not a fixed, but a fluctuating and uncertain quantity; which depends in each case upon a great variety of circumstances, and which is diminished or increased by the greater or less degree of security, of enterprise and of commercial improvement. The causes which influence the demand are evidently too complicated to admit of the quantity being ascertained by previous computation or by any process of theory" (*Effects*, p. 20).

At about the same time as King's original publication, John Wheatley, one of the most penetrating and original, but doctrinaire, writers of the Restriction period, entered the controversy with his *Remarks on Currency and Commerce* (London, 1803). Wheatley represented the extreme bullionist position that foreign payments had no effect on the exchanges, that exchange depreciation was due entirely to monetary expansion, and that monetary expansion could have only price effects and could give no stimulus to production (pp. 18–20, 78–93). He analyzed, in a way that no other writer of the period did, the effect of monetary policy in a single country upon the purchasing power of the precious metals:

The paper of one country has the same tendency to depress the value of money as the paper of another; it is of no consequence where the increase originates; whether London, Lisbon, Paris, or Vienna. But wherever it takes place, and augments the currency of the country above its due proportion, it will either lead to the departure of specie, or will circulate at a discount proportionate to the excess. . . . By the recent state of our unfavourable exchanges, it is evident, that our currency has been augmented in a greater proportion than any. But if all augmented it in the same proportion, the paper currency of the world may be carried to any extent, and the value of money depressed in much greater ratio than it has hitherto been. (pp. 184, 187)

Wheatley also stressed the difference between an internal run and an external run and the need for the Bank to ease credit in the face of an internal run (pp. 216–218).[21]

The Irish Currency Committee and the Bullion Committee

In March 1804 the Commons appointed a committee to investigate the state of the Irish currency and the exchange relations between Ireland and England. After hearings the *Report from the Select Committee on the Circulating Paper, the Specie and the Current Coin of Ireland* appeared in June of that year.[22] It presented extensive factual material, and also gave an analysis of the causes of exchange fluctuations. Henry Thornton played a leading role on the committee, and the analysis, if not written by him, certainly reflected his views: the major cause of long continued exchange depreciation is monetary expansion, although unilateral transfers and structural changes in trade may be a contributing factor, particularly in the short run. Hence the report drew the conclusion that it was within the power of the banking authorities, by appropriate credit policy and by the willingness to use its reserves when needed, to stabilize exchange rates.

The report provoked little discussion, as even before its publication the Irish exchange had improved, and by the end of the year was close to the old Dublin-London parity of £108.33 to £100. The Bank of England note remained almost at par in relation to specie and to the Continental exchanges, and for nearly five years the monetary problem was quiescent, both in and out of Parliament. Early in 1809 the premium on gold rose to about 15 per cent, and there was a comparable depreciation of the Bank of England note as measured by the Continental exchanges. In

[21] Wheatley published nine economic works, in large part dealing with money and banking, between 1803 and 1828. I discuss these in "The Life and Writings of John Wheatley," *Journal of Economy*, L, 357–376 (June 1942).

[22] This report, and a portion of the Minutes of Evidence before the committee, are reprinted in my *The Irish Pound* (London and Evanston, Ill., 1955), where on pp. 125–217 are listed 20 items on the Irish monetary situation that appeared in 1803–1805.

this new setting David Ricardo started his career as an economist with a letter in the *Morning Chronicle* of August 29, 1809, on "The Price of Gold," in which he attributed the depreciation of the pound solely to the inflationary policy of the Bank of England. Further public controversy led to the appointment, on the motion of Francis Horner, of the Bullion Committee in February 1810.[23] The report of the committee, written in large part by Francis Horner, William Huskisson, and Henry Thornton, gave an extended discussion of the relation of monetary policy and of nonmonetary influences on the exchanges, and reiterated the basic thought of the Irish Currency Report: it is within the power of a national bank, by appropriate credit policy and use of reserves, to stabilize the exchanges. In addition to the theoretical analysis the report also made the policy recommendation that specie payments be resumed within two years whether the country were at war or peace, as compared with the existing law that resumption should take place six months after ratification of a peace treaty.

The appearance of the report in August 1810 was followed by a flood of pamphlets, and a full dress Parliamentary debate in 1811. Parliament rejected the committee's policy recommendation for a resumption of payments, and also by resolution repudiated the theory of the committee that it was possible for the Bank of England to control the exchanges.

Henry Thornton and the Real Bills Doctrine

A large part of the controversy raised by both the Irish Currency Report and the Bullion Report centered around theoretical issues that had been discussed by Thornton in his book of 1802, and hence it seems appropriate to take his discussion as a point of departure for an analysis of the argument that reached its climax in the Bullion Report and the subsequent debate. In 1797 Baring had warned that an excessive monetary expansion, no matter from what source, would be inflationary. In 1800 Boyd had claimed that a presumed increase in the issues of the Bank of England had been the cause of the increase in commodity prices. It was Thornton, however, who provided in fully developed form the argument on the relation of bank expansion and prices. When Thornton had testified before the Parliamentary committees in 1797 the inflationary effect of bank expansion was not an issue, and his discussion of bank credit was directed to the depressing effect of a restrictive policy, in time of crisis or of an

---

[23] Details on the appointment of the committee are given in my article "The Politics of the Bullion Report," *Economica*, N.S., XXVI, 99–120 (May 1959).

internal run, on production and trade. The emphasis in his book of 1802 was on the consequence of ill-timed contraction, but his analysis also covered the opposite danger of overexpansion by the Bank. This provided critics of the Restriction, when the price of bullion and of foreign exchange went higher, with material for a powerful case against the Bank of England and the Bank of Ireland, and was the basis for Thornton's major role in the Irish Currency Committee of 1804 and the Bullion Committee of 1810, and his Parliamentary criticism of the credit policy of the Bank of England.

Thornton brought out the difference between the soundness of an individual loan and its desirability in terms of national monetary policy, and the consequent difference in the standards that a country bank and the Bank of England might appropriately follow in extending credit. He denied that confining credit to the discount of bills arising out of real transactions was a satisfactory limitation. After pointing out that, in contrast with the assignats, there was no problem of lack of faith in the Bank of England note, he analyzed the effects of a larger issue of notes resulting from increased loans and drew a distinction between a situation in which monetary expansion increased employment and production and a situation in which it only increased prices. He summarized his discussion thus:

In examining this question, an error into which it is very natural to fall must be developed. When the Bank of England enlarges its paper, it augments, in the same degree, as we must here suppose, its loans to individuals. These favoured persons immediately conceive, and not without reason, that they have obtained an additional though borrowed capital, by which they can push their own particular manufacture or branch of commerce; and they are apt, also, though not with equal justice, to infer, that the new capital thus acquired by themselves is wholly an accession to that of the kingdom; for it does not occur to them that the commerce or manufactures of any other individuals can be at all reduced in consequence of this encrease of their own.

But, first, it is obvious, that the antecedently idle persons to whom we may suppose the new capital to give employ, are limited in number; and that, therefore, if the encreased issue is indefinite, it will set to work labourers, of whom a part will be drawn from other, and, perhaps, no less useful occupations. It may be inferred from this consideration, that there are some bounds to the benefit which is to be derived from an augmentation of paper; and, also, that a liberal, or, at most, a large encrease of it, will have all the advantageous effects of the most extravagant emission.[24]

Thornton then developed, in anticipation of the Wicksellian analysis

[24] *Paper Credit of Great Britain*, pp. 235–236.

of the relation between the market and the "natural" or equilibrium rate of interest, the relation between the current rate of mercantile profit and the Bank's interest rate. He argued that as long as the first was higher than the second there was a motive for expansion of credit, and drew the conclusion that no rule was sound that regarded simply the character of the bills offered for discount, and ignored the state of the foreign exchanges.[25]

The Real Bills Doctrine and the Bullion Debate

The Irish Currency Committee had subjected to searching cross-examination the position of the Bank of Ireland spokesmen, who denied that loans on sound security, no matter how large, could have an adverse effect on the exchange.[26] In the hearings before the Bullion Committee, and in the Parliamentary debates of 1811, the real bills doctrine was stated in an even more extreme way. Under questioning by Francis Horner and Henry Thornton the harassed directors of the Bank of England, in their desire to absolve the Bank from any possible responsibility for exchange fluctuations, overreached themselves in words that Walter Bagehot later described as "almost classical by their nonsense." John Pearse, the deputy governor, after describing the Bank's policy of only discounting "bills of real value, representing real transactions," and "all due within the period of two months," said: "I cannot see how the amount of Bank notes issued can operate upon the price of Bullion, or the state of the exchanges, and therefore I am individually of opinion that the price of Bullion, or the state of the exchanges, can never be a reason for lessening the amount of Bank notes to be issued, always understanding the control which I have already described." And when the question was then put to John Whitmore, the governor, he replied: "I am so much of the same opinion, that I never think it necessary to advert to the price of Gold or the state of the exchange, on the days on which we make our advances." [27]

Ricardo was not concerned with the fine points of theory in Thornton's criticism of the real bills doctrine, although his practical conclusion was substantially the same as Thornton's. In most of his discussion Ricardo simply assumed that any depreciation of the exchanges or a rise in the

[25] *Paper Credit of Great Britain,* pp. 251–259.

[26] *Irish Currency Committee,* 1804: John Puget, p. 21; William Colville, pp. 88–90; Jeremiah D'Olier, pp. 91, 118.

[27] *Irish Currency Committee,* 1804: Pearse, pp. 90, 96–97; Whitmore, pp. 81, 90, 97; Jeremiah Harman, director of the Bank of England, pp. 142–144.

price of bullion beyond the figures possible with redemption was proof of excessive monetary circulation. In his first letter to the *Morning Chronicle* on "The Price of Gold," he contrasted the restraint that redemption and gold exports placed on the Bank expansion with the situation under the Restriction, and concluded: "Whilst the Bank is willing to lend, borrowers will always exist, so that there can be no limit to their overissues, but that which I have just mentioned." [28] He gave no attention to the idea stressed by many defenders of the Restriction and recognized, at least as a theoretical possibility, by every other important critic of the Restriction except Wheatley, that under some circumstances expansion might have production rather than price effects.

The Bullion Report, in words probably written by Henry Thornton, criticized the real bills doctrine in a passage whose theme was given in the opening sentences: "That this doctrine [of the Bank directors] is a very fallacious one, Your Committee cannot entertain a doubt. The fallacy, upon which it is founded, lies in not distinguishing between an advance of capital to Merchants, and an additional supply of currency to the general mass of circulating medium." [29] In the Parliamentary debates on the Bullion Report Horner, Thornton, and Huskisson attacked the real bills doctrine, and Thornton and Huskisson pointed out the similarity of the Bank directors' views to those of John Law.[30]

Nonmonetary Influences and the Exchanges

Closely allied to the controversy over real bills and the influence of monetary policy upon the exchanges was the effect that nonmonetary factors, and particularly foreign transfers, had on the exchanges. As suggested in Chapter I, before 1793 opinion on the effect of foreign transfers on the exchanges was very loosely defined. The experience of England from 1794 to 1796 with loans and subsidies to the Continent added little to theoretical analysis of the problem. The protests from the Bank to Pitt on the threat of foreign payments to their reserves, implying that foreign payments were in large part, or even in full, in specie, simply set up an unresolved difference between two common-sense views: the long-run view of Adam Smith that in some unexplained way the very process of making the financial transfer took care of the real transfer by inducing

[28] *Works*, III, 17. The same argument appears in several other places, and in a particularly strong statement in the *Reply to Bosanquet*, ibid., pp. 214–221.

[29] Edwin Cannan, *The Paper Pound of 1797–1821: A Reprint of the Bullion Report* (London, 1919), p. 50. Citations of the report refer to this edition.

[30] 1 Hansard XIX, 817–826, 912–914, May 6, 1811; 980–982, May 7, 1811.

additional exports; and the short-run Bank view that loans, subsidies, and emergency food imports involved specie exports. There was no real joining of the issue.

The protests of the Bank in 1795 and 1796 against loans and subsidies to the Continent may have created in the minds of the Bank directors and of the public in 1810 and 1811, and possibly of more recent students of the problem, the impression that the directors' warnings of what might happen were an accurate description of what did happen. As already pointed out, the loss of specie was but a small fraction of the foreign war payments in 1793–1796. Furthermore in 1798, and even as late as 1808, the Bank held more specie than it had in August 1792, shortly before the outbreak of war.

In the hearings of 1797 the Bank directors held that any loan or subsidy involved a specie loss to the full amount of the transfer. Daniel Giles, the governor, told the Lords Committee on March 17: "I conceive that all Loans made for Foreign Powers, or Monies given to them, must ultimately go in Specie, although not remitted immediately in Money; but it affects the Exchange so as to occasion Gold to go out of the Country." In response to the question, "If the Exchange should not fall below Par before the Whole of the Money of such Loan is remitted, would any Cash in the Payment of such Loan be necessarily sent out of the Kingdom?" he replied, "It would be sent, or prevent Money coming into the Country" (p. 17). Further examination of Giles and Samuel Bosanquet left no doubt as to their position; and their words, if taken literally, ruled out any possible adjustment of exports through price or income effects of foreign transfers.

Thornton, but only after the exchange was again close to par and controversy had subsided, in his book of 1802 gave the first approach to an analysis of the impact of unilateral transfers and structural changes on the foreign exchanges that distinguished between short- and long-run effects. He pointed out that "ultimately" an "equality between the commercial exports and imports" was reached through the forces of the market—principally income changes. He recognized, however, that "a temporary pressure arises at the time of any very unfavourable balance. To understand how to provide against this pressure, and how to encounter it, is a great part of the wisdom of a commercial state." Without pressing the analysis to the end, and without distinguishing sharply between convertible and inconvertible conditions, Thornton recognized the practical limitations on credit restrictions as an equilibrating force. The essence of his conclusion was:

to limit the total amount of paper issued, and to resort for this purpose, whenever the temptation to borrow is strong, to some effectual principle of restriction; in no case, however, materially to diminish the sum in circulation, but to let it vibrate only within certain limits; to afford a slow and cautious extension of it, as the general trade of the kingdom enlarges itself; to allow of some special, though temporary, encrease in the event of any extraordinary alarm or difficulty, as the best means of preventing a great demand at home for guineas; and to lean to the side of diminution, in the case of gold going abroad, and of the general exchanges continuing long unfavourable; this seems to be the true policy of the directors of an institution circumstanced like that of the Bank of England. To suffer either the solicitation of merchants, of the wishes of government, to determine the measure of the bank issues, is unquestionably to adopt a very false principle of conduct.[31]

This was the analysis of a policy maker, not of a pure theorist or an interested partisan. What Thornton's prescription meant in practice depended on judgment and economic statesmanship. Two persons who accepted Thornton's analysis, or even the same person at two different times under changed circumstances, might have different opinions of how much of the disturbance arose from nonmonetary forces, or how "lean to the side of diminution" was to be translated into practice. But the general policy guides were given.

The influence of nonmonetary factors figured prominently in the discussion of the Dublin-London exchanges in 1803 and 1804. The position of the Bank of Ireland directors and other witnesses before the Parliamentary committee, and of many pamphleteers, was that the depreciation of the Irish exchange was due largely if not exclusively to Ireland's unfavorable "balance of debt" or "balance of remittances." Although these terms had no formal definition, the context generally showed a consistent usage: the difference between the total of current account receipts and long-term borrowing, and the total of current account payments and repayments on long-term loans, thus making the "balance" equal, in modern analysis, to gold movements and short-term capital movements.

Specie movements, which in the Irish situation were negligible and in the case of Britain's over-all balance were certainly less than the "balance of remittances," could not possibly have taken care of an "unfavorable balance" of the dimensions that the spokesmen for the Bank of Ireland, the Bank of England, and the Government talked of. An adjustment through capital movements toward England probably provides the key to explaining a claim in much of the antibullionist literature: a deficit in the "balance of remittances" substantially greater than the net specie

---

[31] *Paper Credit of Great Britain*, pp. 142–143, 259.

export. This situation has been noted by writers as far apart in time as Ricardo, in his *Reply to Bosanquet*,[32] and Viner,[33] both of whom pointed out that some antibullionists felt that the mere existence of a depreciated currency, without specie flow and without commodity trade adjustment, made possible the subsidies and extraordinary foreign payments.

That capital movements toward England in part took care of the "deficit" created by wartime foreign payments was specifically stated by two defenders of the Restriction. John Hill, after assuming a situation where "the country was exhausted of all its exportable treasure," went on to say: "In this state of things it would be literally impossible that the balance of payments should be any longer against us, because we could have no means of paying an unfavourable balance. Our receipts from, and payments to, foreign nations must therefore be reduced to an equality, (or the balance must be turned in our favour) either by an increase in our exports of merchandise, a diminution of our imports and of the foreign expenditure of government, or by some of those inter-national transfers of capital to which I have before alluded." [34] And J. C. Herries, who as commissary general of the army had the responsibility for making large remittances to Wellington's army in the Peninsula and thus knew whereof he spoke, wrote in an anonymous pamphlet: "This is probably the case, with respect to our drafts from abroad at this time:—we are borrowing money to carry on our foreign expenditure, at a high rate of interest." [35] This picture of the transfer process given by Hill and Herries was consistent with the idea that depreciation of the English currency was necessary, not to set up commodity price differences, but to offer profit opportunities to foreigners to invest in Great Britain, or to British holders of foreign investments to liquidate those investments. Material in the Herries papers[36] also suggests that as a result of credits received abroad the net transfers by Great Britain were in many years substantially less than contemporary or subsequent estimates of British foreign expenditures.

[32] *Works*, III, 206.

[33] *Studies in the Theory of International Trade* (New York, 1937), p. 146.

[34] *An Inquiry into the Causes of the Present High Price of Gold Bullion in England* (London, 1810), pp. 8–9.

[35] *A Review of the Controversy Respecting the High Price of Bullion* (London, 1811), pp. 43–44.

[36] These papers are on deposit at the National Register of Archives. Some of the material relating to foreign borrowing arranged by Herries to take care of foreign subsidies and British military expenditures was published in *Memoir of the Public Life of the Right Hon. John Charles Herries . . . by His Son Edward Herries* (London, 1880), but much important information in the papers is not published in this volume.

It is a mistake to think of all critics of the Bank of England as denying that foreign payments and structural changes in trade influenced the exchanges. The one view that all bullionists shared was that, in the situation of the time, expansion by the Bank of England was a cause of the depreciated exchange, but they differed as to how much, if any, of the depreciation stemmed from foreign payments and structural changes in trade. The most extreme position taken by Wheatley and Ricardo was that such developments would have no effect on the exchanges. They seem to have assumed an almost frictionless adjustment to such disturbances solely on the basis of income transfers or price changes. As Wheatley put it, "The remittance of the subsidy would, therefore, be transacted by the dealers in bills, without the slightest innovation in the price of the exchange, which would regularly correspond with the respective value of money in the two places." [37] Ricardo never made a statement quite so categorical, but in *The High Price of Bullion* his criticism of Thornton for arguing that extraordinary foreign remittances would disturb the exchanges because of the difficulty of immediately expanding English exports seems to have involved essentially the same view. [38]

Wheatley[39] and Ricardo[40] in other passages took a less doctrinaire view, while still insisting that subsidies and extraordinary foreign expenditures would not cause exchange depreciation if the Bank followed the proper credit policy. Their position was that if the Bank had a passive policy in the face of such transfers, and depreciation followed that could have been prevented had the Bank contracted credit, then the cause of the depreciation was not the foreign payments but a monetary circulation greater than would maintain the exchange in the face of these foreign payments. Proceeding from such a premise, any depreciation of the exchange is in itself evidence of an excessive monetary supply.

Most of the other bullionists, although criticizing the Bank for a lax credit policy, recognized that the problem was complicated by foreign military payments and changed conditions of foreign trade. Lord King, when he reopened the dispute in 1803 against the background of the Irish situation, brought out as fully as Thornton had the power of subsidies and extraordinary foreign expenditures to disrupt the Hamburg exchanges. The Bullion Report also took into account the existence of unusual foreign payments and their probable effect upon the exchanges,

[37] *An Esssay on the Theory of Money* (London, 1807), I, 180–181.
[38] *Works*, III, 61.
[39] *An Essay on the Theory of Money*, I, 181–182.
[40] *Works*, VI, 87–88.

and its analysis was very different from Ricardo's. Malthus' discussion in the *Edinburgh Review,* after the publication of the Bullion Report, not only made clear his own view of the importance of nonmonetary influences on the exchanges, but also sharpened up the difference between the theory of Ricardo and the theory of the report:

> The great fault of Mr. Ricardo's performance, is the partial view which he takes of the causes which operate upon the course of Exchange. . . . He attributes a favourable or unfavourable exchange *exclusively* to a redundant or deficient currency, and overlooks the varying desires and wants of different societies, as an original cause of a temporary excess of imports above exports, or of exports above imports. . . . We have already adverted to the error (confined, however, principally to Mr. Ricardo, and from which the report is entirely free) of denying the existence of a balance of trade or of payments, not connected with some original redundancy or deficiency of currency.[41]

The Country Banks and the Currency

Closely allied with the question of the influence of the Bank of England's policy upon the exchanges was the effect of the operations of the country banks. In logic there was also a third level of credit expansion that might have affected prices and the exchanges: the nonissuing London banks, with which the country banks kept part of their reserves in the form of deposits. It would have been possible, on the basis of given note and deposit liabilities of the Bank of England, for the reserves of the country banks to increase and thus to foster an expansion of country bank note issues, even though Bank of England credit was unchanged and the country banks maintained the same reserve standards. Only once in the literature of the Bullion controversy have I seen such a suggestion, in Jasper Atkinson's anonymous pamphlet of 1802, *Considerations on the Propriety of the Bank of England Resuming its Payments in Specie* (p. 33), and statistical data for the period are so meager as to make useless any attempt to test such a hypothesis.

Some aspects of the relations between country banks and the Bank of England have already been discussed in connection with the Boyd-Baring debate in 1800, but the controversy revived on a wider scale in 1810. That the increase in country bank notes was exactly proportional to the increase in Bank notes was not argued, to my knowledge, in this new setting by anyone other than Ricardo, and even the individual sentences in Ricardo that might appear to suggest such an exact relation are

---

[41] XVII, 342–343, 361 (February 1811).

not consistent with Ricardo's general argument. He wrote in *The High Price of Bullion:* "When they [Bank of England] increase or decrease the amount of their notes, the country banks do the same; and in no case can country banks add to the general circulation, unless the Bank of England shall have previously increased the amount of their notes."[42] It seems clear, however, that Ricardo was talking primarily of a long-run relation, and also that he recognized that even in the short run there could be changes in the relative importance of the two types of notes in particular areas.[43] The Bullion Report, in a discussion that suggests the hand of Henry Thornton, indicated that the country banks probably had been able to increase their circulation by holding smaller reserves than before the Restriction (pp. 62–65). The position of Ricardo, and in a less dogmatic way of most critics of Bank of England policy in the Restriction, was that the Bank "controlled" the issues of the country banks. By this they meant that an increase in its notes, by making more plentiful the reserves into which every country banker was required to redeem his own notes, gave an encouragement to country bank expansion, and that a contraction of Bank notes was an inducement to credit restriction. They did not picture an unchanging relation between Bank and country bank notes, but rather the ability of the Bank of England to exercise a powerful influence on country bank circulation.

Most bullionists were critical of the country banks for their contribution to the credit expansion. Yet the idea has crept into economic literature of recent decades that the bullionists had a mechanistic concept of the relation between Bank of England and country bank circulation, and that the view of the Bullion Report was simply the view that Ricardo had expressed in his most extreme statements. This idea seems to have originated in the 1920's with N. J. Silberling.[44] More recently it received the approval of Sir John Clapham in his history of the Bank of England, and Silberling's thesis has been brought to the attention of a new generation of economists by the republication of his original article in a collection of readings in economic history.[45] It is time to set the record straight, not only in order to understand the Bullion Report, but to get a better under-

---

[42] *Works,* III, 88.

[43] *Works,* III, 86–88; *Reply to Bosanquet,* ibid., p. 231.

[44] "Financial and Monetary Policy of Great Britain during the Napoleonic Wars," *Quarterly Journal of Economics,* XXXVIII, 397–439 (May 1924).

[45] *Enterprise and Secular Change,* ed. Frederic C. Lane and Jelle C. Riemersma for the American Economic Association and the Economic History Association (New York, 1953).

standing of the forces that brought about the Bank Act of 1844, whose rigid provisions, contrary to a widely held belief, were a denial of and not an acceptance of the doctrine of the Bullion Report.

Silberling writes of the Bullion Report: "Perhaps the most extraordinary single feature of the Report was its complete exoneration of the country banks, despite tremendous increase in their number and the grave abuses in their operations. They were praised for their helpful services to trade and industry, and Parliament was earnestly advised to leave their reckless career free and unmolested."[46] Clapham's verdict on the report is: "There was no word of criticism for the country banks."[47]

Both in contemporary debate and in historical retrospect some of the discussion of the effect of changes in Bank of England circulation upon the circulation of country banks has been confused by the failure to distinguish between two problems: a change in Bank circulation that leaves unaltered the relative roles of Bank of England and country bank circulation, and a change in Bank note circulation that simply represents a shifting public preference for the two types of notes or is a result of a campaign of a particular bank to increase the area of circulation of its notes. In England, unlike the situation in Ireland, the areas of circulation of Bank of England and country bank notes were reasonably well defined, and any changes on the geographic margins of these areas appear to have been gradual and on a limited scale.

Four witnesses before the Bullion Committee—John Whitmore, governor of the Bank, Ebenezer Gilchrist, manager of the British Linen Bank, Thomas Thompson, a banker of Hull and member of the committee, and John Henry Tritton, a London banker—were in substantial agreement that the circulation of the Bank of England had an important influence on the circulation of the country banks and of the Scottish banks (pp. 127, 114, 115, 140–142). A fifth witness, Vincent Stuckey, although less categorical in his statement, gave a general picture that is consistent with what the other witnesses had said. He then volunteered an opinion on a superficially similar, but basically quite different, situation: the withdrawal, for some unexplained reason, of Bank of England notes from an area where they had previously circulated: "As a matter of opinion, I should imagine that in those parts of England where Bank of England notes circulate, if they were to be withdrawn their places would be immediately filled up by the notes of country banks; and I would illustrate

---

[46] *Financial and Monetary Policy*, p. 435.
[47] *Bank of England*, II, 23.

this opinion by the example of the County of Lancaster, where the notes of the Bank of England are the chief circulation for small payments" (p. 140).

Clapham quotes Stuckey's view and then says that it hardly fits Ricardo's thesis.[48] The fact is that Stuckey's statement, dealing with a situation quite different from the situation that Ricardo was discussing, was not even a refutation of Ricardo's position, and much less of the milder and more general view of Thornton and of the Bullion Committee.

Proposals for Regulating Country Bank Issues

The debate over the power of country banks to expand the currency independently of action by the Bank of England was associated with another issue—the weakness of many country banks and the proposals for restricting their issues. The crisis of 1793, the temporary *de facto* suspension of payments in the south of Ireland in December 1796, and the runs of early 1797 that preceded the Restriction had revealed the potential instability of a monetary system where a large part of the means of payment consisted of obligations of small, and in many cases, financially irresponsible, banks. Remarks after 1793 suggest increasing concern about the country bank notes, and there were occasional suggestions of the need for legislative remedies.

In 1797, apparently before the suspension of payments, an anonymous pamphlet, *The Iniquity of Banking,* attributed to William Anderson, had stressed the instability of a monetary supply consisting in large part of bank obligations. It urged that the Bank of England and the country banks be forbidden to issue notes, and recommended a national paper money—presumably redeemable in specie. In 1798 Ambrose Weston published *A Method of Increasing the Quantity of Circulating-Paper,* proposing a system of bond-guaranteed notes issued by country banks. The suggestion that the country bank notes, aside from any inflationary influence, had a deflationary effect in time of crisis cropped up a number of times in the years following. No one stated the problem more succinctly than did John Wheatley in 1803: "I shall endeavour to prove that the paper of country banks must ever form an inefficient and dangerous medium of circulation, from its liability to sudden contraction in the period of alarm; and its tendency to as sudden an increase in the moment of security; and that its continuance is inconsistent with the stability of

[48] *Bank of England,* II, 28.

the national bank, and the general interests of the country." He urged that the right of note issue be taken away from country banks, and that the Bank of England be given a monopoly of issue and be required to make public information on its issues.[49]

William Cobbett does not rank high as an economist, but his influence on the development of British monetary and banking policy should never be underrated. Many critical items in his *Political Register* from 1804 on probably reflected, and certainly stimulated, the distrust of country banks. There are no statistics on this point in which trust can be placed, but it is likely that in 1803 and 1804, and again from 1810 to 1812, commercial difficulties were aggravated by the failures of country banks.[50] Pamphlets, both bullionist and antibullionist, were critical of country banks[51] and give a ring of plausibility to rumors in 1809 and 1810 that the Government was considering restrictions on the issues of country banks. The *Morning Chronicle* reported on May 22, 1809, a story that the Government would suppress all note issues within 30 to 50 miles of London as part of an arrangement for a new loan from the Bank of England. Nothing more was heard of this, but the next year Cobbett[52] claimed that letters appearing in early August in the *Morning Post,* a ministerial spokesman, proposing that the right of note issue be taken away from country banks, were a feeler to test public response to such a measure. If this was the case, nothing came of it.

[49] *Remarks on Currency and Commerce,* pp. 210, 257–258.

[50] Viner, *International Trade,* pp. 162–165, points out the unreliability of the estimates of the country bank circulation in the Restriction period. Even if the available annual estimates could be accepted as accurate, they would throw little light on the short-run reduction in the circulation of notes resulting from failures, or runs on solvent banks. Figures on failures are in Pressnell, *Country Banking,* pp. 535–538.

[51] An anonymous writer, probably Peter Carey, in *The Real Cause of the Depreciation* (London, 1810), in suggesting that the right of issuing notes of £1 and £2 be denied to country banks, said: "They would lose their emoluments as coiners of base money, but would not be deprived of their fair profits as bankers" (p. 38). William Bard, under the pseudonym Danmoniensis, referred to the existing permission to "erect mints innumerable and deluge society with overflows of paper," and suggested that the Bank of England or the Treasury be given some control over the note issues of country banks (*Desultory Reflections on Banks in General,* London, 1810, pp. 6–15). T. Hopkins, *Bank Notes the Cause of the Disappearance of Guineas* (London, 1810), pp. 66–68, urged restriction of country banks more on the ground of their instability than of their inflationary influence. Peter Richard Hoare, in the anonymous *Letter, Containing Observations on Some of the Effects of Our Paper Currency* (London, 1810), spoke of "this new system of money making, not to say coining," and made a sweeping criticism of country banks (pp. 16–21). Henry Boase felt that the evil of country banking was not so much in the expansion of the currency as in the "chasm" that was created by the failure of a country bank and the consequent distrust of the notes of other banks, and "in the displacing the good by bad, or very doubtful notes" (*Remarks on the New Doctrine Concerning the Supposed Depreciation of Our Currency,* London, 1811, pp. 76–80).

[52] *Political Register,* August 11, 1810, 173; August 18, 1810, 205–211.

The Bullion Report and the War

The Bullion Report in its recommendation for resumption in two years took a position that, both then and in critical literature since 1920, has been regarded, and properly so, as a doctrinaire and dangerous policy in a war situation. Yet a discussion of the Bullion Report that concentrates on the economic dangers of deflation misses much that went into the controversy that culminated in that report. It came after thirteen years of the Restriction, during which time spokesmen for the Bank of England and the Bank of Ireland and other defenders of the Restriction had repeatedly said that no credit expansion based on real bills could possibly raise prices or affect the foreign exchanges. In the face of the movements of the exchanges in 1809 and 1810 they had said this with increasing dogmatism.

The Bullion Report recognized that under wartime conditions there was danger of an internal run, and drew a distinction between a restriction resulting from an internal drain of specie, with which the Bank might be powerless to deal, and a restriction to protect against an external drain, with which the Bank could deal (pp. 57–60). Its authors probably would have preferred, in the setting of 1810, restriction to forestall the dangers of an internal run, if restriction were accompanied by a Bank policy that recognized the Bank's powers and responsibilities in the field of foreign exchange. But when the choice was between resumption with the dangers of a repetition of 1797 and continued restriction, with the Bank of England directors claiming that monetary expansion could have no influence on prices or exchange rates, a realist might well have considered the first alternative less dangerous than the prospect of continued inflation. This appears to be the explanation why such men as Thornton and Huskisson, familiar with the details of finance and having a high sense of public duty, supported a proposal for resumption in two years.

As the real bills doctrine was the main argument against the theory of the Bullion Report, so the principal practical argument against its recommendations was that inconvertible paper was necessary to the effective prosecution of the war against Napoleon. Viscount Castlereagh, in probably the ablest Parliamentary attack on the report, brought the deflationary dangers into his "win the war" argument.[53] Spencer Perceval, the Prime Minister and Chancellor of the Exchequer, expressed fears that adopting of the Bullion Report "would be tantamount to a declaration that they would no longer continue those foreign exertions which they

[53] 1 *Hansard* XIX, 986–1011, May 7, 1811.

had hitherto considered indispensable to the security of the country . . . the house, in adopting it, would disgrace themselves forever, by becoming the voluntary instruments of their country's ruin." [54]

Likewise, in the pamphlet literature provoked by the Bullion Report the idea appeared repeatedly that the recommendation to open the Bank in two years, or even to make any attempt to hold a stable rate, would cripple the war. James Cruickshank, in opposing a resumption of payments, gave an unusual twist to the argument for inflation as an instrument of war finance by stressing the increase in the labor supply from forcing real wages so low that workers would have to be continuously employed.[55] However, in the pamphlet literature, as in Parliament, opposition to resumption was more on the advantages of the Restriction as an instrument of war by releasing specie for export than on the stimulus that monetary expansion would give to domestic production.[56]

The bullionists were not blind to the difficulties of restoring the exchange to par in time of war. Many of them, and particularly Ricardo, minimized the difficulties, but against these difficulties they set the dangers of a severe inflation if the Bank were freed from any external restraint on its issues. The critics of the Bullion Report, most of whom were either lost in the morass of the real bills doctrine or were combining their economic discussions with denunciations of the French, did not provide the answer to the country's monetary problems. Henry Thornton's penetrating analysis of the dangers of credit contraction would have made him the ideal critic, in a modern seminar in monetary theory, of the resumption proposals of the Bullion Committee. But in the total atmosphere of theory, politics, personality, and strategy out of which policy emerges, he was a defender of the Bullion Report.

Nature of the Monetary Standard

In addition to the more sharply defined theoretical issues and policy proposals that were fought out from 1800 to 1811, there were two other

---

[54] 1 *Hansard* XIX, 1064, 1076, May 8, 1811. Similar statements were made by Rose, the Secretary of the Navy (891, May 6); Sir Thomas Turton (1052–1053, May 8); the Earl of Harrowby (XX, 875–876, July 8); and Lord Liverpool (XX, 879, July 8).

[55] *Observation on Money* (London, 1811), p. 69.

[56] Sir John Sinclair, *Observations on the Report of the Bullion Committee* (London, 1810), pp. 38–42; Sir John Sinclair, *Remarks on a Pamphlet . . . by William Huskisson* (London, 1810), p. 58; the Earl of Rosse, *Observations on the Present State of the Paper Currency of England* (London, 1811), pp. 33–50; [Coutts Trotter], *The Principles of Currency and Exchanges* (London, 1810), pp. 47–49; F. P. Eliot, *Observations on the Fallacy of the Supposed Depreciation of the Paper Currency of the Kingdom* (London, 1811), p. 5; [Herries], *A Review of the Controversy Respecting the High Price of Bullion*, p. 86.

problems on the fringes of discussion that were to come nearer the center of controversy when the war was over: first, the nature of the British monetary standard, and second, the responsibilities of the Bank of England. There was no clear-cut debate on these issues before 1816, but incidental comments indicated an evolving ferment of opinion, which was ready to break out in controversy after Waterloo had removed Napoleon as the overshadowing consideration in the grand strategy of monetary and banking policy.

Before payments were suspended in 1797 Britain had a legal bimetallic standard that was a *de facto* gold standard, subject only to the qualification that legislation forbidding the melting or exporting of full-weight British coin might at times raise the gold export point above the figure that would have prevailed under the nineteenth century gold standard. The metallic standard, in the sense of redemption in coin that could not be legally melted or exported, was almost universally accepted. Few people defended the legislation against melting and exporting, but there was no concerted move to repeal it. The suspension of payments in 1797 had been accompanied by assurance from the Government and the Bank that this was a temporary measure caused by wartime conditions.

With the Peace of Amiens in 1802, had the statements of Pitt in 1797 been taken literally, specie payments should have been resumed. But the exchanges were against England by around 7 per cent, there was no strong sentiment in or out of Parliament to resume payments, and legislation of 1802 and 1803 extended the Restriction.[57] It is true that Government representatives did not speak with quite the assurance that they had in 1797 of the soundness of the Bank note and that Whigs spoke not so much against extending the Restriction as against doing it without a Parliamentary investigation.[58] But there was nothing to indicate in responsible circles serious discussion of devaluation or of permanent inconvertibility.

Evidently, however, some persons were considering such possibilities. Henry Boase, in an anonymous pamphlet of 1802, *Guineas an Unnecessary and Expensive Incumbrance on Commerce,* suggested that the Restriction be continued *"as a permanent measure of prudence and sound policy"* (p.v.). That others were making similar suggestions is indicated by Francis Horner's comment in a review of Lord King's *Thoughts on*

[57] 43 Geo. III, c. 18; 44 Geo. III, c. 1.
[58] George Tierney, *Parliamentary History,* XXXVI, 545–546, April 9, 1802, and 1149–1150, February 7, 1803; Charles James Fox, 1150–1154, February 7, 1803.

the Restriction in the *Edinburgh Review* of July 1803: "In the great commercial cities, and especially in the metropolis, opinions are gravely avowed, by persons who ought to be acquainted at least with the details of the money trade, that the precious metals are altogether unnecessary, even as a part of circulation; and that the provisional law of 1797 should be established as a permanent system"[59] Yet no witness before the Bullion Committee suggested either a permanent restriction or devaluation, and the theory of the Government and Bank directors was that the Bank of England note would come back to par as soon as foreign war expenditures had ended.

In the Parliamentary debate that followed the Bullion Report Government spokesmen put forward an idea that to some persons seemed dangerously close to a defense of devaluation: the standard of England had never been a given quantity of precious metal, but a coin, which on account of the existing legislation against melting and export was something completely different from the precious metal that it contained. It is small wonder that such a suggestion by the Government should have alarmed even the mildest bullionists. If taken literally it would have meant that no matter how high the premium on specie that could be legally exported—say 100 per cent—this was no evidence of a depreciation of the Bank of England note. This position was taken in Nicholas Vansittart's resolutions, debated and approved by the Commons in May 1811, of which the most important were the first resolution and the third, which stated the equality of the Bank of England note and gold:

1. That the right of establishing and regulating the legal money of this kingdom hath at all times been a royal prerogative, vested in the sovereigns thereof, who have, from time to time, exercised the same as they have seen fit, in changing such legal money, or altering and varying the value, and enforcing or restraining the circulation thereof, by proclamation, or in concurrence with the estates of the realm by Act of Parliament; and that such legal money cannot lawfully be defaced, melted down, or exported.

. . . .

3. That the promissory notes of the said Company have hitherto been, and are at this time held in public estimation to be equivalent to the legal coin of the realm, and generally accepted as such in all pecuniary transactions to which such coin is lawfully applicable.[60]

A similar idea was expressed in numerous pamphlets, some of which

[59] II, 405–406.
[60] The debate on May 13 and 14, 1811, is reported in 1 *Hansard* XX, 1–128; the text of the resolutions is in 69–74.

appear to have been inspired by the Government. A statement typical of many others was that of Francis Perceval Eliot, that the "fundamental mistake" of Huskisson's argument was that "he considers the guinea as the measure and standard of value," rather than the pound sterling, "which is the ideal money of account only which admits of invariable value; because it is not formed of *substantial,* and, therefore, *variable* materials." [61]

Despite Vansittart's resolutions, which seemed almost to invite devaluation or a permanent restriction, up to 1815 no public intimation came from either the Bank or the Government that this might be desirable. Too many hostages had been given by the Bank and the Government, in the real bills doctrine and in the explanation of exchange depreciation and gold premium as arising out of the war situation, to permit any suggestion from those quarters that the end of the war would not quickly bring the pound back to par.

Gold or Silver as the Monetary Standard

The question whether gold or silver was the standard, or which was the preferable standard, was rarely raised in the Restriction period before 1816. Between 1788 and 1815 barely £1700 of silver had been minted.[62] In 1793 the silver-gold ratio had edged above 15.2:1 in Hamburg, and between early 1793 and late 1797 the price of standard silver in London had intermittently fallen slightly below the Mint price of 5s.2d. This had not been sufficient inducement to bring silver to the Mint, but late in 1797 the price of silver, both in bars and in Spanish dollars, fell about 5 per cent below the coinage price, even in terms of the inconvertible Bank of England note. A number of banks sent silver to the Mint and some shillings had already been coined when the Privy Council Committee on Coin ordered the Mint to stop coinage. Charles Jenkinson, first Earl of Liverpool, a leading figure on the Committee, apparently was responsible for this action. Jenkinson had for some years been studying the British monetary situation, with particular reference to the problems of silver coinage. The substance of his conclusion, to adopt a single gold standard and to coin fiduciary silver on government account, although not published until 1805,[63] had been presented in its substance to the Privy Council Committee in 1798, and probably had been urged on his asso-

---

[61] *Observations on the Fallacy of the Supposed Depreciation* (London, 1811), pp. 31–32.

[62] See table in Craig, *The Mint,* pp. 418–419. The account of the silver situation draws on this table, and on the discussion on pp. 261–263.

[63] *A Treatise on the Coins of the Realm* (Oxford and London, 1805).

ciates even earlier. The administrative action of the committee was rati-
field, without debate, by legislation of June 21, 1798,[64] closing the Mint
to coinage of silver brought by the public. By early in 1799, although the
Hamburg ratio remained above 15.2:1, the London price of silver, reflecting the depreciation of the pound in relation to Hamburg exchange, was
again above 5s.2d. and stayed there until April 1816. However, at any
time in this period a resumption of specie payments would have meant,
but for emergency legislation of 1798, a *de facto* silver standard.

In the period from 1797 to 1816 the discussion of the relative merits of
gold and silver as the standard, or of the desirability of the free coinage
of both metals, was a minor issue. In the controversy that headed up in
the Bullion Report, and in Ricardo's writings of 1809-1811, the question
whether gold or silver should be the standard, or even which was the
legal standard, was submerged in the larger theoretical and policy questions: why was the Bank of England note at a discount in relation to
both gold and silver, and when and how should it be brought back to
par? The arguments of both the bullionists and the antibullionists in
large part bypassed the issue of the relative merits of gold and silver.
Most of the bullionists apparently would have gladly accepted any metallic standard, and the antibullionists would have viewed with equal alarm
a proposal to go back to either metallic standard. After Waterloo Ricardo
considered, without great conviction one way or the other, the relative
merits of gold and silver as standards of value.[65] Only after the decision
had been made by legislation of 1816 that the standard would be gold
once specie payments were resumed, was there any extended discussion
of the relative advantages of gold or silver as the standard.

Role of the Bank of England

The crisis of 1793 had raised the question of the responsibilities of the
Bank of England, and the issue was under almost continuous debate for
more than three quarters of a century. Was it just a bank that had been
granted some monopoly powers in exchange for services that it rendered
to the state and that issued circulating notes as an incident of its business,
or was it the basis of the monetary and banking system, with the responsibilities that went with such power? In the interchange, beginning in
1795, between the Bank and the Government over advances and foreign
transfers, the Bank sometimes talked as if it were a sovereign power

[64] 38 Geo. III, c. 59.
[65] For details of Ricardo's shifts in opinion, see Sayers, "Ricardo's Views," p. 37.

negotiating with another sovereign. In the last analysis, however, the Bank apparently always gave in, although its protests may have had a moderating effect on the demands of Government. The issue went much deeper, however, than the Bank's obligation to advance funds to the Exchequer. There was the question of the Bank's responsibilities to the financial and business community and the relation of these responsibilities to its money-making activities. The status of the Bank's notes was uncertain: were they simply a convenient substitute for money, or were they in effect paper coin of the realm, with the privileges of coin and subject to the regulations that might apply to coin? All of these issues were raised during the Restriction, but only on the status of the Bank note was there a clear-cut conflict and legislative action.

In 1797 Sir Francis Baring had recognized Bank notes for what they were—not a substitute for money, but the basis of the monetary system—and wanted them to be legal tender. However, as long as the public would accept the Bank's notes without benefit of legal tender, the Government and the Bank preferred it that way. The Gold Coin acts of 1811 and 1812,[66] intended to stop Lord King's attempt to force his tenants to pay their rents in specie, in effect made Bank notes *de facto* legal tender, but the Government went through legal contortions to avoid the use of the term "legal tender." [67] In the debates in 1797, and again in 1811 and 1812 on the Bullion Report and on the Gold Coin acts, the background of the French Revolution evidently played an important part in this desire of the Tories to avoid the term "legal tender," which was associated in the public mind with the assignats.

The Bank's responsibility to the banking and business community in time of crisis, as distinct from its responsibility to furnish funds to the Government to finance the war, was really not tested in the years 1797–1815. The redemption crisis of 1797 revealed no development of the Bank's philosophy, although after the event it brought from Henry Thornton a prophetic statement before the Parliamentary committees on the Bank's responsibility. Insofar as the Bank did have a concept of responsibility that went beyond what any banker might be expected to have to his customers, the experience of 1797, like that of 1793, would suggest—although this cannot be documented by any specific statement of the Bank—that whatever the Bank's view of its responsibility, it did

---

[66] 51 Geo. III, c. 127; 52 Geo. III, c. 50.

[67] More details on the legal tender issue are given in my "Legal Tender during the English and Irish Bank Restrictions," *Journal of Political Economy*, LVIII, 241–250 (June 1949).

not embrace the entire country. The Government's decision of 1797 to suspend payments meant that the crisis did not revive the controversy of 1793: who should increase the circulation in time of crisis? Between then and the Bullion Report it was clear that the Bank, despite its many protests, was in fact a lender of last resort as far as the Government was concerned. There was no test of its relation to the money market until the late summer of 1810. Then a series of failures followed the speculative boom of 1809 and early 1810 and was aggravated by the death of Sir Francis Baring on September 11, 1810, and by the suicide on September 28, 1810, of Abraham Goldsmid, a leading loan contractor, under conditions that raised doubt as to his solvency. The Bank's total advances, according to Silberling's figures, rose by over £6 million—nearly 15 per cent—between May and July, 1810, and nearly £4 million of the increase was in discounting for private parties.

The Bank's records are silent as to the reasons for the expansion of private discounts in June and July of 1810, the persons to whom they were granted, and why these fell off so sharply in the following seven months. In February 1811 private discounts were down by more than £7 million from the previous July, and advances to Government had declined by about £800,000. Total Bank credit declined by £3,851,420 between August 31, 1810, and February 28, 1811. This decrease in Bank credit was in the face of record bankruptcies in the last quarter of 1810 and the first quarter of 1811. Early in March the report of the Commons Select Committee on the State of Commercial Credit recommended the issue of £6 million of Exchequer bills. It said that the issue of 1793 "was attended with the happiest effects, and the most complete success," and "that similar provisions should be adopted in regard to the relief at present proposed" (p. 5). The recommendation had Government backing, but both Huskisson and Thornton expressed doubts whether the situation was comparable to that of 1793. In Thornton's view the troubles of 1793 were due to a "momentary want," whereas "the failure of this day implied a disease of much deeper and more serious nature." [68] Legislation authorized £2 million of Exchequer bills,[69] and a total of £1,339,000 were issued, of which all but £990 had been repaid by 1813.[70] Aside from the question whether the conditions in early 1811 justified emergency support, when support was given, it came not from the Bank but from the Government.

[68] 1 *Hansard* XIX, 343, March 11, 1811. The debate on the Exchequer bills covers 327–350.
[69] 51 Geo. III, c. 15.
[70] *Report from the Commissioners . . . for the Issue of Exchequer Bills*, P.P. 1813–14 (53), III.

Many actions and statements of the Bank and the Government between 1793 and 1811 are consistent with the idea, never stated in unequivocal terms, that the Bank was considered an essentially private business except for the obligation to make loans to Government. This was particularly true in the attitude toward the Bank's profits and toward information about its operations. After an annual dividend rate of 7 per cent since 1788, the Bank paid 12 per cent in 1805 and 1806 and 10 per cent from 1807 to 1822. There were occasional snipings at this increased rate, but public opinion seemed to acquiesce in the view that any increased profits resulting from the Restriction belonged to the stockholders, and at several meetings stockholders complained that they should receive even larger dividends.[71]

Before Parliamentary committees officials of the Bank withheld many details of their operations, on the ground that this was confidential business information which the committees were not entitled to know. In 1797 Pitt refused, without having the Bank's permission, to tell the Lords Committee when the directors had informed him that their specie holdings were dangerously low (p. 8). In Parliament he successfully opposed George Tierney's motion for information on "outstanding advances made from the Directors of the Bank to the Government" on the ground that "it would tend to divulge the private transactions of the Bank, and thereby prove injurious to public credit."[72] In the hearings before the Irish Currency Committee in 1804, William Colville, a director of the Bank of Ireland, asked whether the Bank of Ireland in 1797 would have had to suspend payments in the absence of a restriction act, replied: "That is a very delicate question, and goes almost the length of asking the quantity of Specie that existed in the Bank of Ireland at that period; and that being a subject upon which I have taken oath not to give any information upon, with great humility I hope it will not be pressed any further" (p. 122). Evidently the committee agreed with his view, for he was not pressed further. In 1810 the Bullion Committee acquiesced in the position of the Bank that it need not reveal the total of its private discounts (p. 56).[73]

[71] The Bank kept no records of the speeches at stockholders' meetings before 1892, but with very few exceptions there was some mention of every meeting the following day in the London press. I have used the accounts as given in the *Times* from 1793 to 1875.

[72] *Parliamentary Register*, I, 786–787, March 9, 1797.

[73] The Bank, however, furnished an index number of discounts from 1790 to 1809, but the committee returned the document to the Bank and the information in it was not published in the appendix of the Bullion Report. A letter signed "A.B." in the *Morning Chronicle* of October 15, 1810, gave what purported to be an extract from this document. The letter, with the editor's comment on it, is in Ricardo, *Works*, IV, 416–418.

A Lull in the Controversy, 1812–1815

The five years after the bullion debate were an anticlimax in monetary and banking controversy. Other economic problems, in particular the Corn Laws, came to the fore. Following the publication of some ninety pamphlets on monetary and banking problems in 1810 and 1811, the next four years inspired barely half that number. Both sides had said about all there was to say on the theoretical issues. The premium on gold and the price of Hamburg exchange, influenced no doubt both by the continued expansion of the monetary supply and by the large foreign expenditures, rose to a maximum in 1813. In July 1813, when the gold premium was nearly 50 per cent, the Prime Minister, Lord Liverpool, assured the Lords that there was "no proof whatever of a depreciation of our paper currency."[74] Bills for continuing the Restriction were passed in 1814, 1815, and 1816[75] with little debate beyond the unsuccessful efforts, in which Francis Horner took the lead, to force the Government to state what its policy was. When George Tierney asked, after Napoleon's retirement to Elba, what the Government intended to do about the Restriction after a treaty of peace was signed, the Chancellor of the Exchequer refused to answer.[76] When a motion for a committee to investigate the state of the Bank of England was before the Commons in 1815, Lord Archibald Hamilton "wished that persons connected with the Bank would state to the House at what price they would attempt to restore the currency of the country." The Chancellor of the Exchequer ignored the insinuation that a devaluation was contemplated, and replied that he hoped that the Restriction would end on July 5, 1816.[77]

Bullionists and antibullionists alike seem to have had a tacit hope that with the defeat of Napoleon the pound would come back to par with little difficulty. For a time it looked as if the hopes of both groups would be fulfilled. The price of gold, which had stood at £5.10.0 at the end of 1813, had fallen to £4.5.0—a premium of barely 8 per cent—by October 1814, less than six months after Napoleon's retirement to Elba. During the Hundred Days the gold premium again almost reached the level of 1813, but fell to £4.9.6 shortly after Waterloo, and by the end of 1815 was only £4.2.0, the lowest figure since 1805. The pound as measured by Hamburg exchange, was higher in March 1816 than at any time since September

---

[74] 1 *Hansard* XXVI, 1178, July 9, 1813.
[75] 54 Geo. III, c. 99; 55 Geo. III, c. 28; 56 Geo. III, c. 40.
[76] 1 *Hansard* XXVII, 525–526, April 25, 1814.
[77] 1 *Hansard* XXIX, 1179–1181, March 2, 1815. The entire debate covered 1177–1203.

1808. By October 1816 the gold price was £3.18.6, a premium of less than 1 per cent. There is no evidence of any conscious policy by the Bank of England of restricting credit in the effort to raise the gold value of the Bank note, and the Bank then, and for more than a decade after, stood firm in its announced belief that its credit policy was powerless to affect the exchanges or the price of gold. But whether the result of policy or of forces outside the bank, in the year after Waterloo total Bank credit declined sharply from £44,854,180 on August 31, 1815, to £34,279,540 on August 31, 1816. Private discounts and advances to Government, a somewhat less comprehensive figure but available twice a month, fell from over £47 million on July 12, 1815, to less than £28 million on December 11, 1816. Bank circulation, over £28 million on July 8, 1815, was a little over £25 million by the end of the year but showed little trend in 1816. Bank deposits fell off by about 15 per cent in the year following August 31, 1815.

The movement of the pound toward par and the consolidation of the gains were complicated by three developments: a world-wide drop in prices on a gold basis; increasing economic distress, particularly in agriculture and in the metal industries in the Birmingham area; and extensive failures of country banks. In contrast to the policy of hoping for the best, there was, beginning early in 1816, a rekindling of popular and Parliamentary controversy over monetary policy and increasing demands for positive policy by the Bank and the Government. The lines of monetary and banking battle were more sharply drawn than at any time since 1811, and proposals for action on the standard, the country banks, and the Bank of England were no longer prevented by the overriding problems of war. The distress associated with the virtual restoration of the pound to parity produced an organized attack, partly against gold convertibility of the pound at the old rate, and partly against the idea of a metallic standard of any kind. The premium on gold, after a low in October 1816, increased later in the year. This new depreciation of the pound, which had been at virtual parity for several months, strengthened the view in many quarters that convertibility was the only sure protection for the currency. The result was a reviving controversy, from 1816 to 1821, over monetary and banking theory and practice.

III

DECISION TO RESUME SPECIE
PAYMENTS, 1816–1819

SIX MAIN developments in theory and policy marked the period from 1816 to 1819:

1. Demonetization of silver in 1816, and adoption of a gold standard to become effective at the end of the Restriction.

2. Increasing acceptance of the idea that the issue of country bank notes created an unstable monetary situation; an abortive attempt by Government to control these issues.

3. Criticism of banks as exploiters of the people and of the Bank of England for the executions for forgery of its notes.

4. Trial and error actions by the Government and the Bank to reconcile the two objectives of relieving economic distress and bringing the pound back to par.

5. Widespread opposition to the attempts to bring the pound back to par.

6. Adoption of legislation for the resumption of payments in stages in 1820–1823 and for the dropping of all prohibitions on the melting and export of British coins.

Formal Adoption of the Gold Standard

The silver circulation, already bad in 1797, had gotten steadily worse in the years following, for the Government refused to make any provision for a new silver coinage. Not only did the very limited mintings of the Restriction years disappear from circulation, but from 1800 on there was a profit in melting almost any British silver coin, no matter how badly worn or clipped. The situation was mitigated by the issue of notes of smaller denominations by merchants as well as by banks, by increased minting of copper coins, and particularly by the issue of tokens—often referred to as stamped dollars—by the Bank of England. These were

Spanish silver coins stamped with the head of George III that were currently accepted as a monetary value above their bullion value.[1] Even these tokens did not solve the difficulty, for the rise in the price of silver in terms of the inconvertible paper drove a large part of the original stamped dollars to the melting pot, and there was the repeated necessity of issuing new tokens and raising the shilling rating at which they were to pass.

From the long view of history the problem of silver coin between 1797 and 1816 was a minor monetary incident, but it probably did more than all the writings on monetary theory to bring the legal adoption of a single gold standard in 1816. The Bank of England's records in the years 1797–1816 have more information on the Bank's difficulties with silver tokens than on all the larger issues of monetary and banking policy with which it is assumed that central bankers are concerned. The Bank repeatedly objected to the role in which it was placed: the issuing of extralegal fiduciary silver on behalf of a Government that was unwilling to authorize fiduciary coins on its own account. The defeat of Napoleon, the virtual end of the gold premium, and the drop in the price of silver to the coinage price did nothing to relieve the silver situation. Continuance of chaotic monetary conditions in time of peace brought increased public criticism and a development galling to British pride. The shortage of British silver led private parties to import French silver that was extensively used as small change. Pascoe Grenfell's charge in Parliament that in change for a pound note "persons usually received one half in French coin, and the other half perhaps in counterfeit coin made at home," if not literally true, was in line with a general picture given in other statements.[2] Alexander Baring, who spoke with authority on financial matters, urged a 10 per cent reduction in the weight of silver coins.[3] Pressure mounted for some action to deal with a situation that was getting steadily worse, and petitions were presented to Parliament by retail traders "praying for a new coinage of silver." [4] The Lords of the Committee of Council, without holding any public hearings, belatedly turned in the report that they had been directed to prepare in 1797 and recommended "that it should forthwith be proposed to Parliament, to pass an Act declaring the Gold Coin alone to be the Standard Coin of this Realm; and that the Silver Coins

[1] A detailed account of these tokens is in Maberly Phillips, *The Token Money of the Bank of England, 1797 to 1816* (London, 1900).
[2] Grenfell referred to the circulation of French coin in speeches in the Commons on March 22 and April 10, 1816 (1 *Hansard* XXXIII, 535, 1148).
[3] 1 *Hansard* XXXIII, 1149, April 10, 1816.
[4] 1 *Hansard* XXXIV, 239–243, May 3, 1816.

are hereafter to be considered merely as representative Coins, and to be a legal tender only in payment of Sums not exceeding Two Guineas." [5]

Debate followed in both houses.[6] Government spokesmen based their case largely on the ground that gold had been the *de facto* standard for nearly a century before 1797, rather than on an analysis of the economic significance of demonetizing silver. Alexander Baring, however, pointed out that a gold pound was worth about 4 per cent more than a silver pound, and "as a silver circulation could be more easily established than one of gold, the resumption of cash payments by the bank could be more conveniently and expeditiously made in the former than in the latter." [7] This discriminating comment did not lead to further discussion of the relation between demonetization of silver and the resumption of cash payments, and there was no debate on the larger economic issues involved. John Wilson Croker's suggestion of a decimal coinage[8] received no support. The legislation, commonly known as Lord Liverpool's Coinage Act,[9] was passed without a record vote, but the Earl of Lauderdale made a protest on the records of the Lords, pointing out the fallacy in the idea that the greater stability in the pound price of gold proved gold a more stable standard.[10]

Under the old legislation, suspended in 1798, anyone could bring silver to the Mint and receive coins at the rate of 5s.2d. per ounce of standard silver, equivalent to 62 shillings per troy pound of standard silver. The new law still permitted the public, upon the issuance of a royal proclamation, to bring silver to the Mint and receive 62 shillings per pound of silver. However, the coins were to be reduced in silver content so that 66 shillings would be coined, of which 4 shillings were to be retained by the Mint "for the Defalcation or Diminution and for the Charge for the Assaying, Coinage and Waste in Coinage." The new silver coins were to be legal tender only up to £2. With the price of silver much above 5s.6d. an ounce (66s. a pound) England would have lost its silver coins— a possibility that had been suggested in the Lords by the Earl of Liverpool and the Earl of Lauderdale.[11] On the other hand, with the price of

---

[5] *Report of the Lords of the Committee of Council, appointed to take into Consideration the State of the Coins of the Kingdom*, P.P. 1816, (411) VI.

[6] The Commons debate is in 1 *Hansard* XXXIV, 946–965, May 30, 1816, and 1018–1027, June 7, 1816; the Lord's debate is in XXXIV, 912–923, May 30, 1816, and 1122–1125, June 17, 1816.

[7] 1 *Hansard* XXXIV, 964, May 20, 1816.

[8] 1 *Hansard* XXXIV, 1024–1025, June 7, 1816.

[9] 56 Geo. III, c. 68.

[10] 1 *Hansard* XXXIV, 1235–1239, June 21, 1816.

[11] 1 *Hansard* XXXIV, 914–916, May 30, 1816.

silver below 5s.2d. an ounce, it would have paid private parties to bring silver to the mint and receive 62 shillings in limited legal tender silver coin.

It is not clear whether, regardless of the wording of the law, it had ever been the intention of its sponsors that private parties were to be free to bring silver to the Mint. Whatever the Government's original idea, its hand was forced by the fact that the price of silver was under 5s. when the law was passed and went as low as 4s.10d. later in the year. Private parties could have made a profit by buying silver at the market price and taking it to the Mint for coinage. The Government, presumably for this reason, did not at the time issue the necessary royal proclamation, and never did, thus forestalling the possibility of legal chaos that could have resulted from unlimited coinage of limited legal tender silver. The new silver coin was minted only on Government account. For most of the next fifty years, and even before the great rise in the silver-gold ratio in the 1870's, the price of silver was below 5s.2d. an ounce. As far as the record shows, however, no one challenged the administrative demonetization of silver until 1870, when a tough-minded British colonel delivered silver to the Mint and demanded coin, and was informed that it had no authority to give him coin because no royal proclamation had been issued.[12]

Proposals for Regulations of Country Bank Notes

The economic distress in 1814, 1815, and 1816 and the collapse of commodity prices had been accompanied by wholesale failure of country banks and a large decline in their note circulation. The previous high for country bank failures had been 22 in 1793, but in 1814, 1815, and 1816 the failures were, respectively, 27, 25, and 37.[13] Figures presented to the Lords Committee in 1819,[14] although subject to a large margin of error, point to a decrease in country note circulation proportionately much greater in 1815 and 1816 than the decrease in the circulation of the Bank of England—£22,709,000 in 1814, £19,011,000 in 1815, and £15,096,000 in 1816. Even Francis Horner, defender of the country banks as against the Bank of England, although attributing the development to a previous drop in agricultural prices, said that the result had been "a destruction of the country bank paper to an extent which would not have been thought possible without more ruin than had ensued."[15]

[12] See p. 198 for a discussion of this episode.
[13] *Bank Charter Committee*, 1832, app. 101.
[14] *Lords Committee*, 1819, app. F.8.
[15] 1 *Hansard* XXXIV, 143, May 1, 1816.

There was, however, little discussion in 1814–1816, either in or out of Parliament, of country banking as a separate problem, although much of what was said about the unduly large profits of the Bank of England may also have represented a feeling that all banks were profiting at public expense. The resistance, beginning in 1816, that developed in some quarters not only to resumption of payments at an early date, but even to a gold or metallic standard of any sort, put the emphasis in controversial writing on the monetary standard rather than on the specific problems of country banks. But the question of country banking, within the structure of whatever larger monetary arrangements might be made, was still an issue. Matthias Attwood, a London banker, in a publication of 1817 that was written and privately circulated early in 1816, pointed out that country bank failures were affecting the total monetary supply and also urged a cut in the gold content of the pound.[16] Sir John Sinclair, sharing Attwood's views on the standard, urged "placing provincial circulation on a safe and solid foundation." [17] Edward Tatham suggested that banks be required to "give *landed or funded* security to the public for the payment of their notes." [18]

Control of country bank notes was an issue that cut across that of the standard or resumption of payments, and Ricardo's views, much as they differed from Matthias Attwood's and Sinclair's on the standard, were of the same general nature on country banking. Ricardo's *Proposals for an Economical and Secure Currency,* written in large part in August and September 1815, and published in February 1816, in addition to its plan for redemption in bullion by the Bank of England and for securing to the Government a large share of the profits of note issue, discussed the need for regulating country bank issues. He recommended that "the public should be protected by requiring of every country bank to deposit with government, or with commissioners appointed for that purpose, funded property or other government security, in some proportion to the amount of their issues." [19]

In April 1818 the Government introduced a bill providing that after July 5, 1820, no private bank outside of Scotland could issue any notes under £5, except against the deposit of Exchequer bills with the Treas-

---

[16] *Observations Concerning the Distress of the Country* (London, 1817), p. 13.

[17] *On the Means of Arresting the Progress of National Calamity* (London, 1817), p. 13.

[18] *Observations on the Scarcity of Money* (Oxford, 1816), pp. 32–34.

[19] *The Works and Correspondence of David Ricardo,* ed. Piero Sraffa (Cambridge, 1951–1955), IV, 73.

ury.[20] The Bank was consulted about the bill and may even have suggested it, although the Bank's record on this is not clear.[21] The Government's proposal evidently had been known in advance to others than the Bank, for over two weeks before its presentation to Parliament Ricardo had written to his friend Hutches Trower: "Mr. Vansittart had a ridiculous project I hear of creating a new circulating medium and legal tender, called stock notes, which were to be advanced, without any limit, on stock, at the rate of £50 for every £100 stock. If such a plan had been carried into execution it was possible that our money might have been increased to 400 millions. I am told that he has now abandoned it, and it is difficult to believe that he ever entertained so ridiculous a project, tho' my authority for the fact is no less than that of Mr. Tierney." [22]

Ricardo's opposition is evidence of the crosscurrents of opinion about country banks and of the fact that views on a particular proposal could be altered greatly because of a difference in the setting in which it was made. Ricardo had made a similar proposal two years before, and much of the argument given by the Chancellor of the Exchequer in presenting the bill sounded like an expanded support of Ricardo's proposal. Yet in this particular setting, apparently because the bill had the support of Government and of the Bank, which were then lukewarm about resumption, Ricardo opposed the Government plan. The bill drew some Whig criticism in Parliament,[23] but it was a united banking opposition rather than party politics that forced the Government to withdraw it.[24]

Criticism of Banks as Exploiters of the People

This unsuccessful movement for a regulation of the issues of country banks was part of a groundswell of criticism of all banks. The idea appeared increasingly that banks had deprived the public of its natural

[20] The debate is in 1 *Hansard* XXXVII, 1230–1254, April 9, 1818, and 1284–1285, April 10, 1818.

[21] The only reference to the bill in the Bank's records is a letter of April 8, 1818, to the Chancellor of the Exchequer, asking for a copy of the bill "if there should be any deviation in the plan from that originally proposed and sent to the Bank" (Bank of England, Letter Book, 4, p. 63).

[22] Letter of March 22, 1818, *Works*, VII, 260.

[23] George Tierney, 1 *Hansard* XXXVII, 1244–1246, April 9, 1818; Sir John Newport, 1284; Alderman Atkins, 1285.

[24] Speech of Nicholas Vansittart, Chancellor of the Exchequer, 1 *Hansard* XXXVIII, 410–411, April 30, 1818; records of meetings of country bankers and of their conferences with the Government are in the British Museum, Add. MS. 38,271, fols. 237–239, 249–252, 257–260, 271–273.

metallic money and had created paper money as an instrument of oppression, in contrast to the view sometimes put forward in the late nineteenth and twentieth century of gold being the instrument by which banks exploited the people. A climate of opinion developed that inconvertible paper money should be abolished for reasons that went beyond the theoretical analysis on such matters as how much deflation might be expected from a return to specie payments. Men who were far apart on most points were in agreement that somebody was making too much money from the paper money system: the restrained criticism of Ricardo, under James Mill's urgings, of the Bank's profits; the strictures of obscure pamphleteers that bankers "appear to be infinitely more mischievous than the coiners of base money,"[25] and that both the Bank of England and the country banks had made "unfair gains from the restriction measure";[26] the wholesale invective of Cobbett against bankers as a class; and the denunciations in Jonathan Wooler's *Black Dwarf*, in Leigh Hunt's *Examiner,* and in *Sherwin's Political Register,* where without benefit of economic analysis these radical journals reiterated that the paper money system was one of the oppressors of the people. In 1819, when Parliament was considering resumption, *Sherwin's Political Register* offered this advice: "Let our tyrants turn their infamous paper into coin of the same weight and fineness, as that of which the people have been deprived, then we may say that they have acted justly, and surmounted at least some of their difficulties."[27]

The Bank, serving the financial needs of government during the Restriction, had prospered. In addition to increased dividends it distributed substantial bonuses in 1799, 1801, 1802, 1804, 1805, and 1806; and in 1816 it paid a stock dividend of 25 per cent and maintained the same dividend rate on the increased stock.[28] The new contract between the Bank and the Government in 1808 was believed to have been extremely profitable to the Bank. Ricardo, and doubtless other men of property who were critical of the Bank, were bothered about whether the relations of the Government and the Bank would justify the abrogation of such a contract.[29] That the Bank had made unprecedented profits during the Re-

[25] John Vance Agnew, *Resolutions drawn up for the Consideration of the County of Wigton* (Edinburgh, 1816), p. 40.

[26] Samuel Read, *An Inquiry Concerning the Nature and Use of Money* (London, 1816), pp. 188–189.

[27] May 8, 1819, p. 7.

[28] *Bank Charter Committee,* 1832, apps. 29, 34.

[29] Ricardo discusses this in *Proposals for an Economical and Secure Currency,* in *Works,* IV, 79–95, as does Sraffa in his editorial note, pp. 45–47.

striction, that it seemed to regard its legal and moral rights to these profits as beyond challenge, and that the continuation of the Restriction probably would be profitable to the Bank cannot be ignored in explaining why political pressure for resumption was so strong in 1818 and 1819, despite the impressive economic arguments against it.

In an extreme way William Cobbett represented the national schizophrenia on the monetary question, compounded by his political views and his powers of demagoguery. As spokesman for an England of rugged yeomen Cobbett was critical of all banks as symbols of exploitation. As a friend of the people he played up the losses that the ordinary man suffered from inflation; and as a political radical he denounced the relations between the Tory Government and the Bank. Ever since the Irish exchange difficulties of 1803 and 1804 his *Political Register* had criticized the Restriction. When in 1815 and 1816 the rise in the gold value of paper was accompanied by economic distress, Cobbett blamed the Bank for deflation with all the vigor he had previously shown in denouncing it for inflation. In the first of a series of open letters to the Chancellor of the Exchequer he charged: "The Bank, in endeavouring to follow the advice, and to act upon the principles, of the Bullion Committee, has plunged agriculture and trade and rents and debts and credits all into confusion." [30] The same idea, with emphasis on the iniquitous role of both the Bank of England and the country banks, appeared repeatedly.

Forgery and the Criticism of Restriction

Another point, logically different from the Bank's profits but part of the general picture of public criticism of the Bank as fattening itself at the expense of the people, was the increasing forgery of the Bank's notes and the executions for that offense. Before 1797 the Bank had issued no notes under £5, and forgery of its notes was almost unknown. Forgery increased greatly after 1797, when following the Restriction the Bank first issued £1 and £2 notes and prosecutions and capital convictions soon reached alarming figures.[31] In 1806 barely 3000 forged notes were presented to the Bank, in 1817 nearly 29,000, of which only 839 were of denominations over £2. In the seven years between 1790 and 1796 there were no prosecutions for forgery of Bank notes, but between 1797 and 1815 there were 257 capital convictions, in addition to 321 convictions for

[30] *Political Register,* October 28, 1815, 100.
[31] Figures by denominations on forged notes presented to the Bank annually from 1806 to 1874 are given in appendix 15, *Committee on Banks of Issue, 1875.* Figures on executions up to 1818 are in 1 *Hansard* XXXVIII, appendix, pp. xxxviii–xxxix.

possessing forged notes. In 1816, 1817, and the first two months of 1818, the total figures were 56 and 200 respectively.

In May 1818, shortly after the Government's country bank note bill had been withdrawn, Sir James Mackintosh moved for the gathering of figures on prosecutions for forgery of the Bank's notes and the appointment of a committee to investigate the problem. Mackintosh's motions were voted down 87 to 75, but the debate showed how closely executions for forgery were involved in public thinking on the Restriction and on the country banks.[32] Not only did the forgery issue sharpen the feeling that the Restriction should end, but it also strengthened the opposition to any limitations on the notes of country banks, which were generally believed to be less easily forged than the Bank's notes. Mackintosh's description of the bill for restricting the issues of country banks as "a Bill for the better promotion of Forgery" and a "bill for the erection and furnishing of gibbets"[33] doubtless was colored by Whig politics, but there is no doubt of the seriousness of the situation, or of the criticism, both in and out of Parliament, that the executions had aroused. The Bank's records in 1818 and 1819 suggest that the forgery of its notes took up more time at directors' meetings than did major issues of monetary policy. The Bank's protest against furnishing information about prosecutions for forgery as an "incroachment on the rights and privileges of the Bank"[34] is further evidence of its feeling that it was a private business into whose affairs Parliament had no right to pry.

Early in 1819 George Cruikshank's famous etching of the Bank Restriction Note both reflected and inflamed public indignation. The note, signed by "Jack Ketch," the popular name for the public hangman, showed eleven men and women hanging from a gallows marked "Bank Post"; and below, the words "During the Issue of Bank Notes easily imitated, and until the Resumption of Cash Payments, or the abolition of Punishments of Death."[35] Clemency in capital convictions for forgery of the Bank's notes seems to have been based on the recommendation of the Bank, which intensified feeling against it.[36] The charge in Parliament

[32] 1 *Hansard* XXXVIII, 671–703, May 13, 1818.

[33] 1 *Hansard* XXXVIII, 275, April 21, 1818.

[34] C.T., 12, April 23, 1818, p. 90.

[35] A copy of this etching is in A. D. MacKenzie, *The Bank of England Note: A History of Its Printing* (Cambridge, 1953), pl. xi. Cruikshank's account of how he came to make the etching after seeing convicted forgers hanging from gallows, and of the popular appeal of the etching, is given in Blanshard Jerrold, *The Life of George Cruikshank* (New York, 1882), pp. 93–94.

[36] This is indicated by a number of items in the Bank's records, which support the charges to this effect made in Parliament, and by William Cobbett in the *Political Register*.

that the Bank's lawyers handling forgery cases were paid on a piecework basis for the convictions obtained may not have been literally true, but it is indicative of public opinion.[37]

The three most powerful radical journalists of the day kept up a steady denunciation of the executions for forgery. Cobbett's criticism of the Bank, like so much of what Cobbett wrote, does not meet the tests of historical scholarship, but it cannot be ignored as part of the stuff out of which monetary history is made: "This villainous Bank has slaughtered more people than would people a *State*. With the rope, the prison, the hulk and the transport ship, this Bank has destroyed, perhaps, fifty thousand persons, including the widows and orphans of its victims. At the shop of this crew of fraudulent insolvents, there sits a *council* to determine, which of their victims shall live, and which shall swing! Having usurped the royal prerogative of coining and issuing money, it is but another step to usurp that of pardoning or of causing to be hanged!"[38]

In one of a series of articles attacking the executions for forgery in the *Black Dwarf*, Wooler said that "the 'Old Hag of Threadneedle Street' must have no repose, until she consents to abandon her infernal traffic in the blood of those who are tempted to imitate her ragged wealth."[39] And Leigh Hunt's *Examiner*, with evident approval, cited a correspondent who "begs to recommend to the notice of Parliament that every person convicted of forging such Notes—*as they are manufactured at present,* —shall be hung by a Bank Director, the said Bank Director himself performing the office of Executioner. Our Correspondent professes to have been some time deliberating with himself, whether it would not be still more effective, if the Forger were to hang the Director."[40]

Public Criticism of Deflation

At the same time that widespread public opinion was building up for ending the Restriction on the ground that it contributed to the exploitation of the public and to executions for forgery, another public sentiment was developing for continuance of the Restriction, a permanent devaluation, or the adoption of the silver standard, on the ground that deflation was contributing to economic distress. Prices fell almost continuously from late in 1814 until the middle of 1816: the Gayer wholesale index[41]

---

[37] 1 *Hansard* XXXVIII, 282, April 21, 1818.

[38] *Political Register,* May 15, 1819, 1071.

[39] II, 617 (September 30, 1818).

[40] April 26, 1818, p. 267.

[41] Arthur D. Gayer, W. W. Rostow, and Anna Jacobson Schwartz, *The Growth and*

fell by over 20 per cent, and the Silberling wholesale index by about 30 per cent. Bankruptcies, which had averaged 105 a month in 1814, averaged 147 in 1815 and 179 in 1816, and in November 1816 reached a new high of 277.

Criticism of the postwar deflation came primarily from two sources: agriculture and the Birmingham industrial area. With the exception of Cobbett, whose monetary views were peculiar to himself, it represented a politically conservative opinion, as did most attacks on the gold standard up to the 1860's. As early as 1814, Peter Richard Hoare, who in 1810 and 1811 had written three pamphlets critical of the Restriction, expressed serious doubts as to the feasibility of a return to specie payments without an adjustment of all monetary contracts.[42] In 1816 an anonymous writer argued that "the present extensive state of distress in England, arises chiefly from the sudden change that has taken place in the circulating medium of the country."[43] In the same year C. R. Prinsep urged that specie payments be restored on the basis of a silver standard, reduced by 20 per cent, and said of such a policy: "It amounts to an act of general bankruptcy; but, like other violent remedies, is fully justifiable on the score of necessity."[44] Edward Tatham combined an attack on banks as "paper-mints" with a suggestion that the gold content of the pound be reduced by 10 per cent.[45] Similarly the conservative *Quarterly Review*, in an article by Robert Southey, was critical of "a further subtraction of currency (too much having already been subtracted)," and asked rhetorically: "What! Is the ghost of Bullion abroad?"[46] The *Quarterly* urged public expenditures to provide employment and relief of economic distress, and although the point was not spelled out in detail, its lukewarmness about monetary deflation evidently was tied in with a desire for greater government spending.

A large part of the criticism of deflation focused on its distributive effects in raising the burden of taxes and benefiting creditors at the expense of the rest of the community, particularly landowners. Representa-

---

Fluctuation of the British Economy, 1790–1850 (Oxford, 1953), vol. I, pt. 3. All subsequent references to prices, production, bankruptcies, and other nonbanking figures, unless otherwise indicated, are taken from the tables in this work, including those in the "Microfilm Appendix" (Ann Arbor, 1953).

[42] *Tracts on our Present Money System* (London, 1814), pp. 7–15.

[43] *An Address to Her Royal Highness the Princess Charlotte,* pamphleteer edition (London, 1816), p. 493.

[44] *A Letter to the Earl of Liverpool* (London, 1816), pp. 22–31.

[45] *Observations on the Scarcity of Money,* pp. 16–17, 32–33.

[46] October 1816, vol. XVI, art. xi, "Parliamentary Reform," p. 260.

tive of the views of many was the statement of John Edye: "Our taxes are being still paid in the currency which is nominally the same, though really so different, the fundholder is wallowing in imaginary and unexpectedly doubled wealth, whilst the landed, manufacturing and commercial interests, which alone support him, are groaning under the doubled pressure of an artificial debt."[47] Some criticism also brought out the idea that deflation reduced the total economic output. This had been suggested in the *Quarterly Review,* but from the Birmingham spokesmen Thomas Attwood, a banker and brother of Matthias Attwood, and Henry James, a merchant, came a more sophisticated analysis, with a statement that would rate high, by the standards of a generation that had read Keynes, of the essentials of a theory of aggregate demand and a theory of employment. As the center of the armaments industry, Birmingham had felt the transition from war to peace with great severity.

The Birmingham protests had comparatively little to say about debts, but much about unemployment. The agricultural protests had emphasized the desirability of tax reduction, the Birmingham protests objected to tax reductions as deflationary. The emphasis of Attwood was on the maintenance of expenditures, both by private parties and by government, and on the employment effects of such expenditures: "It is the chief purport of this letter to show that the issue of money *will* create markets, and that it is upon the abundance or scarcity of money that the extent of all markets principally depends ... The two great evils under which the country has latterly laboured, have been the diminished expenditure of the rich, including that of the Government, and the exhaustion of stocks which, whilst consumption has been diminished, has glutted the markets and increased the general depression and scarcity of Money, which had first caused such exhaustion."[48]

In other publications Attwood reiterated the thought, with emphasis on the need for giving employment regardless of the monetary consequences.[49] He recognized that prices could adjust downward, but was as impatient as Keynes with the idea that an economy could ignore the pains of adjustments to a lower level of prices:

---

[47] *A Letter to the Right Hon. Lord Rolle* (London, 1817), p. 17.

[48] *A Letter to the Right Honourable Nicholas Vansittart* (Birmingham, 1817), pp. 5, 10–11.

[49] *The Remedy; or, Thoughts on the Present Distresses* (London, 1816); *Prosperity Restored* (London, 1817); *Observations on Currency, Population and Pauperism* (Birmingham, 1818); *A Letter to the Earl of Liverpool, on the Reports of the Committees of the Two Houses of Parliament* (Birmingham, 1819); *A Second Letter to the Earl of Liverpool* (Birmingham, 1819).

If human wants could stand still during the action of this fatal principle; if men could live without food and clothing for two or three years, until the reduction of the circulating medium had acted alike in reducing the prices of all kinds of industry and commodities, then the social system might go on again, with no other injury than the secret and unjust transfer of the prosperity of the debtors, into the hands of their creditors; and the far more ruinous transfer of the productive powers of the nation from hands accustomed and competent to do them justice, into other hands totally incompetent to guide them at all.[50]

From Henry James, who before putting his ideas in print had submitted them to Nicholas Vansittart, the Chancellor of the Exchequer, came the same thought that rising prices were a stimulus to the productive elements in the community, and the same demand for action: "Governments ought to legislate for the benefit of the quick, and not solely for the relatively dead (in a national sense); for the industrious and productive, and not altogether for the advantage of those who have ceased to become so."[51]

Development of a Concept of Open Market Operations

While Parliament was debating the single gold standard and the extension of the Restriction, and the public was turning its criticism on both the evils of paper money and the evils of deflation, the Bank and the Government, by a process of trial and error, were carrying on what amounted to open market operations. As early as 1797 Thornton had pointed out, in his testimony before the Parliamentary committees, that as far as the money supply was concerned it made little difference whether the Bank loaned to merchants, loaned to Government, or purchased Exchequer bills. The same point appeared in his *Paper Credit of Great Britain* and in the Bullion Report. As long as the war against Napoleon continued the Bank had little choice but to make the advances that the Government demanded. After Waterloo a larger field of discretion was opened to the Bank.

Total Bank credit reached a high of over £48 million in August 1814, and with three minor exceptions declined at every semiannual reporting date from then up to and including February 1822, when it was less than £16 million. The decrease was particularly great between February 1816 and February 1818, when the total fell from over £43 million to less than £31 million. This deflationary situation was aggravated by the failures

---

[50] *Observations on Currency, Population, and Pauperism*, p. 11.

[51] *Considerations on the Policy or Impolicy of the Further Continuance of the Bank Restriction Act* (Birmingham, 1818), p. 31; *An Inquiry into the Cause of the Distressed State of the Country* (Birmingham, 1817).

of country banks and the sharp reduction in country bank circulation. In view of the seriousness of the country bank situation the argument could well have been made that a moderate expansion of Bank credit would increase employment and production rather than prices, as Henry Thornton had more than once pointed out. But he had died in January 1815. Ardent resumptionists like Ricardo, Tierney, and Horner were so concerned about the long-run dangers of inconvertible paper and so prone to see in any increase in Bank credit, no matter what the justification, an attempt of the Bank to postpone resumption, that they refused to face up to the difficult short-run problem. There is little evidence of positive thinking from within the Government or the Bank on the relation between bank credit, economic conditions, and the restoration of the Bank of England note to par. The imaginative thinking on the relation of the money supply and of government expenditures to economic conditions that came out in 1816 and 1817—in particular the ideas of the Attwoods and Henry James—went to such extremes in policy proposals that it had little effect on the development of an organized theory of Bank or Government action in time of unemployment and distress.

However, regardless of any theory that may have been involved, there were in 1815, 1816, and 1817 two suggestive developments in the Bank's operations: an increase of government credits when distress was at its worst, and a fluctuation of private discounts in inverse relation with government advances. The reduction in Government credit from nearly £35 million on August 31, 1814, to less than £19.5 million on February 29, 1816, seems to have been the result of the accidents of Government finance rather than of fiscal or monetary philosophy, although the Bank's records tell nothing on this point. An increase of over £10 million in "private securities" in the same period still left a net credit decrease of nearly £5 million, or over 10 per cent, in eighteen months. Private credit then fell by over £12 million between February and August of 1816, but was offset in part by an increase of nearly £7 million in public credit. In a less striking degree from 1817 to 1821 there were several cases of a change in one type of advance in large part offset by changes in the other type of advance.

The pressure for government expenditures, particularly from Liverpool and Birmingham, was great. James Mill's mention, in a letter to Ricardo in October 1816, of "some villainous schemes of finance" [52] pending in Parliament probably referred to such proposals. Correspondence of early

[52] Ricardo, *Works*, VII, 85.

1817 in the files of the Liverpool Parliamentary Office shows that leading citizens of that city recommended to the Government a public works program. Henry James and Thomas Attwood, speaking for Birmingham, had urged in correspondence, before their ideas appeared in print, that the Government take action to relieve the distress. In April 1817 the Government proposed an issue of Exchequer bills to finance public works for the relief of the unemployed, and Parliament authorized loans of £1,750,000, of which £250,000 was assigned to Ireland.[53] By the end of the year £750,000 had been advanced to fifty-seven applicants in Great Britain. Possibly Cobbett referred to these transactions when he later charged that the relative prosperity of 1818 was due to the action of the Chancellor of the Exchequer, who, he claimed, as a result of the urging of Matthias Attwood, had "caused bales of paper-money to be poured out, as a *remedy* (now mark what I say) *as a remedy against the workings of those evil-minded and designing men, who were urging the people on for parliamentary reform.*"[54]

Whatever may have been the reasons for changes in the Bank's credit to Government or for the effect of such changes on employment or on the exchanges, the operations of 1816 and 1817 apparently brought home the idea to the banking and business community, in a way that Henry Thornton's earlier reasoned analysis had not, that expansion of Bank credit, no matter what its form, increased the reserves of other banks and eased over-all credit conditions. The witnesses before the committees of 1819 agreed that the important thing was total Bank credit, and not its distribution between credit to Government and credit to private parties. In 1817 Matthias Attwood had stated that the greater abundance of money after the middle of 1816 had been due to the Bank's advance to Government.[55] Particularly illuminating in this connection, even if not technically correct in all details, was the report of Hudson Gurney, a Norfolk banker and one of the few Parliamentary opponents of the resumption act of 1819, in his diary on February 11, 1822, of Matthias Attwood's explanation to him as to just how the then current proposal for an expansion of Bank credit to aid agriculture would operate: "Atwood explained to me what they really mean by borrowing the 4 millions of the

[53] 57 Geo. III, c. 34, June 16, 1817; amended in administrative details by 57 Geo. III, c. 124, July 11, 1817. M. W. Flinn, "The Poor Employment Act of 1817," *The Economic History Review*, ser. 2, no. 1, pp. 82–92 (1961), gives the background and history of the act; the figures on the loans are on pp. 89–90.

[54] *Political Register*, April 25, 1835, 198–199.

[55] *Observations Concerning the Distress of the Country*, pp. 16–17.

Bank. If the agriculturists do not take it—which they think they will not—they will buy stocks—and the Bk. notes coming into the market—will glut the bankers—raise the funds—and move prices generally. In 1816 when all was stagnant Vansittart so borrowed 9 millions—Atwood says all the Bankers without knowing why found themselves flooded with money. Rothschild stepped in borrowed 400,000 of R. G. [probably Richard Gurney] drove up the funds—& the prices of *every* thing started."

Aside from any operations in government debt by the Bank that may have been prompted by a policy of stimulating the economy, the Bank adjusted its private discounts so as to offset seasonal movements in the money market resulting from tax collections and public debt operations. Ricardo, in *Proposals for an Economical and Secure Currency*,[56] appears to have been the first to call public attention to the problem. There is no evidence that the Bank took any action on Ricardo's suggestion that it should give the dividend warrants to the holders of government stock a few days before tax payments were due, and that dividend warrants then be accepted in payment of taxes. The first record of the Bank formally recognizing the need to iron out these fluctuations in the money market was in 1829.[57] But in this, as in many aspects of monetary and banking policy, the problem existed and was dealt with before there was a formal statement of policy. Samuel Thornton's testimony before the Lords Committee in 1819 shows that the Bank then had the practice of adjusting its discounts to offset seasonal movements of tax collections and public debt payments (Q. 33), and Silberling's semimonthly figures on private discounts indicate such a seasonal movement from shortly after 1800.

Faltering Steps toward Resumption

In April 1816, with the Restriction due to end on July 5, 1816, and the price of gold at £4—less than 5 per cent above the Mint prices—the Government introduced a bill for the postponement of resumption for two years. This touched off the first extended debate since 1811 on monetary policy.[58] Even Francis Horner did not oppose the extension of the Restriction for two years, but his demands that extension be "no longer" than two years,

---

[56] Works, IV, 74–76.

[57] J. Horsley Palmer, in his testimony before the Bank Charter Committee of 1832, referred to the Bank's action in expanding near the end of the quarter "for the purpose of relieving the scarcity that be supposed to arise from the payments into the Exchequer," and said that the regulation for this practice had been adopted about three years before (Q. 255, 256).

[58] 1 Hansard XXXIV, 149–167, May 1, 1816; 243–252, May 3, 1816; 404–408, May 8, 1816.

that the Bank "take steps" to prepare for resumption, and that a committee be appointed to investigate the affairs of the Bank were all defeated by large majorities.[59]

The debate produced virtually nothing on the relation of monetary policy to economic conditions, even though economic distress was critical. Horner and other Whig critics of the Restriction were so convinced on over-all political and moral grounds that the Bank should resume, that in their public statements they virtually ignored any possible relation between monetary policy and economic conditions. Ricardo was not in Parliament, but his letter of the following year to Sir John Sinclair is a fair summary of the position of such Parliamentary spokesmen for speedy resumption as Horner and George Tierney: "I agree with you, that a part of our distress has been occasioned by the reduction of the circulation; but I consider it as a necessary price for the establishment of a better system, than that of encouraging an indefinite amount of paper circulation. I cannot think that any but a very small further reduction will be necessary, to enable the Bank to meet any demands that may be made on them for specie. The remedy, grievous as it is, is the necessary consequence of former error." [60] The result was a gap in 1816 and 1817 between the widespread criticism in the pamphlet literature of monetary policy as the cause of depression and the slight attention given to that issue in Parliament. There is substantial truth in a comment of Thomas Attwood in 1817: "It is very remarkable that for the last five years, the situation of the country has been known every where better than in the House of Commons." [61]

While the Bank and the Government were opposing any definite resumption date and even any investigation of the problem, the Bank had started a piecemeal resumption that was the product of historical accident, confused thinking, and public relations. Almost continuously since the suspension of payments in February 1797 the Bank had redeemed some of its notes. The Restriction Act of May 3, 1797, contained a provision, opposed by the Bank but inserted at Pitt's insistence,[62] authorizing the Bank to accept gold deposits of not less than £500, of which three fourths were payable in gold on demand. Under this provision £1,186,160 was deposited

[59] 1 Hansard XXXIV, 166–167, May 1, 1816; 250–251, May 3, 1816; 407–408, May 8, 1816.

[60] Letter of May 4, 1817, Works, VII, 151.

[61] A Letter to the Right Honourable Nicholas Vansittart, p. 105.

[62] C.B., Z, March 23, 29, 1797. The Bank records indicate that Pitt originally wished gold deposits to be repayable in their entirety in gold; however, when the Bank took the position that such a provision "will not be expedient," Pitt acceded in part to the Bank, but insisted on a provision for deposits payable in part in gold.

with the Bank,[63] up to the discontinuance by an order of February 22, 1798, of the practice of accepting such deposits. The Bank also made payments in specie to the Government for specific purposes, in particular foreign subsidies and overseas expenditures.[64]

In addition to payments of specie to depositors and to the Government, the Bank made intermittent and, in the aggregate, substantial specie payments to all holders of particular types of notes and in settlement of small obligations. It did this under an authorization in the Restriction legislation to make payments in specie acquired after February 25, 1797. The Bank announced in January 1798 that it would redeem any £1 and £2 notes dated prior to February 1, 1798,[65] and two months later had paid out more than £800,000 in specie in exchange for such notes and for stamped dollars.[66] Beginning January 14, 1799, it paid in cash "all fractional sums under *Five Pounds*," and starting February 1, 1799, it redeemed in cash all £1 and £2 notes dated prior to July 1, 1798. The Bank, at least as late as 1809, continued to make its traditional payments "to Doorkeepers of the House of Commons"[67] in gold coins. Entries of 1809[68] in its Court Book not only show that the Bank was still paying sums under £5 in cash, but suggest that under a loose interpretation of the redemption started on January 14, 1799, had been making some payments of over £5 entirely in specie.

No figures are available on how much specie the Bank paid out during the Restriction in each of these various ways or on the dates of payments. However, the large profit that could be obtained by obtaining gold for Bank notes with gold above the mint price, and the concern of the Bank about the situation from 1809 on, suggest a heavy drain on the Bank's reserves. In 1812 the Bank reported, in addition to payments of more than £10 million in specie to the Government, a "drain made by the Public, for payments of fractional sums under £5, which amounted to more than Four Millions."[69] The situation was particularly critical in 1811, but the Bank apparently felt that it had no choice but to continue to do so, having

---

[63] This would have permitted £889,620 to be withdrawn in specie by the depositors. As of March 22, 1798, £133,362 of specie had been withdrawn, leaving £756,258 subject to withdrawal (C.B., Z, February 22, March 22, 1798). There is no record as to when, if at all, this was withdrawn during the Restriction.

[64] For example, on October 9, 1799, the Bank authorized the delivery to the Treasurer of the Navy of £152,000 of specie in exchange for Bank notes to pay "the Crews of such of His Majesty's Ships as shall receive Orders to proceed on Foreign Service" (C.B., Aa, p. 176).

[65] The text of Bank notices from 1797 to 1818 for limited redemption is given in *Commons Committee*, 1819, app. 2, pp. 269–270.

[66] C.B., Z, March 22, 1798.   [67] C.B., Fa, June 22, 1809.

[68] June 22 and 29, 1809.   [69] C.B., Ha, October 8, 1812.

once announced that it would pay sums under £5 in gold. It asked the Chancellor of the Exchequer to introduce legislation "to put the Bank in the same situation in which it was placed by the first Restriction bill." [70] The Chancellor, despite the note of urgency in the Bank's request,[71] refused to introduce such legislation "from an apprehension of the disadvantage obviously belonging to it, under all of the circumstances of the present period," which presumably meant that he did not wish to take any action that might add fuel to the charge that Bank of England notes were depreciated. Over a year later the Bank was still complaining of the drain on its cash "thro' the means of fractional payments which can only be remedied by the interference of Parliament," [72] and as late as October 21, 1813, the Court was debating the issue.[73]

On May 3, 1816, the governor, Samuel Thornton, stated in Parliament that the Bank was making preparations to resume.[74] He did not specify what this meant, but presumably he referred to purchase of gold. Since March 28, 1804, the Bank had had a standing offer to buy gold at £4 an ounce,[75] although with the market price above £4 an ounce most of the time it is doubtful whether much was bought on this basis. The Bank also made some purchases by special arrangement at a higher price, although it is not clear in all cases whether these purchases were for its own account or for the Chancellor of the Exchequer.[76] On July 3, 1816, the Bank reduced its standing offer from £4 to £3.19.0 an ounce.[77]

At the same time that the Bank was buying gold at over the coinage price it gave additional opportunity to holders of notes to redeem them in gold at par. On November 28, 1816, with the market price of gold at

[70] C.B., Ga, May 30, 1811.

[71] C.B., Ga, June 13, 1811.

[72] C.B., Ha, October 8, 1812.

[73] C.B., Ia. On May 5, 1813, the Committee of the Treasury had given "directions, that in the Case of any Clerks in this House applying for gold in payment of Dividend warrants they be referred to the Chief Cashier" (C.T., 10, p. 55), and on June 24, 1813, the Court instructed the Committee of the Treasury to put a stop to the practice of "drawing specie from the Bank, by small sums under £5" (C.B., Ia, June 24, 1813; C.T., 10, June 25, 1813, p. 69). It is not certain whether this put an end to all payments in specie for the time being, or only such payments as were not required by its announced policy, for at the same meeting at which the Committee of the Treasury took action to stop these gold payments it again voted to request the Chancellor of the Exchequer for legislation "to put the Bank in the same respect to Cash payments, in which it was placed by the Restriction Bill of 1797" (C.T., 10, June 25, 1813), p. 69).

[74] 1 Hansard XXXIV, 248.

[75] Lords Committee, 1819, app. A.11, p. 317.

[76] C.T., 7, December 21, 1808, p. 153; Bank of England Letter Book, 2, January 25, 1809, p. 23, February 9, 1809, p. 24.

[77] C.T., 11, p. 131.

£3.18.6, the Bank decided that, beginning December 9, 1816, it would redeem all £1 and £2 notes dated prior to January 1, 1812.[78] On May 2, 1817, it began redemption of all £1 and £2 notes dated prior to January 1, 1816, and on October 1, 1817, of notes of all denominations dated prior to January 1, 1817.[79] Under these two orders, the Bank paid out £4,308,833 up to April 6, 1819.[80] On November 26, 1816, just before the first of the three announcements of redemption of notes the Bank held £9,626,100 in specie; on November 26, 1817, after redemption of all notes issued prior to January 1, 1817, had been in effect for nearly two months, its specie holdings were £11,449,100,[81] or over five times what they had been early in 1815.

In February 1817 Pascoe Grenfell again asked for an investigation of the Bank's affairs, primarily on the basis of its profits. His motion, although turned down by a vote of 90 to 40, showed a stronger sentiment than at any previous time for publicity on the Bank's operations.[82] In April 1817 the price of gold rose and went above £4 in August. In January 1818 the Chancellor of the Exchequer said that proposed loans to foreign countries might make necessary a further extension of the Restriction.[83] In April he introduced legislation for a postponement of resumption until February 1819 and referred again to the proposed foreign loans. His statement is a commentary on the prevailing views as to what a government might properly do to implement a monetary policy: "Under these circumstances it would have been impolitic as well as unjustifiable on the part of the British government to prevent any voluntary transaction of its own subjects with the French government."[84] The debates, beyond these general references to foreign loans, produced virtually no information on the causes of the recent fluctuations in the price of gold and of foreign exchange.

[78] C.B., Ma, p. 197.

[79] C.B., Ma, April 17, 1817, September 18, 1817. These announcements are in *Lords Committee*, 1819, app. A.6, p. 311.

[80] *Lords Committee*, 1819, app. D.6, p. 374. The committee published no separate figures on gold payments, beginning December 9, 1816, for £1 and £2 notes issued previous to January 1, 1812. However, any redemptions under this order must have been quite small. The Bank made no payments of gold coin of one guinea or less for any purpose in December, 1816, payments of only £38,021 in January and February 1817, and no further payments until April 6, 1817 (*ibid.*, app. D.3, p. 372. Total gold payments, in coins of one guinea and under, were £6,786,775 from January 1817 to April 6, 1819. Presumably the gold payments of nearly £2.5 million for payments other than redemption of notes were made to Government, although nowhere in the evidence or in the tables presented to either the Commons or Lords committees of 1819 is this made clear.

[81] *Bank Charter Committee*, 1832, app. 88.

[82] 1 *Hansard* XXXV, 447–470, February 19, 1817.

[83] 1 *Hansard* XXXVII, 115, January 29, 1818.

[84] 1 *Hansard* XXXVII, 1235, April 9, 1818.

The Whigs pushed the criticism of the Bank profits, and the position of the Chancellor of the Exchequer shows how great a change has taken place between then and now in public opinion on the relations of government and central bank: "It would not be consistent with the honour or welfare of the country, to make itself a partner in any profits which the Bank of England happened to derive from the restriction."[85] The motion of George Tierney for the appointment of a committee to investigate the Restriction, although defeated 164 to 99, mustered by far the largest vote that a resumption-oriented measure had obtained.[86] The continuance of the debate on the postponement of resumption[87] was notable in one detail: the speech of Hudson Gurney, with the first outright suggestion in Parliament that the gold content of the pound be cut. Legislation postponing resumption until July 5, 1819, was passed without recorded vote.[88] Parliament adjourned in June 1818 and reassembled in January 1819.

Parliamentary Committees on Resumption

The remarks in the debate in April and May of 1818 left little doubt that, when Parliament met again, there would be a move either for positive action on resumption or for an investigation of the Bank. When Parliament reconvened Lord Liverpool "entertained a confident expectation, that but for certain contemplated operations in foreign loans, our currency might have been restored," but he "thought it impossible that cash-payments could with safety be restored on the 5th of July next."[89] He suggested that discussion be put over "till the succeeding session when the whole question might be deliberately weighed and finally decided on." Four days later the Government did an about-face, Lord Liverpool informed the Lords that since his previous statement "a communication had been received from the committee of gentlemen with whom his majesty's government were in the habit of officially communicating, he meant the committee of Bank Directors, which had induced him to bring forward a motion for a committee of inquiry."[90] Presumably the communication was the result of a resolution of the Committee of the Treasury of the Bank, passed January 20:

This Committee having deliberately weighed the Subject, and considered the Improbability that the Foreign Exchanges will be turned and permanently

---

[85] 1 *Hansard* XXXVII, 1284, April 10, 1818.
[86] 1 *Hansard* XXXVIII, 435–498, May 1, 1818.
[87] 1 *Hansard* XXXVIII, 764–783, May 18, 1818.
[88] 58 Geo. III, c. 37.
[89] 1 *Hansard* XXXIX, 32, January 21, 1819.
[90] 1 *Hansard* XXXIX, 78, January 21, 1819.

settled in Favour of Great Britain by March 1820, the Time to which it is proposed to limit the Duration of the Restriction of Cash Payments, think it a matter of the highest Importance that the Public shall not be deluded with an Expectation which is not likely to be realized.

That it appears preferable to submit to the Consequences of a Parliamentary Inquiry, rather than pass a Bill for a Time inadequate to the Circumstances in which the Country may be placed.[91]

In the next three months monetary policy developed with speed, and along lines quite different from those that the Government and the Bank had followed for the previous three years. With the Government now taking the lead in support of an action that the opposition had been urging, there was little substantive dispute. As Tierney pointed out, there was one point of agreement among all, namely, the "necessity of inquiry," and the debate in the Commons was largely on the terms of reference of the committee and on its membership.[92] Committees were appointed by both houses.

The Commons Committee, under the chairmanship of the younger Robert Peel, held hearings from February 11 to May 1, the Lord's Committee from February 6 to April 30. The Commons Committee examined twenty-three witnesses, and the Lords Committee twenty-five. The questioning and statements of the witnesses and the reports centered around five main themes: (1) desirability of re-establishing the old gold parity; (2) ability of the Bank of England to influence exchange rates by its credit policy; (3) relations between the circulation of the Bank of England and the country banks; (4) importance for monetary and credit conditions of the total of Bank credit rather than its distribution as between different forms; (5) amount of deflation needed to restore and maintain parity, and the procedure necessary to minimize the effects of that deflation.

Only four witnesses were hostile to resumption in the near future. Lewis Lloyd, a country and London banker, felt that it would be dangerous to resume in less than four or five years, and saw no objection to a permanent restriction.[93] Thomas Smith, an accountant, favored a permanent restriction.[94] Hudson Gurney,[95] while not stating an opposition to return to gold at the old parity such as he had expressed in Parliament, was apprehensive as to the consequences of a reduction of Bank issues.[96] Alexander

---

[91] *Lords Committee,* 1819, app. A.2, p. 300.
[92] 1 *Hansard* XXXIX, 213–276, February 2, 1819; 276–282, February 3, 1819; 350–360, February 8, 1819.
[93] *Commons Committee,* 1819, p. 172.
[94] *Commons Committee,* 1819, pp. 252–260.
[95] *Commons Committee,* 1819, pp. 249–252; *Lords Committee,* 1819, pp. 92–96.
[96] The difference between the views of Gurney in Parliament and his statements before the

Baring urged caution, and pointed out that the problem was not to re-establish and maintain parity but to do it without disastrous economic consequences.[97]

Recognition of the desirability of resumption was not new, but what was new and significant for policy was the recognition of this in a setting where action was contemplated. The testimony of practically all wit-nesses—Thomas Smith was the one clear exception—other than Bank directors showed a strengthening of the position, which the Bullion Com-mittee had supported and of which Ricardo had become the champion, that entirely aside from the advisability of setting and maintaining a particular rate the Bank could set and maintain a rate. The view that the directors of the Bank of Ireland had expressed before the Irish Currency Committee of 1804, and that the directors of the Bank of England had held consistently since the hearings of the Bullion Committee, was that they were powerless to affect the exchange rate. To a large degree Govern-ment spokesmen had, up to 1819, tacitly accepted that view. The Bank directors, in response to a question from the Commons Committee, had officially restated the Bank's old view in a resolution of March 25, 1819: "That this Court cannot refrain from adverting to an opinion, strongly insisted on by some, that the bank has only to reduce its issues to obtain a favourable turn in the exchanges, and a consequent influx of the precious metals; the Court conceives it to be its duty to declare, that it is unable to discover any solid foundation for such a sentiment."[98] However, as J. Keith Horsefield has brought out,[99] this was not the unanimous view of the Bank directors, and in the setting in which it was made was not the head-on denial of the Bank's power to control the exchanges that the words might suggest.

The testimony showed a clarification of opinion, as compared with 1810,

---

committees may be explained in part by the nature of the questions put to him, which diverted the discussion away from the issue of the standard. He noted in his diary on February 26, 1819: "Was examined before the Lords—I am afraid the evidence is a sad bother—Having so many questions of mere opinion mixed with those as to fact (one fact is they are bringing back the embarrassment of 1816—by their lowering the Bk. Disc.)." This comment by Gurney, the limitation of the questioning of Matthias Attwood, an opponent of resumption, before the Lords Committee, to details of banking practice, and the failure of either committee to examine Thomas Attwood, the most articulate of the critics of resumption, suggest that both in the selection and questioning of witnesses the committees secured an appearance of unanimity of public opinion that was not in accord with the facts.

[97] *Commons Committee*, 1819, p. 195; *Lords Committee*, 1819, pp. 107, 110.

[98] *Commons Committee*, 1819, p. 263.

[99] "The Bankers and The Bullionists in 1819," *Journal of Political Economy*, LVII, 442–448 (October 1949).

on the relations between the Bank's issues and the country banks' issues. There was a sharpening of the distinction between the long-run dependence of country bank circulation upon Bank credit and the short-run fluctuations, but the weight of the testimony was that Bank policy had an effective control over the power of the country banks to expand credit.[100] Noteworthy was the testimony of Ricardo and Stuckey, showing that whatever interpretation might be given to their statements in 1810, there was now substantial agreement on the relations between Bank and country bank circulation. Ricardo, in response to the query "Do you think that the amount of country bank circulation will vary with the amount of Bank of England circulation?" answered:

In all common cases I think it will; but I believe that there are exceptions to that general rule, arising from the more or less credit of the country banks; there is of course always a contention between the country banks and the bank of England, to fill as many districts as they can with their respective notes. The bank of England or the country banks may be more successful at one period than at another, but provided every thing were to remain the same in that respect, I have no doubt that a reduction of the London circulation would occasion a reduction of the country circulation.[101]

Stuckey's comment was: "I consider that country banks generally follow the Bank of England; if they increase their circulation, it has been commonly found that the circulation of the country banks increase."[102] The testimony almost without exception supported the view that Henry Thornton had so cogently urged as early as 1797, and which had been written into the Bullion Report: the important element in the Bank of England's influence on credit conditions, and even on the exchanges, was not the form of its advances, but their total, whether to Government or to business.[103]

When one reviews the hearings and the Parliamentary debates of 1819, it is evident that the economic question of what resumption at the old gold parity would do to prices and to employment was not the dominant

[100] *Commons Committee*, 1819: William Ward, p. 75; Thomas Tooke, pp. 127–128; David Ricardo, p. 134; Lewis Lloyd, pp. 166–167, 170–171; Samuel Gurney, p. 174; Ebenezer Gilchrist, p. 215; Vincent Stuckey, pp. 244–246. *Lords Committee*, 1819: George Dorrien, p. 34; William Haldimand, p. 44; William Ward, pp. 57–58; Lewis Lloyd, pp. 83–85; Matthias Attwood, pp. 86–88.

[101] *Commons Committee*, 1819, p. 134; also in Ricardo, *Works*, V, 375. Hereafter all references to Ricardo's evidence and to his speeches in Parliament will be to the *Works*, which are more readily available to most readers and in some cases give a fuller or more accurate version of his Parliamentary speeches.

[102] *Commons Committee*, 1819, p. 244.

[103] *Commons Committee*, 1819: Charles Pole, p. 35; Jeremiah Harman, p. 51; John Irving, pp. 102–103; *Lords Committee*, 1819: George Dorrien, p. 31; Charles Pole, p. 39; Hudson Gurney, pp. 95–96.

consideration in the decision that was reached. It was not that witnesses and members of Parliament were unaware of the fact that deflation would be involved, and that it would cause some distress. A large part of the articulate public had come to the conclusion that on over-all political and long-term economic grounds the old par should be resumed if at all possible and that the immediate economic consequences were relevant only to the extent that the distress involved to achieve this result should not be too high. An illustration of this attitude, particularly pertinent as coming from a man who was lukewarm toward resumption, was the statement of John Irving, a London merchant and member of Parliament: "It is undoubtedly an opinion, fixed in the public mind, that the resumption of cash payments is the natural and fit course to pursue; and I think also, it is the duty of those who administer the affairs of the country, to pay some attention to that opinion." [104]

Relation of Resumption to Deflation

The hearings, however, brought out the problem that had been touched on repeatedly in the years since Waterloo, but never thoroughly analyzed: the amount of price deflation involved in re-establishing and maintaining parity. This involved four issues, logically separate, but frequently assimilated into a single problem in contemporary discussion: (1) required reduction in the price of gold; (2) reduction in the price of commodities, larger or smaller than the reduction in the price of gold, assuming no change in the purchasing power of gold; (3) probable changes in the purchasing power of gold, for reasons independent of Britain's return to specie payments; (4) effect of Britain's return to specie payments upon the purchasing power of gold.

The first point—the gold premium—was a simple question of fact on which there was no disagreement: whatever the price of gold, it would have to be brought down to £3.17.10½ if specie payments were to be resumed and maintained.

The question whether the reduction in commodity prices would be greater or less than the reduction in the price of gold—or, in modern parlance, whether the pound was overvalued or undervalued on the exchanges —was never analyzed as a separate issue or debated head-on. The question was, however, repeatedly recognized in references to the supposed effects of foreign investments and foreign travel in depreciating the pound below what it would otherwise have been. The implication of many remarks—

[104] *Commons Committee,* 1819, p. 99.

although the conclusion was rarely pointed up—was that if foreign investment were reduced, as seemed to be expected, the foreign exchange value
of the pound would appreciate without a further deflation of domestic
prices, assuming no increase in the purchasing power of gold.[105]

In the early years of the Restriction, Henry Thornton and John Wheatley
had discussed the purchasing power of the precious metals and the influence of British policy on it, and Thornton's view had been given wider
currency by Francis Horner's review in the first issue of the *Edinburgh
Review*. The Bullion Report referred to changes in the relative purchasing
power of gold and silver. In 1815 and 1816, with the gyrations in the price
of gold and silver, it was evident that changes in their prices did not always
parallel changes in the price of commodities, and the developments suggested to a number of persons the influence that changes in the purchasing
power of the precious metals might have on commodity prices.[106] Reduction of the current supplies of silver and gold by the wars of independence
in South America, the restoration of European currencies, and American
monetary policy stimulated further thought on possible changes in the
purchasing power of gold and silver.[107]

Several witnesses touched on the same point. Alexander Baring's concern
about an immediate return to gold was closely associated with his doubts
as to the future of gold and silver production.[108] Jeremiah Harman[109]
referred to the same problem. Ricardo mentioned the possibility of changes
in the purchasing power of the precious metals,[110] but this did not alter his
belief that specie payments should be resumed at par in the near future.
No matter what reservations Ricardo might make under cross-examination
as to the possibility that other influences—such as business conditions or

[105] *Commons Committee*, 1819: Charles Pole, pp. 34, 37; N. M. Rothschild, p. 157; John
Ward, pp. 239–240. *Lords Committee*, 1819, Alexander Baring, p. 127.

[106] Arthur Young, *An Inquiry into the Rise of Prices in Europe* (London, 1815), pp.
192–195; Thomas Read, *An Inquiry Concerning the Nature and Use of Money* (London,
1816), p. 52; Robert Torrens, *A Letter to the Right Honorable the Earl of Liverpool*
(London, 1816), pp. 3–4; Thomas Attwood, *A Letter to the Right Honourable Nicholas
Vansittart*, p. 47; Thomas Attwood, *A Second Letter to the Earl of Liverpool*, pp. 54–55;
Francis Horner in 1 *Hansard* XXIX, 1191, March 2, 1815.

[107] James, *Considerations on the Policy or Impolicy of the Further Continuance of the
Bank Restriction Act*, p. 9; Anonymous, *Remarks on Some Occurences since the Reports of
the Committees* (London, 1819), pp. 33–34; Sir William Congreve, *On the Impracticality
of the Resumption of Cash Payments* (London, 1819), pp. 17–19; B. A. Heywood, *Arguments Demonstrating from Recent Facts* (Liverpool, 1819), pp. 20–21, 24–25; Charles Lyne,
A Letter to the Right Honourable the Earl of Liverpool (London, 1819), pp. 19–21;
Anonymous, *On the Relation of Coin and Currency* (London, 1819), pp. 18–19.

[108] *Commons Committee*, 1819, pp. 180–181; *Lords Committee*, 1819, p. 119.

[109] *Commons Committee*, 1819, pp. 46–47.

[110] *Works*, V, 390–391, 418–420.

foreign developments—might affect the price of commodities, for practical purposes he always came back to changes in the price of gold as the test by which the consequences of resumption were to be measured. This was brought out in his testimony before the Commons Committee of 1819:

Q. Are you aware that there is at present a considerable stagnation in trade, and that there has been a great reduction of prices in consequence?

A. I have heard so; but I am not engaged in trade, and it does not come within my own knowledge.

Q. Would not the effect of a reduction of the issues of the bank be a further reduction in the prices of commodities?

A. I should certainly expect so, because I consider a reduction in the amount of bank paper to be raising the value of the medium in which the prices of those commodities are estimated.

Q. Explain in what degree you think it would take place?

A. I should think, to the amount of about five or six per cent; I measure it by the extent of the excess of the market above the mint price of gold.

Q. Do you think a diminution of the circulation produces a diminution of prices in exact arithmetical proportion?

A. I think it has a tendency to do so, but it does not exactly so nicely as that.

B. Does it reduce the prices of all commodities equally?

A. I think not, in consequence of the inequality of taxation, otherwise I think it would.

Q. Might not the reduction of prices to the amount of five per cent, conse-quent on a reduction of the issues of the bank, be particularly embarrassing, if it took place at a period when there appears to have been so great a reduction of prices in consequence of other causes; namely, the excess of speculation, and the stagnation resulting from that?

A. An alteration in value of five per cent does not appear to me very for-midable; but of this matter I do not profess to know much; I have had very little practical knowledge upon these subjects.[111]

He gave the same view three weeks later before the Lords Committee, but since the price of gold had fallen 6d. in the meantime the meticulous Ricardo now said that the price decrease now called for would be 4 per cent.[112]

The doctrinaire nature of Ricardo's approach, and his lack of concern with the problems of price adjustment, came out in further questioning:

Q. Do the Prices of Commodities conform to the Fluctuations in the Market Price of Gold, or does not a Length of Time elapse before such Conformity takes place?

A. They do not immediately conform, but I do not think it very long before they do.

[111] Works, V, 384–385.
[112] Works, V, 416–418.

Q. If the Prices of Commodities have not already fallen to a Level with the present Market Price of Gold, is it certain there will not be a greater Reduction in their Prices than 4 per cent., on the Market Price of Gold falling to the Mint Price?

A. I think the Prices of Commodities fall from a Reduction of the Paper Circulation quite as soon as Gold falls. If the Prices of Commodities and of Bullion have not already fallen in proportion to the Reduction of paper, I should think that, to make the Value of Bullion and Paper agree, a less Reduction of Paper would be necessary.[113]

The mind of the stockbroker, thinking in terms of small percentage changes in money relations but unconcerned with the problems of commodity price changes, was again revealed in the debate on May 24, 1819, when with the price of gold down another 6d. Ricardo spoke of raising the currency 3 per cent in value.[114]

Ricardo never said that reduction of the price of gold to £3.17.10½ would not be followed by a reduction of commodity prices by more than 6 per cent—or 5, 4, or 3 per cent. He simply said that a reduction in the price of gold, providing the Bank did not raise the purchasing power of gold by unnecessary gold purchases, would not cause a reduction in the price of commodities by more than 6 per cent. But he virtually ignored the complications that might follow from a further reduction of commodity prices due to other causes being added to the price reduction he anticipated from the reduction in the price of gold. Ricardo's whole attitude gives basis for the belief, held both by contemporaries and by later generations of economists, that he underestimated the problem of re-establishment and maintenance of the gold standard at the old parity.

Ricardo's Bullion Plan

Ricardo's neglect of the problems associated with a decline in British commodity prices was a defect in his analysis of resumption. On the other hand, his constructive proposals for British policy to minimize this price decline, by arranging Britain's resumption of gold payments so as not to raise the purchasing power of gold, showed him at his best as an economist. As early as 1811, in discussing Malthus' article in the *Edinburgh Review* of February 1811, Ricardo had suggested that Bank notes be redeemable in gold bars,[115] and this idea had been repeated in his *Proposals for an*

---

[113] *Works*, V, 452.

[114] *Works*, V, 10.

[115] *Observations on Some Passages in an Article in The Edinburgh Review, on the Depreciation of Paper Currency* (London, 1811); this appeared both as a separate publication and as an appendix to *The High Price of Bullion*, in *Works*, III, 99–127.

Economical and Secure Currency in 1816.[116] When Ricardo appeared as
a witness before the committees of 1819 he continued his support of bullion
redemption.[117] His emphasis was on the saving to the Bank and to the
country in being able to carry through redemption with a smaller gold
stock, but he also considered the advantage of not increasing the world
demand for gold.

Ricardo's plan had no strong support in the committee hearings[118] other
than from Alexander Baring[119] and from Swinton Holland, a Baring
partner.[120] The adoption of the ingot plan in the committee reports and
the resumption legislation appears to have been almost entirely the result
of Ricardo's persistence and lucid exposition. The Bank showed no enthusiasm for the plan, but did not oppose it, and to a query from the Lords
Committee replied that it "is not aware of any Difficulty in exchanging, for
a fixed Amount of Bank Notes, Gold Bullion of a certain Weight, provided it be melted, assayed, and stamped by His Majesty's Mint." [121] In
later testimony Jeremiah Harman, a former governor of the Bank, expressed doubts,[122] but Samuel Thornton, a former governor, George
Dorrien, the governor, and Charles Pole, deputy governor, gave restrained
approval.[123]

The Committee Reports

Interim reports of the two committees recommended that, pending
definite action on resumption, the Bank be required to stop the partial
redemption of its notes—those issued before January 1, 1817—and Parliament acted quickly and forbade the Bank to make further redemptions in
gold.[124] The final report of the Commons Committee was submitted on
May 6 and a practically identical report of the Lords Committee on
May 7. The membership of the committees represented a wide diversity of
opinion on monetary policy, and included many who had been opponents
of earlier moves toward resumption and critics of the idea that the Bank
of England could influence the exchanges. But a combination of persua-
sion, and pressure from Tory leaders for the party to present a united front

---

[116] *Works*, IV, 67–68.

[117] *Works*, V, 379–384, 401–415, 422–435, 439–457.

[118] Sraffa's editorial "Notes on the Evidence on the Resumption of Cash Payments," in
Ricardo, *Works*, V, 350–370, summarizes the position of the witnesses on Ricardo's plan
for redemption in bullion.

[119] *Commons Committee*, 1819, pp. 189–190, 199–200; *Lords Committee*, 1819, pp.
134–137.

[120] *Commons Committee*, 1819, pp. 123–125.

[121] *Lords Committee*, 1819, app. A.8, p. 314.

[122] *Lords Committee*, 1819, pp. 221–222.

[123] *Lords Committee*, 1819, pp. 225–234, 243–244.

[124] 59 Geo. III, c. 23.

once the majority had decided that the Restriction should end, produced virtually unanimous support for the reports.[125]

Both reports recommended resumption of gold payments in gold bullion at the old par of £3.17.10½ per fine ounce beginning May 1, 1821. To prepare for this final step the Bank, not earlier than December 1, 1819, and not later than February 1, 1820, was to begin redemption in bullion at £4.1.0 per ounce, and not later than November 1, 1820, at £3.19.6 an ounce. Payment in coin would not be permitted until May 1, 1823, and then only when authorized by Parliament with one year's advance notice. Both reports accepted without question the view, still formally rejected by the Bank, that the Bank could maintain a fixed price of gold by a combination of free redemption and credit control, and recommended a removal of the existing prohibitions on the melting and export of coin. The reports did not mention the alternatives of the silver standard or of bimetallism, made no mention of possible changes in the purchasing power of gold, and assumed, with only passing comment, that long-run advantages of a fixed standard would outweigh any temporary distress. The question of the country banks was not faced by either committee, but the cryptic comment of the Commons Committee showed that the instability of the country bank note circulation was still recognized as an unsolved problem: "Whether it may be practicable further to provide against inconvenience to the Public and the loss to Individuals, which arise from the occasional insolvency of Country banks, and to make such provision, without an interference with the rights of property, and the transactions of the community founded on commercial credit, are questions of great difficulty; respecting which Your Committee could not, without further evidence and considerable delay, have enabled themselves to submit an opinion to the House." [126]

Resumption Legislation

The keynote of the Government's approach was set by Robert Peel in

---

[125] Castlereagh's remarks in the Commons debate indicate that the only members of the Commons Committee to oppose the report were George Tierney, presumably on the ground that it put off resumption too long, and a Bank director, and that only one unidentified member of the Lords Committee opposed the report (1 *Hansard* XL, 706, May 25, 1819). A plausible account of the way in which this virtual unanimity was reached is given by J. L. Mallett in his diary, reprinted in Ricardo, *Works,* V, 365–366. Mallett identified the holdout Lord as Lord Lauderdale, and stated that in addition to Tierney's opposition "from factious motives and ignorance of the question," Manning, "as a Bank director of the old school," also opposed the report. Tierney said that in the committee both he and a Bank director opposed the "plan" (apparently the plan for redemption in bullion), but that only he had voted against it (1 *Hansard* XL, 724, May 24, 1819).

[126] *Commons Committee*, 1819, p. 20.

introducing the Commons Committee reports. He pointed out the change that his own opinions had undergone since 1811 and the need for a fixed standard: "If once a hope should be held out that the suspension might last for an indefinite period, that the amount of the circulating medium was to be left to the discretion of the Bank directors, uncontrolled by any consideration but that of their own profits, it would become impossible to estimate the extent of the mischief that might ensue."[127] The Bank of England submitted a representation against the committee's proposals,[128] and a petition, signed by four to five hundred "Merchants, Bankers, Traders and others" of the City of London and presented by the elder Sir Robert Peel, pictured great distress as the result of the committee's recommendations.[129] But there was no organized opposition in either House.

Peel's critical comments on the Bank, and particularly his reference to the Bank's communication of May 20, 1819, opposing resumption, give circumstantial support to an idea suggested in other speeches as well as in pamphlet literature—that the relations between the Government and the Bank had become less cordial in recent months. The Bank's communications of March 25 and May 20 had appeared to some members of Parliament as a challenge to their authority, and these communications may have been a force in consolidating Parliamentary opinion in favor of a fixed resumption date. Even the comments of defenders of the Bank suggest the extent to which, regardless of party, there was Parliamentary opposition to the Bank. John Pearse, a former governor, plaintively remarked that "while hon. gentlemen were depreciating the character of the Bank in Parliament, that character was the subject of admiration and confidence in every other part of the world."[130] Ricardo's thrust, "The House did not withdraw its confidence from the Bank from any doubt of its wealth, or integrity, but from a conviction of its total ignorance of the principles of political economy," was greeted with "hear, and a laugh."[131]

In the Commons the reports and the resumption legislation were debated at length, but there was almost unanimous support of the resumption, with the criticism directed more at the failure of the bill to provide for speedier action. An amendment to drop the provision for resumption by steps was defeated 166 to 21, and the bill was passed without recorded

[127] 1 Hansard XL, 676–702, May 20, 1819. The quoted passage is on 683.
[128] The text, dated May 20, 1819, is in 1 Hansard XL, 601–604.
[129] The text is in 1 Hansard XL, 598–600.
[130] 1 Hansard XL, 778, May 25, 1819.
[131] Works, V, 14.

vote.[132] In the Lords debate was less extended, but the result was the same.[133] Liverpool presented the case for speedy resumption with the same vigor the Whigs had displayed in previous years urging the same view. Lauderdale's resolutions for a bimetallic standard were rejected, and the bill passed without recorded vote. Its Parliamentary history would seem to support the self-congratulation of the Prime Minister that "the present bill had met with no opposition, and required no defence."[134]

Parliamentary debate added little to monetary theory, but provides political scientists with rich material on the crosscurrents that give the final direction to legislative action. Two points stand out: first, an increasingly critical attitude toward the Bank of England for determining, under the Restriction, policy that properly belonged to Parliament, and second, a feeling that, in view of the political unrest and the widespread criticism of the Bank of England as a monopoly fattening on the profits of the Restriction while it was hanging forgers of its "wretched notes," it was desirable, regardless of the finer points of economic analysis, to settle the monetary standard.

The Whigs had the pleasant opportunity of combining support of the Government's resumption plan with twitting the Tories for their change of views, but on the substantive issue of resumption there was little difference between Whigs and Tories. The fears expressed outside Parliament about the distress that might follow from resumption seem to have called forth a bipartisan Parliamentary loyalty. This public attitude toward resumption, taken against the background of the political unrest of the time, apparently was an argument, not, as logic might suggest, in favor of postponing resumption until further study could be made, but in favor of unanimous action by Parliament to reassure public opinion.

The resumption legislation in final form was approved on July 2, 1819.[135] Had resumption proceeded as there provided, redemption in bullion at the old mint par of £3.17.10½ per ounce would have been reached on May 1, 1821, and redemption in gold coin on May 1, 1823. However, in the two years that followed the almost unanimous approval of this redemption legislation the plan for ingot redemption was wiped out before it had a real test, and growing public criticism of low prices and economic distress brought a serious challenge to the whole idea of the re-establishment of the gold standard.

[132] The debate is in 1 *Hansard* XL, 672–748, May 24, 1819; 750–802, May 25, 1819; 1150–1154, June 14, 1819.
[133] 1 *Hansard* XL, 597–657, May 21, 1819; 1224–1232, June 21, 1819; 1295–1296, June 23, 1819.
[134] 1 *Hansard* XL, 1229, June 18, 1819.   [135] 59 Geo. III, c. 49.

IV

PROBLEMS OF THE NEW GOLD STANDARD

Gold was almost at the parity price when the resumption legislation was passed, and by August 17, 1819, it had fallen to £3.17.10½. Except for a brief period in November of the same year it remained at that figure until the full redemption of specie payments in May 1821. On February 1, 1820, redemption in bullion was to begin at £4.1.0 an ounce. Only three ingots were purchased: "One for Lord Thanet, one for a country banker, from curiosity, and the other, I know not for whom," according to a contemporary letter.[1] The new monetary situation went unnoticed in the press, Parliament, and the records of the Bank. On October 1, 1820, the Bank was obligated to furnish ingots at £3.19.6 an ounce, and it sold three more between then and May 1, 1821, and again without publicity. As compared with the royal funerals and the trial of Queen Caroline for adultery, the technical point that the Bank note was legally redeemable at a fixed price of gold seems to have meant little to the public.

The Bank in the meantime, flaunting the advice of Ricardo that the basis for a firmly established parity was not the holding of a large reserve but proper control of credit,[2] continued to buy gold. Reserves, which had totaled £3,825,900 on May 26, 1819, shortly before the passage of the resumption legislation, were £4,079,000 on November 26 of that year and rose every quarter until they reached £11,988,100 on May 28, 1821. The ingot plan's test would come only after May 1, 1821, when the Bank would be under obligation to redeem at the par rate of £3.17.10½.

---

[1] Quoted in *The Works and Correspondence of David Ricardo,* ed. Piero Sraffa (Cambridge, 1951–1955), V, 369.

[2] One of Ricardo's statements of this view was in his Parliamentary speech of May 24, 1819: "If he might give them [the Bank of England] advice, he should recommend to them not to buy bullion, but even though they had but a few millions, if he had the management of their concerns, he should boldly sell" (*Works,* V, 13).

Abandonment of the Ingot Plan

Before that date new legislation, apparently sponsored by the Bank, was proposed to authorize payment of its notes in gold coin. The reason for this proposal was the continuing problem of forgery. Early in February 1821 Pascoe Grenfell had asked the Chancellor of the Exchequer when new notes less subject to forgery might be expected. The Chancellor's reply and the debate that followed would suggest that the Bank had made little progress in producing a note less susceptible to forgery, and also that criticism of the Bank on the forgery problem was continuing.[3] The question was again raised in the Commons on February 20.[4] On March 19 the Chancellor of the Exchequer proposed that beginning May 1, 1821, the Bank be authorized to redeem in coin,[5] and gave as a reason that "the speedy and progressive substitution of the coin of the realm must necessarily diminish the crime of forgery." Even more clearly than in the case of the act of 1819, the forgery issue was a major consideration in determining this new turn in monetary policy.[6]

By shifting alliances of politics the only strong opposition to the change came from two men who were in disagreement with Ricardo on the question of the standard, Alexander Baring and Matthias Attwood. According to Baring, "The permanent establishment of that plan was peculiarly calculated to relieve the tension which was at present felt in the currency of the country."[7] Attwood stressed the deflationary pressure that the new demand for gold would put on the pound, and turned his criticism of a

---

[3] 2 *Hansard* IV, 286–287, February 1, 1821. The story of the Bank's attempt to produce a note less easily forged is given in Mackenzie, *The Bank of England Note*, ch. 4.

[4] 2 *Hansard* IV, 803–804.

[5] 2 *Hansard* IV, 1315–1317. The March 19 debate continues through 1338; on April 9, in V, 91–148, and April 13, V, 203–208. For the Lords debate, on May 4, see V, 495–508.

[6] Clapham's comment is: "No one asked for bars and the Bank was not interested in them. Feeling sanguine, it saw no reason why it should not cash its notes in the old way as from that date," to which is footnoted: "There is nothing about it in the Bank's records, and it seems that the City was cold" (*Bank of England*, II, 73). This is not supported by the Bank's records: first, on February 21, 1821, the Committee of the Treasury recommended that the Bank "acquiesce" in legislation to permit the Bank to pay in coin after May 1, 1821 (C.T., 13, p. 174), and the Court agreed the same day (C.B., Qa, pp. 244–245). Second, the only reason given for this recommendation was "unforeseen difficulties and consequent delays having arisen, in perfecting the New Note which the Bank intended to issue" (C.T., 13, March 22, 1821, p. 180). Third, the directors on April 5, 1821, defeated a motion: "That this Court can see no objection to the Bank having the option of paying its Notes in Bar Gold at £3–17–10½ the Ounce as proposed by a Member of the House of Commons, and that the Governor and Deputy Governor be requested to communicate this opinion to the Chancellor of the Exchequer" (C.B., Qa, pp. 312–313).

[7] 2 *Hansard* IV, 1325, March 10, 1821.

gold coin circulation into an all-out attack on the re-establishment of the gold standard.[8]

In contrast, Ricardo apparently now did not attach much importance to the permission to pay in gold bullion because he felt that the Bank by its large purchases of gold had undermined the whole idea of the ingot plan, and that it made little difference whether the demand for gold was raised by holding it in the Bank's vaults or by putting it in circulation. On February 8, 1821, he had criticized the Bank as "a timid body" that had made "great and unnecessary purchases of gold."[9] In the debate on the bill to abolish the ingot plan he took a detached view, and said: "He should be perfectly ready to abandon his own plan, if by so doing that most desirable object [putting a stop to the forgery of Bank notes] could be effected."[10] Ricardo's comments to Malthus, barely two months after the ingot plan was given up, in which he described the Bank directors as "indeed a very ignorant set,"[11] suggest that his real regret was not about the formal abandonment of that plan, but about the policy of the Bank in making large purchases of bullion. When the speaking was over no Parliamentary defender of the ingot plan was prepared to put up a last-ditch fight, and the bill was approved in both the Commons and the Lords without formal vote. It became law on May 7, 1821,[12] and the Bank began redemption in coin the following day.

The closing days of the ingot plan provided the only ripple of excitement in the fifteen months of bullion redemption. Seven ingots were paid out on May 1 and the days immediately following—more than in the previous fifteen months. The Bank, which but for a delay in final enactment of the coin payment bill would have been relieved on May 1 of the obligation to redeem in bullion, apparently tried unsuccessfully to avoid bullion redemption. Cobbett on May 4 reported and counseled: "Some bars of gold were *got yesterday,* at any rate, though not without some extraordinary *ceremonies,* of which the public will hear more by-and-by!— Why all this ceremony?—My advice to every one, is to *lose no time.* To make *sure* of some *gold* while it can be got."[13] No further ingot redemp-

---

[8] 2 *Hansard* V, 97–130, April 9, 1821. Attwood's speech was also printed as a pamphlet, *Speech . . . in the House of Commons, April 9, 1821* (London, [1821]).

[9] *Works,* V, 76.

[10] *Works,* V, 96–97.

[11] *Works,* IX, 15, July 19, 1821.

[12] 1 & 2 Geo. IV, c. 26.

[13] *Political Register,* May 5, 1821, 354. Cobbett commented further (May 12, 1821, 397–398) on the problem. The *Morning Chronicle* of May 4 also had an editorial remark suggesting difficulties in getting gold bars.

tions were made after May 7, and redemption in coin began on May 8.

The Bank by August 20 of that year had returned to the Mint for melting some 2000 of its ingots, but for reasons of which there is no record continued to hold 50 ingots until they were melted late in 1824. Of the thirteen ingots paid out no specimen is known to exist, although the Bank of England has a gilded plaster cast of an ingot.[14] Thus ended as a victim of the vagaries of forgery and politics an original and constructive monetary plan that over a century later was to be revived when England resumed gold payments in 1925.

Mounting Opposition to the Act of 1819

It is probable that this anticlimactic death of the ingot plan and Ricardo's unwillingness to make a vigorous defense of it are explained by the revolt against the whole principle of the redemption legislation that was shaping up in Parliament at the same time that the abolition of the ingot plan was under debate. A larger issue was at stake: whether the gold standard at the existing parity was to be maintained in any form.

Opposition in 1819 to resumption at par was much stronger outside Parliament than inside, where politics gave a misleading picture of unanimity. This grass roots opposition, which from 1816 on had been expressed both by conservative landed interests and by the Birmingham spokesmen, was increasingly vocal in 1819, both before and after the reports of the committees. In 1817 about twenty pamphlets had appeared on the currency situation, and about the same number in 1818, but some seventy were published in 1819, and a substantial majority of these were critical of the resumption proposals.

Out of the diverse, and not always consistent, criticism in 1819 two points emerged, which were to be stressed repeatedly in the debates of the next thirty years.

First, there were suggestions that the redemption legislation of 1819, by dropping the prohibition on the melting and export of coin, permitted, when exchanges were unfavorable, deflation greater than could take place if the melting and export of coin were forbidden. As an anonymous pamphlet put it, what the new legislation provided for "is not restoring the antient metallic standard of the country, is not a resumption of cash payments according to that standard; it is going further, it is altering the

---

[14] Further details on the ingot plan are given in Ricardo, *Works*, V, 368–370; in James Bonar, "Ricardo's Ingot Plan," *Economic Journal*, XXXIII, 281–304 (September 1923); and in the editorial note, *ibid.*, p. 591 (December 1923).

standard and raising its value; it is forcing on the Bank of England and the country a greater reduction of its notes in circulation, than a mere restoration of the antient standard, on its antient footing, would require." [15]

Second, there were suggestions that a metallic standard, and in particular a gold standard, was bad because it meant that the action of foreign countries could influence the value of the pound. A succinct statement of this view came from Edward Cooke: "This measure will make the quantity of our currency and the accommodation of our merchants dependent not on their own wants and interests, but on the wants and interests of foreigners." [16]

Baring's Move to Reconsider the Act of 1819

Before Parliament disposed of the ingot plan it had an extended debate on modifying the act of 1819 in a much more fundamental way. In May 1820 the citizens of Birmingham had presented to Parliament a petition picturing the economic distress of the city,[17] which provoked a short debate but no action. The following February the "merchants, manufacturers, and traders" of Birmingham submitted a similar petition, drafted in large part by Thomas Attwood. In the ensuing debates[18] not only did both Whigs and Tories attribute part of the distress to the monetary situation, but there was evidence of substantial sentiment for re-examination of the act of 1819. There was no action, however, beyond the order that the petition be printed.

The following month Nicholas Vansittart proposed the bill to abandon the ingot plan. This brought from Alexander Baring a criticism of the act of 1819, and a proposed amendment: "That it is expedient to appoint a Select Committee, to consider the act of the 59th of the late king, chap. 49, with a view to alleviate the pressure which the due execution of that act

---

[15] *Observations on Bullion Payments, and on a Free Trade in Gold* (London, 1819), p. 6. The same point was made by Robert Torrens, *A Comparative Estimate of the Effects* (London, 1819), pp. 35–57; Thomas Smith, *An Address to the Right Hon. Robert Peel* (London, 1819), pp. 17–18; Samuel Turner, *A Letter Addressed to the Right Hon. Robert Peel* (London, 1819), pp. 77–80; and is implied in Jasper Atkinson's anonymous *Cursory Observations on some Parts of the Evidence before the Committees of both Houses of Parliament* (London, 1819), p. 6; and in his *State of the Circulation and the Currency Briefly Considered* (London, 1826), p. 25.

[16] *An Address to the Public* (London, 1819), p. 15. The same idea is suggested by Erick Bollman, *A Letter to Thomas Brand* (London, 1819), p. 33; Thomas Attwood, *A Second Letter to the Earl of Liverpool* (Birmingham, 1819), pp. 54–55; B. A. Heywood, *Arguments Demonstrating from Recent Facts* (London, 1819), pp. 20–21, 24–25; Charles Lyne, *A Letter to the Right Honourable the Earl of Liverpool* (London, 1819), pp. 19–21.

[17] 2 *Hansard* I, 338–342, May 16, 1820.

[18] The petition was presented to the Lords and debated on February 5 (2 *Hansard* IV, 350–360), and to the Commons and debated there on February 8 (*ibid.*, 523–542).

is likely to produce upon the several branches of public industry." [19]
Baring's amendment was defeated without record vote, but when the
House was in committee on the ingot bill Baring again moved his amendment, seconded by Matthias Attwood, which was defeated 141 to 27.[20]

The result of Baring's proposed amendment was that what started as a
discussion of legislation to abandon the ingot plan turned into a full-dress
debate on the act of 1819. Most of what was said pro and con had been
said before, but the most significant feature of the debate, and far more
important than the technical arguments, was the shift in opinion from
two years before. Some who joined Baring in 1821 had been, like him,
critics of the inflationary policy of the war years, and had been supporters
of the act of 1819. The comment of John Pearse, a Bank director, undoubtedly had an *ad hominem* quality, but also contained a large core of
truth, "that he could not express his surprise that after the measure of
1819 had received the sanction of Parliament and the Bank was ready to
discharge its duty towards the public, the very persons who promoted that
measure, should now be the first to object to its operation." [21] There was
little praise of the act of 1819 on economic grounds, and Matthias Attwood's statement was substantially correct: "There is no party which does
not ascribe some part of the distress of the country to the alterations in our
currency." [22]

The opposition to Baring's motion was primarily on the ground that he
had exaggerated the economic distress occasioned by the resumption; or
that as a decision had been made, whether it had been a good or a bad
decision it should not be challenged. Even Edward Ellice, although he
stated that resumption at £5.10.0 per ounce in 1819 would have been preferable, opposed Baring's motion primarily on the ground that it would
be politically disturbing.[23] Ricardo made two speeches opposing Baring's
motion, but he was on the defensive.[24] As on many other occasions he
practically ignored the problems of price adjustment, seemed concerned
only with the income transfer effects of changing prices, and in substance
denied that inflation or deflation could alter total production. Baring,
however, had both the idea of the difficulties of price adjustment and of the
depressing effects of deflation upon production. He drove home his point

[19] 2 *Hansard* IV, 1317–1328, March 19, 1821.
[20] 2 *Hansard* V, 91–148, April 9, 1821.
[21] 2 *Hansard* IV, 1332, March 19, 1821.
[22] 2 *Hansard* V, 111, April 9, 1821.
[23] 2 *Hansard* V, 141–144, April 9, 1821.
[24] *Works*, V, 91–97, 105–108.

by a dig at the mechanistic Ricardian picture of frictionless price changes: "The Hon. member for Portarlington told them, that the change of the value of the currency immediately had its effect on all commodities. But the effect could not penetrate into all parts of the country, or change habitual expenses. If he were going to York, and gave a post-boy 2s.6d. who was accustomed to get 3s., the man would think him a shabby fellow, in spite of his political economy."[25] Baring's position was that falling prices, in addition to income transfers, led to unemployment in the interval before money wages were reduced. His statement of the problem of adjustment of a worker's wages, "His wages must come down, when his master could find nobody to employ him; and whenever that time arrived, which could not be very far distant, the reduction of wages would no doubt be received with great discontent,"[26] reads much like Keynes's observations over a century later.

Baring, in his discussion of the income transfer effects of changing prices, had an ethical and social-justice approach that was quite different from Ricardo's clinical approach. Aside from any effect on total production, Baring saw in rising prices a transfer of income to the socially more useful members of the community, in falling prices a transfer to the less useful members of the community. As he put it, "The effect [of the act of 1819] was, that the industrious were obliged to labour under difficulties, that the drones might live in the greater affluence."[27] To Baring the prospect that the purchasing power of silver might fall was, contrary to Ricardo's view, an argument for, and not against, silver as a standard of value. But he did not want such a transfer of purchasing power if it involved a breach of public faith, and to him the silver standard was the best working compromise.

This attempt in 1821 by Baring and Matthias Attwood to re-examine the monetary standard, like the earlier opposition to resumption, represented a politically conservative view. Those who agreed with Baring did not speak with one voice, but the idea of maintaining the position of the landed gentry was the most important single theme. The statement of the Earl of Carnarvon, although made some three months after the debates and in connection with a move to reduce public expenditures, is worth quoting as a statement of a conservative view on the economic and political consequences of the act of 1819: "He called upon the House to

[25] 2 *Hansard* IV, 1324, March 19, 1821.
[26] 2 *Hansard* V, 96, April 9, 1821.
[27] 2 *Hansard* IV, 1323, March 19, 1821.

consider the consequences, in a constitutional point of view, of destroying by its means the aristocracy of the country—the gentlemen and the yeomanry of England, on whose existence our institutions alone could rest. The monied interest had been formed by the calls of our finances; they could be removed; they were inhabitants of this or of any other country; but the stability of our institutions, and the safety of the throne itself, depended on our agricultural population, on the *adscripti glebae*." [28]

The radical press gave no suggestion of approval to Baring's efforts to re-examine the gold standard. In 1819 Cobbett had ridiculed Henry James, the Birmingham merchant who was urging a devaluation of some 10 per cent, as "my Lord Little-Shilling of Birmingham," [29] and later criticized James's Birmingham associate Richard Spooner and also Matthias Attwood for wanting to break the act of 1819 while opposing Parliamentary reform.[30] And after gold payments were resumed in May 1821, Cobbett said of the suggestion for devaluation, "For, as to the base, swindling, execrable plan of *lowering the standard;* as to that cruel design, which could have been suggested by nobody but the Devil himself in person, it will not, it cannot, it must not, be adopted, nor attempted." [31]

Agricultural Distress and the Monetary Standard

The monetary issue had come before Parliament in 1821 even before Baring's motion, not directly but as a by-product of agricultural distress. Prices fell from early in 1819 until late in 1822, and the decline was particularly great in agricultural products. Wheat, at 90s. per quarter in April 1818, was 76s. in April 1819, 66s. in December 1819, 53s. in April 1821, and 39s. in December 1822. Oats, pork, and tallow had comparable drops. Petitions on agricultural distress poured into Parliament in 1820, and the resulting Parliamentary Committee on Agricultural Distress turned up much on the details of prices, but neither witnesses nor the committee in its perfunctory report attempted to tie agricultural distress to the monetary situation. The petitions continued as agricultural prices went even lower, and in March 1821 a new Committee on Agriculture, of which Ricardo was a member, was appointed. It held hearings, in large part while the abandonment of the ingot plan was under debate, and presented an extended report. In both the hearings and the report the

---

[28] Hansard V, 1473–1474, July 2, 1821.
[29] *Political Register,* May 15, 1819, 1051–1090; September 25, 1819, 185.
[30] *Political Register,* October 2, 1819, 202–211; February 10, 1821, 391–392; May 5, 1821, 289–351.
[31] *Political Register,* May 12, 1821, 417.

monetary standard was discussed. Thomas Attwood as a witness (pp. 243–276) blamed the act of 1819 for the country's troubles, but his stimulating analysis of the relation between prices and production was mixed with policy proposals that apparently assumed that the low prices of agricultural products were entirely the result of going back to the old par. He claimed that the act of 1819 had reduced corn prices a "full thirty per cent," and favored an increase in the price of gold to £6.6.0 and of silver to 8s.

Emphasis on the influence of the restoration of the pound to par upon commodity prices was not limited to such a confirmed critic of the act of 1819 as Thomas Attwood. Thomas Tooke, a supporter of resumption in 1819, estimated in the hearings of 1821 that British monetary policy had lowered prices by about 10 per cent—4 per cent by raising the value of the pound in relation to gold, and an additional 6 per cent as a result of the "preparation made by the Bank" for resumption (pp. 295–296). Similarly, R. G. Harvey, a farmer and miller, Edward Wakefield, the land agent who had arranged for the purchase of Ricardo's Parliamentary seat, and David Hodgson of Liverpool attributed part of the fall in prices to the act of 1819. None of these four witnesses, however, suggested a repeal of the act, although much of their evidence could have been used as an argument for its repeal (pp. 35, 207–209, 213, 265, 277–278).

The report of the committee, drafted in large part by William Huskisson, was published after Parliament had beaten down Baring's proposal to reopen the question of the standard, and after redemption in coin had begun. It was a compromise that had something for everybody. It agreed with most of the arguments made by those who wanted to break the act of 1819, but its final conclusion that the act should not be changed was acceptable to Ricardo, who wrote to Hutches Trower on July 4, just after its publication: "I hope that you are satisfied with a great part of the Report, there are some absurdities and contradictions in it, but considering how the committee was formed, and the opposition that was given to sound principle by the landed gentlemen, I think it on the whole creditable to the Committee." [32]

Continued Agricultural Criticism of the Act of 1819

Petitions asking relief for agriculture continued to come to Parliament. In 1822 another committee to consider petitions on agricultural distress made two reports that had only a brief mention of the monetary situation. The monetary issue, however, was again raised in Parliament early in

[32] *Works*, IX, 1.

1822 as a by-product of the debate on these petitions and on government expenditures. Much of the argument both in and out of Parliament dealt with technicalities of taxation, including the incidence of tax burdens, and with the legal-ethical question of how far the Government could go in adjusting the burdens between debtor and creditor without being guilty of breach of faith. The emphasis in the discussions of 1822 and 1823, representing the particular concern with the agricultural situation, was on the income transfers of the Restriction and post-Restriction period rather than on the aggregate demand and total employment effect that had been stressed by Baring and the Attwoods. Discussion on the distribution effects was stimulated by William Blake, in his *Observations on the Effects Produced by the Expenditure of Government* (London, 1823), who argued that the fundholder had not, on balance, benefited at the expense of the debtor and the taxpayer (pp. 86–88), and his ideas are mentioned by others, including Ricardo, both in correspondence and in Parliamentary debate. Malthus' criticism of any depreciation of the standard established in 1819 is indicative of his own position on the standard, and coming as it did from a supporter of the concept of aggregate demand is suggestive of the concern in 1823 with income transfers rather than aggregate production: "But whatever may have been the pressure on the owners of land since the peace, they cannot have the slightest pleas for an attempt to indemnify themselves at the expense of the public creditor. In the turns of the wheel of fortune all parties should have fair play, no class of persons can be justified in endeavouring to lift themselves by using unfair and dishonourable methods to pull others down." [33]

The defenders of the act of 1819 made surprisingly little attempt in 1822, or at any time until the late 1830's, to argue the economic merits of the decision made in 1819 to re-establish gold payments at the old par. They argued, rather, that a decision had been reached, and that the decision should stand because it was a symbol of England's political stability and her economic strength. In the Commons, Henry Brougham, a Whig leader, and Viscount Castlereagh, speaking for the Tory government, although exchanging irony in their discussion of the effects of taxation, vied with each other in their insistence that the act of 1819 must not be disturbed. Brougham's statement appears to be a fair summary of the view held by a large part of Parliament, both Whig and Tory:

To tamper with the public faith; to sully the honour of the country; to declare a national bankruptcy!—Good God! Who in his senses could recommend it? ... For it was one thing to have kept the currency where it was a few years

[33] *The Measure of Value Stated and Illustrated* (London, 1823), pp. 80–81.

ago, and another thing, having reestablished it, again to alter the standard. Many persons would have agreed to keep the currency down, where it would have been to the great and equitable relief of the country, if it had remained, who would not now agree to retrace their steps, and to change the state of things once more. And with cause; for the thing itself would be worse, and the example would be ten thousand times worse, as it would be easier to follow it in cases of future difficulty.[34]

In April 1822 Castlereagh announced that the Government, to ease agricultural distress, had arranged with the Bank to purchase £4 million of Exchequer bills, whose proceeds were to be used to expand the circulation by loans to agriculture; and that the Government was proposing an extension of the authority, due to expire in 1825, for country banks to issue notes under £5.[35] C. C. Western argued that these actions were only palliatives and that "nothing but the repeal of the act of 1819 would give relief to the agriculturalists,"[36] and moved for a committee to investigate the effect of the act. Western's motion produced two days of debate.[37] It received no support from any party leader, either Whig or Tory, except the unpredictable Henry Brougham, and was defeated 193 to 40. The following month Western proposed eighteen motions to the effect that the act of 1819 was responsible for the economic distress of the country, but after debate they were defeated without recorded vote.[38]

In the early months of 1823 came more petitions on agricultural distress, and Western returned to the attack on the act of 1819 and moved for a committee of investigation.[39] Two days of debate showed that criticism of the act was concentrated in agriculture even more than in 1821 and 1822, and the idea of its adverse effects on the landed aristocracy was stated in strident tones. If, on the one hand, Western's attack emphasized the politically conservative basis of the agricultural opposition to the act, the debate also suggested that another type of conservatism was coming increasingly to the support of the act: the feeling that whatever may have been the economic wisdom of the act in 1819, the pains of adjustment were largely over and that to tamper with it after four years would be economically and politically disturbing. Symptomatic of this feeling was the position of Alexander Baring, who two years before had headed the move for a reconsideration of the act of 1819 but opposed Western's motion

[34] 2 *Hansard* VI, 253, February 11, 1822.
[35] 2 *Hansard* VII, 157–160, April 29, 1822.
[36] 2 *Hansard* VII, 199, April 29, 1822.
[37] 2 *Hansard* VII, 877–928, June 11, 1822; 928–1028, June 12, 1822.
[38] 2 *Hansard* VII, 1596–1633, June 10, 1822.
[39] 2 *Hansard* IX, 833–901, June 11, 1823; 902–964, June 12, 1823.

primarily on the ground that the passage of time now made it unwise to agitate for a change.[40] Ricardo, in opposing the motion, said: "He had cared little, comparatively, what the standard established was—whether it continued at its then value, or went back to the old standard: his object had been, a fixed standard of some description or other." [41] The Commons rejected Western's motion 96 to 27.

Circulation of Small Notes

The defeat of Western's motion did not end the controversy over the standard, but there was already a shifting of emphasis, with other aspects of monetary and banking policy becoming increasingly important. The effect of the various resumption acts had been to terminate, as of May 1, 1823, the right of country banks to issue notes under £5 but to leave untouched the right of the Bank of England to issue such notes. The provisions that for practical purposes had made the Bank's notes legal tender were to expire on the same date. The Bank, although not required to retire its small notes, beginning with coin redemption on May 8, 1821, replaced them with gold coin. Their circulation fell from £6,692,050 on May 5, 1821, to £925,180 on July 6, 1822, and they decreased every week until the latter part of December 1825.

Economic policy and legislation seldom operate in a steady and consistent manner, so while the Bank was retiring its small notes and Cobbett was urging holders of notes of all banks to demand gold, agricultural distress in 1822 had led to Government-sponsored legislation of July 8, 1822, extending to January 5, 1833, the right of country banks to issue small notes.[42] No figures of country bank issues in which trust can be put are available for the years 1821–1825, but various bits of evidence suggest that they increased proportionately more than Bank circulation in those years, and that after 1822 this increase was particularly great in the small notes.[43] Regardless of how much the country banks may have increased their total issues or their small notes, this problem was soon involved in the larger problems, which were brought to a head by the crisis of late 1825 and early 1826: the legal position of the country banks in relation to

[40] 2 *Hansard* IX, 897, June 11, 1823.

[41] *Works*, V, 310.

[42] 3 Geo. IV, c. 70.

[43] Henry Burgess, secretary of the Committee of Country Bankers, estimated before the Bank Charter Committee of 1832, on the basis of incomplete and questionable evidence, that total country bank issues, after decreasing about 5 per cent in 1822, increased 16 per cent between 1823 and 1825 (Q. 5165). Clapham, *Bank of England*, II, 97, suggests that the increase was around 20 to 25 per cent.

the Bank of England, the growing movement for joint-stock banking, and the public responsibilities of the Bank of England.

Cobbett's Attacks on Country Banks

In February 1821 Cobbett had pictured, on the first page of his *Political Register,* a gridiron on which he promised to be broiled when Peel's act came into full force. He continued to show this after the resumption of payments in gold coin in May 1821, for he claimed that as long as country banks continued to issue small notes—or continued to issue any notes, or even that the Bank of England issued notes, for consistency was not the basis of Cobbett's influence—Peel's act was not fully operative. He ran a series of "Letters to Money Hoarders," urging the public to redeem their notes in gold while they could still get it. Writing as only Cobbett could, his advice on gold, in a special appeal to women, was: "Stayed dames, put it by with those silks and lace, that you have so long preserved as memorials of your early conquests! Lovely maidens, hug it to those bosoms, which would almost warm the metal into flesh and blood!—Faith, I must stop, or I shall be myself on fire." [44] When the bill for extending the circulation of small notes was under debate in 1822, Cobbett stepped up his attack on paper money, and headed his advice to money hoarders "On the Measures now in Progress for partially repealing Peel's Bill," [45] and continued his attacks until the crisis broke in 1825.

Other Proposals for Changes in Note Issues

Criticism of the country banks was not confined to Cobbett. Ricardo as early as 1816 had expressed doubts about their freedom of note issue, and only opposition of the country bankers had prevented the Government in 1818 from pressing for legislation to restrict their issues. Suggestive of an opinion that cut across the conventional divisions of conservative and radical were the comments in 1824, critical of country banks, in the Tory *Quarterly Review*[46] and in the newly established radical *Westminster Review.*[47]

Strong as was the organization of the country banks in defense of their privileges, it is questionable whether that alone can explain the failure

[44] December 8, 1821, 1403–1404.

[45] June 29, 1822, 769.

[46] Vol. XXXI, December 1824, art. vii, "Savings Banks and Country Banks," by George Taylor.

[47] Vol. I, January 1824, art. x, "On the Instrument of Exchange," by Perronet Thompson. The criticism of the country banks is on pp. 197–198.

of positive action against the "ravenous rooks," as Cobbett called them. The lack of any well-developed and generally accepted alternative to the existing system of country bank notes is the major explanation of why the distrust and criticism of country bank notes did not lead to legislative measures. Leaving aside Cobbett's idea of a purely metallic circulation, three major approaches to reform were open: (1) turning over to the government or a government agency the exclusive right of note issue; (2) turning over to the Bank of England the exclusive right of note issue; (3) strengthening of private bank issues, by requiring guarantees of note issues, by permitting the establishment of joint-stock banks, or by some combination of these actions. In practice the matter was even more complex, for in the background of any proposal was the unresolved question of the position of the Bank of England. The Bank's insistence on its monopoly rights, and its refusal, at least in formal statements, to recognize public responsibilities other than those arising out of its direct relation to government, made difficult the logical conclusion that would suggest itself to a twentieth century economist: concentration of the note issues in a bank endowed with the powers and responsibilities of a modern central bank. Developments after 1797 had increased the powers and the profits of the Bank, but with the Bank regarding its profits in the same light as the increased profits of any private bank. A small but revealing bit of evidence of this attitude was the reaction of the Bank to the proposal of Pascoe Grenfell, its perennial Parliamentary gadfly, that it be required to furnish regular information on its note issues. William Manning, a Bank director and former governor, replied that the directors "were clearly of opinion, that he [Grenfell] had no more right to demand the account he had moved for, than he had to call for copies of the books of any private merchant or banking-house."[48] In this the Bank was out of step with the trend of opinion, and without recorded vote the Commons ordered the Bank to deliver its accounts.[49]

Throughout the Restriction period and continuing after resumption, the idea that the right of note issue was a sovereign power of government appeared repeatedly in pamphlet literature and in Parliament. Ricardo, although he expressed his views with less emotion and more analysis than did Cobbett and others who denounced "paper mints," also challenged, both on grounds of safety and of social justice, the existing system of note issue. In 1816, in *Proposals for an Economical and Secure Currency*, he had

---

[48] 2 *Hansard* X, 124, February 11, 1824.
[49] 2 *Hansard* X, 241, February 19, 1824. The debate covered 226–241.

suggested that the right of note issue be taken away from the Bank of England and the country banks and given to a government agency. This idea was developed in his *Plan for the Establishment of a National Bank,* posthumously published in February 1824. The plan called for concentrating all note issue in a board of national commissioners, but would have left to the Bank its deposit business. Both the main outlines of the plan and Ricardo's underlying philosophy are summarized in the opening paragraphs:

The Bank of England performs two operations of banking, which are quite distinct, and have no necessary connection with each other: it issues a paper currency as a substitute for a metallic one; and it advances money in the way of loan, to merchants and others.

That these two operations of banking have no necessary connection, will appear obvious from this,—that they might be carried on by two separate bodies, without the slightest loss of advantage, either to the country, or to the merchants who receive accommodation from such loans.

Suppose the privilege of issuing paper money were taken away from the Bank, and were in future to be exercised by the State only, subject to the same regulation to which the Bank is now liable, of paying its notes, on demand, in specie; in what way would the national wealth be in the least impaired?[50]

Ricardo's proposal had no immediate effect, but from another quarter came a plan aimed at the Bank's monopoly privileges and at the instability of the country bank circulation, but in a form that stood greater chance of political acceptance. This was Thomas Joplin's proposal for the establishment of joint-stock banks with the right of note issue. Joplin first published his recommendation anonymously in *An Essay on the General Principles and Present Practice of Banking; in England and Scotland; with Observations upon the Justice and Policy of an Immediate Alteration in the Charter of the Bank of England, and the Measures to be Pursued in Order to Effect It* (Newcastle, 1822). The *Essay* appeared in new editions under Joplin's name, and he kept up a tireless campaign in support of joint-stock banking. In April 1822 the Government had broached to the Bank the idea of extending its charter, due to expire in 1833, to 1843 in return for concessions by the Bank, including the authorization of joint-stock banking outside of London. The Bank was willing to accept such a compromise, but the Government did not press the matter, apparently because of the opposition of the politically powerful country bankers.[51] But Joplin had planted the idea of joint-stock banking, thus

[50] *Works,* IV, 276.
[51] Further details are given by Clapham, *Bank of England,* II, 87–88.

strengthening two powerful groundswells of public opinion—the dangers of country bank notes and the inequity of the Bank of England monopoly.

The Crisis of 1825

In late 1823, 1824, and early 1825, aside from Cobbett's attacks on the country banks, there was little public discussion of monetary and banking problems. Criticism of the Bank of England was at low ebb, and economic conditions were better than at any time since Waterloo.[52] Brick production, a good index of economic activities in early nineteenth century England, more than doubled between 1821 and 1825, as did timber imports. Agricultural prices rose, and in April 1825 bar iron sold at nearly twice what it had three years earlier. A Birmingham manufacturer, T. C. Salt, reported some years later: "During the whole of 1824 and 1825 the stock went off so rapidly into consumption that we could hardly keep the shop-keepers supplied fast enough." [53] The literary output of the Birmingham economists fell off, and "on the 12th December, 1824, Sir John Sinclair wrote to Mr. Attwood, congratulating him on the prosperous state of the Country, and on the disappointment of their mutual predictions, that the ancient Metallic Standard could not be restored without occasioning universal misery and distress." [54] Bankruptcies dropped, and in 1823 and 1824 were less than in any year since 1806.

The economic expansion in real terms was accompanied by a financial expansion, foreshadowed in 1822 by foreign investments, particularly in South America. Stock market promotion was on a scale previously unknown, and share prices, especially in the mining field, soared. The Bank apparently had no positive policy in the early part of this expansion other than to get its assets into earning form. It is true that private discounts declined from £5,986,000 on January 8, 1823, the highest since July 1820, to barely £2 million in November 1824, the lowest figure since resumption, but owing to an increase in the Bank's mortgage investments and in its holdings of public securities, total credit moved upward after August 30, 1823. From £17,467,370 on that date it increased at the next four semi-annual reporting dates, and reached £25,106,030 on August 31, 1825.

Cobbett kept up his attacks, but persons of less radical views were also prophesying that rough financial waters were ahead. As early as March 1822 Hudson Gurney had recorded in his diary Huskisson's concern "that

[52] Details are given by Gayer and others, *British Economy, 1790–1850*, I, 171–210.

[53] *Committee on Manufactures*, 1833, Q. 4146.

[54] *The Late Prosperity . . . a Correspondence between Sir John Sinclair and Mr. Thomas Attwood* (London, 1826), Introduction.

this universal Jobbery in Foreign Stock will turn out the most tremendous Bubble ever known." Huskisson was also alarmed by the failure of the Bank to take a firmer stand and apparently by its desire to keep its funds profitably invested in 1824 and 1825. On September 4, 1825, he wrote to George Canning: "Once or twice before the end of the session [July 6, 1825], I warned the cabinet to look with suspicion at symptoms, which proved to me that the Bank, in its greedy folly, was playing over again the game of 1817." [55] He added that but for the good harvest there would already have been suspension of payments, and predicted serious trouble within the next three months. In June 1825, Edward Ellice had expressed in Parliament fears over the consequences of the credit expansion: "The least alarm in foreign affairs, or a bad harvest, would inevitably reduce government to the dilemma, in sending down another Order in Council to the Bank to suspend cash payments, or of witnessing, without having any other means of averting it, a convulsion threatening the industry, commerce, and finances of the country, with indiscriminate ruin." [56]

Beginning in late 1824 the exchanges became unfavorable and substantial amounts of gold went abroad. On February 26, 1825, the Bank's reserves were £8,857,730, lower than at any time since August 1820; on July 30, 1825, they were £4,174,830; and on October 29 £3,012,150. [57] The exchanges were again favorable for a short time in September 1825, but in the meantime the Bank continued to lose gold from the internal drain arising from runs on country banks. The situation became critical in late November, and from then until the last days of December the internal demand for gold continued at an alarming rate. In June 1825 a case had been aired in Parliament of the refusal of a bank in Bristol to give gold to a noteholder who objected to payment in Bank notes, [58] and Cobbett publicized the incident. [59] Cobbett's exhortation to all noteholders to demand gold was intensified by his claim that another bank restriction was imminent. [60] A noteholder of the Bristol bank, when the panic was at its worst in December, distributed a broadside reading: "I have the pleasure of being a disciple of Mr. Cobbett," and gave this advice to the inhabitants of Bristol: "As there is no knowing what may happen, get Gold, for if

[55] Augustus Granville Stapleton, *George Canning and His Times* (London, 1829), p. 226.
[56] 2 *Hansard* XIII, 1387, June 27, 1825.
[57] William Ward, a Bank director, discussed the gold losses of the Bank in late 1824 and 1825, in his testimony before the Bank Charter Committee of 1832 (Q. 1883–1892, 1956–1957). The figures on specie holdings are in appendix 6.
[58] 2 *Hansard* XIII, 1381–1400, June 27, 1825.
[59] *Political Register*, July 2, 1825, 14–53.
[60] *Political Register*, May 7, 1825, 359; October 8, 1825, 88.

Restriction come it will be too late." [61] The Bank's withdrawals of its notes under £5 contributed to the crisis, for timid holders of small notes of country banks, who might have been satisfied with Bank notes of £1 and £2, added to the demand for specie.

When the internal runs began, the Bank, though it increased its discounts greatly, at first held to a narrow standard of eligibility and refused to discount high-grade paper for solvent houses. When Henry Thornton's old firm, Pole, Thornton & Company, correspondent for forty-four provincial banks and headed by Sir Peter Pole, with whom Cornelius Buller, the governor of the Bank, was "particularly connected . . . by marriage and other circumstances of relationship," [62] was in desperate straits, the Bank advanced it £300,000 on December 7, 1825, but the firm failed a few days later. Other banks whose claims seemed equally good were turned away, apparently on technical grounds of eligibility, [63] and runs on country banks and demands for gold from the Bank of England increased. Not until December 13 did the Bank raise its discount rate from 4 to 5 per cent.

John B. Richards, the deputy governor, said: "On Monday morning [December 12] the storm began, and till Saturday night it raged with an intensity that it is impossible for me to describe." [64] On Thursday the 15th, the *Morning Chronicle* reported: "Melancholy as was our picture of the state of the City on Monday and Tuesday, the scenes which were yesterday exhibited far surpassed anything we had previously witnessed. It would be impossible to give an adequate idea of the panic which prevailed; and this, added to the curiosity naturally excited in the public mind, rendered the appearances of things still more aweful."

On December 13, at the urging of Government, the Bank authorized the purchase of £500,000 of Exchequer bills, [65] and in the week beginning December 12 total discounts were £5,977,000 as compared with a weekly average of under £1 million in the period November 7–26. [66] Between December 7 and 21 outstanding private discounts, as shown in Silberling's series, increased from £7,834,000 to £14,987,000. Bank circulation increased

---

[61] A copy of this broadside is in the British Museum, Add. MS. 40,385, fol. 123.

[62] Statement of John B. Richards, deputy-governor of the Bank in 1825, *Bank Charter Committee*, 1832, Q. 5006. I have drawn on Richards' testimony, Q. 4956–5091, for this account of the crisis.

[63] I say "apparently," because the Bank's records have practically nothing on any policy decisions by the Bank in the crisis of December, and they are barren as to the reasons for the decisions that were reached, beyond a request from the Government to purchase Exchequer bills.

[64] *Bank Charter Committee*, 1832, Q. 5056.

[65] *Bank Charter Committee*, 1832, app. 4.

[66] Clapham, *Bank of England*, II, 98–99.

from £18,037,960 on December 10 to £25,611,800 on December 24. Jeremiah Harman described the Bank's actions: "We lent it [assistance] by every possible means, and in modes that we never had adopted before; we took in stock as security, purchased exchequer bills, we made advances on exchequer bills, we not only discounted outright, but we made advances on deposits of bills of exchange to an immense amount; in short by every possible means consistent with the safety of the Bank; and we were not upon some occasions over nice; seeing the dreadful state in which the public were, we rendered every assistance in our power." [67]

The crisis continued, despite the purchase of Exchequer bills, the increased discounts, and the inflow of gold from abroad. Only on Monday the 19th did the run slacken, although the Bank's reserves did not reach their low of £1,027,000 until December 24. Aside from that general catchall "restoration of confidence," two developments apparently played a major role in stopping the crisis: the issue of £1 and £2 notes by the Bank, and the belief of the public, toward the latter part of the week, that the Bank was prepared to function as a lender of last resort.

The Bank, which had issued no small notes since the resumption of payments on May 8, 1821, on December 16 paid out pound notes from a supply untouched for years. At the close of business on Saturday, December 17, its circulation of notes under £5 was £383,610; a week later it had risen to £1,149,570, and on December 31 to £1,236,650. Public acceptance of these notes indicated that faith in the Bank of England note was unshaken. This development undoubtedly contributed to the feeling that the Bank note was a more stable element in the currency than were the country bank notes, and gave stimulus to the legislative moves of 1826 and to the forces that led up to the Bank Act of 1844.

The Bank's payment of pound notes at the height of the crisis has given rise to a story, embellishing the evidence of Jeremiah Harman before the committee of 1832,[68] that Bank officials by chance stumbled across a box of unissued pound notes just in time to pay them out and stop the crisis.[69] The Bank records contribute nothing, but it is inherently implausible that for over two weeks of crisis the existence of these unissued notes should have been unknown to the high command of the Bank. Furthermore, as early as November 22 Thomas Attwood, in a letter to Lord

[67] *Bank Charter Committee*, 1832, Q. 2217.
[68] *Bank Charter Committee*, 1832, Q. 2232-2234.
[69] The story appears, among other places, in H. G. Macleod, *The Theory and Practice of Banking*, 4th ed. (London, 1886), II, 118; A. Andreades, *History of the Bank of England* (London, 1909), p. 252; Feaveryear, *The Pound Sterling*, p. 237; and Clapham, II, 100.

THE NEW GOLD STANDARD

Liverpool warning of an impending crisis, had urged the Bank to provide itself with a stock of pound notes.[70]

Advice was coming to the Bank from private quarters, as well as from the Government, that it should apply less rigorous standards in making advances. Thomas Attwood, with a letter from the elder Sir Robert Peel, called upon the younger Robert Peel, who took him to see Lord Liverpool and arranged a meeting with the Chancellor of the Exchequer and one with a committee of the Bank directors. These meetings were on Friday, December 16. Attwood reported that evening to the younger Peel:

In consequence of your recommendation I have seen the Committee of the Bank Directors, and I have represented to them the measure which I deem proper for the relief of the District of Birmingham and its neighborhood; and I think it is my duty to inform you, that they have declined to accede to my suggestion, alleging that it is too great a variation from their usual rules; but they say, that if I wish it, they will present the subject to the Court of Directors tomorrow. I hardly feel justified in putting myself too forward in a public cause, which may be liable to misinterpretation, and therefore I believe that I shall decline it. The measure, and views of these gentlemen are evidently too timid and indecisive to meet the occasion.[71]

Whether Attwood's urging had any influence on the Bank we do not know. Its records are silent on the matter, and the testimony of the Bank directors in 1832 made no reference to Attwood. In any case, Attwood's memorandum in the Peel papers accompanying the correspondence, and which presumably was the substance of his plea to the Bank directors, was a remarkable statement, for its time, of the Bank of England's public responsibilities:

As respects the objection to interfering with the Bank on the ground of its being a private & not a public body, let it only be considered that the Bank has been placed by the Legislature in such circumstances as to perform, in point of fact, functions of a Public Nature, & those of the most important & almost regal nature; & standing indeed, virtually in the situation, & exercising all the power & effect of a Public Mint, in a degree as far beyond those of the Royal Mint as the extent of the Paper Currency exceeds that of the King's Coin at present circulating in the Country. It cannot therefore for a moment be held that so long as the Bank is entrusted with Powers as great as they ought not to be held subject to such control & Interference on the part of Government as

[70] Thomas Attwood, *The Scotch Banker* (London, 1828), p. 164.

[71] Several letters and memoranda relating to this incident are in the Peel papers in the British Museum, Add. MS. 40,384. Part of the material is published in C. S. Parker, *Sir Robert Peel from His Private Papers* (London, 1899), I, 380–382, but differs in details from the original manuscripts.

may be necessary to prevent any great public calamity from the mismanagement of this great public power.

Regardless of what Attwood's influence may have been, his voice was only one of many to urge the Bank to change its old concepts of credit worthiness when the financial world was on the brink of collapse. Joplin "claimed that he had written the leading article in the *Courier* of Tuesday evening, December 13, urging liberal discounting. The following day Vincent Stuckey at seven o'clock in the morning"[72] had written to the Bank urging that the Bank expand credit. Whether the Bank, the Government, Attwood, Joplin, or Stuckey deserves the credit is a detail compared with the fact that action was taken by the Bank in 1825 on a scale far beyond anything that it had done before. Unlike 1793 and 1811 the precedent was set that in time of crisis the Bank, not the Government, was to be the instrument of action; and unlike 1797 the position was taken that depletion of reserves was no reason for a suspension of payments.

The Bank suggested to the Government an Order in Council to suspend specie payments. There were evidently stormy meetings of the Cabinet and the Bank directors, but, as Jeremiah Harman reported, the Government "resisted it from first to last." The account in the diary of Mrs. Arbuthnot, whose husband was Joint Secretary of the Treasury, Patronage Secretary, and a close associate of the Duke of Wellington, catches the drama, and apparently states accurately most of the facts of the crisis days, although her dislike of Huskisson and Canning is evident:

[December] 17th . . . yesterday morning Mr. A. received a letter from Mr. Herries[73] describing the state of affairs in London as so alarming as to require the presence of all those interested in the Govt. We came to London immediately & saw Mr. Herries, who came up to the Duke's House. He told the Duke the Cabinet was sitting, & he immediately set off to it. Mr. Herries told us that such had been the extraordinary demand for gold to supply the country bankers & to meet the general run upon them that the Bank of England was completely drained of its specie & was reduced to 100,000 sovereigns, with which it wd have to open today & meet demands of probably four times that amount. The Bank expects to be obliged to suspend cash payments tomorrow, and they want the Government to step forward to their assistance & order the suspension. Lord Liverpool is unwilling to do this & wishes the Bank to do it upon their own responsibility. By Mr. Herries's account there seems to be considerable irritation between the Govt & the Governors of the bank. They trace all these money difficulties to the encouragement given by members of the

---

[72] T. E. Gregory, *The Westminster Bank through a Century* (London, 1936), II, 149–150. A reference to Stuckey's advice is in *Bank Charter Committee*, 1832, Q. 5012.

[73] John Charles Herries.

Government to the foreign loans & speculations, which all go out of the country in gold, and to Mr. Huskisson's commercial liberality which drains the country of gold in another way. Such is the detestation in which he is held in the City that Ld L[iverpool] & Mr. Canning did not think it prudent to summon him to London till all the Cabinet were sent for &, in the discussions with the Bank, he is kept out of sight. He repays them with equal hatred & told Lord Liverpool that, if they stopped payment, it wd be a good opportunity of taking their Charter from them, although he knows their circulation is but 18 million & we owe them 30 million. Ld Liverpool is so afraid of Mr. Huskisson that he entered into this scandalous scheme & was for letting the Bank break, tho' the consequences wd be ruin both at home & abroad, rather than take any responsibility upon the Govt. Mr. Herries remonstrated with Lord Liverpool & asked him how he meant to pay the Dividends & the Army & Navy? This a little stopped him, & he was frightened again by Mr. Baring[74] who told him all the Bank distresses were caused by the Govt and read him a lecture upon it. Mr. Huskisson has done all he can also to ruin Rothschild by spreading reports that their house was in danger, & he made Mr. Canning write to Paris to enquire into the affairs of that brother. Ld. Granville sent his private secretary to pump Rothschild. R[othschild] found out what he was at & instantly shewed him his accounts & proved to him that he was worth 2½ millions. Rothschild has made most gigantic efforts to assist the Bank & he told Mr. Herries that, if he had been applied to sooner, he wd have prevented all the difficulty. As it is, if they can hold out till Monday or Tuesday, he will have enormous sums over in sovereigns from Paris, & the pressure will be entirely relieved. Mr. Herries, I see, expects that the Bank will suspend their payments tomorrow. They have but 100,000 sovereigns left, tho' they have a large quantity of uncoined bullion in the Mint. Mr Herries said that the City merchants appeared to have the utmost contempt for Mr. Robinson,[75] who was wholly without plan or expedients & who did not appear to have the least idea what to do.

What will happen in the country I don't know. The banks are breaking in every direction &, as the circulation is entirely in local notes, there is now in fact no circulation for gold cannot be supplied & every thing is at a stand. In the manufacturing districts they do not know how to pay the wages & serious riots are expected.

We remained at the Duke's till he returned from the Cabinet which was not till 2 o'clock in the morning. He had taken just the line I expected he wd take. He told Lord Liverpool while there was life there was hope; that there was a chance of the Bank standing & while that chance remained, he wd not despair; that the Government were bound to support them to the very utmost of their power & that, if they were forced to suspend their payments, it must be done in the manner most beneficial to the Bank, for that their interests were those of the country & their difficulties caused by no imprudence on their part but by the fault of the Govt in encouraging foreign speculations & allowing the

[74] Alexander Baring.
[75] John Frederick Robinson, Chancellor of the Exchequer.

country banks to inundate every district with one & two pound notes. Lord Liverpool professed to the Duke great desire to serve the Bank.

20th.—Two or three more anxious days have passed. The Bank have been able to continue cash payments, tho' at one moment they had 60,000 sovereigns left, & yesterday when they closed they had not much more. Rothschild was to receive 200,000 this morning and, as he sent 25 couriers off last week to buy sovereigns wherever they could be got, I hope they will now begin to pour in. The state of the country at this moment is most extraordinary; there is no circulating medium, no means of getting money or of paying for any thing. Sir Chas Knightly, a gentleman of large property near Daventry, came to London two days ago & was obliged to ride part of the way & to borrow a few sovereigns, which his little girl had hoarded, to be able to pay for his journey, and told us that at this moment he had not the means of getting a shilling. The bank he deals with have suspended their payments and, tho' he feels sure they are perfectly solvent, yet the momentary embarrassment is as great as if they were bankrupts.

The Duke's coming up did great good; the Bank Directors & all those who are not under the influence of the Canning part of the Cabinet look up to him as a protector & one who will not be afraid of responsibility & vigorous measures. The Bank & the Treasury were delighted when they heard he was arrived, & said that now at least the country wd not be ruined by cowardice. He told me he is quite sure that he is a *most inconvenient* person in the Cabinet, that they are all afraid of him, that in his presence they dare not *name* even any of their shabby wishes to shirk responsibility, that they know he will always come out with his fair & honest opinion & the consequence is that they sit & look at each other & say nothing. This applies to Messrs. Canning, Huskisson & Robinson. There has not been a word uttered since he came to town about taking the Charter from the Bank, which the Duke said, whether right or wrong under ordinary circumstances, wd be scandalous in a moment of difficulty caused by our own false policy.

.   .   .   .   .   .

26th.—The money matters had improved so much by the 22d that Ld Liverpool went to Coombe, the D. of Wellington went to Sudbourne &, on the 23d, we also went to Sudbourne. At one moment the Bank were reduced to 18,000 Sovereigns, but the tide had turned before we left town & they were receiving more than they were paying.[76]

Refusal of Government to Issue Exchequer Bills

Richards testified before the Bank Charter Committee of 1832 on the Bank's role in 1825: "I am satisfied the Bank would have failed in its duty had not it gone forward with the energy and resolution it did at that moment" (Q. 5096). Yet at the time the crisis was raging the Bank

---

[76] *The Journal of Mrs. Arbuthnot: 1820–1832*, ed. Francis Bamford and the Duke of Wellington (London, 1950), I, 426–428, 431.

management does not appear to have been happy at the idea of meeting a rendezvous with central banking destiny, and two months later it wanted to play a more modest part when the market again needed a lender of last resort. Early in 1826, although the exchanges were favorable, bankruptcies were high, and a group of London merchants petitioned the Commons for an issue of Exchequer bills.[77]

The problem was debated both in the Commons and the Lords, and a discussion of broad principles as to whether action in time of crisis should come from the Government or from the Bank was mingled with partisan thrusts from the Whigs, and the airing of charges against the Bank.[78] Canning, then the Tory leader in the Commons, persuaded the Government, against the wishes of a large number of its own party, to oppose the issue of Exchequer bills, and probably for the only time in British history a Government staked its life on an issue of central banking. He wrote to Lord Liverpool on February 23: "The same confidence, and an infinitely more prompt and valuable relief may be afforded by the Bank, in the instant and judicious use of their undoubted power to lend on goods ... What the Bank has the power to do, it is its duty to do in such an emergency as the present."[79] Canning's letter of March 6 to Lord Granville indicates that the issue went much deeper than the technical economic question whether Exchequer bills or Bank credit were the better means of granting credit in an emergency, being more a basic power struggle as to whether the Government or the Bank had the final word.[80] John Wilson Croker's account to the Duke of Wellington a few days later supports Canning's picture of the tension-charged atmosphere: "During the debate on the Petition I went up to Canning and said, 'For God's sake take care of what you say about this issue of Exchequer Bills, for the whole House is against us, and our best friends are mutinying at our backs.' He replied with considerable nervous excitement, 'So much the better; it will bring matters to a point sooner.'"[81]

No Exchequer bills were issued, and the Bank, evidently reluctantly, agreed to advance up to £5 million on the security of goods "for the relief of the Commercial Distress now prevailing."[82] As it turned out,

---

[77] Printed in 2 *Hansard* XIV, 732–733, February 23, 1826.

[78] The principal debates in the Commons are in 2 *Hansard* XIV, 416–423, February 15, 1826; 698–733, February 23, 1826; 920–963, February 28, 1826; in the Lords, 450–499, February 17, 1826; 1347–1358, March 13, 1826.

[79] The full letter is in Stapleton, *George Canning*, pp. 235–236.

[80] Stapleton, pp. 237–238.

[81] *The Croker Papers*, ed. Louis J. Jennings (London, 1884), I, 315.

[82] C.B., Wa, February 28, 1826.

however, the Bank made advances of only £533,040 on personal security and the security of goods,[83] and at the same time its discounts and holdings of Exchequer bills fell off by more than this amount, so that total Bank credit declined in the weeks after the clash with the Government. But the principle was reaffirmed that if aid were to be given to the money market it should come not from the Government but from the Bank.

Aftermath of the 1825 Crisis

In the controversy that followed there were few suggestions of devaluation or of a paper standard. Renewed proposals for bimetallism were prompted by problems of short-run international adjustments rather than the price level issues that a few years earlier, or a half century later, had been the main arguments of bimetallic supporters. Those who had denounced the deflation of Peel's act now were more concerned with the failure of country banks and the latent instability of a fractional reserve money system. This shift of emphasis from monetary standard to banking structure is symbolized by the exchange of views in 1826 in *The Late Prosperity* between those tireless critics of the act of 1819, Sir John Sinclair and Thomas Attwood. Attwood saw in the events of 1825 additional evidence of the need for a new standard: "Every *shock* that our Circulating System has sustained, *from the year* 1791 *to this day,* can be traced to the pressure of the Metallic Standard" (p. 37). He could see no benefits in the establishment of joint-stock banks in England along the lines of the Scottish banks. In contrast Sinclair, although still more favorable to paper than to a metallic standard, admitted that it was politically useless to push such a view, since "all of the leading political characters, in both Houses of Parliament, were decidedly hostile to paper" (p. 106), and supported bimetallism. But the main point in Sinclair's argument was the weakness of the existing system of country banks and the need under any standard of authorizing joint-stock banking and of requiring security from banks for the issue of notes under £5 (pp. 98–100).

Before Parliament reassembled in February 1826 the Government had acted. On January 13, 1826, Lord Liverpool and Frederick John Robinson, Chancellor of the Exchequer, sent to the Bank a memorandum, which William Huskisson is believed to have drafted in large part, suggesting that the small notes of country banks be forbidden, that joint-stock banks be authorized, and that the Bank establish branches. There followed an

[83] Clapham, *Bank of England*, 108–109.

exchange of views, with the Bank receptive to the establishment of branches, which the Bank's own committee had already recommended to its directors, and to the authorization of joint-stock banks in the provinces.[84]

The Government introduced legislation to carry out its program, and committees were appointed in both the Lords and Commons to investigate the issue of notes in Scotland and Ireland. From early February until May Parliament debated the Government's legislative program, with criticism of some details but little attack on the basic concepts as far as they applied to England and Wales.[85] The events of the years immediately preceding had convinced a large part of the public of the need for such legislation. It simply required the events of 1825 to bring action. An anonymous writer, in a publication of 1826 urging "interference of the legislature" to ensure the safety of the country bank notes, said: "I believe it will be readily conceded to me, that some check is necessary to this dangerous species of our currency. I have never conversed with any person upon the subject , who, however differing upon the mode, had any doubt upon the principle." [86] The extensive pamphlet literature of 1826 supports the essential truth of this statement. With the losses from the failures of country banks and the growing resentment against the Bank of England, it was an easy task for a strong Government to put across its program.[87]

The act of March 22, 1826,[88] forbade banks in England or Wales to issue new notes under £5, or after April 5, 1829, to reissue any notes under £5. The wording of the law was not clear as to whether it also applied to the Bank of England, but the Bank as a matter of policy never issued any notes under £5 after June 1826 until specific authorization was

---

[84] The memorandum of Liverpool and Robinson, the actions of the Bank Court, and subsequent correspondence from Liverpool and Robinson are in 2 *Hansard* XIV, 103–111, February 6, 1826.

[85] The Commons debates are in 2 *Hansard* XIV, 145–152, February 9, 1826; 165–245, February 10; 245–356, February 13; 358–359, February 14; 537–555, February 17; 570–642, February 20; 696–698, February 23; 859–864, February 24; 878–915, February 27; 963–967, February 28; 1184–1192, March 7; 1258–1259, March 9; 1358–1360, March 14; 1379–1388, March 16; XV, 155–157, April 13; 236–244, April 14; 1414–1444, May 26. The Lords debates are in XIV, 132–145, February 9; 450–500, February 17; 556–566, February 20; 864–877, February 27; 1347–1358, March 14; 1392–1400, March 17; XV, 131–132, April 10; 210–218, April 14; 558–562, April 25.

[86] *A Letter to the right Hon. Robert Peel* (London, 1826), p. 58.

[87] Clapham goes into the details of the Government's relations to the Bank in early 1826 (II, 102–109), and the account seems fully to justify his comment that "the Bank was never so inert in the hands of ministers, so much ordered about, as in 1826" (II, 107).

[88] 7 Geo. IV, c. 6.

given in the Currency and Bank Notes Act of 1928.[89] The act of May 26, 1826,[90] authorized the formation of joint-stock banks with the right of note issue, providing the issuing bank had no office within 65 miles of London. The same act authorized the establishment of branches by the Bank of England and the issue of notes at branches, payable at the option of the holder either at the issuing branch or in London.

Controversy over Scottish Note Issues

The one real controversy stirred up by the Government's proposal was primarily a problem of Scottish home rule, not of economic analysis. The original proposal of the Government had called for treating the Scottish and Irish banks in the same way as the English and Welsh banks. The Government had not reckoned on the spirit of Scottish nationalism or the pen of Sir Walter Scott. In *A Letter to the Editor of the Edinburgh Weekly Journal* (Edinburgh, 1826) from "Malachi Malagrowther," and in *A Second Letter* and *A Third Letter* purporting to come from the same "discontented person" of "ill temper" and "hasty and peevish humour," Scott appealed to Scottish history and Scottish pride against any restriction on the banks of his country.

The Scottish situation differed from that below the Tweed in three main points of history and structure, and in one important point of banking practice:

1. Small notes had a much longer history than in England. Even after the resumption of payments in 1821 little coin had circulated; and to a large degree there was a tradition, almost with the force of law, that banks should not be required to redeem their notes in coin. Redemption in London drafts was the usual form of paying noteholders. There was a core of truth in the remark of an anonymous pamphleteer: "Any southern fool who had the temerity to ask for a hundred sovereigns, might, if his nerves supported him through the cross examination at the bank counter, think himself in luck to be hunted only to the border." [91]

2. Banking in Scotland was carried on largely by joint-stock banks.

3. Few Scottish banks had failed since the collapse of the Ayr Bank in 1772.

4. The Scottish banks made a practice of granting small credits on the general character of the borrower. Many Scots believed that this cash

---

[89] 18 & 19 Geo. V, c. 13.

[90] 7 Geo. IV, c. 46.

[91] *A Letter to the Right Hon. George Canning* (London, 1826), p. 45.

credits system had been a powerful stimulus to Scottish economic development, and that to forbid the issue of £1 and £2 notes would limit the ability of Scottish banks to extend cash credits.

This last point, when mixed with Scottish nationalism, was a heady political potion, and British governments more than once over the next century had to reckon with Scots who had quaffed deeply of it. In the hearings before the Commons committee—over which the younger Robert Peel presided at most of the meetings—and before the Lords committee the Scottish witnesses were unanimous in their opposition to the suppression of small notes, and most Irish spokesmen, although less extreme in their views, agreed. Both Scottish and Irish bankers claimed that, if small notes were forbidden, banks would have to restrict credits or even close some offices.[92] James Dunsmore, secretary to the Commissioners for the Herring Fishery, felt that stopping cash credits would be highly injurious to the fisheries.[93] James Gibson Craig, a Writer to the Signet, expressed fears that a suppression of small notes would make it impossible for Scottish banks to continue cash credits on the then prevailing terms. Then followed this question and answer: "Did you ever know the Opinions of all Parties so united upon any subject in the Course of your Life?"— "Certainly never." [94]

As a result of this Parliamentary and literary protest, Scotland and Ireland were exempted from the prohibition on small notes. The complexity of motivations that affect attitudes on economic policy is shown by the reaction of *Blackwood's Edinburgh Magazine,* spokesman for Scottish Toryism and critic of the rising power of London, and of the radical *Westminster Review. Blackwood's,* which combined political conservatism with a defense of paper money and a pride in things Scottish, said: "The admirable Malachi Malagrowther, Esq., has protested against the affairs of Scotland being managed by the people of London and we, in like manner, protest against the affairs of the country parts of England being managed by the people of London." [95] It later published two articles on "The Country Banks and the Bank of England," [96] in which it combined

[92] Representative testimony was that of H. A. Douglas and Thomas Spring Rice, directors of the Provincial Bank of Ireland (*Lords Committee,* 1826, pp. 24, 52); Robert Paul, secretary of the Commercial Bank of Scotland (*ibid.,* pp. 132–134); Alexander Blair, of the British Linen Company (*Commons Committee,* 1826, pp. 41–52); Hugh Watts, cashier of the Arbroath Banking Company (*ibid.,* pp. 187–190).

[93] *Lords Committee,* 1826, p. 211.

[94] *Lords Committee,* 1826, pp. 246–251.

[95] No. CXI, p. 443 (April 1826).

[96] No. CXXXIII, December 1827; no. CXXXV, February 1828.

its three ideas: breaking the gold standard, opposition to the Bank of England, particularly to its branches, and praise of country banks. In contrast the *Westminster,* whose utilitarian approach to life made it unsympathetic to the Scottish nationalist aspect of Scott's argument, and whose economic logic made it stress the irrationality of turning the right of note issue over to private companies, described Scott's letters as "only an exhortation to the sonsy and twice-thinking Scots, to threaten a civil war in defence of the privilege of being plundered." [97]

New Support for Bimetallism

The crisis of 1825 brought from a small group of Tory leaders a renewed interest in bimetallism. On February 8, 1826, William Huskisson, president of the Board of Trade, prepared for the Cabinet a memorandum in which he made favorable reference to Baring's earlier bimetallic proposals.[98] He recommended bimetallism at the French ratio of $15\frac{1}{2}$:1, by leaving the gold content of the pound unchanged and increasing the silver content by about $2\frac{1}{2}$ per cent over the 1797 figure. Huskisson's reasons for advocating the monetization of silver were threefold:

1. The desire to foster commercial relations with the new South American republics, many of which were large producers of silver.

2. The need for a broader metallic basis, if gold coin were to be substituted for small notes, which Huskisson felt to be essential if runs for specie were to be prevented in the future.

3. The need to give the Bank greater freedom in meeting external drains, in particular those arising from war or the threat of war. This international situation was particularly bad, in Huskisson's opinion, because under a single gold standard "the result is that we place ourselves, in matters connected with the foreign exchanges, and the means of supplying our metallic wants at the mercy of a powerful house here [Rothschild], acting in concert with their connexions on the continent, and vest them with a power, the use of which, however profitable to them and their connexions, it is neither desirable for the interests of commerce, nor safe for those of the country, to place in any such hands."

What went on in the Cabinet meeting at which this memorandum was presented we do not know. Peel, however, was sufficiently impressed by

---

[97] X, 366 (April 1829).

[98] *Despatches, Correspondence, and Memoranda, of Field Marshall Arthur, Duke of Wellington* (London, 1868), III, 98–104. The memorandum is reprinted in H. H. Gibb (Lord Aldenham), *A Colloquy on the Currency,* 3d ed. (London, 1894), pp. xlvii–lvi.

the report that Baring intended to move in Parliament for the adoption of bimetallism that he wrote on February 10 to the Duke of Wellington, then on a mission to Russia: "I am satisfied that this proposition, subject to some modification, should not be rejected, at least that it should be most maturely considered." Wellington, replying from Berlin, was unsympathetic on the ground that mining speculations in South America were greatly increasing the output of silver, and concluded: "The truth is that what is going on in the world will make silver useless as a measure of value, and I am afraid that for this evil there is no practical remedy." [99]

Baring did not at the time introduce any motion for the monetization of silver, but in the debates on the banking legislation both he and Huskisson made a number of comments on the advantages of such action. They persisted in their advocacy of silver, and in 1828 apparently won the support of the Duke of Wellington, who had become Prime Minister in January, and the Cabinet. On April 22 the governor and deputy governor of the Bank met with the Board of Trade and were asked about a plan for the Mint and the Bank to issue notes against the deposit of silver, to be redeemable only in silver but receivable in all payments to Government. Four days later the governor and deputy governor met at Downing Street with the Duke of Wellington, Huskisson, now Secretary of the Colonies, and Henry Goulburn, the new Chancellor of the Exchequer. As the Bank records report the meeting, it would appear that the Bank was lukewarm about these silver proposals, although "the Governor stated the readiness of the Bank to meet the views of His Majesty's Government in any manner which might be deemed for the National Interests, with reference to the propositions submitted for the consideration of the Bank on the 22d instant." [100] The Government also asked a series of questions about the greater use of silver in the monetary system and the establishment of bimetallism. The Bank was not enthusiastic, and it could "see no advantage in reverting to the former system of making silver by weight a legal tender to any amount."

At the meeting of the Board of Trade Baring gave testimony favorable to bimetallism.[101] A month later, according to the Bank's records: "The Governor and Deputy Governor attended at the Privy Council to explain the Answers of the Bank to the Queries respecting Silver as a legal Tender.

[99] Parker, *Sir Robert Peel*, I, 394-395.

[100] Committee of the Treasury, Report Book, April 28, 1828, pp. 91-96.

[101] Baring's testimony, and the Government's questions and the Bank's answers, were printed by the Commons in 1830, P.P. 1830, (31) XVII, and reprinted in 1848, P.P. 1847-48 (718) XXXIX.

In the early part of the conversation the impression on the part of the Duke of Wellington appeared to be in favour of the Measure; but no decision was expressed." [102]

The outcome of this discussion was nil, and for reasons that are not clear neither Baring nor any other Government spokesman made any moves in Parliament on behalf of silver. But Baring remained in principle a supporter of bimetallism, and as Professor R. S. Sayers has suggested,[103] it is possible, although there is no direct evidence on the point, that the provision in the Bank Act of 1844 that one fifth of the Bank's reserve could be in silver was the fruit of Baring's arguments for bimetallism.

Controversy without Action, 1827–1830

After the small-note legislation of 1826, for the next six years political controversy over Catholic emancipation and the reform of Parliament overshadowed monetary and banking questions. Discussion of the standard and banking was endemic, but there were no Parliamentary committees, no great legislative battles, no single publication that stands out in the history of controversy. The bimetallic proposals of Huskisson and Baring, important as they may have seemed when discussed in the Cabinet or Bank directors meetings, attracted little public attention.

Petitions on agricultural distress continued to come to Parliament. In 1829, 1830, and 1831 there were indications that many Parliamentary spokesmen for the landed gentry felt that the monetary situation was in some way responsible for their difficulties. Charles Greville, with the opening of the social season, reported in his diary of January 17, 1830: "The Country Gentlemen are beginning to arrive, and they are all of the same story as to the universally prevailing distress and the certainty of things becoming much worse; of the failure of rents all over England, and the necessity of some decisive measures or the prospect of general ruin. Of course they all differ as to the measures, but there appears to be a strong leaning towards an alteration in the currency and one pound notes." [104]

Huskisson, who had never publicly countenanced any change in the act of 1819 beyond a shift to bimetallism, in a private letter in the closing days of 1829 showed a concern about the deflationary consequences of the resumption of gold payments:

[102] Committee of the Treasury, Report Book, May 28, 1828, p. 96.

[103] "The Question of the Standard," *Economic History*, III, 100–101 (February 1935).

[104] *The Greville Memoirs, 1814–1860*, ed. Lytton Strachey and Roger Fulford (London, 1938), I, 358.

At the termination of the War, or at least before Peel's Act, passed in 1819, Government should have looked their difficulties in the face from the passing of the Bank Restriction Act. The wheel of depreciation producing high prices, etc., was turning one way whereby many interests suffered and were ruined; to attempt to turn the wheel back, without some equitable adjustment, which would have reduced the Government expenditure, in which I, of course, include the interest paid on the national debt, and which would have reduced the taxes, and all outgoings, and also rents raised since 1792, has always appeared to me madness.[105]

With such a committed champion of the act of 1819 talking this way in private, it is not surprising that stronger comments should come from others who had no such emotional attachments to that legislation. Not since 1819 had so many pamphlets dealt with the monetary standard as in the early 1830's, and only a small proportion had a good word to say for the act of 1819.[106]

There was a marshaling of arguments and forces in the three-cornered fight between country banks, joint-stock banks, and the Bank of England. In 1827 Henry Burgess was instrumental in forming the Committee of Country Bankers, which soon came to include practically all country bankers.[107] The house organ of the committee, *Circular to Bankers,* edited by Burgess, for over two decades kept up a running attack on the Bank of England and the act of 1819. The first issue spoke of the "effort for protecting the interests of the Country Bankers and the Private Bankers of this kingdom, against the encroachments of the powerful Corporation of the Governor and Company of the Bank of England, and against the measures of the Government, which must go hand in hand with those of the Bank Directors."[108] Although the statements of Burgess were not necessarily the opinions of the individual country bankers, the fact that they would so long support an organ that was so critical of the Bank of England and the gold standard would suggest that many country bankers must have shared the views of the *Circular.* A few samples of these comments are:

Those ignorant, vain, and obstinate, projectors—Huskisson, Peel, and Ricardo.[109]

[105] Letter of December 20, 1829, to J. C. Herries, British Museum, Add. MS. 38,578, fol. 64, as printed in *The Huskisson Papers,* ed. Lewis Melville (pseud. of Lewis S. Benjamin) (New York, 1932), p. 312.

[106] Of 16 pamphlets of 1830 that I examined that discussed the act of 1819, 11 were hostile; in 1831, 1832, and 1833 the hostile pamphlets were, respectively, six, 15, and 11 out of a total of eight, 19, and 14.

[107] See Burgess' testimony, *Bank Charter Committee,* 1832, Q. 5134.

[108] July 25, 1828 (no. 1), p. 1.

[109] January 6, 1832 (no. 181), p. 194.

That stupendous monument of ignorance and folly—the famous Bill of 1819.[110]

We have repeatedly described the danger which the country interest incurs from this grasping dominant money-corporation of the metropolis.[111]

The Political Economists (the curse of the country).[112]

The *Quarterly Review,* torn between the idea that the act of 1819 was injurious to the landed aristocracy and the view that any change in the monetary standard was a threat to the forces of law and order, faced both ways on the monetary standard. The archconservative John Wilson Croker, who wrote in 1830 in criticism of the act of 1819, said of its sponsors: "Impelled by extravagant feeling of honour on the one hand, and misled by abstract maxims of political economy on the other, they precipitately took a step of which no man can foretell the issue," [113] and urged a reconsideration of the standard. Yet shortly before and after Croker's attack on the act of 1819, other articles in the *Quarterly* from the pens of Edward Edwards,[114] H. A. Nilan,[115] and George Poulett Scrope,[116] although critical of the act of 1819, did not believe that a decade later the solution lay in a change in the standard.

The other Tory spokesman, *Blackwood's Edinburgh Magazine,* had no such mixed feelings on the act of 1819 as did the *Quarterly.* In 1829 and 1830 it condemned it without mercy, and continued to do so until the 1850's. In its view those who persuaded Parliament to pass the act of 1819 "gave the Jews, stock-brokers, and attorneys of the country, an enormous advantage, at the expense of classes connected with land . . . The desolation brought upon private families by that cruel and unconstitutional measure, no pen can paint—no tongue can tell." [117]

The small-note issue again gave Cobbett a chance to criticize the country banks. When an amendment to the Small Notes Bill was before Parliament in 1828 he restated his basic monetary philosophy: "Ever since that hellish compound word, Paper-money was understood by me, I have wished for the destruction of the accursed thing: I have applauded every measure that tended to produce its destruction, and censured every measure having a tendency to preserve it." [118] Even Cobbett's attacks on

[110] February 1834 (no. 297), p. 292.
[111] May 2, 1834 (no. 302), p. 330.
[112] August 15, 1835 (no. 469), p. 27.
[113] Vol. XLII, January 1830, art. ix, "Internal Policy," p. 254.
[114] Vol. XXXIX, April 1829, art. vii, "Currency"; Vol. XLII, March 1830, art. vii, "Banking."
[115] Vol. XLIII, May 1830, art. ix, "Distress of the Country."
[116] Vol. XLVII, July 1832, art. v, "The Rights of Industry and the Banking System."
[117] Vol. XXVII, January 1830, "The Effects of Variations in the Currency," pp. 63, 69.
[118] *Political Register,* June 14, 1828, 762–763.

Scots, Quakers, and Jews were not based on racial and religious grounds but simply on the fact that to him these groups were symbols of a hated world of finance. McCulloch's defense of paper money prompted him to speak of "this Scotch stupidity, conceit, pertinacity and impudence" as a warm-up for his judgment that "these Scotch have been a pestilence to England for more than two hundred years, becoming every year more and more destructive." [119] Sir Henry Parnell's pamphlet[120] supporting the country banks as against the Bank of England, praising the Scottish banking system and defending the general principle of "free banking," provoked from Cobbett a reference to "the Scotch monopolists, equally greedy with the Quakers, and the half Jews of England,"[121] followed by a denunciation of the "ravenous Rooks of Scotland."[122] The net effect of Cobbett's attacks on country banking probably strengthened the position of the Bank of England as against the country banks. Evidence of the way in which Cobbett and the Bank, relentless enemies, were nevertheless both giving support to the same movement is the revelation in Parliament in 1827 that a Bank director had written and distributed a letter casting doubt on the solvency of the country banks.[123]

The general satisfaction, despite many local protests, with the expansion of the field of circulation of the notes of Bank of England increased the prestige of the Bank as compared with the country banks. There was no dramatic event to mark the change, but in the years 1826–1832 there was much evidence, both from what was said and what was not said, of a changing attitude toward the Bank. The events of 1825 had impressed on the national consciousness the extent to which the entire banking structure pivoted on the Bank of England. After 1825 there was less discussion of getting rid of the Bank of England and more of making it function with greater effectiveness, a greater willingness to look on its notes as a national currency and not just the currency of London, and an acceptance of the idea that in time of crisis the Bank must act.

Origins of the Currency Principle

Along with this idea of making the Bank operate more effectively developed the thought that all paper money was a disturbing element in

---

[119] *Political Register*, April 26, 1828, 514–516.
[120] *Observations on Paper Money, Banking, and Overtrading* (London, 1827).
[121] *Political Register*, June 21, 1828, 792.
[122] *Political Register*, June 28, 1828, 810.
[123] 2 *Hansard* XVII, 1149–1154, June 1, 1827. John Pearse admitted that the letter had been written by a Bank director, although he did not confirm the charge of Sir John Wrottesley that other directors had been a party to its distribution.

the economy because of the sudden expansion and contraction that it caused in the total monetary supply. This to some extent coincided with, but went much further than, the opposition to the notes of country banks. This was not a new idea, but after 1825 there was increasing evidence of a feeling that, aside from bank failures or bank runs, the issuing of notes on fractional reserves, even by banks of unquestioned solvency, caused undesirable increases and decreases in the monetary supply. The attempt to find some simple way of avoiding these fluctuations led to the development of the currency principle, which was the basis of the Bank Act of 1844.

The currency principle—that the note circulation should fluctuate with changes in the Bank's holding of specie—represented the third stage in the search for a more stable monetary system, in which the monetary supply would not be subject to discretionary control. The first stage had been the restoration of a metallic standard which eliminated any discretion in the price of gold; the second was outlawing the issue of small notes by country banks and extending the field of circulation of Bank of England notes. The experience of 1825 and the years immediately preceding had shown the possibility of great changes in Bank note circulation, independent of changes in gold reserves. Even before 1825, in addition to Cobbett's demagogic outbursts, thoughtful comments had come from more conservative quarters on the inflationary and deflationary influence of Bank policy even with a fixed price of gold. The events of 1825 had given further impetus to suggestions for limiting the Bank's discretion in the creation of money.

The first organized statement of the currency principle came in 1827 from James Pennington,[124] who at the time was a friend of members of the Political Economy Club, of which he was also a member from 1828 until his resignation in 1856. In April 1826, probably at the suggestion of Thomas Tooke, Pennington prepared a memorandum dealing primarily with the problems of bimetallism but also suggesting the need to prevent an undue expansion or contraction of notes convertible into gold. He closed his memorandum with a query and the suggestion that he had an answer: "Are there, then, no means to be found, of preventing those alterations of excitement and depression—of extravagant expectation and

[124] I am indebted to Professor R. S. Sayers for making available to me information based on his research on Pennington. This information has since appeared in his essay "The Life and Work of James Pennington," in *Economic Writings of James Pennington*, Series of Reprints of Scarce Works on Political Economy, No. 17, London School of Economics and Political Science (London, 1963).

disappointed hope—but in the exclusive employment of so expensive a medium of interchange as gold, and the suppression of paper? The difficulty which this question implies, is not insuperable." Pennington submitted a copy to Huskisson, who in a reply on June 1, 1827, spoke of Pennington's mention of the need of "preventing those alterations of excitement and depression which have been attended with such alarming consequences to this country." Huskisson went on to say, "This, for a long time, has appeared to me one of the most important matters which can engage the attention of the Legislature and the Councils of this country. The subject is certainly intricate and complicated; but the too great facility of expansion at one time, and the too rapid contraction of paper credit (I speak of it in the largest sense) at another, is unquestionably an evil of the greatest magnitude." Huskisson asked Pennington for suggestions as to how these fluctuations could be minimized, and Pennington submitted a second memorandum in August 1827.[125]

Pennington did not mention Ricardo in his second memorandum but he followed Ricardo—as opposed to Thornton—in the idea that credit changes affected the direction but not the total of production. He also adopted the Ricardian idea that the note issue should be concentrated in a single agency, but unlike Ricardo favored the retention of the Bank of England as the note issuer rather than the creation of a new note-issuing institution. This theory, and his remedy, are best given in his own words:

When the Bank of England increases or lessens its outstanding paper, by an augmentation or diminution of its advances upon securities bearing interest, no extraordinary exchange of commodities for money, or of money for commodities, with other countries, necessarily takes place. The capital and labour of the country remain unaltered, but an artificial direction is given to both.

. . . .

If the Bank of England were the sole issuer of paper money or if the country banks were, in all cases, directly, and immediately, controlled by the bank, the means of preventing this source of unintended mischief would be obvious and easy. Nothing more would be necessary than that the bank should constantly hold a fixed amount of the same unvarying species of securities. If its outstanding liabilities amounted, at any particular time, to £26,000,000, and if, against these, it held £18,000,000 of government securities, the £8,000,000 of bullion, then, by confining itself to the £18,000,000 of securities, the action of the foreign exchange would necessarily turn upon the gold: at one time the

---

[125] Pennington's original memorandum, Huskisson's reply, and Pennington's second memorandum were privately printed in 1827 with the title *Memorandum*. The portion of Pennington's first memorandum dealing with paper currency, and his second memorandum, were reissued by Pennington in *A Letter to Kirkman Finlay, Esq., on the Importation of Foreign Corn* (London, 1840), pp. 82–88.

bank might have six, at another time ten, and at another time eight millions of treasure; and in all cases, its paper would contract and expand according to the increase or diminution of its bullion.

Pennington's memorandum did not become a subject of public controversy at the time, but its substance almost certainly was discussed in the Political Economy Club, and in this and other ways influenced the shaping of opinion in responsible quarters.

Taken literally, what Pennington said in his memorandum of 1827, and what many other later defenders of the currency principle said, would indicate that they were unaware of the monetary significance of bank deposits. Yet Pennington, in an earlier memorandum of 1826 to Huskisson, had spelled out the monetary role of deposits, and the same analysis was embodied in his memorandum that was published in 1829 as an appendix to Thomas Tooke's *Letter to Lord Grenville*.[126] All of the evidence indicates that the policy proposals of Pennington and others of the currency school were the product not so much of their theory as of their belief about the institutional facts of notes and deposits and their sensing of political attitudes. They apparently thought that there was sufficient difference in the behavior of noteholders and depositors in time of crisis, and a sufficient difference in public feelings and prejudices toward notes and deposits, to make it desirable, in a program that had to pass the political test, to treat deposits and notes differently as regards the need for legislative action.

Shortly after Pennington outlined his program of bank note control, the Bank, so far as is known independently of Pennington,[127] was working out between 1828 and 1830 what came to be known as the Palmer rule. This rule, first explained by J. Horsley Palmer to the Bank Charter Committee of 1832,[128] was that the Bank, when the circulation was "full" —that is, when the exchanges were just on the point of becoming unfavorable—should have a specie reserve equal to about one third of notes and deposits. Starting from this situation all fluctuations in the Bank's

[126] Pages 117–127. A copy of the 1826 memorandum is in the Huskisson papers in the British Museum, Add. MS. 38,761, fols. 201–210, and is reprinted by Sayers.

[127] There is no direct evidence of any connection between Pennington's program and the adoption of the Palmer rule, but it is plausible, in view of the close association in time of the two developments and the influence that the Government had over the Bank after the crisis of 1825, that Government pressure, or at least a desire to fall in line with Government views, influenced the Bank's action. The answer is to be found, if at all, in private papers as yet unworked by economists.

[128] In particular Q. 72–95. J. Keith Horsefield, "The Bank and Its Treasure," *Economica*, N.S., VII, 161–178 (May 1940), traces the background of the Bank's efforts to arrive at a policy on reserve holdings.

notes and deposits should, "excepting under special conditions," be equal to the changes in the Bank's holding of specie. Pennington's proposal and the Palmer rule, although they pointed in the same direction, differed in that under the Pennington proposal changes in the Bank's notes would move up and down by the same amount as did the Bank's specie, whereas under the Palmer rule the total of the Bank's notes and deposits would have this relation to specie. Furthermore, the Palmer rule related only to the liabilities of the Bank of England, whereas Pennington's suggestion, with its provision for suppressing country bank issues or bringing them under Bank control, would have meant that the entire circulation—paper and metallic—would have varied like a completely metallic currency. Important as Pennington's memorandum and the adoption of the Palmer rule were, they played no part in public controversy before the Bank Charter investigation of 1832.

Bank Runs as Political Weapons

The crisis of 1793, runs on the Irish and English banks that had preceded the Restriction of 1797, and runs on country banks in 1810 and 1816 had highlighted the difficulties inherent in the system of fractional reserve banking that had evolved under the motives and pressures of economic self-interest. I find no suggestion, however, until Cobbett's writings in 1821, that these runs had any sinister purpose. There may have been criticism of noteholders for yielding to the mob spirit, but there is no indication of any organized plot to embarrass the existing economic and political order, much less any attempt to extort political concessions from the Government.

The idea that mass exercise of legal redemption rights was a means of putting pressure on the Bank of England or on the Government doubtless occurred to minds more conservative than Cobbett's. There is a record of one such development in the 1820's. In February 1826 a threat from a delegation of Norfolk country bankers to Lord Liverpool to send £500,000 in notes to the Bank of England and demand gold was believed to have forced the Government to amend its proposed small-note legislation.[129]

---

[129] Diary entry of February 17, 1826, in Lord Broughton (Sir John Hobhouse), *Recollections of a Long Life* (London, 1910), III, 126, reporting a conversation with Hudson Gurney. Charles Greville also recorded the incident in his diary on February 20, 1826, but in a slightly different form: that it was Hudson Gurney who had made the threat to the Chancellor of the Exchequer. The editor of the diary says that the entry "Hudson Gurney" was a mistake for "Samuel Gurney" (*Greville Memoirs,* I, 156–157). Broughton's version is much more plausible than either the Greville account or the editorial correction.

In Ireland, following the victory of Daniel O'Connell in the Clare election of 1828, runs for gold were used intermittently for several years, sometimes with specific objectives, sometimes as a protest against the circulation of pound notes, and sometimes for the more general purpose of bedeviling the established order. In late 1828 rent collectors in Wexford, Clonmel, and Kilkenny organized runs on local banks, which were met by rushing gold from London, and in December of that year suggestions were made that Bank of Ireland stockholders sell their stock and convert the proceeds into gold.[130] The following year O'Connell said in a public letter to a Waterford newspaper: "Call, therefore, on the people—the honest, unsophisticated people—to send in the bank-notes of every description, and to get gold." [131]

Some of O'Connell's associates opposed him in this policy on the ground that it injured the Irish, and particularly critical was the Dublin journalist F. W. Conway, who called the runs for gold "O'Connell cholera." Politically inspired demands for gold in Ireland were endemic for several years, but they never created a crisis situation.[132] In 1833, when the Irish Coercion Bill was before Parliament, the question whether O'Connell, then in London, should urge on his countrymen a run for gold to put pressure on the British was considered by him and his advisers. His two letters to P. V. Fitzpatrick show the complex of considerations involved. He wrote on March 8, 1833: "The run injures friends as well as foes. I cannot think without apprehension of the worthy men I may injure if I call for gold. On the other hand, I am quite convinced that a general demand for gold would *now* at once stop the bill. Consult our best friends; ask those who think the most soberly, and let me know what advice they give on this most vital subject. I wish I saw my own way." [133] Five days later, apparently after receiving word from Fitzpatrick that Conway advised against urging a run for gold, he said: "I will not call for a run for gold. I do myself believe that *I ought*. At this moment it would force the Ministry to give up the vile Coercion Bill. But I yield to the authority you mention, and I will not call for Gold; nor have I. But I cannot go farther. I cannot call on the country to refrain from doing that in favour of which my own judgment certainly

---

[130] James A. Reynolds, *The Catholic Emancipation Crisis in Ireland, 1823–1829* (New Haven, 1954), pp. 151–152.

[131] M. F. Cusack, *The Speeches and Public Letters of the Liberator* (Dublin, 1875), I, 65.

[132] Frequent references to these runs are in Irish newspapers, and were reported in the London *Times* in 1831, including January 19, 25, 26, and 29, and February 1 and 2.

[133] William John Fitzpatrick, ed., *Correspondence of Daniel O'Connell* (London, 1888), I, 334.

is. I give up my private judgment, but I cannot reverse it. You may rely on this, that I will not say one word in favour of a run." [134] Without O'Connell's support no major run developed, and the Coercion Bill died from other causes.

In England, however, a run for gold was used in 1832 as a weapon in the campaign for Parliamentary reform, after the defeat of the Reform Bill by the Lords and while the Duke of Wellington was trying unsuccessfully to form a new Government. This run is usually associated with the name of Francis Place, but Place did not originate the idea, and in fact opposed it when it was first urged in reform meetings.[135] The pressure from reformers to make a run for gold increased, and Place adjusted his policy to new circumstances. When the proposal was made in a meeting of reformers on Saturday, May 12, 1832, that a placard be drawn up urging a demand for gold unless the Duke of Wellington give up his attempt to form a Government, it was Place who wrote the historic slogan "To stop the Duke, go for gold." [136]

The run on the Bank drew down its gold by around £1.6 million "in the course of a week or ten days," [137] and in some areas outside of London Bank notes briefly went to a discount in terms of country bank notes. Cobbett wrote on May 17 of the public protest against the formation of a government by Wellington: "Amongst the means intended to defeat the King and the new Minister, was that most effective of all means, *a run upon the Bank for gold.*" [138] Before the week had ended the idea of a Wellington government had been given up, Grey was again asked by the King to form a government pledged to reform, and the run had stopped. What influence the run for gold may have had in forcing the Government's hand is uncertain. Place believed that it was important, and gave a plausible account of a representative of the Bank informing Lord Grey and the Duke of Wellington that the Bank would have to close its doors within a few days if the run did not stop.[139] On the other

---

[134] Fitzpatrick, I, 339.

[135] Letter of Place to Sir John Hobhouse, October 11, 1831, in Graham Wallas, *Life of Francis Place* (London, 1898), p. 277.

[136] Wallas, p. 310.

[137] J. Horsley Palmer's statement, *Bank Charter Committee,* 1832, Q. 745. William Ward spoke of "a diminution of nearly £2,000,000 sterling in consequence of it [the public's run on the Bank in the political crisis]" (Q. 2074).

[138] *Political Register,* May 19, 1832, 383.

[139] An account of the developments between Saturday, May 12, when Place wrote his slogan, and the following Saturday, when Earl Grey was asked to again form a government, is given largely in Place's own words in Wallas' *Life of Francis Place,* pp. 306–323. A number of witnesses before the Bank Charter Committee of 1832 discussed the run,

hand, J. R. M. Butler, the historian who has traced in greatest detail the day by day events that led up to the passage of the Reform Act, expresses doubt whether the run for gold was as important as Place had thought.[140] The Bank's records are silent on the matter.

From the point of view of banking history the important thing was not the exact influence that the run may have had in the political crisis, but its effect in strengthening public opinion that Bank notes should be legal tender. In another way, more difficult to document but suggested by many bits of circumstantial evidence, it is probable that Cobbett's warnings to the public to convert notes into gold, the intermittent runs for gold on the Irish banks, and the run of May 1832 had their effect on English banking history by building up the climate of opinion that culminated in the Bank Act of 1844. These developments, by contributing to the feeling that the Bank should be limited in its note issues to an amount that under the most unfavorable circumstances conceivable it could redeem out of its gold reserves, and by bolstering the basis for trying to differentiate between reserve requirements against notes and against deposits, fitted in nicely with the case for the currency principle.

The Relation of British Prices and World Prices

For several years after the abandonment of Ricardo's ingot plan in 1821 there was little discussion, either of the effect of British banking policy upon the purchasing power of gold, or of the effect of world-wide changes in the purchasing power of gold upon British conditions. These theoretical issues were swallowed up in the wrangles of political controversy. It is true that Zachary Macaulay raised for discussion in the Political Economy Club in March 1823 the question: "In what degree may the purchase of Gold by the Bank of England since the passing of Mr. Peel's Bill be considered as having enhanced the value of Gold and proportionately lowered the value of commodities?"[141] The question, however, appeared to be outside the mainstream of interest of the day, or of the years immediately following.

Revival of public interest in the international aspects of British prices came in the late 1820's and seems to have been associated with discussion of the possibility of raising prices but leaving untouched the act of 1819.

including Charles Smith Forster, a country banker (Q. 1481–1489), John Baker Richards, a director and former governor of the Bank (Q. 4981–4999), Thomas Attwood (Q. 5611–5614), and George Grote, a London banker (Q. 4683).

[140] *The Passing of the Great Reform Act* (London, 1914), pp. 412–413.

[141] Henry Higgs, ed., *The Political Economy Club* (London, 1921), p. 19.

This was reflected in Parliamentary debates in 1828 on legislation to authorize £1 and £2 notes, and particularly in the speech of Sir James Graham, who combined an attack on the act of 1819 with a plea that something be done to raise prices, but without urging a repeal of that act.[142] C. C. Western, with nice irony, later laid his finger on the idea that was becoming enshrined in monetary orthodoxy: deliberate policy to raise prices was praiseworthy if done within the limits of the gold standard, but was wrong if it involved breaking the gold standard. In 1835, referring to Lord Liverpool's claim in 1822 that an issue of notes would raise prices, he wrote: "Now upon what principle it can be justifiable to alter the standard of value by an increased circulation of bank notes, and wrong to do it by *changing the standard from gold to silver,* for instance, is to me perfectly incomprehensible. To alter the metallic standard in any way is, they say, a robbery, and I know not what. To alter the value of every man's property by increasing the amount of bank notes in circulation is highly praiseworthy."[143]

A straw in the wind of thinking that conditions outside of England might alter domestic prices was a motion introduced by Lord Lansdowne, and passed by the Lords, asking the King to have the consuls in South America secure information on the state of the gold and silver mines.[144] Several writers made references to changes in the purchasing power of gold,[145] sometimes as an argument for bimetallism or devaluation, sometimes as an argument for the issue of £1 and £2 notes, sometimes in criticism of Bank policy. One of them suggested platinum as a standard, and in the interest of a larger monetary base urged a tax on the use of precious metals in jewelry.[146] Gerald Graulhie proposed that precious stones be made part of the monetary base.[147]

The most complete and best thought-out statement of the possibility of raising prices within the limits of the gold standard came from George

---

[142] 2 *Hansard* XIX, 992–1012, June 3, 1828. Commons debates: 190–191, April 28; 859–868, May 22; 980–1033, June 3; 1054–1100, June 5; 1380–1392, June 16; Lords debate, 1597–1605, July 3.

[143] *Lord Western's Second Letter to the President and Members of the Chelmsford and Essex Agricultural Society* (Bath and London, 1835).

[144] 2 *Hansard* XXIII, 1048–1052, March 1830.

[145] Sir John Sinclair, *Thoughts on Currency* (London, 1829), pp. 49–51; Alexander Mundell, *An Examination of the Evidence* (London, 1832), p. 31; *What Has Currency to do with the Present Distresses?* (London, 1832), p. 10; Cosmopolite (pseud.), *A Concise Treatise on the Wealth, Power and Resources of Great Britain* (London, 1833), pp. 5–20; *Reflections on the Domestic and Foreign Policy of Great Britain* (London, 1833), pp. 144–165.

[146] Cosmopolite, pp. 118–119.

[147] *An Outline of a Plan for a New Circulating Medium* (London, 1832), pp. 10–13.

Poulett Scrope in books of 1830[148] and 1833,[149] and in his article in the *Quarterly Review* of July 1832 on "The Rights of Industry and the Banking System." He argued for the substitution of bank notes for coin by permitting the use of notes under £5, by strengthening country banks, by making country bank notes convertible into notes of metropolitan banks—for Scrope favored the abolition of the Bank of England's monopoly of the note issue in London—and by permitting all metropolitan banks to redeem their notes in bullion. He believed that as a result "the restoration of this mass of metal to the general market of the commercial world, from whence we have been draining it during the last fifteen years, will everywhere lower the values of the metals, and with them that of money."[150] Much the same idea had been suggested in earlier articles in the *Quarterly*: "Banking," by Edward Edwards, in March 1830, and "Distress of the Country," by H. A. Nilan, in May 1830. The articles in the *Quarterly* and Scrope's books seem to have had little impact on public opinion or policy, possibly because their proposals for decreasing the purchasing power of gold were associated with proposals for an increase in the note issues by country banks and the elimination of the note-issue monopoly of the Bank of England in London, ideas contrary to the increasingly dominant thought of the time.

Proposals for Readjustment of Contracts or a Tabular Standard

In 1807 John Wheatley had proposed that by voluntary arrangement contracts be drafted to take care of price changes.[151] During the Restriction others had made similar suggestions, although more with reference to changes in the price of gold than to changes in commodity prices. In the early 1820's, in addition to the frequent suggestions of some adjustment of the government debt to allow for the decline in prices since the contracts had been made, Joseph Lowe had proposed that contracts contain a provision for the change of money payments on the basis of changes in prices.[152]

After the pickup in commodity prices in 1823, and with the concern about financial excesses after the panic in 1825, such suggestions virtually ceased for several years, but revived around 1830. Cobbett, while opposing

---

[148] *The Currency Question freed from Mystery* (London, 1830), pp. 17–19, 32; *On Credit Currency* (London, 1830), pp. 6–17, 83–84.

[149] *An Examination of the Bank Charter Question* (London, 1833), pp. 36–56.

[150] *Examination of Bank Charter Question*, p. 456.

[151] *An Essay on the Theory of Money* (London, 1807), I, 328–329.

[152] *The Present State of England* (London, 1822), pp. 276–291.

any suspension of specie payments, still talked about "equitable adjust-ment." J. R. McCulloch in 1831 criticized the "dishonest expedient of enfeebling the standard," but gave implicit testimony to the continuing strength of the price level change argument against the act of 1819 by suggesting that in case of necessity "fairly compounding with its credi-tors" would be a better policy for the Government to follow.[153]

In 1832 Charles Jones, in addition to his minor anticipation of Keynes in characterizing the re-establishment of gold payments in 1821 as "pur-suing an *ignis-fatuus*," advocated a policy of price stabilization by a national bank of issue through open market operations, buying public debt when a twenty-commodity price index fell, and selling public debt when the price index rose.[154] This was followed the next year by Scrope's suggestion of an index number standard of deferred payments, to be operated along with a metallic standard, with an option to be chosen by the parties to the contract at the time of making it as to the basis on which it would be settled.[155] William Virgo suggested that debts be settled on the basis of the purchasing power of the pound.[156] John Stuart Wort-ley, later Lord Wharncliffe, discussed the presumed gains and losses to creditors and debtors from changes in the gold premium during the Re-striction. He minimized any inequities of these changes, and opposed any adjustment, but his statement that the increased burden of the public debt "has been administered as a stimulant in speech and print to the passions of all tax-payers from the Land's End to John o'Groat's, and from 1819 down to 1833,"[157] is indicative of the opinion of the time. Henry James, the Birmingham merchant who had been an early critic of the resumption of specie payments, suggested an adjustment of debts and fixed charges.[158] Nothing came of these diverse proposals, but like the renewed interest in the relation between the British monetary situ-ation and the world purchasing power of gold they were evidence of the revival in the early 1830's of discontent over low prices.

The Gold Standard as an Article of Faith

Although criticism of the gold standard continued in pamphlets and in Parliament, and in the *Quarterly Review* and *Blackwood's Edinburgh*

---

[153] *Historical Sketch of the Bank of England* (London, 1831), p. 29.
[154] *A Plan for Realizing the Perfection of Money* (London, 1832), pp. 14–15.
[155] *Examination of Bank Charter Question*, pp. 25–26.
[156] *A Plan for Immediately Reducing the National Debt* (London, 1833), p. 11.
[157] *A Brief Inquiry into the True Award of an "Equitable Adjustment"* (London, 1833), pp. 3–7, 37–39.
[158] *State of the Nation* (London, 1835), pp. 137–138.

Magazine, political economists by the 1830's had practically removed the monetary standard from the area of debate. They simply assumed that the gold standard was the basis from which analysis on policy should proceed. Questions that economists have so often asked since the early 1930's—what is the logic of a monetary standard, and what are the advantages and disadvantages of insisting that the monetary authority's discretion be limited to action within a fixed price of gold—were rarely mentioned between the early 1820's and the debate over international bimetallism in the 1870's. As regards the functions of a monetary standard, one must turn to independent-minded bankers like Alexander Baring and the Attwoods; to a brilliant rebel like Scrope; and to cranks like Richard Cruttwell, John Rooke, and the Taylor brothers, John and James, who combined a great deal of real bills nonsense with occasional perceptive comments on the tests of an adequate monetary supply, to find anything that after the Keynesian revolution would have been considered enlightened analysis in a graduate seminar in monetary theory.

Ricardo, after payments had been resumed in 1821, said little more in defense of the gold standard than that what had been adopted should not be changed. Robert Torrens in 1819 had pointed out the economic evils of falling prices, opposed early resumption, and urged that when a metallic standard was restored it should be silver rather than gold. But once the act of 1819 was in effect Torrens did not urge its repeal, although in principle he continued, until the late 1830's, to favor a silver standard. McCulloch was even more adamant than his master, Ricardo, in holding that the gold standard, once re-established, was not a fit topic for argument as an economic issue.[159]

James Mill pointed out the difficulties of bimetallism and the need to maintain a fixed price of gold.[160] The younger Mill took over the views of his father, and of Ricardo and McCulloch, and added to them a crusading fire about the sanctity of contracts and a moral indignation against those who would break the gold standard. In 1832, after Thomas Attwood had appeared before the Bank Charter Committee and urged a combination of a silver standard and inconvertible paper money, Mill criticized him in the spirit of a New York banker of 1896 attacking William Jennings Bryan's proposals for free silver: "The gigantic plan of confiscation which at present finds some advocates,—a depreciation of the currency . . . That men who are not knaves in their private dealings should understand

---

[159] A forceful statement of McCulloch's view was in the *Edinburgh Review,* vol. XXXV, July 1822, art. xi, "Pernicious Effects of Degrading the Standard of Value."

[160] *Elements of Political Economy,* 2d ed. (London, 1824), pp. 136–138, 163.

what the word 'depreciation' means, and yet support it, speaks but ill for the existing state of morality on such subjects."[161] Malthus took no part after 1811 in the controversy over the standard, beyond a couple of philosophically detached remarks in the 1820's approving the resumption of cash payments.[162] Nassau Senior, who entered economics after the resumption of specie payments, appears to have accepted unquestioningly the ideas of Ricardo and McCulloch.

Other important figures of the classical tradition who came into economics in the 1820's and 1830's—Archbishop Whately, Richard Jones, Mountifort Longfield—as well as the lesser-known men who held professorships at Cambridge, Oxford, London, and Trinity College (Dublin), do not appear to have questioned the gold standard. Only once did the Political Economy Club discuss an outright cut in the metallic content of the pound in the question proposed on April 5, 1830, by Perronet Thompson: "Whether the cost of production of Gold and Silver, relatively to that of all other commodities, has not increased; and if such be the case, would it not be advisable to reduce the standard in the United Kingdom?"[163] In the light of Thompson's expressed views on the standard it is probable that he raised the question only to provide a forum for criticism of devaluation. Among economists from the 1820's on the gold standard was a matter of economic theology rather than economic analysis. Other aspects of monetary and banking policy might be treated in analytical terms, but questioning the standard was not a proper subject for discussion for a man who called himself an economist. Western's judgment in 1822 on the defenders of the act of 1819 became increasingly applicable to economists in the decade that followed: "A degree of something like superstitious veneration has been created for what they [Bullionists] called a SOUND METALLIC currency at the ANCIENT standard of value; a sort of priesthood is exercised by the learned on this subject, by which, as in the case of religious superstition, unassuming patient men are induced to believe that there are mysteries beyond the reach of common sense, and in like manner, give up the use of their own understanding, thus undergoing the fate of all honest dupes."[164]

Why the rising fraternity of political economists not only should have

---

[161] "The Currency Juggle," *Tait's Edinburgh Magazine*, January 1833, reprinted in J. S. Mill, *Dissertations and Discussions: Political, Philosophical, and Historical*, I (New York, 1874), 68–81. The passage quoted is on page 69.

[162] *Principles of Political Economy* (London, 1820), pp. 514–515; see his statement of 1823 quoted above on page 105. The passage in the *Principles* appeared unchanged on page 412 of the posthumous second edition of 1836.

[163] Higgs, *Political Economy Club*, p. 34.

[164] *Second Address to the Landowners of the United Kingdom* (London, 1822), p. 23.

been unquestioning supporters of the gold standard, but should have practically dismissed it as a subject for serious discussion, is a puzzle. In view of the philosophy of enlightenment and rationalism of most of the economists, we might have expected them to have given an understanding analysis of the possible contributions that a silver standard or bimetallism might make to greater price stability or to have considered how a conscious policy of the Bank of England could contribute to a greater stability in the purchasing power of the pound than did the accidents of geology and mining. Instead, we find that the economists, most of whom were apathetic toward religious faith and critical of a hierarchical concept of society, applied to the monetary standard a devotion to creed and dogma that they deprecated in religion and in social philosophy.

For this apparent paradox there seem to be three main explanations: first, a distrust of Bank of England policy in the Bank Restriction, and particularly of the defense of the real bills doctrine by the Bank and the Government; second, the feeling that any monetary arrangement that gave discretion, either to Government or to a monopoly like the Bank of England, was bad in principle; and third, the assumption that changes in prices affected the distribution of income, but had little if any effect on the total of income and employment.

The first two bases of the economists' critical attitude toward any tampering with the gold standard were associated with recent "lessons of history" and with a philosophy of government and monopoly. The third involved a basic question of economic theory, but a theory that may have been influenced by contemporary events. Ricardo, when examined by the Lords Committee in 1819, had been asked whether an expansion of bank credit might not permit the borrower to expand production and increase employment. His categorical denial was representative of the prevailing economic orthodoxy: "Impossible; he can purchase Machinery, &c. with Credit, he can never create them. If he purchases, it is always at the Expence of some other Person; and he displaces some other from the Employment of Capital." [165]

Such a statement is likely to make the modern economist who knows his Keynes and is familiar with the history of the Great Depression wonder at the lack of enlightenment of an earlier generation. In this connection three observations are relevant.

1. Several of the most serious economic disturbances in the 1820's and

---

[165] *Works*, V, 438. The same idea that monetary expansion could have no aggregative production effects, developed in more detail, is in *Works*, V, 446–447.

1830's were associated with speculative expansion of credit, rather than with deflation of commodity prices.

2. The worker at the time did not believe that his troubles were due to the gold standard, and insofar as he had any views on monetary policy they were associated with criticism of banks and of the actions of a government of the aristocracy. Strip Cobbett's remarks on banking of their purple language and what is left is the essence of Ricardo's view: expansion of the monetary supply cannot increase total production, and a limitation of the monetary supply affects the distribution of income but not its total. From a quarter even more radical than Cobbett—Henry Hethrington in the *Poor Man's Guardian*—also came, along with a picture of the privileged classes dividing the profits of exploitation, the Ricardian idea that monetary policy did not affect total production:

> All the currency-mongers can say (if they speak truth) is, that to expand the currency would be to relieve all debtors at the expense of all creditors, to the exact amount of the depreciation. This would be, decidedly, a great boon to debtors; but it is also to be remembered, that prices would rise faster than wages, and that during the transition the labourers would suffer bitterly before things could adjust themselves to the new standard.
>
> No, no, Messrs. of the *Herald* and *Standard*, your currency choppings will not go down. They might do very well for scheming bankers, and half-bankrupt mortgagors; but the millions want something else besides a mere transfer of plunder from one set of schemers to another.[166]

3. The strength of Say's law, with its assumption of full employment, probably was the result rather than the cause of monetary thinking. Instead of being responsible for the monetary ideas of the economists of the period, it appears to have been accepted by them as a means of bolstering monetary thinking that had emerged out of their observance of recent history and out of their distrust of discretion by a Government dominated by an aristocracy and by a Bank run by a "company of traders."

[166] July 4, 1835, p. 583.

V

BANK CHARTER INVESTIGATION OF 1832 AND CONSOLIDATION OF THE GOLD STANDARD

T HE BANK of England charter was to expire in 1833, and in 1832 Lord Althorp, leader of the House of Commons in Lord Grey's Whig Government, moved for an investigation. He made clear the premise on which the Government was proceeding: the question of the standard was settled; and "the issuing of money was the prerogative of the State, and, therefore, the Legislature had the right to say on what conditions individuals should be allowed to issue money." [1] Althorp's statement, by highlighting the note circulation, in a negative and undramatic way presented another proposition that was becoming basic to British thought and policy: the State had the right and responsibility to regulate bank notes, but this did not apply to deposit currency.

The Bank Charter Committee hearings of 1832 were the most extensive review up to that time of the British banking situation. The 5978 questions put to 21 witnesses, and their answers, took up 474 printed folio pages, and 120 pages of appendixes gave details never before published about the operation of the Bank of England and of private banks in London and in the country. The committee, in reporting the evidence to the House, said (p. 3) that in questioning witnesses "the principal Points to which they have directed their attention are:

First. Whether the Paper Circulation of the Metropolis should be confined, as at present, to the Issues of one Bank, and that a Commercial Company; or, whether a competition of different Banks of Issue, each consisting of an unlimited number of partners, should be permitted.

Secondly. If it should be deemed expedient that the Paper Circulation of the Metropolis should be confined, as at present, to the issues of one Bank, how far the whole of the exclusive privileges possessed by the Bank of England are necessary to effect this object.

[1] 3 *Hansard* XII, 1358, May 22, 1832.

Thirdly. What checks may be provided to secure for the Public a proper management of Banks of Issue, and especially whether it would be expedient and safe to compel them periodically to publish their Accounts.

With respect to the Circulation of Paper in the Country, the Committee have examined—*First,* into the effect produced by the establishment of the Branch Banks of the Bank of England; and *Secondly,* into the expediency of encouraging the establishment of Joint Stock Banks of Issue in the Country.

The committee reported: "On all these, and on some collateral points, more or less information will be found in the Minutes of Evidence; but on no one of them is it so complete as to justify the Committee in giving a decided opinion." In fact, however, the questions and answers covered a greater field than the committee's terms of reference or its report would indicate, and on most major issues there was a substantial agreement on principles that was far more significant for the course of British monetary and banking thought and policy than were the disagreements on details.

The Monetary Standard

The Government had made clear its support of the gold standard, and only two witnesses questioned that position. Henry Burgess (Q. 5536–5555) and Thomas Attwood (Q. 5776–5777) preferred a silver standard, and in addition Attwood indicated that his ideal of currency was one divorced from the precious metals and regulated for the purpose of creating "full employment" (Q. 5644–5650, 5698, 5722–5727). Attwood, as well as Joseph Chesborough Dyer, a merchant of Manchester and director of a joint-stock bank, also discussed the effect of British policy upon the purchasing power of gold (Q. 4212, 5627). But these views were outside the committee's main line of investigation. It was the issues raised by the panic of 1825 with which most of the questions dealt: the responsibilities and the policies of the Bank of England; the relation in time of crisis between country banks and the Bank of England; and the relation between the Bank, the country banks, and the joint-stock banks as note issuers.

Reserve Policy of the Bank of England

At the hearings, John Horsley Palmer, governor of the Bank, explained (Q. 72–89) the Palmer rule, already described.[2] The rule, narrowly interpreted, raised more questions than it answered—the definition of

[2] The most important part of Palmer's testimony is reprinted in T. E. Gregory, ed., *Select Statutes, Documents & Reports Relating to British Banking, 1832–1928* (London, 1929), I, 3–6.

"special circumstances," the latitude to be given to "about one-third"—and it was a far call from the rigid reserve requirements of the act of 1844. Nevertheless it was a landmark in the public recognition by the Bank of the responsibility to keep a substantial nonearning asset, larger than an ordinary bank would keep. The rule related to notes and deposits combined, but Palmer's reply—"Less dangerous"—to the question: "Do you think the liability arising from the deposit to be more dangerous to the Bank as to sudden calls, or less dangerous to it than the same amount out in paper?" (Q. 77) could easily suggest to those who wanted to translate ideas into legislation that a distinction between notes and deposits had a solid pragmatic basis.

No witness disagreed with the general philosophy expressed by Palmer. The only question was whether the Bank should be under legislative mandate to maintain such a reserve, and whether the Bank should be required to make a periodic statement of its condition. The view of Thomas Tooke that there should be no statutory requirements, and that "it would be sufficient, I should think, if by a regular publication of the state of its affairs it were under the constant check of public opinion" (Q. 5415), was a fair statement of contemporary consensus.

Only one witness, Dyer, felt that the Bank's notes should not be legal tender (Q. 4489), and there was probably some connection between the testimony of a number of witnesses in favor of legal tender and their view that the Bank should hold substantial reserves. That the Bank should have the monopoly of note issue in London was generally accepted. The relation between the issues of the Bank of England and those of other banks was mentioned a number of times, but there was no extended discussion and no consensus. Samuel Jones Loyd suggested that it would be well to have a single bank of issue for the entire country, but added that "the expediency of now attempting to make the change is a very serious question" (Q. 3455). Henry Burgess, speaking for the country bankers, opposed the idea that they be required to put up security for their note issues (Q. 5143–5145, 5176–5183). Yet the testimony gave the impression that time was running out on the note issues of the country banks and of the joint-stock banks, and that the future would bring their regulation, if not their abolition. The statement by William Beckett, a banker at Leeds, that notes were "not one-fourth" of deposits (Q. 1282), by Charles Smith Forster that notes were "about one-sixth" of deposits (Q. 1459), and by Henry Burgess that "many bankers" had deposits "tenfold the amount of their issues" (Q. 5178), although probably not representative of country banks, would suggest that some country bankers no longer considered the note issue essential, or even important.

The Country Banks and the Foreign Exchanges

The relation of country bank policy to the foreign exchanges came up repeatedly. The events of 1825 had sharpened a feeling that went back to 1793, and that had been expressed in an organized way by Wheatley as early as 1803, that the country banks' notes were an unstable element in the circulation; and that in the short run they expanded and contracted with little reference to Bank of England credit. But as long as there was no agreement as to what standards the Bank of England should follow in relation to the foreign exchanges, any criticism of the country banks for failing to conform to Bank action of necessity had no firm base. When the Bank had to redeem its notes at par in 1821, and particularly after 1827, when it recognized that its policy could affect the foreign exchanges, the question whether country bank action was in line with Bank policy took on new meaning. The Bank Charter Committee put to six country bankers the question whether they paid attention to foreign exchanges. Of these only Vincent Stuckey, who headed a joint-stock bank in Somerset with close London connnections, admitted that the foreign exchanges played a role in credit policy (Q. 1015).[3] Such a view on the part of country bankers, although in the mainstream of thought in 1810, was increasingly an anachronism after the Bank's new look in 1827. It was further evidence, with London's growing role in international finance, of the cleavage between provincial and City thinking.

Bank of England Policy and the Foreign Exchanges

When the Bank directors in 1827 rescinded their resolution of 1819 that changes in the Bank circulation could not influence the foreign exchanges, the stage was set for a discussion of the ways in which the Bank could influence the exchanges, and the conditions under which it should try to influence them. Palmer raised the problem several times during the committee hearings, and one statement might appear as the epitome of the specie-flow price-adjustment mechanism:

---

[3] William Beckett (Q. 1386, 1415), Charles Smith Forster (Q. 1462), John Parry Wilkins (Q. 1652), and Joseph Chesborough Dyer (Q. 4210) said categorically that they paid no attention to the exchanges. John Easthope (Q. 5914) was more guarded, but the general picture was the same: "Country bankers, I conceive generally, have more reference to the state of the money market in London, than they have to the state of the Foreign Exchanges."

What is the process by which the Bank would calculate upon rectifying the Exchange, by means of a reduction of its issues?—The first operation is to increase the value of money; with the increased value of money there is less facility obtained by the commercial Public in the discount of their paper; that materially tends to limit transactions and to the reduction of prices; the reduction of prices will so far alter our situation with foreign countries, that it will be no longer an object to import, but the advantage will rather be upon the export, the gold and silver will then come back into the country, and rectify the contraction that previously existed. (Q. 678)

The reference to credit to the "commercial Public" is significant, however, as implying what many other witnesses in 1832 and in later years said specifically, that the price effect was primarily on already produced goods rather than on new production. William Ward, another Bank witness, agreed with Palmer in considering changes in commodity prices induced by changes in circulation of Bank notes, an influence on prices and on the exchanges (Q. 1987–1989).

Other witnesses took a less Ricardian view of the mechanism of exchange adjustment. Jeremiah Harman, who had been a witness before the Bullion Committee and the committees of 1819, but was no longer a Bank director, had reservations about the effect of changes in the Bank's circulation upon the exchanges (Q. 2365–2368). In response to the question: "Supposing that the issues of the Bank were to be increased to any great extent, do you believe that the foreign Exchanges would immediately feel the influence?" he replied, "That involves a question which, if I may be excused, I would rather not enter into." George Carr Glyn, a London banker, doubted whether credit restriction by the Bank reduced commodity prices. His statement (Q. 2978–2980) is representative of what witnesses before committees, pamphleteers, and financial journalists continued to say for the next forty years:

2978. Has that pressure upon the money market been accompanied by lowering the prices of commodities?—I cannot remember any particular instance in which the diminution has brought about at the time any lowering of prices; the general effect may have been subsequently to lower prices, but probably other causes have acted with it to produce that effect.

2979. Then the circumstance of a diminution of issues on the part of the Bank of England not operating immediately upon the price of commodities, would have produced no immediate effect upon the Exchanges?—Except that of rendering money more scarce in London, which of itself always has an effect upon the Exchanges, without immediately acting upon commodities.

2980. How does scarcity operate upon the Exchanges?—It is done by anticipation of its effect upon prices; it is not the actual fact that a certain large amount of Bank notes is taken out of the money market on any particular day, but it is the expectation on the minds of people, that from the course of the Exchanges a diminution of the currency and a reduction of prices will eventually follow, which prevent orders from going abroad; the effect is not produced by any immediate operation upon the price of commodities, but rather by the anticipation of the probable consequences.

Similarly Samuel Gurney, than whom few were wiser in the ways of the City or more judicious in statement, saw the impact of Bank policy as producing "caution in the first place, in money dealers, and through them to the dealers in goods," and further answers showed the great importance that he attached to Bank policy as affecting international credit operations (Q. 3525-3536). Thomas Tooke thought that the contraction of Bank issues affected exchanges in two modes: "By its tendency, *caeteris paribus,* to reduce prices and to raise the rate of interest; it therefore tends ultimately, though perhaps not immediately, to increase the export and to diminish the import of commodities and to check the transmission of capital" (Q. 3948). Nathan Rothschild, whose mind ran to financial paper rather than commodities, could see the effect of Bank policy on credit operations, but minimized the effect on the movement of commodities (Q. 4798-4898). And insofar as he recognized the effect on commodities, he laid the emphasis on the fact that "the manufacturers and persons in working business are obliged to send their goods abroad, and to sell at any price" (Q. 4799).

Different Types of External Drains

Recognition by the Bank that it could control the exchanges by credit operations, and acceptance by the financial community of this situation, was closely related to another problem: to what extent should the Bank treat all demands for gold in the same way, to what extent should it attempt to distinguish between demands of different origin and adjust its policy to the nature of the demand? As early as 1797 Henry Thornton had explained the difference between an external and an internal demand for coin. The panic of 1825 and the political run of May 1832 had driven home the point that there could be a demand for gold that had no relation to the foreign exchanges. This was reflected in the growing feeling that Bank notes should be legal tender and in the increasing recognition, both by the public and the Bank, that in the face of such an internal demand for gold a restriction of credit would simply make matters worse. The proposition that an internal run was different from an external drain, and that the Bank should not contract but generally should expand credit in the face of an internal run, was not questioned by any witness. But the distinction between different types of foreign drains raised the issue over which so much ink had been spilled in 1810 and 1811: what are the causes of fluctuations in the foreign exchanges?

The resumption of the payments in 1821 had been a victory for the long-run objectives for which the bullionists had argued, and the Bank's rescinding in 1827 of its resolution of 1819 on its power over the exchanges had placed the capstone on that victory. The Bank was required to maintain specie payments, no matter what the cause of external drain, and it was to take action to stop the drain before it endangered specie payments. These strategic decisions still left unanswered the tactical question whether there might not be different reasons for drains, and if so whether the Bank should attempt to differentiate between drains and then to adjust and to time its policy accordingly. The implications of what Wheatley and Ricardo had argued—but not of what Henry Thornton, Malthus and the Bullion Report had said—was that it was the duty of the Bank to restrict credit and to endeavor to stop the drain no matter what its cause. There was no necessary conflict in the short-run between the view of Thornton and the Bullion Committee and the view of the anti-bullionists. Thus it was still possible for the Bank in the long run to accept the Ricardian view that credit policy and prices controlled exchange rates, but in the short run to act on the anti-Ricardian view that the exchange rates were the result of influences independent of prices, and in large part independent of Bank policy.

In the hearings of 1832 the question was put to almost every witness associated with the City of London whether the Bank should treat alike all foreign drains of specie, and if it did recognize a distinction, what criteria it should use in adjusting policy to deal with individual situations. The statements of witnesses, although they varied in focus and in their implications for policy in a given setting, showed a unanimous opinion that the Bank had a responsibility in the face of an external drain. But as to whether that responsibility was primarily to follow a rule or to exercise discretion, there was no consensus.

J. Horsley Palmer, in answer to a question about the foreign drain of specie decidedly from "political discredit" abroad and "not to be traced on an over-issue of paper here," said that he would not favor "purchasing Exchequer bills" to offset the contraction in the circulation from the public turning in notes to get gold for export (Q. 416–417). William Ward was even more specific in his view that as a matter of principle the Bank should reduce its note issues to deal with an unfavorable exchange, no matter its cause, and should even try to anticipate disturbances (Q. 2073–2096). Ricardo could not have been more doctrinaire: "The position I take is, that whether it is a bad harvest, or whether it is a war, or whatever circumstances might occasion an extraordinary demand for money to send abroad, instead of waiting till I saw the effect produced upon the Exchanges, I should anticipate the event by a small alteration of the notes" (Q. 2093). Yet to Ward the situation was not as simple as this statement would suggest, as this earlier question and answer indicate: "Do you hold the opinion to be a correct one, that the Bank should conduct itself, in its issues, with reference to the state of foreign Exchanges and the bullion market?—Certainly; I do not think there is one person in the Bank of England who denies it, or is disposed to act in opposition to it; but over and over again I have been responsible myself for violating it, when some extraordinary case has arisen" (Q. 2073). Jeremiah Harman, possibly speaking as an unreconstructed antibullionist, was more circumspect. When pressed as to whether the directors should contract their issues in the face of any unfavorable exchange, he replied: "Yes; but then comes another question, and that is, the risk that it may occasion to the commercial world; and the possibility that, by omitting to take that measure, some favourable turn would take place, and render the convulsion that might ensure from the measure itself unnecessary" (Q. 2254). Another Bank director, John B. Richards, while recognizing that a reduction of notes and deposits would follow an export of specie if the Bank followed the Palmer rule, indicated that an expansion of credit might be necessary in the face of a loss of specie due to a succession of bad harvests (Q. 4973–4980). Vincent Stuckey took the position that no matter what the rule might be, "on extraordinary occasions, and particularly in cases of panic, the principles cannot be acted upon" and made clear that there were occasions when the Bank might properly extend credit in the face of either an internal or a foreign drain (Q. 1195–1201). The remarks of George Grote on the policy of the Bank in the face of a loss of reserves were specific only as regards an internal run (Q. 4648–4651), but his observation on the Bank's expansion of credit in 1825 was broad enough to cover Bank policy in the face of any special circumstances:

In the particular case of 1825, I apprehend that the Bank have in their favour what is the best and most complete justification, the actual result as it ensued. But if I am asked whether, if I had been a Bank Director at that moment, I should have been disposed to approve of such conduct, I cannot answer the question without a variety of considerations, which nobody except a Director could have possessed the means of going through, and which could only have been suggested by all of the circumstances taken together at that actual moment. (Q. 4667)

Responsibility of the Bank of England

Closely allied to the specific question of Bank policy in time of external pressure was the broader question of the responsibility of the Bank of England. Henry Thornton and Francis Baring had preached the doctrine that the Bank not only was the pivot of the nation's banking system and the holder of its ultimate gold reserves, but that it was the lender of last resort and that in time of crisis it must accept the responsibilities of this role unless the banking system was to collapse. In practice the problem was more complex than stating a principle of what the Bank ought to do. The Bank operated in a setting of law, tradition, and public opinion. It was a private corporation, and its stock was widely held, for generations having been an investment for trustees and institutions in England as well as on the Continent. In pamphlets and in stockholders' meetings the Bank had often been criticized for actions that were considered against the best interests of stockholders, and its spokesmen before Parliamentary committees, both before and after 1832, repeatedly referred to its responsibilities to its stockholders. It was also the holder of the nation's gold reserve. The country and joint-stock banks, and the Scottish and Irish banks, either directly or through the London money market, turned to it in time of crisis. At the same time it was competing with these banks in many areas. It was a monopoly, but it was not clear either to Government, the public, or the management and the stockholders of the Bank whether the price that it paid for that monopoly was simply the direct services rendered to Government, or whether it had a larger responsibility to the banking community, and even to the entire economy. The answers to these questions, ever present though rarely presented directly, were made increasingly complex by the shift in public opinion, gathering strength in the 1820's and reaching high tide in the 1850's, that anything savoring of monopoly, of state direction, even of action that was not directed to the maximizing of profit, was undesirable. It is no wonder that in such a situation there was no clear and consistent opinion about the Bank's responsibilities, and that even if an approach to agreement might seem to be reached at one period, its basis could easily be eroded by shifting views on the role of competition or be blasted away by a banking crisis which led to a major change in public opinion as to what it expected of the Bank of England.

The hearings of 1832 documented what had been suggested in many general statements in speeches and pamphlets of the decades preceding: everyone believed that the Bank had responsibilities greater than an ordinary bank, but there was no agreement as to exactly what they were. Palmer's testimony on the relation between the Bank and its stockholders, and between the Bank and the Government, has much to interest the student of corporate control and the theory of political sovereignty. The picture emerged of the Bank's management as a self-perpetuating oligarchy that, as long as it followed the "code" in its relations to stockholders and Government, was to be free from control from either source.

In the hearings Palmer could not recall how long it had been since there had been a contested election (Q. 239–240). The Bank never presented to its stockholders any record of its operations: "The question has been frequently submitted to them, and always left to the Proprietors to decide, and they have conceived it to be their interest not to demand the Accounts . . . Demands have occasionally been made, but they have been rejected by such immense majorities, that there has been no possibility of entertaining the question." (Q. 228, 233). When asked "what means have the Government of controlling the management of the Bank?", he replied: "None" (Q. 712). This was followed by a revealing dialogue:

713. Then what is the security that you contemplate in the Government being informed of the management of the Bank, that the affairs of the Bank shall be properly controlled?—I contemplate no other advantage than the knowledge on the part of His Majesty's Ministers that the Bank is managed upon a correct principle, and that they are supplied with adequate means of meeting the demands which are likely to be made upon them.

714. Supposing that it appeared to His Majesty's Ministers that the Bank was not adequately supplied with means, or that in any other way His Majesty's Ministers did not approve of the mode in which the Bank was managed, have they any means of inducing the Directors of the Bank to alter their system of management?—Not of enforcing, but I should think it quite impossible that any suggestions could be made by His Majesty's Government to the Bank, which would not have a full and complete consideration.

715. Do you consider that His Majesty's Ministers would be acting according to their duty in interfering with the management of the Bank?—In expressing their opinion upon that management, I should think they would.

716. The Government is not in the least responsible for the management of the affairs of the Bank?—No.

717. Who are responsible for the management of the affairs of the Bank?—The Directors.

718. Who are they responsible to?—I believe that there are certain penalties attending to their conduct, either individually or collectively, upon certain occasions; but I do not remember what those precise occasions are.

719. Under the terms of the Charter, are they responsible to Parliament for

the conduct of the affairs of the Bank, in reference to the questions which have come under the consideration of this Committee?—No, I should think not; I believe the cases are defined in which the personal responsibility of the Directors is concerned, but I do not remember what they are at the present moment, certainly not for the general management of the affairs of the Bank.

720. At present, then, the management of the affairs of the Bank, so far as relates to the management of the circulating medium of the country, is under the control of the Directors of the Bank, who are not responsible to the Public for the correct management of the monetary system?—I believe so.

721. Then the whole security which the Public have that the monetary system shall be well managed, depends upon the discretion of the Directors of the Bank?—Yes, as far as the action of the Bank is concerned.

Palmer never faced up to the question of how far the Bank should go in passing up profits in order to be in a position to act as a lender of last resort. However, the implications of the Palmer rule calling for substantial reserves, when taken in conjunction with his statement to the committee as to the Bank's responsibility to grant credit freely in time of crisis, were a policy with which Bagehot could have agreed: "The Bank of England is required to provide a requisite supply of paper money for the average circulation of the sphere in which it acts, and to uphold public and private credit when called upon. When commercial credit is affected, it is in such times that the credit of a great body like the Bank of England is available, and has the power to uphold the credit of the country" (Q. 198).

Richards, in answer to a more direct question than was put to Palmer, came up later with a categorical answer:

5081. In the management of the Bank, do you and your brother Directors hold yourselves responsible to the Public and to the Government for the management of the concerns of the Bank, or to the Proprietors?—We are the elected and sworn servants of the Proprietors, our responsibility is to them; but I conceive that we can hardly perform our duty to them as we ought to do it, without performing a duty also to the country.

5082. In cases where the immediate interest of the Public and of the Proprietors may happen to be at variance, as a rule of management, would you hold it to be your duty to consult the interests of the Public, to whom you are not responsible or the interests of the Proprietors, to whom you are responsible?—It has happened to us to feel it our duty to our Proprietors to postpone their interests in order to effect some important good to the Public at large, in which their interests might be mixed up; but I mean to say that it has not been the practice of the Bank to sacrifice the wishes and the expectations of the Public merely to a dry consideration of the interest of the Proprietors, because they are so blended that it is hardly possible to keep them distinct.

5083. In cases of conflicting duty, would not the principle of action adopted by the Directors, depend upon the view taken of their conflicting duty by the parties that happened to be the Directors at the moment?—Of course it would depend upon circumstances; they would give the circumstances their best deliberation, and their action would be the effect of that deliberation. But I am satisfied that the Bank would never look to the dry question of profit and loss, where the general welfare was at stake; I am sure there are repeated instances where they have shown that. Had the Bank pursued a different conduct, I should have imagined their profits must have been upon a much larger scale; but I must always contend that the Bank have used their power with moderation.

And after further questions on the responsibility of the directors, Richards closed with the statement: "I humbly venture to say, however unpopular the idea may be, that it is impossible for us to serve our masters well, without serving the country, who are our great customers, well at the same time; I am sworn to my proprietors, but I know there is a monitor besides the oath taken upon the Gospel, that tells me, although I am not sworn to His Majesty's Government or the country, what my duty is to the country" (Q. 5096).

The evidence (Q. 2369-2373) of Jeremiah Harman, whose services as director had run from 1794 to 1827, suggests more concern for proprietors and more conflict of interest than was apparent in Richards' statement. It also suggests that public opinion and Parliamentary inquiries in recent years had made the Bank more sensitive about its public responsibilities. His reply to the last of the series of questions on this problem apparently reflected the experience of a witness whose examination by many a Parliamentary committee had convinced him that, much as the Bank might like to operate with Olympian grandeur, no longer could it ignore public opinion: "Is it not the fact, that to the Proprietors the Directors are responsible, but to the Public and the Government they are not responsible:— Indeed they are; the Bank Directors will henceforth never make a blot that will not be hit."

The Bank spokesmen might recognize their public responsibilities and set up for themselves standards of conduct different from those applicable to private bankers. However, other witnesses, in the spirit of Adam Smith of looking with cynical eye on anyone who disclaimed a desire to maximize profits, were skeptical about the idea that the Bank would or should pass up profit opportunities on behalf of the larger interests of the economy. Tooke was doubtful whether the Bank should attempt to be a lender of last resort (Q. 3860-3865). Dyer found no reason to criticize the Bank for refusing discounts to his Manchester bank while granting them to a Liverpool bank: "We considered that in attending to their own interests they were justified in refusing us" (Q. 4145). Similarily he assumed that the Bank's action at a time of adverse exchange was based on a very narrow view of protecting its own solvency, and indicated that he did not take seriously such professions of concern for the public welfare as Richards had given (Q. 4461–4462). What Dyer said probably reflected a common feeling of the provincial bankers toward the Bank of England, but the statement of George Grote more nearly represented the opinion of the London financial world: "During moments of distress, private Bankers and brokers will assist none but their own permanent connexions; and if at such a moment a man is thrown out of his accustomed line of discount, he will not know where to find a substitute. If the Bank is open for discount, a substitute is in some measure provided, for a man can get to the Bank without that special, permanent and exclusive connexion which he preserves with his own Banker, and which cuts him off from all other Bankers" (Q. 4773).

Legislative Results of Bank Charter Investigation

The immediate legislative results of this national field day on monetary and banking policy were meager. The legislative program that Lord Althorp presented to the first session of the reform Parliament[4] was not what the Government thought best, but what in view of British history and present political pressure would be most likely to receive legislative approval. The program called for renewing the charter of the Bank and adjusting the financial arrangements between the State and the Bank, making Bank notes legal tender, repealing the Usury Laws, and extending joint-stock bank regulations.

More important than the specific provision of the Government's program were what Althorp said in defense of it and what others said in defense and in criticism. What was said, as well as what was not said, showed an unmistakable drift in public opinion. Althorp, in presenting the proposed legislation, said that since the hearings of 1832 "the public have been more inclined to look favourably on the management of the Bank of England than they did before that inquiry." He indicated that he would prefer that all note issues be made by a single agency, but either out of political expediency or respect for precedent he reached the conclusion that "whatever may be the opinion of any man on this subject in the abstract, I feel certain that in the existing circumstances and state of the country it would

---

[4] Althorp's speech is in 3 *Hansard* XVIII, 169–186, May 31, 1833, and his resolutions are on 186–187.

be insanity to attempt to enforce such a system." He opposed a State Bank, and on the matter of the Bank's relation to Government offered the judgment: "I feel confident, that persons standing so prominent as the Bank Directors will be as completely controlled by public opinion as if they were acting under legal responsibility."

There was almost no opposition in the committee to continuing the Bank's charter,[5] although in the debate Joseph Hume and Robert Torrens[6] in their preference for a State Bank as the sole note issuer, and George Poulett Scrope, in his denunciation of the Bank as a private monopoly endowed with power greater than that of a legislature, said much that foreshadowed the act of 1844.[7] However, there was criticism of the financial arrangements with the Bank on the ground that they were too favorable to the Bank. The preponderance of opinion favored a single bank of issue, certainly in London, and probably for all of England. Alexander Baring, with his ability to get to the heart of a problem in a short statement, passed this judgment on Althorp's position that a single bank of issue was preferable, but that Althorp would not, at that time, press legislation to stop the issues of country banks: "Though the noble Lord deprecated the use of force towards the country bankers, he suspected that the noble Lord would not be unwilling to accelerate and extend Bank of England issues by a gentle shove, or a species of Quaker propulsion, which would effect the object the noble Lord had in view, and drive country bank paper out of circulation." [8]

The country banks were still a power to reckon with, and even the prospect of a "gentle shove" brought their lobby, as powerful as in 1818, into action. A committee of them met with Althorp in early June, and the chairman, W. W. Hobhouse, reported to his fellow country bankers that Althorp admitted "that he had a decided preference for *One Bank of Issue in lieu of many rival banks,* as calculated to keep the circulation of the whole country less fluctuating, and *that his measures were intended to accomplish such a state of things in process of time.*" Hobhouse's judgment was: "There can be no doubt that it is the intention of the proposed Plan to supplant the Country Circulation altogether; and the only chance in favour of preventing such an effect is to use all the influence we possess, individually and collectively, with members of Parliament, to oppose its

[5] According to Sir Henry Parnell (3 *Hansard* XVIII, 1331, June 28, 1833), he was the only member of the committee to oppose renewing the Bank's charter.
[6] 3 *Hansard* XVIII, 198–202, May 31, 1833; 1306–1314, June 28, 1833.
[7] 3 *Hansard* XVIII, 1314–1320, June 28, 1833.
[8] 3 *Hansard* XVIII, 187, May 31, 1833.

passing into Law."[9] The influence was effective and Althorp reported to the Commons that the Government would not press the provision that joint-stock banks could not issue notes, since the power of the country banks was so great that they probably would defeat it.[10] The next day Denis LeMarchant, who was reporting the debates for the Whig Cabinet, entered in his diary: "The outcry of the country bankers caused the Cabinet to yield to them, and Lord A. was so mortified at being deserted by his colleagues that he wished to resign."[11]

Repeal of the Usury Laws was in line with the increasing free trade sentiment, but it is significant that Althorp, reflecting the now almost universal acceptance that the Bank could control the foreign exchanges, gave as a special reason for this recommendation that it would facilitate action by the Bank to restrict credit to deal with external drains.[12] Althorp's presentation of the problem of external drains revealed the same situation that had appeared in the hearings—the question whether every external drain called for a restriction of credit or whether the Bank should use its discretion and adjust its action on the basis of its judgment as to the cause of the drain. His statement indicated that he belonged to the no-discretion school: "So long as you have a complete convertibility of paper into coin, the foreign exchanges will rectify the depreciation by the drain of bullion they will create, and by the change of currency consequent upon it. It is therefore most desirable, that in any arrangement that may be made, as little interruption as possible should be given to the effect of the foreign exchanges upon the currency of the country."[13]

The recommendation that provoked the most general debate, and took up much more space in *Hansard* than problems such as note issues by country banks, or the establishment of a State Bank, which in historical retrospect seem more important, was the legal tender provision for Bank notes. As Althorp explained, if the Bank's notes were legal tender it would be in a stronger position to deal with the foreign exchanges, and to many the provision seemed, for better or for worse, a symbol both of the supremacy of the Bank of England in the British banking system and of the concern over preserving international financial equilibrium. The legal tender provision not only had overtones for emerging issues but also had

---

[9] "Minutes of the Most Material Part of Lord Althorp's Communication to the Delegation of Country Bankers, on the 11th of June, 1833," broadside dated June 13, 1833.
[10] 3 *Hansard* XIX, 82–83, July 3, 1833.
[11] *Three Early Nineteenth Century Diaries*, ed. Arthur Aspinall (London, 1952), p. 343.
[12] 3 *Hansard* XVIII, 180, May 31, 1833.
[13] 3 *Hansard* XVIII, 172, May 31, 1833.

emotional associations with issues that meant much to older members: the depreciation of the legal tender assignats of revolutionary France, and the bullion controversy of 1810 and 1811 in which the Government of the day had indulged in legal gymnastics to avoid making Bank notes legal tender.[14] It had been the boast of Edmund Burke, re-echoed many times in the Restriction period, that the Bank note was all-powerful on Exchange because it was powerless in Westminster. Alexander Baring, although opposed in 1833 to any proposal for a devaluation of the currency, supported legal tender because he felt that this would contribute to the smoother working of a metallic standard.[15] Peel, champion of gold convertibility, quoted Burke on the dangers of legal tender, and in legal tender saw weakness where Baring saw strength.[16] Some were against legal tender because it gave a superior status to the Bank of England note; others favored it because it strengthened the position of country banks in case of panic. When the final vote came many supporters of the gold standard, including Peel, Parnell, and Herries, voted against legal tender, and had it not been for support from critics of the gold standard it is doubtful whether the Government could have carried its legal tender clause.[17]

Attwood Motions for Committees on Economic Distress

The debate on the Bank Charter Act had raised the question of the monetary standard only in passing, as an incident to the discussion of legal tender. Yet before the debate in late May 1833 the Whig Government had fought off two attempts to reopen the question of the standard that seriously threatened the Whigs' control of Parliament and split the Tories wide open: first by Thomas Attwood, now an independent member from newly enfranchised Birmingham, and then by his brother Matthias, a Tory veteran of the Parliamentary wars against the act of 1819.

On March 21, 1833, Thomas Attwood broke up debate on the Whig legislative program for dealing with the Irish disturbances by moving that "a Select Committee be appointed to inquire into the causes of the general distress existing among the industrious classes of the United Kingdom, and

---

[14] Parts of this discussion follow closely the discussion in my article "Legal Tender during the English and Irish Bank Restrictions," *Journal of Political Economy* LVIII, June 1949, where the subject is treated in more detail on pp. 250–252.

[15] 3 *Hansard* XVIII, 1359, June 28, 1833.

[16] 3 *Hansard* XVIII, 1368–1374, July 1, 1833.

[17] The resolution to retain legal tender was approved in the Commons by a vote of 214 to 156 (3 *Hansard* XVIII, 1399–1400, July 1, 1833).

into the most effectual means of its relief."[18] Although the motion made
no reference to the currency, it was clear from Attwood's speech that he
expected that the proposed committee would review the monetary standard. Possibly it was this motion that prompted Althorp's remark on about
the same date to Richard Raikes, governor of the Bank: "A gross robbery
on the public was committed by Mr. Peel's bill in 1819, and we will not
sanction a similar robbery in 1833 by repealing it."[19] Motives were mixed
in the support and opposition to the motion, but the vote on the resolution
was regarded as a test of attitudes on the act of 1819, both at the time and
later by two political historians who have treated the incident, Professor
George Kitson Clark[20] and Professor Arthur Aspinall.[21] The Government
opposed the motion, as did a large part of the Tory leadership. But over
half of the Tories, and well over half of the Tory country members,
including two Tory leaders, Sir Edward Knatchbull and the Marquess of
Chandos, and most of the Irish members lined up in support of the
motion, which was defeated 192 to 158.[22]

Thomas Attwood's motion was hardly out of the way when Matthias
Attwood introduced an even more direct and ominous challenge to the
act of 1819. Thomas Attwood's motion had been sufficiently general to win
support of members, particularly from Ireland, who were not critics of
Peel's act. The new motion from Matthias Attwood called for a commission
whose terms of reference included inquiring how far "general distress"
had "been occasioned by our present monetary system."[23] Matthias
Attwood's motion was immediately followed by a countermotion of Althorp "that it is the opinion of the House that any alteration of the monetary system of the country, which would have the effect of lowering the
standard of value, would be highly inexpedient."[24] The debate was
complicated, with the arguments not always meeting head-on. Matthias
Attwood's motion on its face was not a request for a repeal of the act of
1819, and he sought support on the ground that it simply called for fact-
finding. Althorp, on the other hand, warned the Commons that to pass
the motion was to announce an intention to suspend specie payments,

---

[18] 3 Hansard XVI, 938.

[19] Diary entry of Thomas Raikes, brother of the governor, on March 24, 1833, in
A Portion of the Journal Kept by Thomas Raikes (London, 1856), I, 171–172.

[20] *Peel and the Conservative Party* (London, 1929), pp. 105–108.

[21] *Three Early Nineteenth Century Diaries*, pp. xlii–xliii.

[22] 3 *Hansard* XVI, 918–963, March 21, 1833.

[23] 3 Hansard XVII, 384–462, April 22, 1833. The debate continued on April 23 (466–
537) and April 24 (540–591).

[24] 3 *Hansard* XVII, 416, April 22, 1833.

with ruinous consequences for business, finance, and the condition of the worker.

The speeches of the Tories, Peel and Baring, and Torrens, the independent with Radical leanings, highlighted a difference of opinion among those against a suspension of specie payments. Peel defended the act of 1819 and was critical of anything that he felt would in the slightest way change the act or remotely endanger convertibility. Although Baring's substantive position on the resolution was the same as Peel's, Baring's theoretical defense of his position alarmed the uncompromising Peel. The incongruous result was that Peel directed more attention to criticizing the logic of his principal Tory ally than to attacking the specific proposal that they both opposed. Baring hoped that the Attwood resolution would be rejected "so as to calm the fears and alleviate the evils which agitating it had so extensively produced," [25] and rhetorically asked the Commons "whether they had heard enough from the hon. member from Whitehaven [Matthias Attwood] and from his hon. relative, to say if they would trust themselves with such pilots on a sea so stormy?" [26] He added an obiter dictum that was heresy to Peel, "that the main difficulties of the country had arisen from the struggles which it had then [1819], so much to its honour, though not perhaps so much to its opulence, thought proper to make," [27] and urged bimetallism, legal tender for the Bank notes, and legalization of £1 and £2 notes. Peel characterized these as "some doctrines which excite in my mind so much doubt and apprehension." [28] Torrens took much the same position as Baring. He was even more critical of the act of 1819, and with an oratorical flourish that few economists have acquired, "he was prepared to show that the act of 1819, for restoring the ancient metallic standard of value, was, perhaps, the most extraordinary instance of rash, precipitate, and mischievous legislation, which the history of Parliament contained." He "could not support a proposition for lowering or degrading the ancient standard," on the ground that "lowering the value of currency reduced the real wages of the working classes," but he would support the silver standard with redemption in silver ingots on the principle of Ricardo's program for redemption in gold ingots, and the reissue of £1 and £2 notes. On the basis of this analysis Torrens gave his approval to the resolutions of both Attwood and Althorp.[29]

[25] 3 *Hansard* XVII, 506, April 23, 1833.
[26] 3 *Hansard* XVII, 501, April 23, 1833.
[27] 3 *Hansard* XVII, 499–500, April 23, 1833.
[28] 3 *Hansard* XVII, 506–507, April 23, 1833.
[29] 3 *Hansard* XVII, 540–548, April 24, 1833.

The net result of this free for all debate was three divisions: defeat, 331 to 139, of a motion to consider Attwood's resolution without amendment; defeat, 271 to 134, of the motion that to Althorp's resolution on the standard should be added a provision for a committee to "inquire into the general distress"; and approval, 309 to 49, of Althorp's resolution "that it is inexpedient to lower the standard of value."

Despite the decisive victory of Althorp's resolution, the debate, as well as what was being said outside of Parliament, indicated a continuing dissatisfaction with the monetary situation. But for Peel's refusal to make political capital by a support of any motion that could even remotely be considered a criticism of the gold standard or a threat at convertibility, Tory revolt might have been a political force. The vote on all of these motions suggests a Tory cleavage between the more reactionary landed gentry group, intransigent in devotion to the England of the past, and the group that was becoming more closely associated with commercial, financial, and industrial interests—a division that came to a decisive split with Peel's support of Corn Law repeal.

New Parliamentary Investigations

The defeat of the two Attwood resolutions was followed by a maneuver that is as old as the processes of government. The Whig Government did not object to an investigation of economic conditions, but it did object to any investigation sponsored by the brothers Attwood, however innocent its wording might be. On May 3, 1833, Lord Althorp moved for two select committees, one on manufactures, commerce, and shipping, and the other on agriculture. The spirit of the Government is indicated by Althorp's speech: "He owned, however, that he would do wrong if he led the House to expect any great public benefit would arise from the labours of these Committees. Their appointment would have the effect of showing that the expectations of the country of the subject of a redress of grievances in the way desired were impossible." [30]

Both committees were controlled by the Government, and it would appear that little encouragement was given to witnesses who felt that monetary policy was a cause of economic distress. In the evidence to the Manufactures Committee there was a regional pattern in the picture of economic conditions. Samuel Gurney's statement that the "trading interest is in a sound state" (Q. 4) was in line with the view of almost all who spoke for London interests, although with candor Gurney added "we have

[30] 3 *Hansard* XVII, 958–959.

had time of equal, if not greater prosperity, certainly" (Q. 5). Spokesmen for Manchester gave a similar picture,[31] and leading questions, apparently from the currency critics on the committee, brought scant support, except from spokesmen for the metal trades, for the idea that currency was the cause of distress. A Lancashire cotton manufacturer[32] felt that currency expansion would help but "would rather have the taxation reduced and keep the currency as it is"; and a handloom weaver, to the question, "Do you think that the change of the currency has any effect upon the fall of wages?" replied: "It is a question that is too high for me; but all I can say is, that ever since it took place my situation has been getting worse."[33]

Representatives of the metal trades gave the Manufactures Committee a picture of serious economic distress, and four specifically blamed their troubles on the monetary situation,[34] giving the impression that this was the prevailing opinion in the metal trades.[35] The committee simply transmitted its evidence and submitted no report.

The witnesses before the Agriculture Committee of 1833 had little to say on monetary conditions. The picture was that agriculture was in better condition than a few years before, that the agricultural laborer when employed was better off than before, but that many workers were not in "constant employ." The committee's report, believed to have been written by Sir James Graham, had all the earmarks of a compromise and recommended no action. It said something to conciliate every point of view, including this judgment on the monetary situation: "It is impossible to overlook, and it would be criminal to disguise the fact, that the depreciation and restoration of the value of Money consequent on the Bank Restriction of 1797, have unsettled the habits, disturbed the fixed engage-

---

[31] Lewis Lloyd (Q. 390–617, and in particular 393–396); William Haynes (Q. 4917–5187, and in particular 4959).

[32] James Grimshaw (Q. 10,164, 10,166, 10,181, 10,112).

[33] Richard Needham (Q. 11,899).

[34] John Dixon, a brass founder of Wolverhampton (Q. 4226–4535); Thomas Clutton Salt, brass founder and lamp manufacturer in Birmingham (Q. 4536–4760); William Mathews, in coal and iron trade near Dudley (Q. 9600-9993, and in particular Q. 9940–9942); W. H. Sparrow, iron manufacturer in Staffordshire (Q. 10,789); and John Milner, spring-knife cutter in Sheffield (Q. 11,665–11,666). Dixon made no comment on the monetary situation.

[35] William Mathews (Q. 9971) referred to the memorial, which he said was signed by seven eighths of the iron trade of Staffordshire, presented to Lord Grey on October 4, 1831, asking "the speedy establishment of some just, adequate and efficient currency, which may properly support the trade and commerce of the country, and preserve such a remunerating level of prices as may ensure to the employers of labour the fair and reasonable profits of their capital and industry, as well as the means of paying the just and necessary wages of their workmen."

ments, and injured alternately the interests of large classes of the community" (p. x).

Increasing Acceptance of the Act of 1819

Sniping at the act of 1819 continued, but outside of Birmingham any organized sentiment for an inconvertible currency or for a devaluation of the pound appears to have played out by 1837. The House had tired of Thomas Attwood's beating of the currency drum, and when in July 1834 he moved for a currency inquiry this was disposed of by members walking out.[36] The recovery of nonagricultural prices late in 1835 and of agricultural prices early in 1836 was taking the drive out of attacks on the monetary standard. The iron industry revived in 1835 and 1836. The increasing rivalry between various types of banks and the question of the proper role of the Bank of England were again, as after 1823, shifting interest away from the standard to the behavior of banking institutions on a given standard.

Yet there remained one latent focus of opposition to the act of 1819—the idea, based more on sentiment than analysis, and lacking concrete form, that doing something about silver might help economic conditions. The vitality of this notion is shown by the surprising support in May 1835 for E. S. Cayley's motion for a select committee on "the subject of silver, or a conjoined standard of silver and gold," [37] and the debate that it provoked. Despite Peel's warning that "the main object of this Motion . . . is the depreciation of the standard of the currency," it mustered 126 ayes against 226 noes.

[36] 3 *Hansard* XXIV, 1116, July 3, 1834.
[37] 3 *Hansard* XXVIII, 244–338, June 7, 1835.

VI

CURRENCY AND BANKING SCHOOL
CONTROVERSY AND THE BANK ACTS
OF 1844 AND 1845

T HE IMPROVEMENT in economic conditions that started late in 1835 was accompanied by, and in some areas was preceded by, a financial expansion. Joint-stock companies in all fields were formed on an unprecedented scale. Speculative activity was particularly great in the shares of railroads and of joint-stock banks.

Formation of Joint-Stock Banks

Joint-stock banks had first been authorized in England in 1826, but only fourteen had been established between 1826 and 1830.[1] Forty-four were added in 1831–1835, and late in 1835 their formation became almost a speculative mania. Fifty-nine were established in 1836, and of these fifteen were between April 30 and June 15—more than in the first five years after the legislation of 1826. Some of these banks were started with practically no paid-in capital, by men with no banking experience.

The Bank of England looked jealously on these institutions which, with the establishment of the London and Westminster Bank in 1834, had broken its monopoly of joint-stock banking in London. At the same time the Bank's liberal credit policy must have contributed to the urge to start joint-stock enterprises of all types, including banks, and to the ease with which their stocks were sold. Its private discounts increased from £1,009,000 in April 1833, to £3,387,000 in July 1835, and by the end of that year were over £11 million. Total credit, which had been running around £24 million in 1833, had an upward trend for the next three years and was over £35 million after the quarterly advances in January 1837. The Bank's circulation changed little between 1833 and 1837, but the trend of its deposits,

---

[1] S. Evelyn Thomas, *The Rise and Growth of Joint Stock Banking*, I (London, 1934), app. M. A number of other details on joint-stock banks are taken from this source.

both public and private, was slightly upward in those years.[2] These developments took place in the face of a decline in the Bank's reserves from around £11 million in 1833 to less than £4 million in November 1836. This was a far call, both from the Palmer rule of holding securities constant and letting deposits and notes vary with specie, and from the Pennington suggestion that notes alone should vary with specie.

At the same time that the Bank was expanding its credits in the face of declining reserves, the circulation of country banks increased from barely £10 million in the last four months of 1833 to over £12 million in the second quarter of 1836.[3] This growth came entirely from the joint-stock banks—£1,315,301 to £3,588,064—and their notes continued to increase in the second half of 1836, when the notes of the Bank and of the private banks were declining.

Parliamentary Investigations of Joint-Stock Banks

The problem of the joint-stock banks, although related to the role of the Bank of England, became a public issue independently of any question of Bank of England policy. In May 1836 the Government, stimulated by the reports of malpractice by some joint-stock banks, and apparently also by the opposition of the politically powerful private country bankers and of the Bank of England[4] to their new competitors, moved for and secured the appointment of a Secret Committee on Joint Stock Banks.[5]

The evidence before this committee revealed extensive abuse in the organization and operation of joint-stock banks. It indicated the continuing conflict between the view that banks were private businesses into which the government had no right to pry and the view that if they issued notes they were, simply at government sufferance, performing a royal function of creating money. A threatened refusal by some bankers to give information about their operations was met by a firm stand of the committee, headed by Thomas Spring Rice, the Chancellor of the

---

[2] Figures on the Bank's notes, deposits, reserves, and advances are given in appendix 16 of *Report from the Select Committee on Banks of Issue*, 1840. This and other material on the Bank's operations in 1832–1847 is reproduced in the charts in Elmer Wood, *English Theories of Central Banking Control, 1819–1858* (Cambridge, Mass., 1939), charts i–xii.

[3] An act of August 28, 1833 (3 & 4 Will. IV, c. 83) had required private and joint-stock banks to make weekly returns of their issues. The returns through 1839 are summarized in appendix 2 of the *Report from the Select Committee on Banks of Issue*, 1840.

[4] 3 *Hansard* XXXIII, 840–882, May 3, 1836, reports a debate, marked by charges and counter charges about the motives back of the motion. Matthias Attwood's suggestion that the committee should investigate the entire monetary situation received no support.

[5] The larger part of the committee's report is reprinted in Gregory, *Select Statutes, Documents & Reports*, II, 219–229.

Exchequer (p. iii). Yet at the same time there was almost no interest on the part of either the committee or the witnesses in the problems of deposit banking.

The committee was continued the following year, and after Victoria had come to the throne another committee on the same subject was appointed in 1838. These hearings of 1837 and 1838 strengthened the impression of the 1836 hearings that many dangerous practices existed in English banking. The 1838 hearings gave much attention to the Irish banking situation and revealed that Irish runs were in large part from noteholders, and not from depositors. What was said about the Irish situation was specific confirmation of what was suggested indirectly in the hearings of all three years: the Bank of England was the foundation of the British banking system, and in time of trouble the solvency of all banks depended upon the ability of the Bank of England to grant credit and, if necessary, to supply gold.

The hearings and reports of all three committees, however, were more important as influences on public opinion than as formulators of legislative policy. The one positive recommendation—that Parliament give early consideration to a law governing joint-stock banks—deceptively underplays the forces of opinion that were emerging in the banking field.

Torrens' Letter to Melbourne

The position of the joint-stock banks was discussed largely in Parliamentary committees, but the controversy over Bank of England policy raised by the financial pressure in late 1836 and early 1837 was fought out in pamphlets and in the press. This was opened by Robert Torrens, in one of the most amazing productions of that brilliant and erratic controversialist, *A Letter to the Right Honourable Lord Viscount Melbourne* (London, 1837). As this pamphlet played an important part, both in the public debate that culminated in the Bank Act of 1844, and in the endless bickerings and confusions over the relation of notes and deposits, a full understanding of the issues of the act of 1844 calls for a background and analysis of the pamphlet.

Torrens in 1833 had been critical of the Bank for permitting its note issues to fluctuate without reference to its specie holdings. He also attacked the Palmer rule on the same ground—that it related the Bank's reserves to deposits and notes combined, rather than to notes alone.[6] In the face of rising credits and of falling reserves the Bank left its discount

---

[6] 3 *Hansard* XVIII, 199–202, May 31, 1833; 1306–1314, June 28, 1833.

rate unchanged at 4 per cent until July 21, 1836, when it was raised to 4½ per cent, followed by an increase to 5 per cent on September 1 of that year. In late 1836 and early 1837 economic conditions, particularly in the Birmingham industrial district, deteriorated. The situation was made worse by bank runs, especially in Ireland, and even when there were no runs prudent country bankers apparently added to their reserves of gold and Bank notes and restricted credit. Physical production declined, stock prices collapsed, unemployment increased, and there were widespread failures of banks and businesses.

The situation provided for Torrens an ideal opportunity to attack the Bank's delay in dealing with the expansion of the years 1834 to 1836, and he made the most of it. The result was a mixture of Torrens the economic analyst at his best and Torrens the former colonel of marines, discarding as a hindrance to his policy proposals all of this acute analysis and advancing to attack the Bank with every debating weapon at his command. The first part of the *Letter* was a penetrating discussion, in which he paid tribute to James Pennington, of the process of deposit creation and the role of bank deposits in the monetary system. The tone of the analysis was set in this statement:

Now, it will be found, that in consequence of the system of banking which prevails in this country, our money is composed of two distinct and different elements, namely of circulating money, and of credit money; the circulating money consisting of the coin and bank notes actually in circulation; the credit money consisting of the deposits placed in the hands of bankers, and of the cash credits granted by them.

The manner in which that portion of the medium of exchange, which consists of coin and of bank notes, acts upon prices, and, through prices, upon the foreign exchanges, is sufficiently apparent, and needs no explanation. But neither the members of the Government, nor the directors of the Bank of England, appear to be aware of the extensive influence which is exerted upon prices, and, through prices, upon the foreign exchanges, by that portion of the medium of exchange which consists of deposits and cash credits. This *terra incognita* of our monetary system it therefore becomes necessary to explore. (pp. 5–6)

The two sections that follow carried the headings "Bank Deposits perform the functions of Money" and "A given amount of Circulating Cash becomes the basis of a much greater amount of Bank Deposits." Torrens illustrated his point by the example of the shift of bank liabilities from notes to deposits, and said: "Now this change in the manner of keeping the cash required to meet the current demands of the market, would not leave the merchant and dealer with a less command of money, with a less power of making payments and of making purchases, than they possessed" (*Letter,* pp. 8–9).

Torrens' discussion so far seemed to support the view, expressed in the Palmer rule, that the Bank's reserves should be related to its total liabilities, and not simply to its notes. But at this point Torrens the economic analyst was carried away by Torrens the controversialist. The case against the Bank, on the ground that extension of credit had allowed its total notes and deposits to expand in the face of falling reserves, was a strong one, but Torrens chose to criticize the Bank not on this basis, but on the same ground he had taken in 1833—that the Bank's notes had not moved in line with its specie. Torrens' position was based largely upon an assumption—that seemed contrary to other parts of the *Letter*—that the Bank and not the public decided how the Bank's liabilities were to be divided between notes and deposits. It also involved a further assumption, never fully spelled out, that the Bank's notes, but not its deposits, served as the reserves of other banks, and hence that changes in its notes had a greater influence on the country's means of payment than did changes in its deposits. On this basis Torrens moved to the attack: "Therefore, the Bank directors, in allowing the foreign exchanges to act, not upon their circulation, but upon their deposits, exhibit a lamentable ignorance of the principles upon which the issue of Bank paper ought to be regulated" (p. 29). From there on out Torrens played fast and loose with the term "circulating medium." Analysis which in the beginning had been applied to "circulating medium" that included bank deposits was now transferred to a "circulating currency" that excluded bank deposits.

Torrens recognized that the Bank might also face an internal drain. He talked of the need, in such a situation, for the exercise of the fullest banking discretion, in words that would seem to make him one of the architects of the Bagehot principle: "The Bank directors are justified in disregarding the principle of regulating their issues by the foreign exchanges, and in making such advances as may be necessary to restore commercial credit" (*Letter,* p. 43). At this point in the argument came an idea that for the next twenty years was basic to the currency school case: the need for using discretion would never arise if the Bank directors had not previously misguidedly used their discretion in ignoring their declining reserves, thus creating a crisis which could be cured only by a further use of discretion. The problem was stated in the full flower of Torrensian rhetoric: "But does the necessity under which the Bank directors are occasionally placed, of resorting to extraordinary measures for the purpose of mitigating a pressing mischief, afford a justification of the previous deviations from principle by which that mistake was created? Could a surgeon, who had wounded an artery, instead of having opened a vein, vindicate his professional reputation, by showing that he had secured the blood vessel before the patient bled to death? Could an incendiary escape condemnation, by proving that he had laboured at the engine by which the conflagration which he had kindled was at length subdued?" (p. 43).

Torrens summarized his conclusions as a preamble to his policy recommendation: "That the interposition of the Bank of England for the purpose of supporting commercial credit, is necessary in those instances only, in which a previous departure from sound principles by the Bank directors themselves, may have occasioned a sudden contraction of the currency, and have produced a crisis in the money market" (p. 63). He recommended that, "failing a separation between the business of issuing paper and the business of holding deposits and making advances, it will become necessary for the Legislature to place the medium of exchange under the management of competent functionaries, qualified by the possession not of Bank stock, but economical science; appointed, not by the holders of Bank stock, but by the Government; responsible, not to their co-proprietors, but to Parliament; and having for their object and primary duty the protection, not of their own corporate property, but of the general interest of the nation" (p. 64).

Continuing Controversy over Bank Notes

Shortly after the appearance of Torrens' pamphlet J. Horsley Palmer came to the defense of the Bank. He argued that much of the loss of specie in 1834 and 1835 had been the result of foreign loans and internal runs, that the Bank expansion in those years was justified to offset the withdrawal of funds by the payments for the West India Compensation Loan issued in connection with the emancipation of the slaves, and to utilize special deposits made by the East India Company on which the Bank had agreed to pay interest.[7] He also claimed that the situation had been complicated by the reckless credit policy of English and Irish banks. His conclusion was that the Bank must have a monopoly of the note issue, and—evidently thinking only of banks of issue—"So dangerous

[7] *The Causes and Consequences of the Pressure upon the Money-Market* (London, 1837), pp. 12-36.

does the system appear, *as it now stands,* that it becomes questionable whether the Bank of England and the bodies in question can *permanently exist together."*[8]

Palmer's pamphlet was soon challenged by Samuel Jones Loyd[9] and by Samson Ricardo.[10] Loyd added little to what Torrens had said, but unlike Torrens he did not allow his policy proposals to be compromised in any way by doubts about the absolute difference between notes and deposits. He stated as a fundamental that no man in his right mind could question that note issuing and deposit business were completely separate and that a mixed circulation of coin and notes should fluctuate exactly as would an all-metallic circulation. Despite its theoretical vacuity, there was no denying the effectiveness of Loyd's argument in an atmosphere of increasing distrust of monopoly and in the setting of widespread public opinion that the Bank had misused its discretion. Loyd's prestige as a successful banker undoubtedly made his words carry conviction to many who had little interest in the specifics of his proposal, but who felt that something ought to be done about the Bank of England and that a man who had made money in banking must understand banking. Samson Ricardo took the same general position as Torrens and Loyd, and in particular challenged Palmer's view that the Bank was justified in allowing credit to expand in the face of a gold flow. He urged a single note-issuing agency, and stressed the conflict between the responsibility of the Bank directors to the stockholders, and the Bank's responsibilities as a regulator of the currency.

Palmer returned to the argument in *Reply to the Reflections . . . of Mr. Samuel Jones Loyd* (London, 1837); Loyd countered in *Further Reflections on the State of the Currency and the Action of the Bank of England* (London, 1837); and early in 1838 Samson Ricardo re-entered the controversy with *A National Bank the Remedy for the Evils Attendant upon our Present System of Paper Currency,* and republished his brother David's *Plan for the Establishment of a National Bank.* The more than forty pamphlets on money and banking that appeared in 1837—the largest output on the topic since 1826—added little light but much heat. In 1838, in addition to Samson Ricardo's second pamphlet, George Warde Norman made a politically, if not theoretically, important contribution in *Remarks upon Some Prevalent Errors, with Respect to Currency and*

---

[8] *Causes and Consequences,* p. 50.
[9] *Reflections Suggested by a Perusal of Mr. J. Horsley Palmer's Pamphlet* (London, 1837).
[10] *Observations on the Recent Pamphlet of J. Horsley Palmer* (London, 1837).

Banking. Norman, a director of the Bank of England, and like Pennington, Loyd, and Torrens a member of the Political Economy Club, had
been a witness before the Bank Charter Committee of 1832, and this
pamphlet of 1838 was a revision of a pamphlet first written in 1832 and
privately printed in 1833. Norman held that notes and deposits were
"things in their nature distinct" (p. 97), agreed with the position of
Torrens and Loyd that the Bank should regulate its notes with reference
to its specie, and recommended separation of the Bank into an issue and
a banking department. He also said that it would be wise to outlaw all
note issues other than those of the Bank, but doubtful whether that would
be politically feasible at the time urged that no new banks have the right
of note issue, and suggested that all issues of existing banks be abolished
within ten to twenty years (pp. 95–107).

Pennington, Torrens, Loyd, Samson Ricardo, and Norman had provided the theory and most of the specific proposals of the act of 1844.
It is true that Torrens' analysis of deposits could easily have been turned
against the whole idea of the separate nature of notes and deposits, and
that his view in 1837 on country bank note issues did not agree with the
view of Norman. Although Torrens continued, even in his last publication in the *Edinburgh Review* in 1858, to recognize the importance of
deposits in the monetary situation, he never let this interfere with his
advocacy and defense of the legislative measures that regarded them as
separate.[11] By 1844, however, Torrens had come around to the view that
the country bank issues were an unstable element in the monetary situation.[12]

Committees of 1840 and 1841

The widespread interest in the problem of note issue and in the powers
and responsibilities of the Bank of England resulted in the appointment
in 1840 of a Select Committee on Banks of Issue, which held hearings
and prepared a report, and the reappointment of the Committee in 1841,
further hearings, and two more reports. The hearings of 1840 were notable
for the testimony of Samuel Jones Loyd in support of his view and of
Thomas Tooke in support of the contrary view, which came to be known
as the banking principle, that notes and deposits had the same economic

---

[11] See the discussion in Lionel Robbins, *Robert Torrens and the Evolution of Classical Economics* (London, 1958), pp. 105–116, on "The Rôle of Bank Credit in the Currency Theory."

[12] *An Inquiry into the Practical Working of the Proposed Arrangements for the Renewal of the Charter of the Bank of England* (London, 1844), p. 39.

function. Loyd, in answers to more than 800 questions that cover over a hundred pages, reiterated with plaintive persistence the idea that notes and deposits were different. His analytical position is summarized in the answer to Joseph Hume, who with illustrations of business practice and behavior of depositors stressed the point that depositors and noteholders, and not the Bank, controlled the relation of deposits and notes, and then asked: "Is it not, therefore, from these two instances, proved, that the Bank of England has no power to increase or decrease its circulation, and that that rests alone with the depositors who have money in their coffers?" To this Loyd replied: "I think it does not follow from that, and that not the slightest evidence to that effect has been adduced" (Q. 3252).

The Committee on Banks of Issue pressed Loyd as to the possible consequences for business conditions of requiring note issues to fluctuate with the specie holdings, and replied, "I must admit that I have never reflected upon such topics; because I am quite sure, that if I was to make the attempt, I should only lead my own intellect into great confusion, or come to no satisfactory answer or useful result, either to myself or the community" (Q. 3043). At another point, in evident annoyance at Hume's questions on the relation of notes and deposits, he said: "If the distinction which I clearly draw is not recognized by any other mind, then that mind and my mind are so differently constituted, that we are incapable of reasoning upon any common datum, and therefore cannot hope to come to any mutual understanding" (Q. 3152).

In light of subsequent central bank theory and policy, Loyd's testimony in the hearings of 1840 was a weak performance in comparison with that of Thomas Tooke. Tooke not only assimilated notes and deposits in their economic significance, but insisted that in the face of a foreign drain the Bank should not be "perfectly passive," but should exercise its discretion on the basis of the size of the drain and its cause (Q. 3742–3791). Tooke, however, made it clear that this discretion was never to be exercised if it would endanger specie payments (Q. 3792, 3799).

Relation of Free Trade Movement and Monetary Policy

Aside from the more technical arguments on the relation of notes and deposits, some trends in public opinion that were preparing the way for the act of 1844 were evident in the hearings of 1840 and 1841 and in the pamphlet literature. There was an increasing feeling that the note issue should be concentrated in a single agency, either the Bank of England or a newly created National Bank; and that discretion by the Bank of

England was wrong in principle as violating the tenets of free competition, and that in practice it had been bad. Spokesmen for the country banks tried to make the most of the idea that there was a conflict between the principles of free trade and a monopoly of the note issue. They had little success, and at the same time that free trade sentiment was gaining ground in the field of trade and business there was a growing acceptance of the idea that note issue was not a business activity, but a function of government. The idea was expressed in many ways, and by many people, but the summary statement of Thomas Spring Rice, Chancellor of the Exchequer, in the debate on the Bank of Ireland bill in 1839, gave what appears to have been the preponderance of public opinion: "I deny the applicability of the general principle of the freedom of trade to the question of making money." [13]

The feeling against discretionary action by the Bank was increased by developments in 1839. Economic conditions improved slightly in late 1837 and 1838, and the monthly average of bankruptcies fell from 139 in 1837 to 82 in 1838. The iron and coal trade, following the collapse in 1836 of the boom market for iron products, was in a depressed state for several years, eased only by a mild pickup in 1838. Beginning late in 1838 bankruptcies again increased, and several country banks failed. The Bank's bullion increased throughout 1837 and early 1838, and was relatively stable until near the end of the year, but fell precipitously in December 1838 and 1839—from £9,794,000 on December 18, 1838, to £2,406,000 on September 3, 1839—the lowest figure since the crisis of 1825. The Bank, however, expanded credit in late 1838 and early 1839 in the face of declining reserves. The drain had been accentuated by the loans to the United States, by financial pressure on the Continent, and by large imports of wheat in 1839.

The increase in Bank credit in the face of declining reserves is not prima facie evidence of poor management, and is even consistent with modern central banking concepts. In this particular situation, however, the Bank's action appears rather to have been the result of lack of foresight and absence of policy, as suggested by Sir John Hobhouse's report on the Cabinet meeting of August 10, 1839: "At our Cabinet today Rice brought before us the state of Bank of England, and told us that, if we had a bad harvest we should be obliged to have recourse to a Bank Restriction Act. The Governor and Deputy Governor of the Bank, who had

[13] 3 *Hansard* XLIX, 778–779, July 25, 1839.

hitherto made light of their difficulties, now began to be frightened." [14]
The Bank's absence of policy is further indicated by its credit action in
1839. In February 1838 it had lowered its discount rate to 4 per cent, and
in the face of a decline of its reserves by over two fifths it left this rate
unchanged until May 1839. In the meantime it had, in November 1838
and February 1839, made quarterly advances at 3½ per cent.[15] On May
13, 1839, the rate was raised to 5 per cent, then to 5½ per cent on June 20,
and to 6 per cent on August 1. When the Bank raised the rate to 5½, at
the same time it refused discounts on exchequer bills. The Bank had an
ad hoc policy of dealing with a crisis when it arose, but less of a philosophy of lender of last resort than it had shown under Cabinet prodding
in December 1825 and early 1826.

The crisis of July 1839 was eased, and possibly a suspension of payments averted, by the good offices of the Bank of France in making credit
available by the discounting of British bills.[16] The Bank also arranged
for a £900,000 credit in Hamburg, but details of the transaction are not
known.[17] In retrospect the Bank's arrangements in Paris and Hamburg
may be looked on approvingly as an early example of central bank co-
operation. In the circumstances, however, the appeal to a former enemy
to tide over difficulties that many British felt were in larger part caused
by the Bank's own mistakes weakened the Bank's prestige.

Manchester Opposition to Monetary Discretion

From the experience of the late 1830's, it would have been possible,
with equal logic, to have drawn the conclusion that the Bank should
have a broader concept of its discretionary philosophy, or that discretion
was a dangerous weapon with which it should not be trusted. The increasing free trade sentiment was, however, even before any specific
proposal was presented to Parliament, tilting the scales toward the less
discretion rather than the better discretion answer.

In the hearings of 1840 the opposition of the Manchester spokesmen to
anything that savored of discretion, either in the standard or in the action

[14] *Recollections of a Long Life* (London, 1910), V, 221–222.

[15] Evidence of J. B. Smith, *Committee on Banks of Issue,* 1840, Q. 10.

[16] Part of the story of the negotiations by which French credits were obtained was told
in the 1840 hearings by G. W. Norman (Q. 1896–1902), and by J. H. Palmer (Q. 1368–
1388, 1436–1471). Clapham, *Bank of England,* II, 168–170, gives further details based on
information in the Bank's records.

[17] J. H. Palmer referred to the operation in the 1840 hearings (Q. 1437–1438), but
according to Clapham there are no details in the Bank's records.

of the Bank, was unmistakable. John Benjamin Smith, president of the Manchester Chamber of Commerce, was concerned about the fluctuations of the issues of the Bank of England and of other banks, and said that "it is desirable in any change in our existing system to approximate as nearly as possible to the operation of a metallic currency; it is desirable also to divest the plan of all mystery, and to make it so plain and simple that it may be easily understood by all" (Q. 365). He proposed a National Bank, with powers and responsibilities essentially the same as those to be given in 1844 to the Issue Department of the Bank of England. Richard Cobden held that anything that substituted discretion for the forces of the market was unsound:

> I hold all idea of regulating the currency to be an absurdity; the very terms of regulating the currency and managing the currency I look upon to be an absurdity; the currency should regulate itself; it must be regulated by the trade and commerce of the world; I would neither allow the Bank of England nor any private banks to have what is called the management of the currency. . . . I should never contemplate any remedial measure, which left it to the discretion of individuals to regulate the amount of currency by any principle or standard whatever . . . I should be sorry to trust the Bank of England again, having violated their principle [the Palmer rule]; for I never trust the same parties twice on an affair of such magnitude. (Q. 519, 520, 527)

The third Manchester spokesman, William Rayner Wood, presented the same idea that Torrens had advanced three years before: that there would be little need for the Bank to exercise discretion unless it had already disturbed the money market by unwise use of discretion (Q. 670).

John Benjamin Smith also used the monetary discussion of 1840 as a basis for urging repeal of the Corn Laws, on the ground that the irregular imports of wheat under existing law led to spasmodic specie exports with consequent monetary disturbance; this situation would be corrected by a continuous import of wheat, paid for by a regular export of manufactured goods (Q. 10). This view set the pattern for many statements in the next six years, particularly in the *Economist* and in *The League* (the organ of the Anti-Corn Law League), arguing that repeal of the Corn Laws would contribute to monetary stability.

Significance of Parliamentary Investigations, 1836–1841

The immediate legislative results of the investigations of 1840 and 1841, like those of 1836, 1837, and 1838, were nil. The report from the 1840 committee was little more than a transmission of evidence, but with a Delphic closing paragraph that forecast the shape of things to come. The committee suggested that if the Palmer rule was not satisfactory the Bank might appropriately adopt "any other principle of management which, after their further experience, and upon mature consideration, they may consider to be better adapted for the primary object of preserving, under all circumstances, the convertibility of their notes" (p. v). The reports of the following year were limited to recommending more frequent statements from banks of issue, including those in Scotland and Ireland, on outstanding notes, and from the Bank of England on its bullion.

Over the years 1836–1841 five committees had asked witnesses over 16,000 questions, which with the replies covered more than 1200 folio pages. From this mass of evidence almost any program could have been justified on the basis of a given premise of economic and social philosophy. The increasing strength of the view that the creation of money was a function of government, the rising free trade sentiment, and the opposition to economic discretion in high places made it pretty certain, however, that when action was taken it would restrict or abolish the note issues of country banks, and would either impose some sort of a reserve requirement upon the notes of the Bank of England or turn over the note issue to a newly created government agency.

Renewal of the Birmingham Attack on Gold Standard

Two other trends in public opinion help to explain why Peel sponsored, when he did, the provisions that became the act of 1844: renewed opposition from Birmingham to the gold standard in the early 1840's and the increasingly favorable attitude toward bimetallism or a silver standard. The agricultural interests, who up to the middle 1830's had been the strongest critics of the act of 1819, by the late 1830's in large part had become supporters, or at least had ceased to be vocal critics. The *Circular to Bankers* reported early in 1838 that agricultural conditions in the past two years were better than at any time in the previous twenty years.[18] Thomas Attwood, disillusioned that the reform Parliament did not share his view on monetary policy, resigned from Parliament in December 1839.[19] With some improvement in economic conditions in the Birmingham area, and with Attwood's retirement from public life, the Birmingham movement appeared to have lost its drive.

When economic distress again struck the Black Country in 1841 Bir-

---

[18] No. 499, February 2, 1838, pp. 241–245.

[19] His farewell letter of December 9, 1839, to his constituents at the time of his resignation is printed in C. M. Wakefield, *Life of Thomas Attwood* (London, 1885), pp. 355–365.

mingham returned to the attack in a way that, from the point of view of a dedicated supporter of the gold standard like Peel, must have been more ominous than the earlier Birmingham criticism. Before it might have been possible to regard Thomas Attwood as a well-meaning crank, to whose currency ideas his fellow citizens of Birmingham gave support out of loyalty to a man whose efforts had done so much to further the passage of the Reform Act. Events soon made it clear, however, that Birmingham views on currency had a foundation more solid than the enthusiasm of a single man. Attwood's Parliamentary colleague from Birmingham, Joshua Scholefield, shared his currency views. Attwood's successor at the by-election in 1839 was George Frederick Muntz, a merchant and manufacturer, who agreed with Attwood on currency matters. In 1841 Muntz and Scholefield were re-elected, and the defeated Tory candidate, Richard Spooner, was a banking partner of Thomas Attwood and also a critic of the gold standard. In August 1842 the Birmingham Chamber of Commerce passed a resolution critical of the gold standard, and at a meeting at which Richard Spooner presided unanimously approved the sending of the memorial to Peel "with an expression of reget and disappointment on the part of the Chamber, that it is inconvenient to Sir Robert Peel to afford the Deputation an opportunity of personally expressing to him, the appalling state of the productive Classes in this District, and the urgent necessity which, in their opinion exists for some prompt, and immediate remedial measures."[20] This was followed by the sending of four letters to Peel between August 3 and December 9, 1842, which were published in pamphlet form in January 1843, together with Peel's replies and a further statement by the Birmingham Chamber. Peel's reply that "after mature consideration, I have the misfortune of having drawn conclusions respecting them [the matters presented by the committee] at total variance with those to which the committee have arrived" was unyielding.[21]

Muntz in 1843 brought out a second edition of his pamphlet *The True Cause of the Late Sudden Change in the Commercial Affairs of the Country*, which had first appeared in 1837, and Thomas Attwood, after several years of little to say on monetary matters, published in *Aris's Birmingham Gazette* a criticism of Peel's replies to the Birmingham Chamber of Commerce, in private letters urged his view on Peel and

[20] British Museum, Add. MS. 40,513, fol. 73.
[21] *The Currency Question. The Memorials Addressed by the Birmingham Chamber of Commerce to Sir Robert Peel, with his Replies* (Birmingham, 1843).

Lord Palmerston, and wrote several letters to the London *Times* and other papers. The most influential manifestation of the renewed Birmingham unrest was the anonymous *Gemini Letters,* addressed to Sir Robert Peel. These thirty-five letters by two Birmingham men, Thomas Barber Wright and John Harlow, first appeared in the *Midland Counties Herald,* between February and November 1843, and early in 1844 came out in book form in London and Birmingham as *The Currency Question: The Gemini Letters.* The plea was for an inconvertible paper money, issued in the amount necessary to ensure full employment. The emphasis was on the evils of a contracted currency rather than on a positive program for regulating the currency. It had, however, along with much nonsense, some shrewd analysis of the limitations of the precious metals as a standard of value, as well as some *ad hominem* arguments that undoubtedly carried weight with unemployed artisans, and with distressed manufacturers facing bankruptcy. Its general approach is indicated by these passages: "The proper plan, it appears to us, is to raise the capacity of the consumer, by securing high wages and ample profits, and by these means making light the fixed national obligations of the people. It is idle to talk of over-production when we have a population clothed in rags, and most sparingly supplied with the mere necessaries of life . . . The only limit they [the Birmingham economists] would affix to the issue of paper money would be the degrees of prosperity which the different amount of issues would produce; and this amount can only be ascertained by careful experiment" (pp. 92, 328).

The authors of *The Gemini Letters* made the point, in answer to the charges that the Birmingham proposals would foster speculation, that "the leading currency men of Birmingham are perhaps the most cautious and careful men of business which the town possesses, and by no means disposed to inconsiderate speculation . . . It is not likely that careful men of business would advocate a system which would render their capital and their profits insecure; while, if they were really disposed to exchange the prudent management of their business for a career of wild speculation, it is shown that the means are already provided, and that they need seek for no change" (p. 253).

We do not know to what extent Peel's decision to move for new currency legislation when he did, and in the way he did, was affected by *The Gemini Letters* and the discussion that they stimulated. However, as an able politician and a defender of the act of 1819, it would have been strange had he not been influenced by these developments. The first of the letters had opened with the statement: "It is scarcely probable that the calculations and statements we are about to make, for the purpose of drawing public attention to the currency system of this country, will ever meet your eye" (p. 9). The authors were wrong in this, for Peel, regardless of whether he read the letters as they appeared, owned the book and marked several passages, including one that read: "It is right to mention, that although some of the great principles which we have brought forward have been stated to be the principles of the Birmingham Economists, we are by no means desirous to have it understood that to Birmingham alone must be conceded the honour of drawing public attention to our unjust Monetary System. We feel that in so restricting these views we should be doing an acceptable work for the enemy. The real fact is, as the newspapers of the day fully prove, principles similar to those advanced by us, find able advocates in every part of the United Kingdom" (p. v).[22]

At the same time items were appearing in the London press about attacks on the currency standard, and although most of the articles defended the act of 1819, the very fact that the *Times* spent so much space in criticizing "unsound" ideas suggests that these ideas had a wide circulation. The *Circular to Bankers,* still hostile to the act of 1819, used the correspondence between Peel and the Birmingham Chamber of Commerce as a springboard for again criticizing the gold standard. The newly founded *Economist,* as enthusiastic about the miracle-working qualities of free trade as the most extreme Birmingham spokesmen were about a more abundant currency, was firm in support of the gold standard, but its efforts to make this clear showed that it was aware that many wanted to seek prosperity through more money rather than through free trade.[23]

Parliamentary Discussions of Economic Distress in 1842 and 1843

A variety of forces, both in the Bank and outside, had for several years been building up to some measure that would regulate or abolish the note issues of private banks, and that would either establish a National Bank with a monopoly of note issue or subject the Bank of England to some reserve requirement. But there was nothing inevitable about the legislative result that these forces would produce, or the time of the legislation.

[22] A note by Professor Foxwell in Peel's copy in the Goldsmiths' Library at the University of London states that the markings were made by Peel.

[23] In particular, see the issue of January 13, 1844, p. 387.

Under the act of August 29, 1833, the Bank's charter was to run for twenty-four years, with the option to the Government, at any time within six months after a lapse of ten years, of giving notice that the charter was to terminate within one year. In the summer of 1842 and early in 1843 there were extended discussions in both Houses of the distress of the country.[24] The main focus was on the Corn Laws, but Muntz and Matthias Attwood put in their word on the currency, and Peel, in answer to a question, said that he had no intention to seek new monetary legislation in the current session of Parliament.[25]

Favorable Comments on Silver and Bimetallism

The last serious Parliamentary move for a silver standard or bimetallism had been in 1835, but in the years between then and 1844 suggestions that silver should have a more prominent place in the monetary system came from many persons of widely diverse views on other aspects of monetary and banking policy. In 1836 a Commons Select Committee to Inquire into the State of Agriculture and a Lords Select Committee to Inquire into the State of Agriculture in England and Wales held hearings at which more than 24,000 questions were asked. These hearings revealed little agricultural enthusiasm for devaluation or an inconvertible currency, but particularly from bankers and businessmen in the provinces came a number of statements that showed a surviving, and even a reviving, feeling that silver should be part of the monetary base.[26]

The standing, if not the strength, of the silver movement is shown by the continuing support of Alexander Baring, now in the peerage as Lord Ashburton. He insisted before the 1836 Commons committee that there should never be any "tampering with the standard of value," but

---

[24] In the Lords: 3 *Hansard* LXIV, 1239–1289, July 11, 1842; LXVI, 261–305, February 9, 1843. In the Commons: LXIV, 861–936, July 1, 1842; 1015–1087, July 6, 1843; 1171–1240, July 8, 1842; XLV, 517–568, July 22, 1842; XLVI, 448–525, February 13, 1843; 578–634, February 14, 1843; 636–694, February 15, 1843; 706–762, February 16, 1843; 769–892, February 17, 1843.

[25] 3 *Hansard* LXVI, 419, February 13, 1843.

[26] The following witnesses made favorable comments either on a silver standard or on bimetallism: John Langhorne, banker at Berwick-upon-Tweed, *Commons*, Q. 8943, *Lords*, Q. 3771; George Calthrop, general merchant in Spalding, Lincolnshire, *Commons*, Q. 7942–7948; Richard Spooner, banker in Birmingham, *Commons*, Q. 15,717–15,738, *Lords*, Q. 4399, 4441; Henry Burgess, secretary to Committee of Country Bankers, *Commons*, Q. 16,007–16,009; William Debonaire Haggard, chief clerk of the Bullion Office of the Bank of England, *Commons*, Q. 16,223–16,226; George Frederick Muntz, merchant and proprietor of a metal-rolling mill in Birmingham, *Commons*, Q. 16,468–16,477, *Lords*, Q. 4536–4541; Earl of Radnor, *Commons*, Q. 16,755–16,757; Lord Ashburton, *Commons*, Q. 17,618–17,771; E. S. Cayley, a member of the Commons, *Lords*, 3670; Bickham S. Escott, *Lords*, Q. 5079–5080; Matthias Attwood, *Lords*, Q. 5547–5602.

that the standard would be on a solider basis with a silver standard or bimetallism: "My apprehension is, that by the attempt to maintain a gold instead of a silver, or a mixed standard, you will some day or other come to the lamentable condition of an irredeemable paper" (Q. 17,760). In the hearings before the Committee on Banks of Issue of 1840 George Frederick Muntz (Q. 1099) and Richard Page (Q. 969), a writer on currency, urged a silver standard or bimetallism; and in the hearings before the Committee on Banks of Issue of 1841 Henry W. Hobhouse, chairman of the Committee of Country Bankers, favored a silver standard (Q. 384–385). Between 1837 and 1843 at least sixteen pamphlets had made favorable comments on either bimetallism or a silver standard. Speaking favorably of silver was, by 1844, something which almost all could do without abandoning their convictions. Those who wished to break the act of 1819 could suggest some sort of silver standard as an alternative less alarming to more conventional thinkers, and defenders of the act of 1819 could allay criticism of that act by saying friendly words about silver without really committing themselves to any positive action.

Negotiations between Peel and the Bank

When Peel decided that it was time to move for new banking legislation, he did so with a dispatch and with a political genius that quickly turned his recommendations into law. James Pennington, Robert Torrens, and Samuel Jones Loyd had provided most of the theoretical support of the act of 1844. As far as is known, however, Torrens and Loyd never had any conversations with Peel about the act, and the services of Pennington, who since 1831 had been an occasional adviser to ministers and government departments, were limited to helping on technical details after Peel had already determined the main provisions of the act.[27] What

---

[27] Loyd stated in testimony before the Select Committee on Bank Acts of 1857: "I had no connexion, political or social, with Sir Robert Peel. I never exchanged one word upon the subject of this Act with Sir Robert Peel in my life, neither directly or indirectly. I knew nothing whatever of the provisions of the Act until they were laid before the public. The Act is entirely so far as I know the Act of Sir Robert Peel" (Q. 4020).

There is nothing in the Peel papers to suggest that Torrens had any direct contact with Peel, although in May 1844 he had sent to Peel a copy of his recently published *Inquiry into the Practical Working of the Proposed Arrangements for the Renewal of the Charter of the Bank of England* (British Museum, Add. MS. 40,544, fol. 262). Two months later he asked Peel for office, because "I had been one of the earliest propounders of the principles regarding the regulation of the currency which were advocated by Mr. Lord and Mr. Norman before the Parliamentary Committee of 1840" (British Museum, Add. MS. 40,548, fols. 211–213). Peel answered that he was unable to comply (*ibid.*, fols. 215–216). After Peel's death Torrens in 1852 was given a Civil List pension of £200 "in consideration of his valuable contributions to the Science of Political Economy" (P.P. 1852 (563), XXVIII).

emerged as the act of 1844, even when due recognition is given to the writings of others, or to the economic philosophy of the time, was in the full sense of the name "Peel's Act."

Early in January 1844 Peel asked William Cotton, governor of the Bank, and J. B. Heath, deputy governor, to meet with him and Henry Goulburn, Chancellor of the Exchequer.[28] Out of their discussions came a memorandum from Cotton and Heath that was in effect an outline of the act that finally emerged, plus a provision not in the final act that would have permitted the fiduciary issue to be exceeded on the authorization of three Ministers of the Crown. Word of these negotiations seems to have gotten around, and on January 26 the *Circular to Bankers* reported that the "great advance" in the price of Bank Stock was "universally attributed to a belief prevailing among the friends of the Bank Directors that they have concluded an advantageous bargain with the Government for the renewal or extension of their charter" (p. 261). The Queen's speech of February 1, 1844, suggested in general terms that the Government was considering banking legislation,[29] but no further word came from Peel until early in May. Peel in April submitted a memorandum[30] to the Cabinet, in which he presented three alternatives: first, "maintenance of the leading principles of the present system"; second, "the prohibition for the future of all issues of paper payable to bearer on demand, by the Bank of England and every other Bank whatever," and the establishment of a Board independent of Government, but responsible to Parliament, charged with the issue of paper, convertible into gold, to be a legal tender; and third, "an intermediate one, between complete acquiescence in the present system, and radical subversion of it," which he stated more specifically in an outline of note issue provisions almost identical with those of the bill presented to Parliament the following month. Peel on grounds of logic favored the currency board, of which he said: "If we were about to establish in a new state of society a new system of currency, it would be very difficult to contest theoretically the principles on which this plan is founded or the equity of the practical application of them."

---

[28] In this account of the negotiations between the Government and the Bank I have drawn on J. Keith Horsefield, "The Origins of the Bank Charter Act, 1844," *Economica*, n.s., XI, 180–189 (November 1944), reprinted in *Papers in English Monetary History;* and on Clapham, *Bank of England,* II, 178–185.

[29] 3 *Hansard* LXXII, 4.

[30] An extract from the memorandum is in C. S. Parker, *Sir Robert Peel from His Private Papers* (London, 1899), III, 134–139.

It was evident that Peel, though in form asking for the Cabinet's judgment, favored the third alternative, and his statement in the memorandum of the arguments that would be brought against it, and his request for Cabinet opinion, reveals that nice blending of fixed principles and of flexible policy in achieving those principles that is the mark of the master politician:

> It is impossible not to foresee that it will be encountered by a formidable combination. It will be resisted by those who are for the rigid application of sound principle without reference to times or circumstances, and who think that all paper issues should proceed directly and exclusively from the Government; by those of the opposite opinion, who think there ought to be unlimited competition as to issue, provided there be the security of the immediate convertibility into gold; by those who charge the Bank of England with being the chief cause of the past derangements of the currency, and consider that on that account it is entitled to no favour; by the country bankers, and those whom the country banks can influence.
>
> The Cabinet must weigh deliberately the several considerations which present themselves. My advice is that they should determine to propose the course which they may conscientiously believe to reconcile in the greatest degree the qualities of being consistent with sound principle and suited to the present condition of society, and should encounter the risk which it is impossible not to foresee must attend any proposal for guarding against eventual dangers at the expense of personal interests and in disregard of private feelings.

The Cabinet approved the third alternative. There followed a letter from Goulburn to the Bank, which the Bank directors had previously seen, and a reply from the Bank, a draft of which Goulburn had seen and commented on. Goulburn's official reply to the Bank took a stiff attitude on some financial details, and at the same time he wrote privately to Cotton that he had wanted to make it clear—presumably for public relations—"that we have not altogether yielded to you." A letter of May 3 from Cotton and Heath to Goulburn, after stating that the directors felt that a better treatment of the Bank on the financial arrangement "might reasonably have been expected, they have resolved, in order that no obstacle may be presented by them to the measures which are considered desirable by Her Majesty's Ministers to place the Currency on a sounder footing, to recommend to the Court of Proprietors to accede to the proposals of the Government."[31]

---

[31] The official exchanges between Goulburn and the Bank are in P.P. 1844 (246), XXIII, and are reprinted in Gregory, *Select Statutes, Documents & Reports*, I, 117–128.

Parliamentary Discussion of Peel's Proposals

With the Cabinet and Bank in agreement, Peel on May 6 presented to the Commons the bill that with trifling changes became the Bank Act of 1844. Its main provisions, aside from details relating to financial arrangements between the Bank and the Government, were:

1. The Bank of England is divided into an Issue Department and a Banking Department (art. I). The Issue Department may issue £14 million of notes upon the security of Government debt, but except as the Bank may acquire lapsed note issue rights of private and joint-stock bankers all issues in excess of £14 million are to be made only in exchange for gold coin, or gold or silver bullion (arts. II, IV, V).

2. Silver bullion held by the Issue Department may not exceed one-fourth of its holding of gold coin and bullion (art. III).

3. If any issuing banker ceases to issue notes the Bank of England may increase its fiduciary issue by two-thirds of the authorized issue of that banker (art. V); no banker in the United Kingdom not now issuing notes may issue notes in the future (art. X).

4. Bankers now issuing notes in England and Wales may not exceed their present issues (art. XI).

5. The Bank of England may agree with bankers to take over their existing notes, and to make to such bankers "a Composition at the Rate of One *per Centum per Annum* on the Amount of Bank of *England* notes which shall be issued and kept in circulation by such Banker" (art. XXIV), but any such payments are to cease on August 1, 1856, "or on any earlier Day on which Parliament may prohibit the Issue of Bank Notes" (art. XXV).

Peel in introducing the bill made clear that it was political realism, not economic theory, that had determined its provisions: "The true policy in this country is to work, so far as it is possible, with the instruments you have ready for your hand—to avail yourselves of that advantage which they possess from having been in use, from being familiar from constituting a part of the habits and usages of society. They will probably work more smoothly than perfectly novel instruments of greater theoretical perfection. If we disturb that which is established, let us have some good practical reason for the change." [32] Peel did not go into fine points of theory, but left no doubt that on policy he accepted the beliefs

[32] 3 *Hansard* LXXIV, 742, May 6, 1844.

of the currency school: "Our general rule is, to draw a distinction between the privilege of Issue and the conduct of the ordinary banking
business. We think they stand on an entirely different footing." [33] He was
adamant in his determination to resist issues of private and joint-stock
banks. Spokesmen for banks of issue, who evidently knew the main outlines of Peel's proposals weeks before, had protested and Peel had made
up his mind against them.[34] The Parliamentary debate that followed
added little to analysis of the relation between notes and deposits.[35]

Public Discussion of Peel's Proposals

The predominant opinion outside of Parliament approved concentration of the note issues in the Bank of England, but a number of sources,
and particularly London banking spokesmen, criticized the rigid restrictions on its issues. The *Economist* opposed the bill, but at the moment
its interest was more in the repeal of the Corn Laws, and its article "The
Practical Effects on Commerce of New Currency Proposition. Sir Robert
Peel—Colonel Torrens" [36] used the occasion as much to attack the Corn
Laws as to criticize the Bank bill. The *Westminster Review* of June 1844
in a long article by John Stuart Mill on "The Currency Question" gave
a reasoned criticism of the proposed legislation, stressing the fact that
notes and deposits both affected prices, pointing out that the demand for
gold for export "takes place in most cases mainly by drawing out deposits," and arguing that the Bank's gold should be available to meet all
of its liabilities. Like other critics of the bill, Mill defended the existing
gold standard and went out of his way to attack the Birmingham currency ideas. And like many other supporters and critics of the bill both
in and out of Parliament, Mill proceeded to say that no one paid any
attention to the Birmingham currency ideas. Regardless of any deeper
significance of this constant criticism of an idea that it was claimed almost
no one supported, Mill's words are worth quoting, not only for their
substance but as showing that a rationalist and logician in the heat of
controversy could almost match the "indefatigable Colonel Torrens"—
the phrase is Mill's—in wealth of rhetoric:

[33] 3 *Hansard* LXXIV, 743, May 6, 1844.
[34] The *Circular to Bankers* has many references to protests to Peel in March and April
1844, and Peel in introducing the bill quoted from a protest of the country bankers.
[35] The Commons debate is in 3 *Hansard* LXXIV, 720–755, May 6, 1844; 1330–1413,
May 20, 1844; LXXV, 318–319, June 6, 1844; 777–872, June 13, 1844; LXXV, 1308–1319,
June 24, 1844; LXXVI, 58–73, June 27, 1844; 118–119, June 28, 1844; 315–319, July 4,
1844. The Lords debate is in LXXVI, 704–738, July 12, 1844.
[36] May 18, 1844, pp. 793–796.

There are at this day numerous persons who can read and write, and some who think themselves oracles of wisdom, who see no harm in emancipating a paper currency from the restraint of convertibility . . . There are writers of pretension, not only out of Bedlam, but even, we can assure Sir Robert Peel, out of Birmingham, who think it the duty of the legislature periodically to degrade the standard (or to authorize an issue of inconvertible paper exactly equivalent) in proportion as the progress of industry creates an increase of productions and a multiplication of pecuniary transactions. But it is not against these extreme aberrations that it is now necessary to contend. (p. 581)

Before the bill was formally introduced, but after the Queen's speech, Thomas Tooke had published another attack on the currency principle, *An Inquiry into the Currency Principle*.[37] Samuel Jones Loyd came to the defense of the bill in a reprinting, with an Introduction and a few changes, of his privately circulated anonymous pamphlet of 1840, *Thoughts on the Separation of the Departments of the Bank of England*. Robert Torrens, at his polemical best when dealing with a specific proposal and an opponent who personified the argument, challenged Tooke in *An Inquiry into the Practical Workings of the Proposed Arrangements for the Renewal of the Charter of the Bank of England and the Regulation of the Currency: with a Refutation of the Fallacies Advanced by Mr. Tooke,* and joined battle with Mill in *Reply to the Objections of the Westminster Review to the Government Plan for the Regulation of the Currency*.[38] While the debate was on John Fullarton criticized the currency principle in *On the Regulation of Currencies,* although it was not published until August 1844, after the passage of the act.[39]

Theoretical Issues in Controversy between the Currency and Banking Schools

It is doubtful whether these arguments altered the bill in any way. They added little, if anything, to the theoretical case already made for and against the idea that the Bank of England's notes should fluctuate with its holdings of specie, but they helped to sharpen the issues. Three main points were brought against the note issue proposals of Peel:

1. The total of notes and deposits, and not notes alone, is the significant element in the monetary situation.

---

[37] The Introduction to the first edition is dated March 1844, to the second edition May 15, 1844.

[38] A second edition of *An Inquiry* and a new printing of the *Reply* appeared in a consecutively paged volume in 1844.

[39] Fullarton's work appeared in a second edition in 1845, with a Preface dated December 20, 1844. All citations are to the second edition.

2. In time of internal drain, and of external drain which is the result of commercial or financial disturbances and not of domestic inflation in relation to other countries, it is not sound policy to require that notes (or even notes and deposits combined) fluctuate exactly as a metallic currency would.

3. Increase in the note circulation is a result, and not a cause, of price changes, and therefore the regulation of notes is not a means of controlling prices.

Logically these were quite separate propositions, and it was unfortunate, both for the purpose of policy proposals at the time and for the sake of clear understanding by later economists of the issues involved, that they were all packaged together in the setting of 1844 under the term "banking principle." On the first point the banking school was clearly right. As Fullarton presented the case: "Why, the whole bank-note circulation of this country might be turned tomorrow into a system of book-credits transferable by cheque, or all our banking accounts might be commuted, on the contrary, for promissory notes, and in neither case would the course of monetary transactions be essentially disturbed or altered. . . . Bank notes are the small change of credit, the humblest of the mechanical organizations through which credit develops itself" (*Regulation,* pp. 41, 51). Tooke said practically the same thing (*Inquiry,* p. 19).

The question whether deposits were money was not, however, the heart of the problem. The objections of the banking school to the regulation of notes went much deeper, and would not have been met simply by treating deposits and notes like. Their basic opposition was to any legal reserve requirement against the Bank's liabilities—either notes alone or notes and deposits combined. Since critics as well as supporters of the act of 1844, regardless of their ideas on the relation of notes and deposits, avoided the slightest suggestion of any reserve requirements against deposits of the Bank of England or of any other bank, the views of the banking school on this point are revealed only inferentially. It seems clear, however, that if Peel had proposed a legal reserve requirement against both notes and deposits the banking school objections would have been even greater. In the setting of the controversy Fullarton, Mill, and Tooke trained their guns on the logically weakest point in the analytical defenses of Peel's bill, and this concentration on the reserve requirements against notes obscured the fact that their basic theoretical criticism was of any reserve requirement.

Fullarton's objection to reducing the note circulation as a means of restoring international equilibrium on the ground that this would create a crisis (*Regulation,* pp. 124–130), his argument that an increase of notes be permitted in time of emergency (pp. 109–110), and his warning that the new arrangement "must have the effect of very much disabling it [Bank of England] for the performance of what has hitherto been considered the duty of the Bank in time of difficulty and pressure" (p. 199), would apply to deposits as well as to notes. Mill was not specific, but the whole trend of his discussion indicated that a rigid reserve requirement against deposits and notes would be objectionable, as compelling the Bank to contract when it lost specie whether as the result of an internal run, of too high a domestic price level, of foreign loans, or of a temporary disturbance in the commodity trade.

Tooke gave the most penetrating and discriminating analysis on this point in his *Inquiry into the Currency Principle.* He started from the assumption that there were some drains, even external, that should not be immediately offset by a reduction of notes. His basic criticism of the proposed legislation was not that it required notes to fluctuate with specie but that it required that the Bank's liabiliies—regardless of whether they took the form of notes or deposits—be restricted when specie moved out. His arguments in the last analysis amounted to opposing any reserve requirement other than that set by the good judgment of the Bank.[40] He reiterated the view, which he had expressed in 1838 and again in 1840, that the Bank should strive to maintain "a high average amount of bullion," which he estimated would be about £10 million (pp. 114–120).

The two first points in the controversy—whether deposits should be regarded in the same light as notes, and whether notes (or notes and deposits combined)—should be rigidly tied to specie, presented clear-cut issues, with head-on clashes of argument. The third question, the relation of notes and prices, produced a complex and muddled argument, the net effect of which has been to befuddle the issue, both for contemporaries and for later economists who have tried to interpret the battle between the banking principle and the currency principle. The currency school assumed that the quantity of money had some relation to the maintenance of international equilibrium, and that those who controlled the monetary supply could correct a pressure on the exchanges by monetary contraction. The emphasis in 1844 was on the commodity price effects, although the currency school, to some extent before the act of 1844 and to a greater degree in its

[40] See in particular ch. 15, "Review of the Currency Principle in its Application to our Banking System."

subsequent defense, recognized that at least in the short run the corrective influence of monetary restraint would come more from changes in the international flow of capital than from changes in the flow of commodities. This was not the straw-man quantity theory, on which so much irrevelant argument had been expended, that there is an exactly proportional relation between money and prices. It was not even a theory that in the short run prices necessarily move in the same direction as antecedent changes of money. It was a long-run monetary theory of prices in the sense that it assumed that the monetary authorities held the final power, as against the nonmonetary influences acting on the exchanges. It held that no price increase could long continue unless the monetary authorities acquiesced; that if a price increase had taken place the monetary authorities could force a price reduction by appropriate credit policy; and that a reduction of domestic prices was a means of correcting an unfavorable exchange no matter what the originating cause of that unfavorable exchange had been. And then, on pragmatic grounds, the currency school translated a long-run theory of prices into a short-run policy of Bank behavior.

Fullarton and Tooke—but not Mill—attacked the whole idea of bank-created money as an influence on prices, and on the basis of their analysis and their version of the "lessons of history" came up with the confident conclusion that Peel's Act was all wrong. Their argument was not a single proposition, but two different, though related, ideas: (1) Notes do not have any effect on prices, but simply adjust to price movements; (2) The limitation on deposits and notes from wise banking policy is the real guarantee of price stability, and this would be the case even in the absence of specie convertibility.

The first point was simply a variation of the idea that notes were only a part of the total means of payment. Fullarton drove home his argument by speaking of "the utter hopelessness" of attempting to influence prices "by any officious tampering with the free supply of so comparatively insignificant a portion of the whole mass of circulating credit as the bank-notes, and that portion the least of any affinity with those operations of trade by which the course of prices and exchanges is really directed" (*Regulation*, pp. 50–51). Tooke made much the same point in his *Inquiry* (pp. 38, 123–124).

Both Fullarton and Tooke drew a distinction between changes in the money supply arising out of banking policy, and changes arising from gold production or issues of government paper money, and both granted that monetary expansion from the latter sources was inflationary. But as regards the effect of bank-created money it is never quite clear whether the banking school spokesmen's fundamental idea was that changes in note issues alone had no effect on prices, or that a change in the total means of payment created by banks that loaned only on real bills had no effect on prices.

On one occasion Tooke spelled out the argument that no bank-created money could influence prices, yet at the same time apparently accepted the idea that an increase in the precious metals would lead to a proportional increase in prices.[41] In other settings the banking school spokesmen simply said that the note circulation did not influence prices. The explanation of this vagueness, if not inconsistency, is that the banking school was not trying to develop monetary theory for later generations, but was attempting to make effective arguments against specific proposals for regulating notes. For the banking school's purposes it was sufficient to argue that changes in the note circulation were not the originating cause of price changes, and in the setting of the controversy anything it might say about the effect upon prices of the total bank created money supply was generally by way of obiter dicta.

Tooke and Fullarton in their controversial zeal to show that there was no basis for restriction of note issues came very close to building up a case that the abuses of deposit banking called for regulation. As Tooke put it: "The truth is, that in all the flagrant cases of mismanagement of banks, the resources of the business, that is, the deposits and the capital of the shareholders or partners, have been brought in aid of the efforts to get a share of the existing circulation, not to add to it, for that is impossible" (*Inquiry,* p. 95). Fullarton went even further in *Regulation of Currencies* in suggesting that deposit banking had the effect on prices and the foreign exchanges that the currency school had associated with notes alone:

We, on our part, deny that, in point of fact, such overissues [of notes] are possible. But assuming, for the sake of argument that they have a real existence, we contend, that the same action on prices which you attribute to the occasional excesses of a circulation of notes, over which you profess to possess effectual means of control, must be exercised in a far greater degree by the excessive use of other forms of credit, which perform precisely the same offices in exchange that are performed by the notes, but probably to ten times the extent, and which are wholly beyond the reach of control or limitation . . . Nothing so preposterous can ever be maintained, as that the same payment, which contributes to a rise in the market, when made through the instrumentality of banknotes, will have no consequence if effected by the transfer of a bill of exchange, or by an adjustment of set-off in a banker's books; or, to put the absurdity at

[41] Committee on Banks of Issue, 1840, Q. 3261-3306.

once in its most glaring light, that the action of any given facility of credit on prices depends not at all on the essential nature and tendency of the transaction, but simply on the particular piece of paper on which the amount of the credit may happen to be inscribed. (pp. 40–41)

The Banking School and the Gold Standard

If the banking school had stopped its argument on the point that, within the limits possible with a gold standard, the judgment of bankers was preferable to the rules of government, there might have been ground for compromise. But in their efforts to build up the argument against rules and in favor of trusting the judgment of the Bank of England, Tooke and Fullarton overreached themselves. A principal reason for Peel's proposal was his belief that this would make more solid the foundations of the gold standard. The leading spokesmen for the banking principle claimed also to be uncompromising defenders of the gold standard. Mill's views on this subject have already been quoted, and Fullarton's and Tooke's statements were equally emphatic. Tooke, in criticism of a suggestion of J. W. Bosanquet, of the London and Westminster Bank, that in time of crisis it might be better to suspend specie payments,[42] had made a statement in defense of convertibility that should have satisfied even Peel: "How any well-informed person, not of the Birmingham School, could seriously propose to have cash payments suspended, rather than that the mercantile community should be subjected to some inconvenience from an advance in the rate of interest, and what he chooses to consider as a necessary consequence, a fall of prices, is to me a matter of unutterable surprise" (*Inquiry,* p. 105).

Tooke, while protesting his devotion to the gold standard, came to the very brink of the proposition that the only limitation needed on the monetary supply was that banks lend only on real bills. He held that government paper money, "while it is in the course of augmentation, acts directly as an originating cause on prices and incomes, constituting a fresh source of demand in money, depreciated in value as compared with gold, but of the same nominal value as before," but stated that bank notes had no such effect on prices because they differed from government paper money "not only in the limit prescribed by their convertibility to the

---

[42] Bosanquet had developed this idea in a series of letters in the *Times* in 1841 under the signature "A Lombard," and had republished this material, with some additions, in *Metallic, Paper, and Credit Currency* (London, 1842). He was a signer of the petition of the Committee of London Bankers against the proposed legislation, and in a letter of June 7, 1844, to Peel (Parker, *Sir Robert Peel,* III, 140–142), in which he approved of much of the bill, Bosanquet had suggested that in time of great pressure the Bank be allowed to issue inconvertible notes.

amount of them, but in the mode of issue" (*Inquiry,* pp. 70–71). He argued that "a reduced rate of interest has no necessary tendency to raise the prices of commodities. On the contrary, it is a cause of diminished cost of production, and consequently of cheapness" (p. 123).

All of this raises theoretical issues familiar to readers of Keynes and Hansen as to the existence of unemployed labor and the shape of the supply curve of resources and labor, which may be implicit in Tooke but were not spelled out. An economist skilled in model building can show that under appropriate assumptions things would happen as Tooke claimed, and there may have been real short-run situations in which a reduced interest rate had been a cause of lower prices. But what Tooke was saying had been said by the defenders of inconvertible money from John Law to the most extreme of the Birmingham spokesmen, and Torrens was too keen at seeing the weakness in an opponent's case to miss the debating opportunity that Tooke had given him:

> After a careful examination of Mr. Tooke's recent publication, I cannot discover any very essential or practical difference between his principles and those of the Birmingham economists. Once deviate from the golden rule of causing the fluctuations of our mixed circulation to conform to what would be the fluctuations of a purely metallic currency and the flood-gates are opened, and the landmarks removed. Between the abandonment of a metallic standard as recommended by the Birmingham economists, and the adoption of arrangements hazarding the maintenance of a metallic standard recommended by Mr. Tooke, the difference in the practicable result might ultimately be nothing. (*Inquiry,* pp. 53–54)

If Peel had any doubts about the dangers that the banking school might be but Birmingham economists in sheep's clothing, the clincher to Torrens' claim was furnished by Fullarton: "And, much as I fear I am disgracing myself by the avowal, I have no hesitation in professing my own adhesion to the decried doctrine of the old Bank Directors of 1810, 'that so long as a bank issues its notes only on the discount of *good* bills, at not more than sixty days' date, it cannot go wrong in issuing as many as the public will receive from it.' In that maxim, simple as it is, I verily believe, there is a nearer approach to truth, and a more profound view of the principles which govern circulation, than on any rule on the subject which since that time has been promulgated" (*Regulation,* p. 207).

If we take the statements of Fullarton, Mill, and Tooke in conjunction with their avowed devotion to the gold standard, the area within which their views differed from those of the currency school was, in the light of history, narrower than is often supposed. Much of what the banking school said may sound to economists of the mid-twentieth century like a rejection of shackling rules and an enlightened defense of a managed currency. The banking school wanted to avoid credit restriction, if that could be done and at the same time specie payments be maintained, but once the gold standard was in danger they were ready, if one can take them at their word, to make as great sacrifices to maintain specie payments as would the currency school zealots. The only difference was that the currency school said that it was worthwhile paying a price early in the form of monetary restriction as insurance against not being able at a later date to maintain the gold standard no matter what price was paid. That was, after all, a matter of judgment, and keen analysts and levelheaded men may differ in judgments.

Passage of the Act of 1844

Peel's bill affected Scotland and Ireland only in the provision, applicable to the entire United Kingdom, that no new banks of issue were to be established after May 6, 1844, but it left untouched the note-issue privileges of existing banks in Scotland and Ireland. Peel, introducing his bill, had said of Scotland and Ireland: "I propose to reserve for separate legislation the state of the currency of each of those parts of the United Kingdom . . . the single measure I have to propose is so extensive, and affects such numerous and powerful interests, that I have been unwilling to encumber it with enactments requiring separate consideration, or to cloud the prospects of success by having to encounter too powerful a combination of opponents." [43]

Peel's strategy of not taking on a two-front war in 1844 was successful. There was only scattered Parliamentary opposition. A motion by Benjamin Hawes, Jr., that "no sufficient evidence has been laid before this House to justify the proposed interference with Banks of Issue in the mangement of their circulation," was defeated 185 to 30,[44] and Muntz's motion that the House postpone discussion of the bill was beaten 205 to 18.[45] The bill was passed in both the Commons and the Lords without recorded vote and became law on July 19, 1844.[46]

Legislation on Scottish and Irish Banks

With the principal legislation out of the way Peel turned to the other items on his banking agenda. The bill to regulate joint-stock banks,

---

[43] 3 *Hansard* LXXIV, 751–752, May 6, 1844.
[44] 3 *Hansard* LXXV, 870–872, June 13, 1844.
[45] 3 *Hansard* LXXV, 1312–1319, June 24, 1844.
[46] 7 & 8 Vict., c. 32.

which he had referred to when presenting his program to Parliament on May 6, was introduced on July 4 and became law on September 5, 1844,[47] in "An Act to Regulate Joint Stock Banks in England." This was a technical act relating to the conditions under which joint-stock banks might be established and to their legal responsibilities, and imposed no restrictions on note issue. It was generally believed that the purpose of the legislation was to make difficult the establishment of joint-stock banks. In this the act was successful, as only one joint-stock bank—the Royal British Bank, which failed in 1856—was established in the next eight years.

Peel was now prepared to move in on the Scottish and Irish banks, in the strong position of having the English banks on his side. The Scots saw what was coming and did not like it. *Blackwood's Edinburgh Magazine,* in an article in December 1844, "The Scottish Banking System," raised the alarm against any attempt to regulate Scottish banking.[48] It recalled the successful resistance in 1826 to the proposals of the Government of the day to outlaw the pound note: "All ranks, from the peer to the peasant, rose up in wrath at the proposed innovation; and from every county, city, town, village, and corporation in the kingdom, indignant remonstrances were forwarded to the foot of the Throne, and to the Imperial Parliament of Great Britain. It was assuredly a dangerous experiment to make with a proud and jealous people . . . Were it for that good work alone [Sir Walter Scott's protest], his name ought for ever to be immortal . . . Scotchmen have long memories; and although the days of hereditary feuds have gone by, they are not the less apt to remember to cherish injuries" (pp. 673–674, 686).

The Queen's message in 1845 contained a general statement indicating that Peel intended to do something, but did not reveal his hand.[49] In response to Thomas B. Macaulay's request for more details as to what the Queen's speech meant in terms of specific legislation, Peel replied in language that showed the veteran legislative general who would join battle not when his opponents challenged him, but when he was ready: "I shall reserve to myself the opportunity of stating the nature of these measures until the time arrives for bringing them fully before the House."[50]

On April 25, Peel introduced his proposed legislation—again, a com-

[47] 7 & 8 Vict., c. 113.

[48] LVI, 671–686. The article was written by W. E. Aytoun, lawyer and professor of rhetoric and belles lettres at the University of Edinburgh.

[49] 3 *Hansard* LXXVII, 4, February 4, 1845.

[50] 3 *Hansard* LXXVII, 165–166, February 6, 1845.

promise recognizing that pressure groups and emotions were powerful forces that could not be swept away by economic logic, and recognizing that it was better to yield on details as long as this did not prevent the attainment of the major objectives. Peel's ideal was to have a single note issue for the entire United Kingdom, and barring that to have all note-issuing banks, other than the Bank of England, subject to the same regulations, with the hope that eventually their note issues would lapse. His speech stated that the Bank Act of the previous year had been based on the assumption that "this House had a perfect right at any time to subject the issuers of that paper to such restrictions as might be deemed expedient for the public good." [51]

Peel, having staked out a principle which would provide for him or future Governments a beachhead from which to move against the Scottish and Irish banks when the Government's majority was more secure or memories of 1745 had become dimmer, then made clear that the pleas voiced in *Blackwood's*, by Scottish members of Parliament, and by delegations of Scottish and Irish banks had been listened to and heeded: "I think that, in considering whether or not the enactments [of 1844] should be applied, it is perfectly fit for us to take into the account the peculiar habits and customs of those countries—to take into the account their local peculiarities—and not to attempt rigidly to enforce a principle at the hazard of deranging the long-established habits of business, or I may say, shocking the feelings, or even the prejudices, of the people of those countries." [52] The pound note was the point on which the Scots were most sensitive, and Peel had no intention at the moment of waging a legislative battle over this detail: "Without guaranteeing, therefore, the continuance of these notes, all I can say is, that we do not propose to prohibit them at present. I say nothing, however, as to the future. The discretion of Parliament must be left unfettered in respect to them." [53]

In contrast to the rigid limit of the existing circulation on the note issues of English banks in the act of 1844, Peel proposed that the issues of Scottish and Irish banks not exceed existing circulation plus holdings of gold and silver coin. Since no reserve requirement applied to deposits of Scottish and Irish banks, Peel's proposal imposed no real restriction on note issues. One Scottish member, P. M. Stewart, pointed out: "It

---

[51] 3 *Hansard* LXXIX, 1323, April 25, 1845.
[52] 3 *Hansard* LXXIX, 1327, April 25, 1845.
[53] 3 *Hansard* LXXIX, 1332, April 25, 1845.

would not compel the banks of Scotland to keep one sovereign more in their coffers . . . what was now proposed in meddling with the Scotch banking system, amounted scarcely to any alteration at all." [54]

Apparently the Scottish members were pleased with the substantive content of Peel's proposal, but as Peel for the record had made clear that as a matter of principle the Government could do anything it pleased, whenever it pleased, about Scottish and Irish notes, so Scottish members put in their protest for the record. P. M. Stewart, voicing a view that seemed widely held by those from north of the border, "had no intention to oppose the introduction of the Bill, but rather to express his surprise that the right hon. Baronet had thought it necessary in any degree, however slightly, to interfere with a system so perfect and unobjectionable as experience had proved the Banking system of Scotland to be." [55]

In further debate six weeks later on the bill[56] Scottish members repeated their praise of the Scottish banking system as above reproach. A few amendments on details were introduced, but the Government had the situation well under control. The amendments were decisively defeated and the bill was passed without formal vote. Companion legislation for Ireland, practically identical in its provisions, was also passed[57] and the two measures became law on July 21, 1845.[58]

[54] 3 *Hansard* LXXIX, 1350, April 25, 1845.

[55] 3 *Hansard* LXXIX, 1349–1350, April 25, 1845.

[56] The Commons debate is in 3 *Hansard* LXXXI, 140–149, June 5, 1845; 241–246, June 9, 1845. The Lords debate is in LXXXI, 1022–1030, June 23, 1845; 1342–1343, June 30, 1845.

[57] The Commons debate is in 3 *Hansard* LXXXI, 245–267, June 9, 1845; 437–442, June 12, 1845; 620–626, June 16, 1845. The Lords debate is in LXXXI, 1430–1431, June 3, 1845; LXXXII, 2–3, July 4, 1845.

[58] The Irish law is 7 & 8 Vict., c. 37; the Scottish law, 7 & 8 Vict., c. 38.

VII

CONSOLIDATION OF EXISTING LAW, 1845–1875

THE THREE laws of 1844 and 1845 were the last substantive changes in British monetary and banking legislation before 1914. The authority of the Bank of England to agree with a bank of issue to take over its note issues, which was to lapse on August 1, 1856, was continued,[1] but was finally repealed in 1875;[2] legislation of 1857 made the general joint-stock company law applicable to joint-stock banks;[3] and technical changes in the coinage provisions were made in 1870, 1889, and 1891.[4] The important developments, however, came not from the halls of Westminster, but from the practices and traditions of the City.

In the next thirty years many legislative changes were proposed by the Government, by private members, and in pamphlets and the press: a decimal system, seigniorage on gold coins, closer regulation of Scottish and Irish banks, restriction of branches of Scottish banks in England, and repeal or fundamental change of the Bank Act of 1844. In 1870 Colonel George Tomline, a member of Parliament, delivered silver to the Mint and requested, under the provisions of the law of 1816, that it be coined for him. The Mint refused on the ground that it had no authority to coin silver for the public, as the necessary royal proclamation had not been issued.[5] Shortly afterward Government-sponsored legislation for consolidating existing coinage laws dropped the provision in the act of 1816 authorizing coinage of silver for the public.[6] The new supplies of gold from Australia and California revived suggestions that the single gold standard be given up in favor of silver, but now on the ground that

---

[1] 19 & 20 Vict., c. 20.
[2] 38 & 39 Vict., c. 66.
[3] 20 & 21 Vict., c. 49.
[4] 33 & 34 Vict., c. 10; 52 & 53 Vict., c. 58; 54 & 55 Vict., c. 72.
[5] The exchange of correspondence between Tomline and the Mint was privately printed by Tomline the following year in a pamphlet called *A Free Mint*.
[6] 33 & 34 Vict., c. 10.

the gold standard might be inflationary. Five Parliamentary committees investigated the banking system,[7] put over 30,000 questions to witnesses, and assembled masses of figures. The Commons Select Committee on Decimal Coinage (1853), the Royal Decimal Coinage Commission (1857), the Commons Select Committee on Savings Banks (1858), and the Royal Commission on International Coinage (1868) held hearings and submitted reports. The substantive legislative result was nil. Increasingly, with the passage of years, existing legislation, no matter how weak its logic, became a symbol of the stability of the British monetary and banking system, and even of the British Empire.

James Wilson and the Act of 1844

The most important of the unsuccessful attempts to amend legislation was in connection with the separation of the Bank of England into an Issue Department and a Banking Department. Except for a series of nine articles by James Wilson in the *Economist* in the spring of 1845 while the Scottish and Irish bills were under discussion—articles which with subsequent articles were reprinted in 1847 in his book *Capital, Currency and Banking*—there was little further discussion of monetary and banking theory until 1847. The year 1846 was close to an all-time low for the period 1797–1875 in the output of pamphlet literature on money and banking.

Wilson's articles presented much the same argument against the currency principle as had Tooke and Fullarton. However, since they were not written in the heat of controversy and came from a more skilled pen, they were a better statement of the theoretical case against the act of 1844. Furthermore, Wilson was not emotionally involved by having fought the act of 1844, and he had a more detached attitude that soon made him, when he surveyed the whole picture, come to the conclusion that, all things considered, it was better to leave legislation unchanged.

While the act of 1844 was before Parliament the *Economist* had commented unfavorably on it, but it was free trade as a principle, and not banking legislation, that was Wilson's great interest at the time. The articles entitled "Currency and Banking" that began in March 1845, although making the point that notes were but a part of the means of payment, put the argument on a broader basis by stressing the influences

---

[7] Secret Committee on Commercial Distress (1848); Secret Committee of the House of Lords on Commercial Distress (1848); Select Committee on the Bank Acts (1857); Select Committee on the Bank Acts (1858); Select Committee on Banks of Issue (1875).

unrelated to price changes, and in particular the effect of a bad harvest, that could put pressure on the exchanges. Wilson, with his devotion to free trade in all its aspects, objected even to the mild restrictions in Peel's proposals for the Scottish and Irish banks as "the system of interference in which Sir Robert Peel appears determined to persevere, with respect to the Currency of the United Kingdom."[8] In principle, Wilson supported multiple note issues by competing banks: "We have never been able to discover any good ground for the powerful objections which appear to exist in the minds of a large portion of even the most uncompromising free traders, against the application of the same principles to Banking, and especially to the issue of notes payable on demand. Nor have we ever been able to elicit from such, any satisfactory reasons for their objections; which the more we have considered the more we are satisfied are based upon groundless fears and misapprehensions."[9] He recognized that his views had no chance of adoption, and as an alternative suggested that the Issue Department of the Bank be converted into a bank of issue, to be managed by three commissioners appointed by the Government.[10]

Many sentences in Wilson's article in 1845 and 1847 read like the words of Tooke and Fullarton; for example: "The impossibility of increasing the quantity of paper in circulation (when convertible), except as the effect of a corresponding increase of internal trade, or of any depreciation of its value taking place."[11] But when Wilson is read in his entirety, there is evident a continuing emphasis that this situation applied only under convertibility and a recognition that monetary expansion in a single gold standard country might raise prices in that country and throughout the world. To Wilson convertibility was the assurance that, no matter what mistakes of judgment banks might make, there could be no permanent inflation in relation to gold; to Tooke and Fullarton it was a matter of minor importance as compared with the qualitative standards of bank credit. Torrens never could have said of Wilson's ideas, as he did of Tooke's, that "the flood-gates are opened, and the landmarks removed." It is no accident that he should have called Wilson "the most able of the opponents of the act of 1844,"[12] or that Wilson, in 1847 and

---

[8] *Economist*, May 3, 1845, p. 405.
[9] *Economist*, May 29, 1847, p. 601.
[10] *Economist*, May 29, 1847, p. 601.
[11] *Economist*, April 26, 1845, p. 385.
[12] *The Principles and Practical Operation of Sir Robert Peel's Bill of 1844 Explained* (London, 1848), p. 119.

1848, when popular feeling against the act ran high, should have stopped short of joining the clamor for its repeal.

Responsibilities of the Bank of England under the Act of 1844

Renewed criticism of the act of 1844 came with the crisis of 1847 and with the Government's letter of indemnity to the Bank authorizing a suspension of the note issue provisions of that act. However, the developments that culminated in that crisis had their origin not in any specific provision of the act of 1844, but in the apparent belief of the Bank management that the act had freed them from certain restrictions which public opinion had previously imposed on them. Large in the background of the act was a critical public attitude toward the Bank's use of discretion. There was no specific provision in the act, however, repudiating the philosophy of Bank responsibility that Henry Thornton had preached with such force, that a large part of the City of London agreed with, and that the Bank—although reluctantly—had followed in 1825 and 1826. The act gave no indication whether the Banking Department had an obligation to hold a larger reserve than would be dictated by accepted standards of banking prudence.

The supporters of the act in large part had disposed of the problem of the Bank's responsibility by assuming that it would no longer arise under the new legislative dispensation. What Charles Wood, who had been chairman of the committees of 1840 and 1841, said in the debate in 1844 in answer to the criticism that the Bank would be restricted in granting assistance in crises such as had occurred in the recent past, was essentially the same idea that Torrens, Loyd, and Peel had advanced: "The argument against the application of the new system is, that it would be incompatible with a state of affairs produced by the old one. But this, in fact, admits all that we ask, and the simple answer to this and all similar arguments is, that if the sound principle had been acted upon steadily from the first, the Bank never would have been found in that position. The very object of applying sound principle is to prevent the possibility of such a state of things ever being produced." [13]

Bank of England Policy and the Crisis of 1847

The Bank of England management soon acted in a way that was consistent with the view that the new legislation had relieved them of, or at least had minimized greatly, their previous responsibilities to the

[13] 3 *Hansard* LXXIV, 1379, May 20, 1844.

banking system. The Bank shortly took steps to increase its discount business, both by reducing its rate from 4 to 2½ per cent to bring it in line with the market rate, and by repealing a rule of 1840 against rediscounting bills endorsed by banks of issue. The newly established *Bankers' Magazine* commented: "Notwithstanding the well founded predictions of many, that the Bank would adopt this course of action, directly she was relieved from the responsibility of managing the circulation, the recent proceedings have taken the monetary world entirely by surprise." [14]

On September 7, 1844, the date of the first statement required of the Bank under the new act, private discounts of the Banking Department were £2,116,000 and total earning assets £21,837,000.[15] For the next three months there was little change, but beginning in January 1845 both bills discounted and total earning assets started upward, and by February 28, 1846, the figures were, respectively, £13,137,000 and £35,825,000. Much of this increased credit seems to have gone in support of speculative, or at least questionable, enterprises, in particular domestic railroads. In 1845 over £50 million of railroad construction was authorized and in 1846 over £132 million, a total about double that of the previous decade. The *Economist,* looking back on developments from the vantage point of 1848, moralized: "It would now be of little utility to refer to the mad scenes of 1845 and 1846, and to prove to demonstration that the present prostration and dejection is but a necessary retribution for the folly, the avarice, the insufferable arrogance, the headlong, desperate, and unprincipled gambling and jobbing, which disgraced nobility and aristocracy, polluted senators and senate houses, contaminated merchants, manufacturers, and traders of all kinds, and threw a chilling blight for a time over honest plod and fair industry." [16]

A letter of January 28, 1847, from Samuel A. Goddard of Birmingham to Lord John Russell may have been simply the conditioned reaction of

[14] October 1844, p. 57.

[15] Beginning September 7, 1844, the Bank was required to publish each week in the *London Gazette* a statement of the condition of the Issue Department and of the Banking Department. These figures, however, do not give the detailed breakdown of deposits and assets that is in the statements subsequently furnished to the Parliamentary committees of 1848, 1857, and 1858. The relation between these two types of Bank reports is explained in Wood, *English Theories of Central Banking Control,* pp. 186–190.

[16] October 21, 1848, p. 1187. A similar picture of the speculative developments in late 1845 is given by Tooke in *A History of Prices* (London, 1848), IV, 65–66. An account of credit developments in 1844–1847 is in W. T. C. King, *History of the London Discount Market* (London, 1936), pp. 102–160.

Birmingham to all monetary developments, but was better prophecy than the views of more conventional thinkers:

It is hardly possible this country can escape a monetary panic and a commercial revulsion, through the abstraction of gold and the consequent necessary curtailment of the paper circulation and money facilities of the Bank of England.

This probably will be more severe than any panic previously known to this generation. It is even questionable whether the Bank of England will have the power to stay the efflux of gold in season to sustain its own credit.

The panic and its subsequent evils will ruin thousands, and throw thousands out of employment.[17]

Note circulation in the hands of the public increased moderately through most of 1845, as did deposits. Deposits rose sharply beginning late in 1845, and on February 21, 1846, private deposits reached £18,647,968 and public deposits £6,296,535, as compared with £8,644,000 and £3,631,-000, respectively, on September 7, 1844. A large part of the increase in private deposits was in special "railway deposits" made in connection with payments for new securities. These had been only £162,000 on December 27, 1845, but rose to £10,705,000 less than six weeks later, were down to £14,000 by September 1846, and then up to £1,796,000 by January 23, 1847. Even if one puts the most extreme interpretation on the idea that the Bank should compete just like any other bank, wise heads might well question whether any bank should have expanded credit the way the Banking Department had done in 1845 and 1846. This expansion was accompanied by falling reserves of the Banking Department from March 1845 until the closing months of the year, and then, after a pickup in late 1845 and the first half of 1846, by a precipitous decline that culminated in October 1847 in the suspension of the Bank Act.

The ratio of the Banking Department's note and coin holdings to its deposits had been approximately 68 per cent in the statement of September 7, 1844.[18] By October 18, 1845, the ratio had fallen to 38 per cent. The

---

[17] Samuel A. Goddard, *Miscellaneous Letters on Currency, Free Trade, &c.* (London, 1847), p. 23.

[18] Following R. H. I. Palgrave's procedure in his paper of 1873 before the London Statistical Society, "On the Relation of the Banking Reserves to the Current Rate of Interest," published in the *Journal of the Statistical Society*, XXXVI, 529–564 (1873), I have considered the reserve ratio of the Banking Department as the ratio of notes and coin it held to total deposits plus short bills outstanding. On pp. 552–559 Palgrave gives this ratio for the dates nearest to changes in discount rates, and I have used his figures. For dates for which he does not give ratios I have used the table in the appendix of Ernest Seyd, *Reform of the Bank of England Note Issue* (London, 1873), in which he gives for every week from September 7,

situation, already serious from the overexpansion of credit that had fed speculation, was complicated by the imports of grain in 1846 on account of the shortage of the potato crop in Ireland, and the heavy gold exports fell upon deposits rather than notes. An even more serious crop failure in Ireland later in 1846 further increased the pressure for foreign payments, and this again fell primarily on the deposits. Although the discount rate was raised to 3 per cent in October 1845 and to 3½ per cent the following month, it was again dropped to 3 per cent in August 1846, when reserves were up to 58 per cent. Shortly after this rate reduction banking reserves once more declined: from around £10 million in August 1846 to under £7 million in January 1847, and to barely £3 million on April 17, 1847—a reserve ratio of only 20 per cent. Even by the standards of a bank that had no responsibilities to anyone but its stockholders, maintenance of such low rates in the face of falling reserves was most questionable.

A two-step increase of the rate to 4 per cent in January 1847 still left it well under the market, and between January 9 and April 10 the Bank's discounts rose by nearly £3.8 million, and its total earning assets £4.5 million. Not until April 8, when the market rate had reached 7 per cent, did the Bank again raise its rate, and then only to 5 per cent. At the same time that it increased the rate the Bank imposed a number of arbitrary limitations on discounts that must have suggested to many in Lombard Street that, even for those with the finest security, the Bank had no intention of acting as a lender of last resort. Rates above the published rate were charged on all but bills with only a few days to run, quarterly advances were called in, and an absolute limit was placed on the total of bills regardless of their quality or the standing of those asking for credit. Tooke's judgment is in accord with all of the evidence: "This last circircumstance—the entire rejection of bills without reference to their character—it was, which brought on the extreme severity of the pressure in April." [19] Evidently some of the Bank's directors did not like this procedure. As early as November 1846 a minority of the directors, including the men who were the governor and deputy governor in 1848, had wished to raise the rate in view of the failure of the potato crops and the un-

---

1844, to December 27, 1871, a statement of total deposits and seven-day bills, and notes and coin in the Banking Department. The substance of Seyd's publication originally appeared in the *Journal of the Statistical Society*, XXXV, 458–540 (1872), under the title "Statistical Critique of the Bank Charter Act of 1844," but without the detailed figures given in the appendix of the reprinted version.

[19] *History of Prices*, IV, 74.

favorable exchanges and the outflow of gold.[20] Before the increase in the rate to 5 per cent was belatedly announced in April 1847—still well under the market—a proposal to raise the rates to 7 per cent was turned down, as the majority of the Bank Court preferred a lower rate and rationing of discounts.[21] Clapham's remark, "One must hope that the Committee of Treasury's delays had no connection with the needs of any of its prominent members," [22] is suggestive in view of the fact that the firm of the governor, W. R. Robinson, stopped payments in July 1847, and in September the firm of two other directors, Sir John Rae Reid, a former governor, and A. L. Gower, went under.

The restrictive actions of the Bank were followed by a severe credit stringency. Tooke reported: "There were instances of rates as high as 12 and 13 per cent per annum being paid for unexceptionable six months' paper; and of similar bills beyond that date not being discountable at all. To apply the term 'panic' to the state of affairs as it existed during the last three weeks of April, and the first four days of May, would convey a very inadequate idea of the suffering of that period." [23] Business temporarily weathered the difficulty, and by the end of May the pressure had eased. Regardless of the wisdom of the Bank's action, the gold outflow stopped temporarily, but resumed again in July on a small scale.[24] However, the Bank rate was well under the market rate, rationing continued, and there was no assurance that the Bank would lend to good risks at any rate.

Up to June or July of 1847 it is doubtful if the act of 1844 placed any real restriction on the Bank's ability to help the market. Insofar as the new legislation at first affected the Bank's policy it apparently had been to encourage the Bank to extend credit when it should not have done so,

---

[20] Testimony of James Morris and H. J. Prescott, *Commons Committee*, 1848, Q. 2657–2662.

[21] Testimony of H. J. Prescott, *Commons Committee*, 1848, Q. 2641. Apparently the proposal to raise the rate to 7 per cent did not come to a formal vote, for Clapham, citing the Bank's records, mentions only a proposal to raise the rate to 6 per cent (*Bank of England,* II, 201n).

[22] Clapham, II, 200–201.

[23] *History of Prices*, IV, 305–306.

[24] It is difficult to reconcile contemporary statements about specie movements in these months, because with the United States on a *de facto* gold standard and most of Continental Europe on a *de facto* silver standard, it was possible for one metal to be moving out while the other metal was moving in. For example, John Horsley Palmer reported to the Commons Committee of 1848: "During the whole period from the middle of May to the day of withdrawing the limitation of 14,000,000 l. [October 25, 1847] the foreign exchanges were in favour of the country" (Q. 1944). Yet Tooke shortly after the event, and Clapham in reviewing the period, spoke of the flow of gold to America in July, and from the weekly accounts in the *Economist* it would appear that gold was coming from the Continent and at the same time going out to the United States.

rather than to prevent it from extending credit when credit was needed. The reserve position improved in June as reserves increased faster than liabilities, although it is probable that the weakened position of a number of firms, going back to the speculation of the preceding two and a half years, was sensed in the City. When the "Petition of the Merchants, Bankers, and Traders of London against the Bank Act" [25] was presented on July 3, 1847, the statistical situation was not alarming. The banking reserve was £5,992,474—around 32 per cent of total liabilities of the Banking Department. For close to half the time, in the twelve years between the Bank charter investigation of 1832 and the Bank Act of 1844, the reserve ratio against notes and deposits combined had been as low as the reserve of the Banking Department in July 1847. This petition was, strictly interpreted, not a protest against the provisions of the act of 1844, but against the policy that the Bank had chosen to follow even though not required to do so by the act: rationing of credit rather than raising of the rate, and refusal to buy silver on any terms or to make advances on it.

Since the principal European countries were on a *de facto* silver standard, and since silver was extensively used in payments to and from the Orient, previous to 1844 the Bank not only held substantial amounts of silver, but its turnover of silver was greater, in relation to holdings, than its turnover of gold.[26] The Issue Department had made extensive use of the authority in the act of 1844 to include silver in its reserve, and in several weeks in 1846 and 1847 silver holdings had been over 20 per cent of its gold. This created a peculiar problem for the Bank. It could count silver as part of its reserve, but it could not redeem its notes in silver. Hence there was the possibility that the Issue Department, having acted legally and holding, say, a silver reserve of only 22 per cent of gold, would

---

[25] Reprinted in Gregory, *Select Statutes, Documents & Reports,* II, 2–7.

[26] A breakdown of the Bank's bullion in terms of gold and silver is given as of approximately the end of each year from 1833 to 1839 in appendix 24 of the *Report from the Select Committee on Banks of Issue,* 1840; and of its total bullion and coin in gold and silver on an average quarterly basis for 1825–1835 in appendix 14 of the *Report from the Select Committee of the House of Lords on the State of Agriculture,* 1836. Beginning September 7 1844, the Bank published each week the total gold coin and bullion and silver bullion in the Issue Department.

From 1825 to 1834 the percentage of silver to gold fluctuated widely; 11 per cent in the first quarter of 1825; 41 per cent in the last quarter of 1825; 25 per cent at the end of 1832; 4 per cent at the end of 1834; 16 per cent at the end of 1839; and 13 per cent on September 7, 1844. Monthly figures on purchases and sales of bullion from 1832 to 1857, given in appendix 8, *Committee on Bank Acts,* 1857, show that in a majority of the months through April 1848 turnover in relation to holdings was substantially greater for silver than for gold. Between then and the end of 1857 the Bank made no purchases of silver, except for £2500 in September 1852.

be put in the position of breaking the law by demands for redemption in gold that would raise the silver ratio to, say, 28 per cent. The Bank, apparently fearful that a demand for redemption of notes might create such a situation, in the words of the petition "refused either to buy or to lend money on this silver [that had arrived from the Pacific in payment for British manufactures] to the merchants who received it, stating that it held the full amount of silver bullion on which by law it was permitted to issue notes, and that it could take no more. Thus merchants, with silver in their possession, could not obtain bank notes to meet their engagements."

There was a touch of the dramatic, either in what the Bank told the merchants, or in what the merchants reported, for it is most unlikely that the Bank ever "held the full amount of silver bullion on which by law it was permitted to issue notes." In only two weekly statements in the three months preceding the presentation of the petition had the silver ratio exceeded 20 per cent, and in the six weekly statements immediately preceding the petition the ratio had not been over 18 per cent. There is no doubt, however, that the Bank was using the provisions of the act of 1844 as a reason for refusing to buy silver—it had bought none since October 1846, except for £58,678 in May 1847—or for extending credit to merchants holding silver, and that this was the principal grievance of the merchants against Bank policy at that time. Amending the silver rule was one of the two specific recommendations of the petition—"the expedience of so amending the Bank Charter Act, that a relaxing power may be lodged in the hands of the executive Government, and that the Bank may be permitted to issue notes on silver bullion without restriction."

This petition and its reception are symbolic of the situation that led to widespread protests against the Bank Act but failed to effect any legislative change. The signers of the petition were practical men and little concerned with the well-thought-out analysis of Wilson or with the possibility that the Bank, by making credit freely available but at a higher rate, could have supported the market even with the restrictions of the Bank Act. Their proposals, based on a particular experience with silver, had implications that, if the attitude in the *Economist* is typical, must have scandalized many influential critics of the Bank Act. The *Economist,* in a leading article on "The City Petition—The Bank Act of 1844," [27] gave its principal attention to the silver recommendations of the petition, and its reaction to even this mild straying from gold standard

[27] July 3, 1847, pp. 749–750.

purity is worth quoting as forecasting the increasing concern of the gold standard banking theorists about the ideas of many who were attacking the Bank Act: "That Lord Ashburton or any other advocate of the extra-ordinary doctrine of a double standard of gold and silver, should enter-tain the notion of the Bank of England issuing notes 'without restriction' on silver bullion we can well understand, but that those who demand that the Bank should 'retain its responsibility to *pay* its notes in gold'— should expect to receive notes in any amount in exchange for silver ap-pears to us a most inexplicable and unreasonable proposition." The anonymous answer to the petition,[28] drafted by Samuel Jones Loyd and Robert Torrens, added nothing of theory to the defense of the Bank Act, but was a persuasive piece of polemical writing. Its closing paragraph probably added to the doubts of many critics of the Bank Act as to how far a gold standard supporter, no matter how much he might disapprove of the theory of the act, should go in furthering the currency ideas of Birmingham: "The Birmingham philosophers are consistent reasoners, and have the sagacity to perceive that an arbitrary extension of the paper circulation is incompatible with the maintenance of a metallic standard. The inferior logicians who have signed the London petition, while de-manding the establishment of a double metallic standard, are unable to perceive that an extension of paper money through the exercise (under a protracted drain of bullion) of the relaxing power for which they pray, would render impracticable the maintenance of any metallic standard."

At the time the petition was presented the Bank appeared to have ridden out the storm insofar as it came from overseas. Harvest prospects were good, and gold was moving in. In late July there was again a small outflow of gold to the United States, but it was on the domestic scene that the trouble came. The decline in the price of wheat was, in the long run, doubtless an influence increasing the nation's specie reserves, but in the immediate crisis it created difficulties for merchants and foreign traders who had made commitments at higher prices. Early in August the Bank raised its minimum rate to 5½ per cent, still under the market, but continued its April policy of charging higher rates on some paper and refusing to handle other paper at any price, so that even the best firms had no assurance that they could count on credit in a crisis. In August several corn merchants failed and in September the crisis broke, and London failures were widespread in that month and in October.

---

[28] *The Petition of the Merchants, Bankers and Traders of London, against the Bank Charter Act; with Comments on each Clause* (London, 1847).

Tooke reported: "These *mercantile* failures, in number, and in the amount of property involved in them, were beyond all precedent in the commercial history of this country."[29] There were no bank suspensions until October, when eleven banks in the provinces went under, but none in London.[30]

Discounts went up from £8,528,000 on September 11 to £12,492,000 on October 23, but in this period the Bank sold government securities and reduced advances, so that its total credit increased by less than £1 million in these six weeks. Credit seems to have been largely on an *ad hoc* basis, without any clear-cut philosophy that would give assurance to merchants that sound assets could be turned into cash at a price. Some high-class acceptances that the Bank refused to discount paid a rate of 13 per cent in the market.[31] It was an internal demand for notes or gold that brought matters to a crisis. Thomas Birkbeck, a Yorkshire banker, told the Commons Committee of 1848 that the loss of public confidence and the fear of bank runs was such that he and other country bankers kept 75 to 100 per cent more reserves of notes and gold than was usual, and hence accommodations to the public had been materially lessened.[32]

In this situation the argument over which so many lances had been broken in preceding years, as to whether the Bank should differentiate between different types of foreign drains, was beside the point. On October 23, when the internal situation was at its worst and the Government was on the point of issuing its letter of October 25 authorizing the suspension of the Bank Act,[33] gold was flowing in, but the Banking reserve was slightly less than £2 million, or about 14 per cent of deposits and short-term liabilities. The situation was serious, but it was a public attitude rather than a banking statistic that made it critical. The Banking Department's reserve ratio not only was larger than the reserve ratio against notes and deposits of the undivided Bank had been in the crisis of 1825, but it was higher than it had been for several weeks in 1837 and again in 1839. It was not so much the low reserve of the Banking Department that brought on the troubles of 1847, but the knowledge of the large reserve in the Issue Department that could not be used. The prevailing sentiment was epitomized by an item in *Punch,* "The Obstruc-

[29] *History of Prices*, IV, 316.

[30] Clapham, *Bank of England*, II, 206.

[31] Tooke, *History of Prices*, IV, 317–318.

[32] Q. 5771–5773. Further evidence on the increase in holding of Bank notes by country banks and of hoarding by private parties was given by R. C. L. Bevan, a London banker (Q. 2265–2268).

[33] The letter is in Gregory, *Select Statutes, Documents & Reports,* II, 7–8.

tion in Threadneedle Street," and a cartoon on the facing page showing John Bull paralyzed by Peel waving the Bank Charter Act, and unable to touch £9 million close at hand:

Yesterday, Mrs. Banke, well known in the City as the "Old Lady of Threadneedle Street," came before the Lord Mayor to complain of an obstruction which had been laid at her door by a person by the name of Peel. The Court inquired whether she, in return, laid the obstruction at Peel's door. The old lady hoped the Court would not make fun of her. It was no joke.

The Lord Mayor asked what was the nature of the obstruction complained of?

Mrs. Banke said that it was a heap of rubbish which prevented her from getting into her cellar. She had upwards of nine millions of bullion in that cellar, of which she was unable to get at a mite or morsel; whilst, owing to the badness of the times, she was actually at her wits' end for a sovereign.

· · · · · ·

The Lord Mayor wished to know the nature of the rubbish, which, as she alleged, had been shot at her cellar-door by Peel.

The old lady said it was a parcel of stuff which was called Bank Charter. The rubbish had been carted at her door by Peel, at a time when he was the Government head-carter.

The Lord Mayor suggested that Mrs. Banke should apply to the present driver of the Government cart.

Mrs. Banke said that she had done so, but to no purpose. The one was as bad as the other; there was not a pin to choose between them; for what this one said, that one stuck to. She would be glad if his Lordship would order Peel to take his rubbish away.

The Lord Mayor regretted, that though he was the sovereign of the City he was not an absolute monarch: he had no power to remove an obstacle which was sanctioned by Act of Parliament.[34]

The Government action was taken only after delegations from Liverpool, members from Scotland and the northern counties, where the credit stringency was having serious employment effects, and the London private bankers had brought pressure for action. The *Circular to Bankers* also charged that the London bankers had contemplated, on the day the Government issued its letter of indemnity, a bankers' version of Francis Place's move of 1832, and had planned almost as a body to withdraw their deposits from the Bank.[35] The Bank, assured that the letter authorizing a suspension of the Bank Act would be issued on Monday the 25th, had discounted freely on Saturday. For a week discounts increased and the Banking Department's reserve fell further, but at no time

[34] Vol. XII, May 22, 1847, p. 220.
[35] No. 1049, October 29, 1847, p. 171.

did the Bank exceed the note-issue limit of the act of 1844. Before the end of October notes started to come back to the Bank, and by November 20 Banking Department reserves were over £4.5 million. On November 22, when the Government released the Bank from the obligation of the minimum rate of 8 per cent required by the letter of indemnity, the rate was dropped to 7 per cent. By the end of the year the Banking Department's reserve was over £8 million, higher than at any time since the first week of the year, and only a few hundred thousand pounds less than it had been when the Banking Department made its first report on September 7, 1844.

Controversy after the Crisis of 1847

The crisis left in its wake a renewal of the controversy over the principle of separation of the Bank into an Issue Department and a Banking Department and over the reserve requirements against notes. Parliamentary oratory flowed again in 1848, both Houses held investigations, and after the lean literary year of 1846 there was an outpouring of controversial pamphlets. This debate, as well as the one that followed the suspension of 1857, is a rich source of information on the theory, the attitudes, and the social philosophy that gave final form to the main outlines of pre-1914 orthodoxy. But on the technical point at issue—whether bank deposits should be considered as money, and whether there should be special reserve requirements against notes—little new was said. No one who had been active in the controversy up to 1844 came out and said that he was wrong. Even among those who had not been vocal on one side or the other, the frankness of Samuel Gurney, who told the committees of 1848 that he had originally believed in the act of 1844, but had changed his view in the light of experience,[36] was the exception. Critics of the act saw in the experience of 1847 confirmation of their worst fears, while its supporters saw in the Bank's policy up to the breaking of the crisis new evidence for their old contention that the Bank's discretion was a dangerous thing. Samuel Jones Loyd, George Warde Norman, J. Horsley Palmer, and Thomas Tooke told the committees that what had happened was a proof of the soundness of their respective views. Robert Torrens, in addition to writing a pamphlet around the middle of 1847 attempting to show that the Bank Act had not been repsonsible for the April crisis—*On the Operation of the Bank Charter Act of 1844*—and cooperating with Loyd the same year in drafting an answer to the Lon-

[36] *Commons Committee*, 1848, Q. 1617; *Lords Committee*, 1848, Q. 1166, 1274.

don petition, came to the defense of the act in *The Principles and Practical Operation of Sir Robert Peel's Bill of 1844 Explained* (1848). John Fullarton had a hand in a *Quarterly Review* article, "The Financial Pressure," [37] which praised "Mr. Fullarton's masterly treatise" and saw in recent events a confirmation of the warnings of Fullarton and Tooke.

From the point of view of modern banking theory and practice the case for treating all of the Bank's liabilities alike, or at least for vesting a discretionary power to exceed the fixed fiduciary issue in the Government or in the Bank in consultation with the Government, is so strong that it is hard, without sensing the crosscurrents of opinion of the time, to understand why no change was made. In the first place, Torrens, Loyd, and the Parliamentary defenders of the Bank Act exploited to the full the idea that the difficulty in which the Bank found itself in 1847 was the result of its reckless action in the two previous years. They made much of the idea that but for the restrictions of the Bank Act the situation that the Bank faced in 1847 would have been worse. The failure in the crisis of the governor and of two other directors of the Bank undoubtedly strengthened the position of the currency school by raising doubts in the minds of some who may not have understood the technical arguments whether it was wise to give more discretion over the nation's monetary affairs to those who could not handle their own finances.

It is probable, however, that the decisive influence in the decision against any change in the Bank Act was the feeling of many of its critics that an all-out attack on it would strengthen the hand of Birmingham and revive throughout the country latent forces that wanted to abandon the gold standard. Possibly critics of the act of 1819 boasted strength they did not have, and supporters of the act of 1844 may have used these critics of the gold standard as bogeymen to frighten gold standard men into standing by the act of 1844. Yet even when full allowance is made for this possibility, the evidence is impressive of widespread embers of dissatisfaction with the act of 1819, which would have needed but little to be fanned into major fires of revolt. Perronet Thompson, former editor of the *Westminster Review*, wrote in April 1847 to John Bowring: "I hold to my opinion that there will be mischief on the Currency question. I receive more half-mad pamphlets from Birmingham." [38] Matthias Attwood's anonymous pamphlet of 1823, *A Letter to Lord Archibald Hamilton, on Alterations in the Value of Money*, was reprinted in 1847. A

---

[37] Vol. LXXXI, June 1847, art. viii.
[38] L. G. Johnson, *General T. Perronet Thompson* (London, 1957), p. 265.

Birmingham delegation headed by George Frederick Muntz waited upon Lord John Russell, and the *Times* felt the event to be of enough significance to carry a leader criticizing the Birmingham ideas; the Birmingham Currency Reform Association sent a memorial to the Queen; the activities of the Liverpool Currency Reform Association prompted the *Economist* to expose its fallacies in two issues;[39] and the National Anti-Gold Law League held an organization meeting in Glasgow attended by 3000 persons.[40]

A number of pamphleteers, though concentrating on the act of 1844, spoke unfavorably of the act of 1819. The *Economist,* which had given the most reasoned criticism of that act, did not now join in the clamor for its repeal, said that its benefits and evils had been greatly exaggerated, stressed the importance of convertibility, and gave much attention to the activities of the Birmingham spokesmen. The position of Alexander Baring, now Lord Ashburton, although creditable to his independent powers of analysis and his freedom from narrow partisanship, probably weakened the drive against the act.[41] His remarks add to the picture of the Birmingham economists being considered enough of a menace so that the public should be warned against them: "Even the, to me, always unintelligible theories of the Birmingham school of philosophers are still maintained with perseverance by persons of great ability, who seem unconscious that, beyond the circle of their own town, the whole world is against them." [42] He indicated, however, that he still favored bimetallism. This put Ashburton in the position of being taken to task by the *Economist,*[43] whose analysis of the act of 1844 was much the same as his, and being praised for his criticism of the act of 1844 by *Blackwood's Edinburgh Magazine,* which was still calling for breaking the gold standard.[44]

In Parliament the Birmingham views received renewed publicity, principally from those who held them up to ridicule. Disraeli, in a long oration against the act in May 1847, before the crisis had broken, asked with rhetorical flourish of the protest of London bankers in 1844 against the Bank Act, "Who, did the House think, signed that document? Did

[39] November 4, 1848, p. 1246; November 18, 1848, pp. 1302–1303.

[40] See Jonathan Duncan, *The National Anti-Gold Law League* (London, 1847).

[41] *The Financial and Commercial Crisis Considered* (London, 1847).

[42] *Financial and Commercial Crisis,* p. 4.

[43] July 3, 1847, p. 750.

[44] "Sir Robert Peel and the Currency," vol. LXII, July 1847, p. 119. The article was written by W. E. Aytoun.

they think it was even the two members for Birmingham?"[45] The remark undoubtedly was intended to be clever, but the emotions, if not the logic, of many members did not give the negative answer that Disraeli expected, but rather a troubled "Yes." When the Commons considered the proposal for a committee, James Wilson, in his maiden Parliamentary speech, spoke of the increasing doubts among members about a fixed price of gold;[46] several members put in a good word for the silver standard; and J. C. Herries, though opposed to the act of 1844, feared that criticism of it might lead to an attack on the act of 1819 and voted against appointment of a committee.[47]

Parliamentary Committees of 1848

In the two committees of 1848 Loyd and Bank of England officials defended the acts of 1844 and 1845, but the majority of other witnesses were critical of the act of 1844. The Scottish witnesses were at one in opposition to the acts of 1845, although their general approach was more a defense of Scotland against legislative interference from Westminster than an economic analysis. The *First Report* of the Commons Committee recommended that "it is not expedient to make any alteration in the Bank Act of 1844," and the *Second Report* recommended, "With regard to the Acts of 1845 . . . it is not expedient to make any alteration in their provisions."[48]

The Commons Committee by a vote of 13 to 11 rejected Joseph Hume's motion: "That in the opinion of this Committee, the laws for regulating the issues of bank notes payable on demand aggravated the commercial distress in England in the year 1847." A series of other amendments to the same effect were defeated by about the same vote. The minority was a strange coalition that included two critics of the act of 1819, Richard Spooner and E. S. Cayley, who shared an opposition to the repeal of the Corn Laws, and two others who were friendly toward silver, Thomas Baring and Lord Bentinck. All of the majority were defenders of the gold standard. Neither a report by Spooner calling for a repeal of the act of 1819 nor one by Cayley, which, though less specific, pointed the same way, came to a vote. Substitute motions by Hume and Spooner, critical of the act of 1845, were defeated 5 to 4 and 8 to 4.

---

[45] 3 *Hansard* LXXXXII, 652, May 10, 1847.
[46] 3 *Hansard* XCV, 417, November 17, 1847.
[47] 3 *Hansard* XCV, 627–628, December 3, 1847; 1032–1034, December 13, 1847.
[48] The *First Report*, the proposed amendments, and the voting on the various amendments are in vol. I, pp. iii–xxii; the *Second Report*, the proposed amendments, and the voting are in vol. II, pp. ii, xiii–xiv.

The Lords Committee report, though stressing "the Duty and Obligation of maintaining at all Times the practical convertibility of the Bank Note," held that "the recent Panic was materially aggravated by the Operation of that Statute [Bank Act of 1844] and by the Proceedings of the Bank itself," and that "the Inflexibility of the Rule prescribed by the restrictive Clauses of the Act of 1844 is indefensible, when equally applied to a State of varying Circulation." It recommended amendment "so far as its restrictive Clauses are concerned," [49] which included leaving the Bank free to decide how much of its reserve to hold in silver. In support of the view that the Bank should expand its issue in the face of an internal run it quoted the Bullion Report, and further bolstered its position by citing the individual opinions of the three authors of that report—Francis Horner, William Huskisson, and Henry Thornton.

Parliamentary Discussion of the Bank Acts and Committee Reports

In the meantime, while the 1848 committees were hearing evidence, the Commons defeated 163 to 142 a motion by J. C. Herries that called for repeal of the limitations of Bank issues in the act of 1844 and for repeal of the acts of 1845. Almost every "soft currency" man supported the motion, from outright opponents of the metallic standard, like Muntz and Spooner,[50] to those who simply had kind thoughts for silver. After the reports of the committees had been presented, Herries moved that the Commons consider them.[51] Two of the principal speeches supporting the motion came from C. N. Newdegate and Spooner, Tory supporters of the Corn Laws and critics of the act of 1819, while more moderate critics of the act of 1844 had little to say. In answer to Spooner's speech Peel said: "It may be thought by some that these are needless comments on the doctrines of my hon. Friend—that those doctrines meet with few supporters. That may be true so far as this House is concerned. In this House my hon. Friend may be in a small minority; but out of this House, of those who talk about the currency, and write about the currency, the vast majority is with my hon. Friend. Nine tenths of these, out of this House, who want a change in the currency want substantially that which my hon. Friend wants, namely, issues of paper without the check of convertibility." [52]

Peel's desire to secure the support of gold standard men may have made

[49] The section of the Lords Committee report entitled "Remedial Measures recommended by the Witnesses" is reprinted in Gregory, II, 36–46.

[50] The debate is in 3 *Hansard* XCVI, 803–867, February 17, 1848.

[51] The debate is in 3 *Hansard* CI, 388–432, August 23, 1848.

[52] 3 *Hansard* CI, 418–419, August 23, 1848.

him exaggerate the "vast majority" that was simply waiting for a chance to restore an inconvertible currency. In any case, however, despite a Lords report calling for amendment of the act of 1844, and a Commons report that with a turn of two votes would have done the same, Herries' motion was negatived without a formal vote. Gold standard defenders who believed that the act of 1844 should be changed apparently held back from pressing the attack when they considered their Birmingham supporters. The situation is suggestive of the attitude that tradition associates with the Duke of Wellington—he had no fear of the enemy, but the very thought of his allies filled him with terror. For close to a decade after 1848 latent fears of renewed Birmingham attacks on the act of 1819 had a restraining influence on many who questioned the theory of the act of 1844. There are suggestions of this in the *Economist*,[53] and James Pennington wrote to Sir C. E. Trevelyan on November 22, 1855: "There is just now a widespread clamour calling for the repeal of that Act [Bank Act of 1844], which clamour, if it prevails, will I think, be followed by a clamour, equally loud, for doing away altogether with the obligation of specie payments."[54]

It is well to put the Birmingham currency movement in historical perspective. In the late nineteenth and early twentieth century the Birmingham economists, insofar as they were even remembered, were generally regarded as simply one aspect of the lunatic fringe found in all societies. After the deflations of the early 1920's and the 1930's, and the discussion of aggregate demand stimulated by Keynes, they came to be considered as original but erratic thinkers who in an unorganized way had sensed problems that economists had virtually ignored for three quarters of a century. But Birmingham ideas were not important in the sense that they influenced the revival of thinking on deflation and aggregate demand, and in any post-1920 discussion of these problems they figure only in footnotes. The significant influence of Birmingham on economic policy was the negative one of ensuring the maintenance of the act of 1844 and of creating not only in England, but in many parts of the world where the names of Attwood, Muntz, Spooner, and Scholefield were unknown, the picture of the Bank Act of 1844 as the pattern for a central bank.

Increasing Acceptance of Existing Legislation

The investigations of 1848 and the Parliamentary debates were the last

[53] In particular the article "The Bank Charter Act, 1844," October 20, 1855, pp. 1145–1146.
[54] Letter in collection of James Pennington's papers at University of Chicago Library.

organized and substantial challenge to the act of 1844, although there were new Parliamentary committees in 1857 and 1858. In 1857 and 1866 came further authorizations to suspend the Bank Act. But from 1848 until the 1870's the legislative history is simply a repetition of abortive attempts at change. Increasingly the forces of tradition and the spirit of Scottish nationalism were the deciding influences, with the decision, whether today regarded as good or bad, made not because of economic analysis but in spite of it.

The idea of a State Bank, proposed by David Ricardo and often mentioned in the discussion that preceded the act of 1844, was one that many, including solid citizens of conservative views, played with over the next thirty years.[55] In 1854, when the act of 1844 permitted the Government to amend the Bank's charter, remarks in the Lords would suggest that in the clubs and banking circles the possibility of a State Bank was being noised about, but Lord Granville denied that the Government had any intention of asking for such an arrangement.[56] It is evident, however, that in 1854 and for over a decade after persons high in the Government gave serious consideration to having all notes issued by a State Bank.[57]

In 1856, the Commons defeated 115 to 68 a motion by Muntz, seconded by Spooner, "to inquire how far the present monetary system was in accordance with the requirements of the country, and to consider if it could not be improved and amended."[58] A similar motion in the Lords, but not under Birmingham aegis, was withdrawn without coming to a vote.[59] The Chancellor of the Exchequer, Sir Cornewall Lewis, shortly afterward informed the Commons: "The Government had no intention

---

[55] Since the question of a State Bank was closely associated with the controversy about the role of the Bank of England, discussion of the theory back of these suggestions is postponed until Chapter IX.

[56] 3 *Hansard* CXXXIII, 1215–1225, June 2, 1854.

[57] In the Kress Library at Harvard University are six Confidential Prints, printed at the Foreign Office for the use of the Cabinet, of correspondence and memoranda between 1856 and 1865 on the legal, economic, and political issues involved in turning the note issue over to a State Bank. One of these, *A Memorandum on the Question of Establishing a National State Bank*, by George Arbuthnot, an official of the Treasury, was published as an appendix of the *Report from the Select Committee on the Bank Acts*, 1858, but to my knowledge the others have not been publicly printed or noted by economists: (1) Report on the Privileges of the Bank of England, December 22, 1854; (2) Correspondence between Earl Grey and Mr. G. Arbuthnot, August 1 and 2, 1856; (3) Correspondence between Mr. Gladstone and Mr. G. Arbuthnot, August and September 1856; (4) Correspondence between Lord J. Russell and Mr. G. Arbuthnot, 1857–1858; (5) Correspondence between Mr. Gladstone and Mr. Arbuthnot on the Bank Act and Money Market in 1864. Most, and possibly all, of this material was printed in 1867 and 1868, suggesting that the Government was then again considering a State Bank.

[58] 3 *Hansard* CXL, 1481–1544, February 28, 1856.

[59] 3 *Hansard* CXLI, 551–564, April 7, 1856.

at present to propose any measure for altering the Bank Charter Act of 1844," [60] and two months later said that the Government "had come to no decision" as to whether it intended in the coming session to move for a committee to investigate the bank acts.[61] In February 1857 the Government moved for and secured the appointment of a committee to investigate the acts of 1844 and 1845.[62] Later in the year, after a crisis in November had again led the Government to issue a letter of indemnity to the Bank, the Government asked for a new committee. This motion produced a debate[63] that gave Lewis, still Chancellor of the Exchequer, an opportunity to say that Peel had hoped to get rid of all English bank notes but those of the Bank, and had probably wanted to get rid of Scottish and Irish notes, and that there had been strong suggestions in 1844 that the state issue all paper money. But he added that the Government now had no intention of proposing any of these changes.[64] Disraeli used the occasion for sallies at the act of 1844, and although he looked on "the Parliamentary literature of England as one of the proudest products of the national mind" he was against a committee that would simply whitewash the act.[65] Gladstone also opposed a committee on the opposite ground that it might call in question the act of 1844,[66] but the Government rode over this opposition 295 to 117. The hearings before the committees of 1857 and 1858 tell much about the development of monetary and banking thinking, but their reports were not debated in Parliament. In 1861 the financial arrangements with the Bank for handling the public debt were continued with minor amendment.[67] In 1864 a bill to permit new banks in Scotland to issue notes on a 100 per cent gold reserve inspired more praise of Scottish banking, but it was withdrawn before coming to a vote;[68] and proposals to make Bank of England notes legal tender in Scotland produced nothing beyond more evidence—if that was needed—that north of the border local pride and not economic theory called the tune on banking legislation.[69]

[60] 3 *Hansard* CXLII, 277, May 9, 1856.

[61] 3 *Hansard* CXLIII, 1040–1042, July 18, 1856.

[62] 3 *Hansard* CXLIV, 259–321, February 6, 1857.

[63] 3 *Hansard* CXLVIII, 580–672, December 11, 1857.

[64] 3 *Hansard* CXLVIII, 580–604, December 11, 1857.

[65] 3 *Hansard* CXLVIII, 604–632, December 11, 1857.

[66] 3 *Hansard* CXLVIII, 644–654, December 11, 1857.

[67] 24 & 25 Vict., c. 3. The correspondence between Gladstone and the Bank that preceded these arrangements is published in P.P. 1861, (12) XXXIV. Clapham, *Bank of England*, II, 255–256, summarizes the negotiations over the arrangements.

[68] 3 *Hansard* CLXXIV, 1727–1752, April 27, 1864.

[69] 3 *Hansard* CLXXV, 602–603, May 13, 1864; CLXXVI, 109–126, June 22, 1864. Similar proposals were made at other times but produced little debate.

In 1865, for the first time since 1845, the Government sponsored substantive banking legislation. The act of 1844, while freezing maximum note issue in England and Wales at the then existing level, had provided not only for the Bank to take over two thirds of the lapsed issues of failed banks, of banks that liquidated, and of partnerships that increased their partners above six, but also had contemplated the voluntary discontinuance of private note issues by agreement with the Bank of England. Peel and those who shared his views were disappointed in their hopes that these issues would soon disappear. By November 1855 the issues of 54 of 280 issuing banks had lapsed, but in large part they were smaller banks, and the total of lapsed notes was only £828,227 out of a total authorized issue in 1844 of £8,631,647.[70] In 1855, Lewis, the Chancellor of the Exchequer, was in correspondence with the Bank about the remaining private issues, but nothing came of it.[71] By January 1857 only eight private banks, and no joint-stock banks, had voluntarily compounded with the Bank of England for the discontinuance of their issues.[72] In the late fifties and early sixties lapsed issues were about the same as in the previous decade. In 1865 the Government moved to do by direct action what time and attrition had not done. A bill, amended from its original form because of banker objections, provided for a 1 per cent tax on all private issues. After a debate that indicated powerful opposition by bankers, which the Government apparently could have defeated but decided not to on grounds of higher political strategy, the bill was withdrawn.[73]

Several private bills to change the banking laws and the coinage laws made little headway over the next ten years. In 1866, Gladstone, Chancellor of the Exchequer, in reply to a question whether the Government had any intention in that Parliamentary session of proposing an amendment to permit the Bank "to increase its issues against securities," said that the Government "would not be disposed to enable the Bank to resume that system [discretionary issue] either in the present Session or in any other."[74] Birmingham spokesmen offered no more challenges to the gold standard, although Philip Henry Muntz, brother of G. F. Muntz, criticized the Government for having the Maria Teresa dollar needed in

[70] Details are given in *Committee on Bank Acts,* 1857, pt. ii, app. 9.

[71] Clapham, II, 250, cites the Bank's records.

[72] *Committee on Bank Acts,* 1857, app. 21, p. 238.

[73] The bill was introduced by the Chancellor of the Exchequer on February 10, 1865, 3 *Hansard* CLXXVII, 150–155; debated on February 23, 1865 (CLXXVII, 608–632), May 1, 1865 (CLXXVII, 1247–1273), May 25, 1865 (CLXXIX, 800–828); and withdrawn on June 1, 1865 (CLXXIX, 1123–1124).

[74] 3 *Hansard* CLXXXI, 448, February 13, 1866.

connection with the Abyssinian War coined at the Mint instead of by private enterprise in Birmingham.[75] The third authorization to suspend the Bank Act, at the time of the Overend, Gurney crisis in 1866, produced no Parliamentary investigation. In view of the nature of the crisis—an internal panic associated with the collapse of the greatest private banking house in England, which under new management had carried on most questionable operations—the public discussion that followed in large part bypassed the banking system. There was no extended debate on monetary and banking policy between 1865 and 1873. The stronger became the economic argument for overhauling the acts of 1844 and 1845, the stronger became the political case for leaving them untouched. Probably few would have put the case in the language that John Culmer used in an anonymous publication in 1869, but he expressed a national attitude: "If a committee of twelve or twenty good business men (I don't mean philosophers or professors) could be selected, and were to study the subject closely for a twelve-month, and could find a plan that could compare with our British coinage and currency (or, in comparison, to come within a hundred miles of it), the writer would be willing to submit to any forfeiture of penalty or liberty." [76]

Debate over Proposal for a Royal Commission

On March 25, 1873, the Commons had a field day on money and banking.[77] George Anderson, member for Glasgow, which had been a center of continual restlessness about the restrictive provisions of the act of 1844, moved for a royal commission on the bank acts:

We have set up gold for our idol—we worship it with a senseless superstition. If a few millions of gold go out from the Bank we straightway plunge into insane panic, depreciate all our property, except gold—probably a hundred times the amount of gold that has gone out; raise our hire for money four or five times what it was before; and at last, when our commerce is in collapse, when one half of our merchants are ruined and the other half on the brink of it, we give the Bank leave to issue a few more credit notes, as the only refuge from universal bankruptcy. Greater folly, greater insanity, greater crime could hardly be. More poverty, more misery, more broken hearts and more desolated homes, are due to this one cause than to all others put together.[78]

Before the day was over more than a dozen members had gotten in on

---

[75] 3 *Hansard* CCI, 1869–1875, June 10, 1870.
[76] *A Defence of the British Currency* (London, 1869), p. 42.
[77] 3 *Hansard* CCXV, 111–157.
[78] 3 *Hansard* CCXV, 117.

the debate. Suggestions were made for requiring the deposit of consols against the issue of private banks, for a State Bank, for larger reserves for the Bank of England, and for a relaxing power in the act of 1844. An amendment was proposed for a select committee rather than a royal commission. After the members had talked themselves out, the Chancellor of the Exchequer, Robert Lowe, took things in hand. He "gathered from the views expressed that the House had no wish to interfere with or alter the main principles of the Act of 1844. Such a declaration, supported as it had been by such admirable reasoning, was not only an intellectual treat, but of real solid advantage to the commercial and free institutions of the country." [79] On his promise that he would make an inquiry into some of the problems that had been raised, both the motion and the amendment were withdrawn. Just what the Chancellor did is not clear, but presumably he had some private talks at the club with the management of the Bank of England and with the heads of the joint-stock and private banks. In any case, it must have satisfied the interested members, for in the next two years nothing more on banking legislation was discussed in Parliament.

Controversy over Branches of Scottish Banks in England

The final challenge to the Peel program came in 1875, and this time it was the Scots who threatened the live and let live attitude toward existing legislation. The combined effects of the acts of 1844 and 1845 had been to leave the Scottish and Irish banks with privileges that the English banks did not have. English banks could under no circumstances issue additional notes; Scottish and Irish banks could make such issues on the basis of 100 per cent reserve, but this was no real restriction, in view of the lack of any reserve requirement against deposits or against the note issues as of 1845. Aside from this purely legal situation, the difference in the banking customs north and south of the Tweed made the impact of legislative provisions, on their face nondiscriminatory as between England and Scotland, unequal in the two countries. At least so it was claimed by some in Scotland. In England the prohibition on the creation of new banks of issue apparently was no serious obstacle to the establishment of banks of deposit. Deposit banking was increasingly important in relation to note issue, and the legal tender Bank of England notes were readily accepted throughout England. In Scotland a larger proportion of bank advances were made in notes, and Bank of England

[79] 3 *Hansard* CCXV, 147.

notes were not legal tender and in fact were almost boycotted by public opinion. It was argued with considerable plausibility that it was impossible, as a practical matter, for any new bank to be established in Scotland, and that hence the eleven Scottish banks existing in 1844 had been given a monopoly. The appeal of this argument was increased by the fact that no new bank had been established in Scotland since 1844. The controversy, however, was one between Scots, for law or no law it was unlikely that any one south of the border would have invaded the Scottish banking field. A few comments had come out of Scotland about monopoly,[80] but the Scots who were unhappy seem to have been a minority, and the English were too practical a people to interfere, simply on grounds of theory, when it was reported that some Scots were exploiting other Scots.

The picture took on a new aspect when in 1874 the Clydesdale Bank established branches in Cumberland and planned to establish branches in London. The City of London moved to challenge the invaders from the North. George Goschen, with the joint sponsorship of Thomas M. Weguelin and Thomas C. Baring, introduced the Bankers' Act Amendment Bill, which would have applied substantially the same regulations to Scottish as to English banks. Then followed a familiar Parliamentary maneuver: Sir S. H. Northcote, Chancellor of the Exchequer, felt that the subject should be referred to a select committee, and on this understanding Goschen agreed not to press the bill. But the Pandora's box both of Scottish local pride and of the principle of Peel so long muffled by political expediency—that in the last analysis the State had full and absolute rights over paper money—had been opened. Before the speeches were finished more words had been used than in any monetary and banking debate since 1858, and some strong statements of principle had been made on behalf of both views.[81] The Scottish position was stated by Lyon Playfair, representing the universities of Edinburgh and St. Andrews: "The Scotch banks have no fear that any Government will interfere with their paper currency. If a Government desired to make the Scotch people Home Rulers, I can give them a double receipt for their speedy conversion. Threaten to suppress Presbytery, and threaten to suppress

[80] As was suggested in the Commons debate of April 27, 1864, 3 *Hansard* CLXXIV, 1727–1752. This idea also appears in Robert Somers, *The Errors of the Banking Acts of 1844–45* (Glasgow, 1857), p. 65, and in his *Scotch Banks and System of Issue* (Edinburgh, 1873), p. 166; and in the testimony before the Committee on Banks of Issue, 1875, of Charles Gairdner, manager of the Union Bank of Scotland (Q. 955, 1422), and of Walter Bagehot (Q. 8244–8245).

[81] The discussion is in 3 *Hansard* CCXXII, 1969–2030, March 17, 1875.

the £1 note. One would be about as dangerous a proceeding as the other."[82]

Gladstone in reply did not raise the question of the Presbytery, but said that, speaking as the only living member of the Cabinet of 1844, he knew that Peel had proceeded on the principle that "the State ought ultimately to get into its own hands the whole business of issue, and that that course should be taken upon the first favourable opportunity." [83] The Chancellor of the Exchequer was emphatic that the Government "will maintain the principle, that the issue of notes is the right of the State, and ought to be granted only upon such terms as are compatible with the public safety and convenience, while, on the other hand, banking should be as free and open as possible."[84] He showed no desire, however, to provoke the legislative battle that almost certainly would have followed had the Government tried to translate principle into action, and the Select Committee on Banks of Issue was appointed.

Select Committee of 1875 on Banks of Issue

Over 8000 questions and answers brought out much detail on banking practices but added little to the theory of banking. The one basic discussion of banking principles came in the examination of Walter Bagehot, the last witness, who as an aftermath to the real concern of the committee about the Scottish situation was asked some searching questions about English note issue. His judgment was: "It is not such a system as anybody would propose to establish but I do not think it does any harm to the community; and, as compared with the total abolition of the provincial issues, I should think it had better be left as it is" (Q. 9979).

The questions that Goschen put to Charles Gairdner, manager of the Union Bank of Scotland, designed to bring out that the "monopoly" of Scottish banks set up by the Bank Acts was limiting competition, raised no fundamental issue of banking theory, but are revealing as showing that "nonprice competition" is not a twentieth century invention:

928. Q. Will you explain to the Committee the phrase "there is a keen competition amongst the Scotch banks" as used in one of the statements put forward by one of the Scotch banks; and will you also explain how that competition acts?

A. In the first place it has been explained that the banks agree upon a tariff, as it were, of rates; and upon the basis of that tariff a very keen competition is

[82] 3 *Hansard* CCXXII, 1983–1984, March 17, 1875.

[83] 3 *Hansard* CCXXII, 1985, March 17, 1875.

[84] 3 *Hansard* CCXXII, 2024, March 17, 1875.

maintained; the tariff, as I think I have shown, brings to the banks a very small margin of profits, and the competition is based upon the tariff.

929. Q. In a general sense, competition means that by offering either higher or lower terms you compete against each other; but, as I understand, you all offer the same terms to the public?

A. The same terms.

930. Q. Will you explain what form the competition takes; you do not either raise or lower your terms against each other, as I understand?

A. No, we do not.

931. Q. Neither as regards interest nor as regards commission?

A. No.

932. Q. There is the strictest agreement, I believe between the banks?

A. Quite so.

933. Q. Is there any bank in Scotland that stands aloof from the combination.

A. No.

The apparent understanding by English and Scots alike that the question of the control of deposit banking was taboo resulted in a theoretical sterility in much of the discussion. The more firmly the Government stated the principle of the absolute right of the State over the note issue, the more completely it seemed to abdicate any claim to regulate, or even to ask for information about, deposits. The committee of 1837 had made clear that it expected information from banks of deposit and enforced its demands, but when in 1875 the question was put to Frederick Seebohm, a private banker, "May I ask what is the amount of your deposits?" he replied: "Being a private banker I am afraid that I must decline to answer that question" (Q. 4927). No member of the committee challenged this position.

The committee simply transmitted its hearings to the House, with the comment, "They have not had time to prepare a Report thereon in the present Session, and they consequently recommend their reappointment next year." The Commons did not reappoint the committee, there was no further Parliamentary discussion of the invasion of the Scottish banks, and undoubtedly some suitable compromise was worked out at the clubs and on the long weekends. The acts of 1844 and 1845 remained untouched by new legislation, and were not even threatened by select committees, until the aftermath of Sarajevo created a situation where the old order had to go, no matter how well it had served its generation or how hallowed the traditions that hung over it.

VIII

EVOLUTION OF MONETARY AND BANKING THEORY, 1845–1875

THE decision after 1845 to make no substantive legislative changes
was not the result of analytical apathy. The failure to act was
accompanied by a continuous discussion in Parliamentary debate
and committees, in periodicals and newspapers, in books and pamphlets,
and in the new societies that were giving increasing attention to economic
problems.[1] This literature not only helps to explain the theory back of
the conclusion that it was better to leave well enough alone, but it also
throws light on the adjustments in practice and tradition that made it
possible for the developing center of world finance to grow and prosper
with its old legislation unchanged.

Theory of International Adjustment

Belief in the gold standard, on which all supporters and most critics
of the act of 1844 were in agreement, of necessity called for some theory,
explicit or implicit, of the appropriate action necessary to alter the relation
of international receipts and payments when there was pressure on the
foreign exchanges. To a large degree the banking school simply evaded
this issue. John Fullarton, and to a lesser extent Thomas Tooke, seemed
to have assumed that if banks loaned only on sound assets British prices
never would get out of line with world prices, and hence that drains of
gold would never be a serious problem. Underlying this idea were traces
of an almost mystical belief in a manifest economic destiny of Great

---

[1] The Cambridge Philosophical Society, although its *Transactions* date from 1819, published almost no economic material until the 1850's, with the exception of William Whewell's "Mathematical Exposition of Some Doctrines of Political Economy," and "Mathematical Exposition of Some of the Leading Doctrines in Mr. Ricardo's *Principles of Political Economy*," in 1829 and 1831. The British Association for the Advancement of Science was founded in 1831; the Manchester Statistical Society in 1833; the Statistical Society of London, which later became the Royal Statistical Society, in 1834; and the Dublin Statistical Society, which soon became the Statistical and Social Inquiry Society of Ireland, in 1847.

Britain, and consequently in a long-run pound shortage. If banks acted wisely practical men need not worry about the long-term condition of the British exchanges.

The currency school, and in particular Samuel Jones Loyd and Robert Torrens, had based much of their argument on the assumption of an adjustment through price changes induced by monetary policy. With the continuation of the act of 1844, by the 1860's there was a tacit acceptance on the part of a large part of the public—both the man of affairs and the academic economist—that this was the case. This seems to have come about as follows. The British balance of payments, under the act of 1844, had adjusted reasonably well. Since the supporters of the act argued that adjustment was brought about by price changes induced by monetary policy, to a practical-minded people the proposition that price changes were the adjusting mechanism was a satisfactory explanation. As the years passed after 1850, and as the inconvertible currencies of the United States and many countries of Europe and South America were depreciated on the foreign exchanges, observation of this strengthened the British view that it was in monetary expansion, and not in the subtleties of demand change or crop failure, that the cause of balance of payments disturbances was to be found.

This explanation of the maintenance of international equilibrium through price changes was given prestige by its acceptance and lucid explanation by John Stuart Mill in his *Principles of Political Economy*. Mill had lined up with the banking school against the act of 1844, but his basic theoretical position was different from that of Tooke and Fullarton, or even of James Wilson. Mill recognized the monetary significance of deposits, and felt that not all short-term disturbances were to be handled by commodity price changes. But on the ability of the monetary authorities to affect prices and on the necessity to do this, even at the expense of deflation, if the exchanges were to be restored after a disturbance of international price relations, Mill's analysis was closer to that of Loyd and Torrens than to that of Tooke, Fullarton, and Wilson. He wrote, in a passage since read by tens of thousands of students:

And if the balance due is of small amount, and is the consequence of some merely casual disturbance in the ordinary course of trade, it is soon liquidated in commodities, and the account adjusted by means of bills, without the transmission of any bullion. Not so, however, when the excess of imports above exports, which has made the exchange unfavourable, arises from permanent cause. In that case, what disturbed the equilibrium must have been the state of prices, and it can only be restored by acting on prices. It is impossible that prices should be such as to invite to an excess of imports, and yet that the exports should be kept permanently up to the imports by the extra profit on exportation derived from the premium on bills; for if the exports were kept up to the imports, bills would not be at a premium, and the extra profit would not exist. It is through the prices of commodities that the correction must be administered.

Disturbances, therefore, of the equilibrium of imports and exports, and consequent disturbances of the exchange, may be considered as of two classes; the one casual or accidental, which, if not on too large a scale, correct themselves through the premium on bills, without any transmission of the precious metals; the other arising from the general state of prices, which cannot be corrected without the subtraction of actual money from the circulation of one of the countries, or an annihilation of credit equivalent to it; since the mere transmission of bullion (as distinguished from money), not having any effect on prices, is of no avail to abate the cause from which the disturbance proceeded.[2]

It is little wonder, when spokesmen for the act of 1844 said that credit policy regulated the exchanges by altering commodity prices, and the leading economist of the age, though a critic of the act, apparently supported the idea, that economists of the twentieth century should talk of the classical "specie-flow price-adjustment mechanism."

To my knowledge no one made any attempt in the year 1845–1875 to test statistically the mechanism of international adjustment, with the exception of a very simple and casual analysis by J. G. Hubbard, comparing specie movements and the prices of fifteen commodities in the period 1834–1856.[3] However, witnesses before the committees of 1848, 1857, and 1858, and articles in the *Economist* and the *Bankers' Magazine,* would suggest that men who knew the City, whether supporters or critics of the act of 1844, when pressed as to details, stressed not commodity price changes but interest rate changes as the cause of international adjustment. And insofar as they did talk about commodity price changes they generally had in mind changes in the prices at which merchants sold already produced goods, and not changes in the costs of production of new goods.

James Morris, governor of the Bank of England, was one of the few Parliamentary witnesses to give a close approximation[4] of the twentieth century version of adjustment through changes in the monetary costs of production in England and abroad based on Mill's *Principles* and

---

[2] Bk. III, ch. 20, sec. 3. The quotation is from the seventh edition (London, 1871).
[3] Hubbard turned over his tables of bullion flows and price movements to the Committee on Banks of Issue, 1857, Q. 2400, but they were not published.
[4] In particular Q. 2277–3315.

amplified by Professor F. W. Taussig.[5] And in the case of Morris, who was not a particularly acute witness, what he said about commodity price changes was not so much in organized analysis as in statements forced out of him by the persistent, adroit, and leading questions of E. P. Cayley, a critic of the act of 1819, who was trying to establish the point that restriction of credits by the Bank in the face of an unfavorable exchange created unemployment and drove down prices. Furthermore, Morris also mentioned security movements as a contributing factor in adjustment.

In the statements of virtually all other witnesses, even supporters of the currency principle, the picture of adjustment was through international capital movements; increased exports because of the urgency to raise funds; or decreased imports because of the unavailability or high cost of credit to importers. Loyd might write in his pamphlets about price changes restoring the exchanges, and might tell the Committee on Bank Acts of 1857: "I have never seen any reason to alter any of the opinions which I have ever expressed upon the subject of the monetary affairs of the country, from the commencement of the year 1837 down to the present time; every opinion which I have expressed consecutively, appears to me to have been fully verified by the course of public events" (Q. 3644). But under cross-examination it became evident that in Loyd's view higher discount rates restored the balance primarily through security movements and the inability or unwillingness of importers to finance imports (Q. 3806–3809), although when the question "The natural effect of money being more stringent is to lower the price of goods?" was then put, he replied, "Yes, that is the principle at the bottom" (Q. 3810). Yet one gets the feeling that in the mind of Loyd the banker, as distinguished from Loyd the spokesman for the act of 1844, "the principle at the bottom" rarely was called into play. Later in the same hearings he gave an outline of short-run adjustment through capital flows (Q. 4044–4046), which differed but little from the explanation of such men as Horsley Palmer and Thomas Tooke.

The closest approach of any witness to an organized presentation of the familiar stereotype of specie-flow price-adjustment analysis came from J. G. Hubbard, governor of the Bank in 1853–1855, to the Committee on

[5] This was first stated in detail by Taussig in "International Trade under Depreciated Paper: A Contribution to Theory," *Quarterly Journal of Economics*, XXXI, 380–403 (May 1917), and further developed in his *International Trade* (New York, 1927), ch. 17. The familiarity of American economists with the specie-flow price-adjustment analysis and the belief that this was the accepted classical analysis also owes much to Taussig's influence as a teacher, by which this analysis became part of the oral tradition in the United States.

Bank Acts of 1857. But Hubbard presented the analysis simply to ridicule it. Much of what he said is suggestive of modern criticism, based upon elasticity assumptions, that monetary policy cannot influence favorably the relation of the value of exports and imports of goods and services:

If a drain of bullion does take place, and if, according to their theory, the value of all commodities were affected, the result would be, according to their idea, an export of goods in order to restore the amount of our claims upon the rest of the commercial world, and to recover our treasure; but if you measure the effect of a fall of prices upon the value of such commodities, you will find that it has the contrary effect, lowering the amount of our claims upon the rest of the world, instead of increasing it. Imagine, for instance, that our exports were 100,000,000 l. annually, and that a fall of prices of 10 per cent took place in consequence of the export of bullion, according to the prices theory, so far from our having a larger claim upon foreigners we should have a less claim, because we should reduce *pro tanto* the amount of value of the goods sent to them. And supposing that the prices of our exports would be lessened, the effect which took place here (according to that notion of a fall of prices by the export of bullion) is reversed abroad. There they have got our bullion, and therefore their prices would be higher; so that we should have at home to take a diminished price for our imports; so that the theory appears to me really to break down with reference to the effects which are supposed. I believe that the effect of the export of bullion upon the rate of prices has no reference whatever to the prices of commodities. It has an effect, and a very important one, upon the price of interest-bearing securities, because, as the rate of interest varies the value of commodities which embodied that interest is necessarily powerfully affected . . . But the action upon prices I totally disbelieve; I think it is untenable in theory, and irreconcilable with facts. (Q. 2400)

The position of Hubbard in 1857 is indicative of the mixture of analysis, tradition, and political realism that, with the passage of years, influenced views on the act of 1844. Hubbard was critical of the theory originally used to justify it, yet in 1857 was an enthusiastic supporter of the act. He felt that the separation of the Bank into two departments "has been, both in a scientific and in a practical view, of the utmost importance and highly beneficial," and spoke of "the moral influence which the Bank Act now has in enforcing the prudent conduct of all banking and commercial operations" (Q. 2325, 2384).

Other witnesses also emphasized capital movements, with the commodity trade coming in only as holders of already produced commodities were forced to sell because of restricted credit, or as merchants were forced to cut down imports, either because credit restriction had cut down their ability to finance imports or had reduced the ability of the public to pay for imports. The testimony of J. Horsley Palmer before the Commons Committee of 1848 is an example of these views:

2105. Mr. T. Baring] Supposing a great and sudden demand for corn, and the profit of the parties importing it to be very large, would you be able to check those imports by any rate of interest?—I think you could.

2108. Then it is not merely by the high rate of discount that the discounter is exposed to, but by the discredit that that high rate occasions, that you check the import of the article?—The high rate of interest that you allude to would itself tend to act most powerfully upon the foreign exchanges; but if that high rate of interest did not have that effect, the next course is to reduce the *echéance* upon bills.

2109. But the effect is produced, not because the party will not pay that which would be less than 1 per cent for his bill when he could get 50 per cent profit upon his corn, but because the measures adopted by the Bank occasion a discredit in commercial proceedings?—The high rate of interest, and the reducing of the *echéance* on bills, would bring the capital back to this country; by withdrawing credit, and stopping a large importation of commodities, and in various modes, you would turn the exchange in favour of the country.

2110. By producing a great pressure upon the commercial community?—Yes.

2111. Mr. Wilson] And also by altering the value of foreign securities?—Yes.

2112. Mr. T. Baring] It is by producing a fall in the value of all commodities in this country that you would correct the exchange?—Yes; not merely in that way, but you would bring capital to this country; by the high rate of interest you stop credit; many persons trading with America, or with India and China, have found money so extremely scarce in this country that they have been forced to stop their operations.

2117. Mr. Cayley] And the pressure produces forced sales?—It stops credit, and the British merchant sells his goods for the purpose of carrying on his payments, and brings back his capital at an earlier period than it would come in the ordinary course of trade.

A similar bypassing of any basic analysis of the long-run problem, and presentation of the short-run problem in terms of capital flows or the behavior of merchants, was in the testimony of Thomas Tooke before the same committee (Q. 5449–5450), of David B. Chapman, managing partner in Overend and Gurney, before the Committee on Bank Acts of 1857 (Q. 5079–5086); and of Robert Slater, partner in the firm of Morrison, Dillon and Company, and John Torr, a Liverpool merchant, before the committee of 1858 (Q. 2376–2386, 4984–4991).

Outside of the Parliamentary committees little was said on the subject. The pamphlets were concerned with more immediate problems than the theory of adjustment, the societies devoted attention to the effect of the new gold and the merits of free banking or a State Bank, and no one seemed concerned over the difference between the theory of adjustment stressed in Mill's *Political Economy* and the explanation given to Parliamentary committees.

Basis of the Gold Standard

Discussion of adjustment was virtually all in terms of the gold standard, but most of it left untouched the question why adjustment should be on the basis of the gold standard. If the visitor to England in the 1850's and 1860's had tried to find out from its economists, its men of affairs, and its press the economic rationale of the gold standard, he would have searched in vain. He could have learned something about the advantages of gold over silver, of the effects of a change in the supply of the standard metal upon prices, of the relation between notes and deposits, of the relation between Bank of England credit and the credit of other banks. As to the basic question why a fixed quantity of gold should be the standard of value he would have learned practically nothing beyond the idea that it was natural and moral, and therefore in line with free trade principles, to have the size of the monetary base determined by the accidents of gold production.

Many items in the *Economist* in the 1840's and 1850's suggested that free trade and the laws of nature were on the side of the gold standard. The dialogue between Richard Spooner, as a member of the 1857 Committee on Bank Acts, and George Warde Norman as a witness before that committee, even though the point at issue was discretion within the gold standard rather than discretion as to the standard, is an illustration of this association of the existing monetary arrangements with the order of nature:

3589. You have stated that you are averse to any artificial mode of interference with the currency in any way?—I am; I think the currency should be regulated entirely by natural causes.

3590. Do you call an Act of Parliament a natural cause?—Yes, if all that the Act of Parliament does is to place transactions of the Bank under the operations of natural causes.

Critics of the gold standard occasionally claimed that a fixed price of gold was not in accord with free trade principles, but free traders denied that the gold standard really involved fixing the price of gold. Richard Cobden took this view in 1848,[6] and one of many other specific statements

---

[6] Exchange of letters with Francis Bennock, of the Anti-Gold League, in *Bankers' Magazine*, February 1848, pp. 79–80.

of this position came in 1857 from another Manchester defender of the gold standard, T. H. Williams. He said that the law "attempts no such absurdity" as fixing the price of gold. "It simply requires that the Bank of England shall receive anybody's raw gold, and hand over its promises to hand the same quantity back, whensoever required to do so, abetting only so much as will cover interest during the time necessary for coinage."[7]

Defense of the gold standard had become by the 1850's a matter of faith rather than analysis, and in trying to find out its basis it is hard to get much beyond the idea of the law of nature and the sanctity of contracts. However, behind this teleological concept of the gold standard there were traces of a special twist to the real bills doctrine, which served a quite different purpose than had this doctrine as expounded by the Bank directors at the time of the Bullion Report. In the setting of inconvertibility the policy thrust of the real bills doctrine was that if banks loaned only on good short-term assets there was no danger of inflation. In the setting of the gold standard there were subliminal traces of the idea that if banks continued to loan on good assets the total means of payment would increase with the volume of business, and that hence, even though the gold supply did not increase as rapidly as production, there was no danger of price decline from an inadequate monetary supply.[8]

A historical factor also helps to explain why, in the late 1850's, 1860's, and early 1870's, the gold standard and the rigidity of the act of 1844 came to be increasingly accepted and praised by British opinion. Only a small minority blamed the economic troubles in the 1850's and 1860's, and particularly the dramatic failure of Overend, Gurney & Co., leading to the suspension of the Bank Act in 1857 and 1866 either on the gold standard or on the act of 1844. The main difficulty was that many persons had taken speculative chances and had gone into questionable, if not fraudulent, enterprises. The general sentiment seems rather to have been that it was fortunate that the country was on the gold standard and that the act of 1844 had restrained credit, with the almost whimsical result that these economic crises apparently strengthened faith in the legislation under which they occurred.

As late as the 1860's diehard Birmingham critics, and *Blackwood's*

---

[7] *Transactions of the Manchester Statistical Society*, 1857–58, p. 51.

[8] It is true that no one specifically expressed the view here suggested but I believe that it was an implicit premise of much banking and business thinking.

Edinburgh Magazine, which combined with opposition of Scots and landed gentry to the financial dominance of London the spirit of the court jester toward reigning economic ideas, might say that it would be better to have an inconvertible currency, but it is doubtful if they then really felt strongly about the matter or took themselves very seriously.[9] How much water had flowed over the dam in a half century, and how far the gold standard was now part of the accepted order, is shown by the position of the *Quarterly Review.* In 1816 it had protested against the idea the currency should be contracted to restore specie payments: "What! Is the ghost of Bullion abroad?" and in 1830 it had suggested that devaluation would have been desirable in 1819. In 1872, in an article favoring the appointment of a royal commission to examine the banking system, the *Quarterly,* without a reference to its earlier views, could say as if speaking eternal verities:

> We need scarcely say that no party in the country entitled to a moment's notice—least of all ourselves—would expect such a Royal Commission as is proposed to entertain any controversy relative to the principle of cash payments, happily re-established by the great and wise measure of 1819. We yield to none in our conviction of the necessity of founding all our banking and currency legislation on the rigid condition of the punctual payment in gold of specified fineness of all engagements in exact accordance with the terms of the several contracts. A currency of inconvertible, and almost of necessity, therefore, of depreciated, paper is one of the most destructive and penetrating calamities which can befall any people, and is especially oppressive to the poorer classes. In this country, however, the Brummagen doctrine of the 'little shilling' is practically as obsolete as the non-jurors.[10]

Criticism of the Gold Standard

Another indication, of a negative sort, of the almost unquestioning and universal acceptance of the gold standard—or at least of a metallic standard—was the low analytical quality of the criticisms, after the 1840's, of a metallic standard. The closest English approach in the first three

[9] In 1867 a special committee of the Birmingham Chamber of Commerce recommended that the Bank Act be repealed, that both gold and silver be legal tender, and that the government issue inconvertible notes receivable for taxes and other payments to government. The whole Chamber took no action on the resolutions, but simply recorded them in the minutes (*Birmingham Chamber of Commerce Resolutions of January 31, 1867,* Birmingham, 1867). The same year *Blackwood's,* in an article on "Monetary Reform," defended, largely on real bills grounds, the principle of inconvertible paper money by competing banks, but added, "we do not believe that the country is ripe for such a system" (vol. CII, October 1867, p. 449).

[10] Vol. CXXXII, January 1872, art. v, "The Bank of England and the Money Market," p. 122.

quarters of the nineteenth century to what the economist of today would consider a theory of an inconvertible currency came not from those who favored an inconvertible currency, but from a supporter of the gold standard, Henry Thornton. His discussion of the relation between the market rate of interest and the Bank rate, and the significance of this for prices and for employment, provided the analytical tools for a theory of a managed currency.[11] To a large degree the Bullion Report followed the Thornton analysis and had an analytical approach that could have served well a theory of a managed currency, despite the fact that it recommended specie resumption and later became a symbol of gold standard orthodoxy. The bullionists believed that the Bank could manage the currency and control prices so as to bring the exchange back to par and hold it there. Thomas Attwood and Henry James had much this same idea about the ability of the monetary authorities to control prices, but because of differences in temperament, and because the impact of post-Napoleonic depression had been particularly acute in Birmingham, they drew a quite different policy conclusion: the gold standard should not be reestablished at the old gold par.

In Thomas Attwood's writing there was a tremendous amount of chaff, mixed with the wheat of aggregate demand analysis. Yet Attwood even at his worst had an idea that economists of the post-1929 years would consider worthy of examination, even though they might not agree with him: the use of monetary policy to raise prices immediately after deflation, and to relieve unemployment even though this might involve an increase in the price of gold or even of commodity prices. Attwood's statements in the 1830's became increasingly hysterical, and though there were occasional flashes of his former stimulating analysis, much of what he said was nothing more than a plea for more money, without any real analysis of the effects of more money. Some of the Birmingham currency proposals of the 1840's had a defensible analysis on price and employment grounds, but in large part they simply claimed that more money would make people better off. Alexander Baring continued to have a theoretical approach that could have been the basis for support of bimetallism or even of an inconvertible currency, but his conservative political views stopped him from pressing the policy implications of his own economic thinking.

The result was that the better theoretical minds of economics, whether

---

[11] See Hayek's Introduction to his edition of Thornton's *Paper Credit of Great Britain*, pp. 49–50, 56, and Thornton's exposition on pp. 251–256.

in academic halls, business, or banking, simply were not interested in considering any analysis that would call in question the desirability of the gold standard. Political radicals and labor spokesmen showed little interest in monetary policy one way or the other, and certainly there is no evidence of any appreciable feeling in such quarters that the gold standard was injurious to the workers. Such criticism as there was of the gold standard had a middle-class origin, and appears to have had its greatest strength among small businessmen and bankers of the provinces. Most of the theoretical arguments in England between 1848 and 1875 in support of an inconvertible currency were sorry stuff that would not be accepted today by any economist: the idea that money should bear some fixed relation to population, to the total wealth of the country, to its landed property, or to its foreign trade, and that the monetary authority should maintain this ratio regardless of the state of prices or employment. Popular was the idea, frequently associated with some form of the real bills doctrine, that currency should be issued on the basis of national wealth or of annual taxes; or that currency should always be redeemable in gold at the market price, without any consideration of the fact that in the absence of convertibility monetary policy was an important influence on the price of gold.[12] One such proposal was bolstered by theological blessing of the real bills doctrine: "The law by which paper-money, issued in excess, cannot be kept out in excess, the excess always returning to the issuer, is a law, in the nature of things, established by the Almighty Father of the Universe."[13]

Probably the most persistent and prolific writers in support of a new

---

[12] Representative of more than a score of such writings are the following: John Finch, *Town Dues & Currency, Free Trade and Protection to British Industry* (Liverpool, 1850), urged notes of a National Bank of Issue convertible into gold at the market price (p. 29); James Harvey, in letters originally published in the *Liverpool Courier* and reprinted in *Remunerative Prices the Desideratum, not Cheapness* (London, 1851), wanted notes that would not exceed the annual taxes; John Twells, *How Can a Paper Money Increase the Wealth of a Nation?* (London, 1851), proposed a money supply based on the wealth of the country (p. 12); Charles Haward, *Currency Reform; the True Remedy for our Present Agricultural Distresses* (London, 1852), wanted gold to find "its real or *natural* value in the market" (p. 15); the anonymous *A Few Remarks on the Currency* (London, 1873), urged inconvertible notes "judiciously fixed in amount," and supported his proposals with this reasoning: "Such inconvertible notes would assuredly be free from depreciation. For if there be even thirty millions of notes ever applicable to payment of taxes, while the revenue is seventy millions, how could they be depreciated?" (p. 5); the anonymous *Money, Its Use and Abuse* (London, 1850), in proposing that the currency should be regulated by the rate of interest (p. 10) expressed a point of view that appeared increasingly after the middle 1850's, for public concern at all levels was more about high interest rates than about low prices.

[13] Alexander Gibson, *A Paper on the Circulating Medium* (London, 1856), p. 16.

monetary dispensation were the Taylor brothers, James, a country banker, and John, a London publisher who gave evidence before the Commons Committee of 1848. Between 1821 and 1864 they turned out close to fifty pamphlets, many anonymous, in support of inconvertible money, marked by religious overtones and by a nativist preference for English money over foreign gold. One of John Taylor's productions was a poem in epic form, *Money for the Millions* (London, 1857), and his defense of inconvertible paper money and fiscal policy as the key to full employment probably would get a more serious hearing from the economist of the 1960's than it did from his contemporaries:

> O would the State resume its ancient plan,
> And levy Taxes on the Englishman
> In Money of the Realm, Gold would not have
> The Power to make one honest Heart its Slave.
> Is there Distress? with Legal Tenders chase
> All Fear of Want from Labour's hardy race;
> Bid Aqueducts be form'd to bring the rills
> Of purest Water from the neighboring Hills;
> Bid Lakes expand, where Youth may safely float;
> Bid deepen'd Streams the Health of Towns promote;
> "Bid Harbours open, public Ways extend;
> "Bid Temples worthier of the God ascend;
> "Bid the broad Arch the dangerous Flood contain;
> "The Mole projected break the roaring Main;
> "Back to her Bounds the subject Sea Command;
> "And roll obedient Rivers thro' the Land:
> "These Honours PEACE to happy Britain brings—
> "These are Imperial Works, and worthy Kings!"*
>
> But let Discretion o'er the Task preside:
> When Trade declines, let Public Works provide
> With private Enterprise increased Employ;
> But when the Plough, the Loom, the Sail, enjoy
> Prosperity, let Public Works give way
> Till Time bring round a less propitious day.
> Lastly, let Government such Wages give
> On Public Works, that *all who toil may live!*

Economists either ignored or ridiculed most such arguments, and this absence of contemporary analysis meant that no light was thrown on what element of truth these proposals might have had or on the technical or political requirements for a successful managed currency. The English were not going to waste their time discussing the theoretical bases of

---

* Pope's Epistle to the Earl of Burlington.

proposals for altering the accepted monetary order. Lord Robbins well summarized the situation: "Speaking broadly, the members both of the Currency School and of the Banking School did not trouble to argue very much with the advocates of inconvertible money, speaking of them always merely as if they were lunatics or enemies of society." [14]

International Complications of the Gold Standard

A general argument against the gold standard was that it tied the monetary supply of England to foreign economic, political, and military developments. To a large degree this view was associated with the provincial opposition to the increasingly international character of British finance and banking, with the feeling in Birmingham and some other manufacturing areas that the interests of production were being sacrificed to the interests of high finance, and with a yeoman-oriented nationalism that felt that the political safety of the country was endangered by tying its economic life to the vagaries of foreign developments. The spirit of Cobbett lingered on in much of this argument. Russia's importance as a gold producer provided in the Crimean War, and the many years of tension before and after, an opportunity to point out the dangers that this created for England's gold standard.

A representative statement of this type came from William Blacker, whom Spooner had wished to be a witness before the Commons Committee of 1848, and who, after the committee by a vote of 4 to 3 had refused to have him appear, published the evidence that he would have given:

Gold . . . is in the present day the *very worst* [basis for a currency] that could be selected, because the universal estimation in which it is held, and its facility of transport, render it the fittest commodity to be hoarded in time of alarm, or the first to be resorted to for the settlement of international balances under an adverse exchange, in either of which cases a denial of discount with all its attendant evils must take place . . . The currency adopted by any country ought not to be liable to be acted upon by any external influence, or by the financial operations of other governments over which no control can be exercised.[15]

Similarly an anonymous writer in the same year argued that gold convertibility was for the benefit of the foreigner,[16] and C. N. Newdegate, a Tory member of Parliament who regarded free trade and the gold

---

[14] *Robert Torrens and the Evolution of Classical Economics*, p. 253.

[15] *Statement of Evidence which would have been given to the Committee of the House of Commons on Commercial Distress* (London, 1848), pp. 18, 27.

[16] *The National Distress: Its Financial Origin and Remedy* (London, 1848), pp. 159–165.

standard as twin evils, attacked the monetary system as tied to the accidents of foreign trade.[17] The Liverpool Currency Reform Association said that "violent fluctuations are inherent in a circulating medium, controlled by FOREIGN EXCHANGES and consisting of a COMMODITY which becomes abundant or scarce without reference to the monetary requirements of trade."[18] Samuel A. Goddard, who classed himself as a "Birmingham economist," attacked as "absurd" a system "whereby the energies of the whole people may be neutralised, and even prostrated, without any fault on their part or without any real necessity" as a result of monetary contraction when gold left the country.[19] Reuben Browning, writing under the pseudonym of "Persius," in a pamphlet of 1865 urged that currency should be "removed from external or foreign influence,"[20] and three years later came back to the theme that the trouble with gold as a standard "arises only from its susceptibility of its being withdrawn for *foreign demand,* not for domestic purposes."[21] Similar ideas stressing the lack of logic in tying the domestic monetary supply to foreign developments came from other pamphleteers.[22]

The same idea was put forward by two witnesses before the committee of 1858: George Holgate Foster, a retired merchant (Q. 2211–2214), and Sampson Samuel Lloyd, a Birmingham banker (Q. 2719–2725). Their statements indicated provincial sentiment that there was something wrong about a monetary system that tied the credit available to provincial business to the interests of London finance and foreign trade. Joseph Pease, a manufacturer and mine operator in Durham, and the first Quaker to sit in the House of Commons, before the Commons Committee of 1848 referred to the oncoming of the crisis of 1847 and said that many businessmen in his area, "being aware that their trade was dependent upon what many in the manufacturing and mining districts consider an arbitrary course of things; viz. the exchanges, over which they have no control, were in some degree of alarm of the danger, that there would be a decided balance of trade against this country, and that the consequences of that upon trade were sure" (Q. 4587). Ten years later John Smith, a Leeds merchant, appearing before the Committee on

---

[17] *A Letter to the Right Hon. H. Labouchere* (London, 1849), p. 5.

[18] *Suggestions for a New System of Currency* (London, 1849), p. 4.

[19] *Letters to the Edinburgh Chamber of Commerce* (London, 1857), pp. 5–7.

[20] *Remarks on the Late Monetary Crisis* (London, 1865), p. 10.

[21] *Addenda to Pamphlet on the Currency* (London, 1868), p. 4.

[22] Hamer Stansfeld, *The Bane and Antidote of our Monetary System Suggested* (London, 1857), p. 6; Henry Brookes, *The Bank Act of 1844* (London, 1861); Sir Archibald Alison, *The Currency Laws* (London, 1859), p. 1.

the Bank Acts of 1858 on behalf of the Leeds Chamber of Commerce, seems to have startled the chairman, Edward Cardwell, by his suggestion that the residents of Leeds were not particularly concerned about the convertibility of the Bank note, and this dialogue followed: "Do you mean to represent to the Committee on the part of the inhabitants of Leeds, that the convertibility of the Bank of England note is to them a matter of no importance, and no consideration?—The class of people who are manufacturers, and others, do not enter into these minute questions; they look simply to the mode of getting money to meet their obligations" (Q. 5744).

It would be easy to dismiss these criticisms of letting gold flows determine domestic credit as the futile struggles of provincial Britain against the rising power of the Britain of the world economy. I would suggest, however, that just as the Birmingham economists of the 1840's left their mark on history by consolidating support of the act of 1844, so these outcries in the 1850's and 1860's of provincial business against the credit stringency caused by foreign developments made their contribution to the emerging picture of pre-1914 orthodoxy. Much of this criticism against letting international events disrupt English economic life came from men not interested in the fine points of economic analysis but able in managing business. They were troubled because apparently they were unable to secure credit, or had to pay exorbitant rates, when London bankers were making loans abroad, France was having a political crisis, or banks were failing in the United States.

A large part of this man in the street criticism against the acts of 1819 and 1844 was not concerned with commodity prices—and certainly after 1848 not with long-run price movements—but with intermittent high interest rates or lack of credit at any price. These protests, even though they may have referred to the gold standard or to the act of 1844 as the cause of their troubles, in essence were criticism of the Bank's policy of carrying such a low reserve that in time of gold flows credit had to be severely tightened, if not denied at any price. The result was that from three different groups—the currency school, the banking school, and critics of the gold standard—each in open theoretical warfare with the other two, pressure was converging for a single policy: keeping of a larger reserve by the Bank of England, so that in time of pressure on the exchanges from short-run influences the Bank could absorb the shock by expansion of credit, accompanied if necessary by only a moderate rise in the Bank rate.

Effect of the Gold Discoveries

The discovery of gold in California in 1848, and three years later in Australia, rekindled suggestions that silver might be a better standard than gold. In the Restriction years the silver standard or bimetallism had had support, at least temporarily, from men of intellectual stature or standing in the world of affairs, including Ricardo, Malthus, Torrens, Alexander Baring, and Thomas Attwood; and after the panic of 1825 from William Huskisson. In the background of a large part of the discussion pro and con from 1815 to the late 1840's had been assumptions as to the relative production prospects of gold and silver, or, in more sophisticated analysis, of the total supply and demand situation of the two metals. The increase in gold production in the Urals in the 1830's occasionally was brought into this discussion.

The outpouring of gold from California and Australia put the silver controversy on a new basis. Figures on the new gold confirmed or even exceeded the first and apparently extravagant reports.[23] In the early years of the nineteenth century annual gold production had been slightly over £3 million, and of this about £2.5 million had been added to the supplies of the Western world. Following the increased output in the Urals annual production was around £8 million, even before the California and Australian discoveries. By 1850 annual production was close to £40 million— nearly fifteen times what it had been at the turn of the century, and five times what it had been in 1848. In the five years 1849–1853, gold production exceeded the world's total production between 1800 and 1848, and between 1849 and 1858 the new gold was about equal to the total production between the time of Columbus' discovery of America and the discovery of Californian gold.

The situation suggested an expansion in the British monetary supply and a rise in prices greater than anything that the Birmingham spokesmen had asked for. Critics of the gold standard could not restrain their delight. *Blackwood's,* in an article in January 1851 on "The Currency Extension Act of Nature" by Sir Archibald Alison, critic of the act of 1819 and spokesman for the idea that the fall of Rome was due to monetary deflation, was lyric over the prospects for prices.[24] The next month

---

[23] In the following discussion I have made use of the figures in Richard Cobden's translation of Michel Chevalier's book, published in English under the title *On The Probable Fall in the Value of Gold* (New York, 1859). I have also found helpful in giving an over-all picture of the controversy R. S. Sayers, "The Question of the Standard in the Eighteen-Fifties," *Economic History (A Supplement of the Economic Journal)*, II, 575–601 (January 1933).

[24] Vol. LXIX, January 1851, pp. 1–8.

Alison wrote: "The Bullionists are struck in the very heart of their power. True to their motives, though not to their principles, they are already in their journals decrying gold as a standard, and proposing silver in its stead." [25] He followed with this judgment on the results of the act of 1819: "The case of mankind and industry seemed hopeless; nothing but a long and painful decline, like that which, from similar causes, overtook Rome, seemed to await the British empire, when Providence in pity to mankind interposed. The Americans conquered California—a few grains of gold were discovered in digging a mill-race—human folly was arrested —the destinies of the world were changed." [26]

In 1847 Holland, apparently in response to the increased production of Russian gold, closed its mint to the free coinage of gold and Belgium took similar action in 1850. In France, where gold was rapidly replacing silver at the existing legal ratio of 15.5:1, there was serious discussion of demonetizing gold, but the only concrete result was the appointment of a committee which recommended against any change. In England no committees were appointed and no action was taken. But for over a decade there was public discussion of the inflationary possibilities of the new gold.

Contemporary British opinion on the effect of the new gold came from three main groups: (1) the public at large; (2) bankers and businessmen; (3) economists. The initial reaction of many, as reflected in letters to the papers, in editorials, and in the pages of *Punch,* was that the new gold might lead to a great increase in prices. A cartoon in *Punch,*[27] "Startling Effect of the Gold 'Diggins,' " showing an impoverished goldsmith seeking customers—"Now then, Here you are!—a handsome gold snuff-box and a ha'porth of snuff for a penny!" had a basic weakness in its economic analysis, but the thought was evident. Letters to the *Economist* showed concern about what might happen to prices. Pamphlets, either in praise or apprehension, prophesied important price consequences. C. N. Newdegate, a tireless but undiscriminating critic of the gold standard, said: "If the discovery of the Californian gold should so far counteract our legislation, and the increasing disproportion between the value of labour, produce, property, and payments in this country, as compared with gold, and consequently with our money, it will be an act of mercy by the Great Disposer of all events, upon which our modern statesmen could not have calculated." [28] Major J. H. M'Donald, as an argument for a stable inconvertible

[25] Vol. LXIX, February 1851, p. 199.
[26] Vol. LXXI, January 1852, p. 17.
[27] Vol. XXIII, July 17, 1852, p. 46.
[28] *A Letter to the Right Hon. H. Labouchere,* p. 25.

paper based on national wealth, played up the fear that gold would fall to one twentieth of its value;[29] and William Austin, a lawyer, took a similar alarmist view as to the future value of gold.[30] Two French writers, Léon Faucher and Michel Chevalier, whose books appeared in English translation, gave a more discriminating analysis but arrived at the same conclusion: there would be a substantial fall in the value of gold.[31]

Men of affairs, and economists like Torrens and Mill who had been active in the controversy of the 1840's over the bank acts, had little to say on the effect of the new gold on its purchasing power. Only after the middle 1850's, and then from a younger generation of economists who had not been involved in the debates of the 1840's, and who had new techniques of analysis to apply, was any really penetrating thought applied to the gold problem. The almost universal initial reaction of business and banking opinion was that the new gold would have little effect on prices, and that any effect would be largely on employment and on interest rates. Also in Parliament the new gold was thought of as affecting the ability of the Bank to deal with financial pressure, rather than as raising commodity prices. According to Disraeli, "When the crisis was at hand, and when all those acquainted with these affairs were looking about with terror and alarm, came those golden galleons from Australia, and those rich Californian argosies."[32] And insofar as any possibility of a price increase was admitted, the trend of the argument was to minimize the disturbances and the distributive injustice of rising prices. This man of affairs attitude seems to have been part of the moralistic approach to the gold standard, combined with a belief that all would be for the best if the laws of nature were left to operate. The same people who had been aghast at the Birmingham proposals for enlargement of the monetary base looked with approval, or at least with equanimity, on the likelihood of a greater enlargement from California and Australia.

There is no evidence that the Bank of England regarded the increased gold imports as presenting a problem different from gold from foreign bank reserves, or that it entertained any notion of even considering a shift to a silver standard. Two attempts to raise the question in the Commons were summarily disposed of by the Government, which apparently had no intention of encouraging any discussion that would raise

[29] England Rescued from her Present Dilemma (London, 1857), pp. 12–37.

[30] On the Imminent Depreciation of Gold, and how to Avoid the Loss (London, [1853]).

[31] Léon Faucher, Remarks on the Production of the Precious Metals (London, 1852); Michel Chevalier, Remarks on the Production of the Precious Metals (London, 1853).

[32] 3 Hansard CXLVIII, 613, December 11, 1857.

the slightest doubt about the gold standard. In June 1852 Perronet Thompson, whose long-time opposition to any tampering with the gold standard had been largely on the ground that inflation was a particular injustice to the worker, moved twenty-one resolutions asking that the Government take action to protect the public against depreciation in the value of gold. There was no debate and the resolutions were negatived without a division.[33] The following year, when Henry Drummond raised the question of "a Committee to inquire into the altered value of the standard, and to suggest some remedy for any evil that might be likely to arise," he was told by Gladstone, now Chancellor of the Exchequer, that the Government "have no intention, under present circumstances, and as at present advised, of appointing any Committee to inquire into this subject."[34] The committees of 1857 and 1858 gave little attention to the gold situation, but what was said stressed the importance of the gold in providing relief from the financial pressures associated with the act of 1844, and paid almost no attention to commodity prices. William Newmarch, secretary of the Globe Insurance Company and disciple of the aging Tooke, concluded a statement on the benefits of imports of new gold: "In truth, I might appeal to the observation of almost any member of the Committee, whether the natural and complete solvent to which we have got into the habit of looking for any financial pressure, is not the arrival of a gold ship."[35] The same emphasis was in the testimony of D. B. Chapman the following month:

5310. We have looked to the arrival of these steamers from Australia as much almost as to anything else, to know whether we were safe in going on with our business.

5311. Mr. Cayley] The destinies of the country seem to have hung upon their arrival?—No question of it. If we had not had those arrivals to an enormous extent which we have had, I defy any person to say what would have been the consequences under this Act.

The *Economist* from the beginning minimized the significance of the new gold,[36] but its argument was largely a mixture of legalism and a general philosophy that no monetary arrangements based on the laws of nature could be injurious. It never came to grips with basic supply and demand concepts. It stressed the sanctity of existing contracts: "Nothing,

---

[33] 3 *Hansard* CXXII, 899–901, June 17, 1852.

[34] 3 *Hansard* CXXIV, 1385, March 10, 1853.

[35] *Committee on Bank Acts,* 1857, Q. 1509.

[36] January 4, 1851, pp. 1–4; October 25, 1851, pp. 1176–1177; December 27, 1851, pp. 1425–1427; March 29, 1859, pp. 337–338.

therefore, in our mind could be more unwise or unjust than to attempt in any way to tamper with the standard; or to readjust existing obligations." [37] It saw in the developments, no matter what particular form they took, another example of the beneficent influence of free trade, and even suggested that the new gold would ease the white man's burden: "The discoveries in California and Australia have a close relation to and connection with the want of the inhabitants of Europe of necessary instruments of exchange, and they have come approximately, though they go not to them immediately, to supply those backward people with the means of civilisation, and hasten forward the increase of the wealth of the world." [38] In line with its general policy of treating almost everything as a text on the virtues of free trade, it preached: "The worst that will happen to him [the creditor] will be, that some small portion of the many advantages he has gained, and will hereafter gain from Free-trade, from the ingenuity, the science, the toil of others, will be lost by a fall in the intrinsic value of gold. [39] The *Bankers' Magazine,* although less vocal than the *Economist,* shared its approach, and felt that the gold discoveries "will not comprise any sudden ruinous alteration in the standard value of gold." [40]

The most reasoned statement of the belief that the new gold would have at most a moderate price effect came not from the City of London, or from economists, but from one of England's leading geologists, Sir Roderick Murchison. Murchison, an authority on the Urals, had been struck by the similarity between formations in Australia and the Urals. In 1848, before any great strikes had been made in Australia, he called the attention of Earl Grey, the Colonial Secretary, to the gold prospects. Murchison reported that Grey was not interested: "As his lordship has since informed me, he feared that the discovery of gold would be very embarrassing to a wool growing country." [41] After the discoveries

[37] January 4, 1851, p. 4.
[38] October 25, 1851, p. 1177.
[39] January 4, 1851, p. 4..
[40] March 1850, p. 137.
[41] This account is based on "Gold Discoveries," *Quarterly Review,* vol. XCI, September 1852, art. vii, by David Trevena Coulton. The original of Grey's letter, dated November 24, 1851, is in the Kress Library at Harvard University, and the relevant passage reads:

"It is singular how completely this discovery fulfils your anticipations which you were so good as to communicate to me two or three years ago, as to the probable discovery of gold in Australia if it were searched for.

"I hope that in the end this discovery may be productive of good but in the first instance I fear its effects will be very embarrassing to the wool growers whose interests I regard as the most important both to the Colony and to us. I should therefore not have been sorry had the gold remained undiscovered."

Murchison wrote an article "Siberia and California" in the *Quarterly Review,* in which he minimized the amount of gold that existed in, or could be profitably extracted from, quartz rock after the placer deposits had been worked out. To the question that he posed "whether California is to change the whole aspect of the civilized world, and *inter alia* to free our nation of 800,000,000 l. of debt in a quiet and imperceptible manner?" he answered that "we hold that such a result is utterly at variance with the great natural fact attested and established by history and science." [42]

Regardless of the theoretical merits of the arguments, the fact that prices in the early 1850's were no higher than in the years before the gold discoveries was evidence, to the ordinary man, that his hopes or fears about the effects of gold were groundless. The Crimean War (1854-1857) turned attention elsewhere and also provided a ready explanation for the higher prices after 1853; and the crisis of 1857, with a decline of prices to but little above those of 1847, diverted public concern away from the commodity price to the interest rate aspect of gold supplies. By 1857 the idea that the gold discoveries might call for any change in the monetary standard was, with the public at large, virtually dead. There was a temporary renewal of popular interest following Cobden's translation in 1859 of Michel Chevalier's new book, *On the Probable Fall in the Value of Gold* (New York, 1859), with its analysis of the supply and demand situation of gold and silver, particularly the absorption of much of the new gold by France and the suggestion of a delayed price effect of the new gold. The *Economist,* prompted by the book, published three articles on the possible depreciation of gold,[43] and in 1863 returned to the topic during the controversy between Stanley Jevons and J. E. Cairnes, with letters from Cairnes, one from Jevons, and two articles.[44] There is no evidence, however, that at this time bankers or businessmen cared much one way or the other about what had happened or what would happen to prices, and much less that they felt that the developments called for any action other than the exercise of prudent business judgment. The *Economist's* verdict in the second article, "A Common Sense View of the Gold Question," represents about as high a level of the theory of changes in the purchasing power of gold as men of affairs were interested in at any time between the middle 1850's and the new problems that emerged in the middle 1870's: "It is certain that in the current business of mercantile life

[42] Vol. LXXXVII, September 1850, art. iv, p. 429.

[43] March 26, 1859, pp. 337-338; April 16, 1859, pp. 419-420; April 23, 1859, pp. 450-451.

[44] May 30, pp. 592-593; June 27, pp. 704-706; September 12, pp. 1011-1012; September 19, pp. 1041-1042; September 26, pp. 1067-1068.

men run greater risks than any which the depreciation of gold is likely to cause them, and that if they choose these risks with judgment, they get money rather than lose it." [45]

The Economists and the Gold Discoveries

In 1849, 1852–1855, and 1857–1859, the British Association for the Advancement of Science issued papers and communications on the gold discoveries.[46] The preponderance of the academic opinion was that the value of gold either had fallen or was likely to fall. From the business world William Newmarch and J. Crawfurd stressed the production stimulus rather than the price effects, and Henry Fawcett, the only academic skeptic on the price significance of the new gold, emphasized the gold-silver ratio rather than the movement of commodity prices.

This argument by the economists was without benefit of systematic analysis of price data, much less of index numbers. Cairnes, however, had put the discussion on a more sophisticated level and suggested the thought, which Jevons was soon to develop, that "considering the propitiousness of the seasons, the action of free trade, the absence of war, the contraction of credit, and the general tendencies to a reduction of cost proceeding from the progress of knowledge, were there no other causes in operation, we should have reason to look for a very considerable fall of prices at the present time, as compared with, say eight or ten years ago." [47] Cairnes was probably right, but to the ordinary citizen, to the Cabinet member, or even to those who had been alarmists in 1850, the

[45] September 26, 1863, p. 1068.
[46] The following articles appeared in the Association's *Transactions:* W. N. Hancock, "On the Discovery of Gold in California," XIX (1849), 94–96; W. N. Hancock, "Should our Gold Standard of Value be Maintained if Gold becomes Depreciated in Consequence of its Discovery in Australia and California?" XXII (1852), 116–117; Francis Bennock, "Some Suggestions for an Improved System of Money and Banking," XXIII (1853), 97; William Newmarch, "On New Supplies of Gold," XXIII (1853), 110–111; William Newmarch, "Facts and Statements connected with the Question, Whether . . . the Exchangeable Value of Gold in this Country has Fallen Below its Former Level," XXIV (1854), 143; Richard Hussey Walsh, "The Price of Silver of Late Years Does Not Afford an Accurate Measure of the Value of Gold," XXV (1855), 198–199; J. Crawfurd, "On the Effects of the Gold of Australia and California," XXVII (1857), 160; J. E. Cairnes, "On Some of the Principal Effects of the New Gold as an Instrument of Purchase, on the Production and Distribution of Real Wealth," XXVII (1857), 156–158; J. E. Cairnes, "On the Laws, According to Which a Depreciation of the Precious Metals Consequent Upon an Increase of Supply Takes place Considered in Connexion with the Recent Gold Discoveries," XXVIII (1858), 174–175; Henry Fawcett (later Alfred Marshall's predecessor as professor of political economy at Cambridge), "On the Social and Economical Consequences of the New Gold," XXIX (1859), 205–209.
[47] "On the Laws," p. 175.

proposition that the new gold had raised prices because in its absence price would have fallen was a theoretical refinement, intriguing as it might be to economists. The publication in 1857 of the sixth and final volume of Tooke and Newmarch's *History of Prices* had, however, material to fire the imagination of anyone interested in the scientific aspects of the gold problem: a mass of data on prices and the precious metals, and the reaffirmation of the conclusion that these authors always reached when they examined price data: "It does not appear that the Prices prevailing in the early part of 1857, when compared with the Prices prevailing in 1851, justify the inference that, in any manifest and appreciable degree, the increase in the quantity of Metallic Money, by means of the New Gold, had raised the Prices of Commodities;—in other words, in every instance of a variation of Price, a full explanation of the change is apparently afforded by circumstances affecting the Supply or the Demand" (pp. 232–233).

A new turn to the discussion of gold depreciation was given in 1862 by young Stanley Jevons, recently returned to England after six years as an assayer of the Royal Mint in Sydney, who brought to the gold problem a first-hand interest, and a mathematical competence possessed by no other British economist of the day. In a paper at a meeting of the British Association in 1862, "On the Study of Periodic Commercial Fluctuations," he developed a concept previously almost untouched by economists—fluctuations around a norm.[48] The following year he published a monograph, *A Serious Fall in the Value of Gold Ascertained, and its Social Effects Set Forth*.[49] Taking as a point of departure Chevalier's book and Newmarch's discussion in the last volume of *History of Prices,* he compiled an index number of English prices since 1845. Jevons reached the conclusion, using his concept of "periodic fluctuations" to interpret the significance of price changes, that as prices were at a cyclical high in 1847, the even higher prices of recent years, and particularly in 1862 "at the very low water of the commercial tide," showed a substantial depreciation in the value of gold (p. 49). He estimated that gold had already fallen "some 15 per cent," and was "inclined to think the fall will be arrested at, perhaps, 30 per cent" (pp. 73–74). Jevons' conclusion as to policy, however, was no different from what it would have been if his figures and analysis had shown no depreciation in the purchasing power

---

[48] An abstract of the paper is in *Transactions,* XXXII (1862), 157–158; the full text was published posthumously in *Investigations in Currency and Finance,* ed. H. S. Foxwell (London, 1884), pp. 5–11.

[49] Reprinted in *Investigations,* pp. 13–118. Citations in the text refer to this reprinting.

of gold. He minimized the distributive injustice, opposed any arrangement for compensating creditors, and with the judgment, "but whether gold be a good or bad standard, it is to be questioned whether silver is a better one," concluded that the gold standard had better be left untouched (p. 103). In his philosophic approach to the limitations of any metallic standard Jevons soared on a high speculative level: "But in itself gold-digging has ever seemed to me almost a dead loss of labour as regards the world in general—a wrong against the human race, just such as is that of a Government against its people, in over-issuing and depreciating its own currency" (p. 104). Yet Jevons, either because he was the pure scientist unconcerned with policy making, or because as the child of an era he was not prepared to fight its myths and its idols, made no public suggestion for a better standard, although he wrote but did not publish a proposal for a tabular standard of value.[50]

After Jevons' stimulating analysis Cairnes returned to the controversy, agreeing with Jevons in large part but believing that the depreciation of gold to date had been greater than Jevons had estimated.[51] This was too rich a theoretical diet for the public to take for long. The judgment of the *Westminster Review,* in an article the following year on "The Depreciation of Gold," summarized a prevailing attitude: "The interest which all economists feel in its solution is accurately balanced by the profound disregard by which it is met by almost all those who are engaged in the active prosecution of the details of commerce; nor is this to be wondered at, for the question is more scientific than practical."[52]

Even the economists soon lost interest in the topic. The shape of the coming controversy, as silver standard countries moved to gold, is suggested by the question that Professor Herman Merivale of Oxford proposed to the Political Economy Club on June 3, 1864: "The obligations of a State having been contracted in a Silver Currency, is there any foundation for the opinion that there is a breach of faith committed towards the holders by substituting or adding Gold as a standard?"[53] And the completely new set of problems in the relation of gold and silver, that were to produce the bimetallic controversy of the last quarter of the

---

[50] Published posthumously in *Investigations,* pp. 297–302, under the title "An Ideally Perfect System of Currency."

[51] See letters in the *Economist,* May 30, 1863, pp. 592–593, and June 27, 1863, pp. 704–706.

[52] N.S., vol. XXV, January 1864, art. iv, pp. 88–89. "The New Gold Mines and Prices," *North British Review,* vol. XLII, June 1865, also comments on the lack of public interest in the gold situation.

[53] Higgs, *Political Economy Club,* p. 83.

century, is dramatized by the statement of George Goschen in 1876, in a review of the problems associated with the depreciation of silver: "The financial world is in tribulation. Political economists are at their wits' end. Economical heretics are at the height of enjoyment." [54]

Revival of Controversy over Banking

By the early 1860's the gold standard was out of the way as a subject of controversy, and even the question of gold's purchasing power had ceased to arouse excitement. As these problems were fading out the old question which Peel had presented to the Cabinet in 1844, the possibility of multiple banks of issue or of a State bank of issue, was taking on new life. For a time these proposals threatened to change British monetary arrangements.

The legislation of 1844 had taken away the ability of the English banks to increase note issues, and had placed at least a nominal restriction on the issues of Scottish and Irish banks. This still left untouched the larger problem, which became of greater substantive importance as deposit banking increased, whether the country banks could ignore the exchanges. On this point there is little specific discussion after the 1850's, but it seems to have been tacitly recognized by almost everyone that no banker could ignore the exchanges. A number of factors contributed to this shifting opinion: the decreasing importance of private country banks as compared with joint-stock banks, which even if their head offices were in the provinces had more of the City view of the world than did the old-time country banks; free trade and the improvement in transportation, which made all of the kingdom more conscious of what went on in London and in every corner of the seven seas; and the gradual weakening of the criticism of the country's international orientation, of which the gold standard was the most sacred symbol. The banks may not have liked the effect of the flow of gold or of the policy of the Bank of England on their ability to extend credit, but by the 1860's there was no longer any question that the effect was there.

Discussions in the third quarter of the century added virtually nothing on the economic significance of deposits, despite the increasing importance of check payments. The strategies of controversy increased, if anything, the intellectual sterility with which the subject of deposits had been treated in the debates of the late 1830's and the 1840's. One of the few discussions of the role of deposits again came from that old campaigner of the mone-

[54] *Edinburgh Review*, vol. CXLIV, October 1876, art. vii, "The Depreciation of Silver," p. 501.

tary wars, Colonel Robert Torrens, whose increasing doubts about the virtues of free trade left him, even as he approached eighty, with a flexibility of thought that a dedicated free trader could not have. Torrens, in his last publication—just fifty years after he had written *The Economists Refuted*—although extravagant in praise of the act of 1844, in his flamboyant style criticized the abuses of deposit banking. He pointed out that such abuses "excite a temporary doubt whether the advantages of discount banking, even when conducted under a metallic currency, balance the evils it inflicts, [55] and suggested, in general terms, legislative remedies. But this was not the prevailing opinion, which was better represented by the statement of another currency school champion, George Warde Norman, before the Committee on Bank Acts of 1857: "It has never entered into my mind that there should be any legislative restriction applicable to deposits . . . A bank has to deal with the money of the country which exists, but it has properly nothing to do with the issue of money" (Q. 2921). And a free trader wrote in the *British Quarterly Review:* "It is allowed on all hands that it would be absurd and out of place for the State to take security from a bank for its deposits." [56]

Occasionally suggestions were thrown out that fractional reserve deposit banking meant that the whole economic system rested on a dangerously unstable foundation. In Ireland might appear the statement, possibly with tongue in cheek, "If there must be gold enough to meet every obligation to pay in gold, the whole community, City and all, are living over the burning fires of a volcano," [57] but the general reaction of economists, bankers, and businessmen to such ideas was that things were going pretty well, and that it was better to concentrate on the day's work than to worry about the possibility of volcanic eruptions. The comment of the *Westminster Review,* in an article on "Political Economy as a Safeguard of Democracy," although made about the whole economic scene would also apply to any fears of a day of judgment for fractional reserve banking: "The English people are ballasted by their naturally practical and unexcitable temperament." [58]

A new opinion that for a time threatened the hopes of the sponsors of the act of 1844 that time would take care of the note issues of the country banks was gaining ground, however. It was not simply that few banks had given up their issues, either voluntarily or by merger or failure, or that the

---

[55] *Edinburgh Review,* vol. CVII, January 1858, art. ix, "Lord Overstone on Metallic and Paper Currency," p. 270.

[56] Vol. XLV, April 1867, art. iii, "Banking Reform," p. 365.

[57] *Dublin University Magazine,* March 1870, p. 343.

[58] N.S., vol. L, October 1876, art. iii, p. 390.

Government was not prepared to take action to unify the note issue. A sentiment, particularly strong outside of London, was developing against the prohibition on new banks of issue or on the increase of issues of existing banks. John G. Kinnear, secretary of the Chamber of Commerce and Manufactures of Glasgow, had urged free banking in 1847,[59] and for the next twenty years Scottish opinion was predominantly to the same effect. The *Economist,* which contrary to the dominant opinion in the City had favored multiple note issue in 1844 and 1845, continued to preach the same doctrine in the 1850's. James Wilson, the editor, as a member of the Committee on Bank Acts of 1857, had without success pressed questions on T. W. Weguelin, recently governor of the Bank, that evidently were intended to produce answers favorable to free banking (Q. 788-797).

With the exception of the *Economist,* dedicated under Wilson to the principle of free trade across the board, the support of free trade in banking came largely from Scotland and the provinces, although William Newmarch supported free banking in his testimony before the committee of 1857 (Q. 1399-1419). The *Circular to Bankers* continued to attack the Bank of England monopoly and to plead the cause of multiple issues. In "The Great Monetary Sebastopol" it dramatized the feeling of many country bankers: "The Sebastopol of Russia is not more dangerous to the liberties and rights of Europe, than the great monetary Sebastopol of Threadneedle-street . . . The allied forces of Liverpool, Nottingham, Birmingham, and other towns, are again meditating an attack upon its fortifications; they declare that it is dangerous to the liberties and freedom of commerce to permit such a power to exist in the United Kingdom." [60] After the *Circular to Bankers* ceased publication in 1860 the same position was expressed by other spokesmen for country bankers.

Before the Bank Acts Committee of 1858 William Rodwell, chairman of the Association of Private Country Bankers, urged the case of the country bankers to at least retain, and preferably to have enlarged their right of issue (Q. 1274-1335). The merchants of Liverpool petitioned for a return to free banking.[61] Professor Bonamy Price, Nassau Senior's successor at Oxford, championed the cause of multiple note issue on the guarantee of government bonds.[62] Articles in a number of journals de-

---

[59] *The Crisis and the Currency* (London, 1847), pp. 56-59.

[60] No. 1516, November 26, 1855, p. 328.

[61] *Economist,* January 27, 1866, pp. 89-90.

[62] Letter in *Economist,* February 27, 1864, pp. 257-258; "The Bank Charter Act of 1844," *Fraser's Magazine,* June 1865, pp. 688-701; "Banks and Banking," *ibid.,* February 1867, pp. 187-204; "The Controversy on Free Banking," *ibid.,* January 1868, pp. 102-120; "What is Money?" *Contemporary Review,* May 1870, pp. 236-259. The last article by Price was a paper read before the Liverpool Chamber of Commerce in April 1870.

fended multiple note issue as in accord with lofty principles.[63] R. H. Patterson, in the higher reaches of eloquence, put the problem this way: "We have to undo Restriction, and we have to abolish Monopoly . . . Such an abolition of the reactionary system of restriction and monopoly in our monetary affairs—such an application of the principle of free trade to banking in all its functions—will be as genial in its effects upon free trade and national well-being as the advent of spring relaxing the icy fetters of a protracted winter." [64] Even John Stuart Mill, although in more measured tones, in his testimony before the committee of 1857 spoke favorably of permitting the country banks to continue and to extend their note issues (Q. 2039–2044).

All evidence would support the substantial accuracy of the statement in 1865 of Jevons, who was opposed to multiple note issue, on the widespread support of the movement: "It is well known that many merchants and gentlemen of influence in Glasgow, Liverpool, and elsewhere, have a strong desire to unsettle our monetary system again. They spare no pains in urging upon us that the Bank of England is the cause of all our troubles, and while some go so far as to propose an inconvertible currency, the others advise a return to a free issue of notes, the convertibility of which shall be dependent on the credit and discretion of the issuing banks, according to the system which used to prevail in Scotland, for instance." And turning on the supporters of a multiple issue system, who claimed that it was in accord with the spirit of free trade, Jevons added: "And I venture to take this auspicious expression, Free Trade, from those who use it wrongly and confuse the free manufacture of currency with free trade in capital, the true business of the banker." [65] The literary output against free banking was less voluminous, but the opponents also felt that high principle was also on their side, because the issue of money was a royal prerogative.[66]

This discussion, pro and con, was carried on largely on deductive

[63] *British Quarterly Review*, vol. XXVII, January 1858, art. vii, "The Bank Acts, and the Credit Crisis of 1857"; *ibid.*, April 1858, art. iii, "Credit-Currency, and Banking"; *ibid.*, vol. XLV, April 1867, art. iii, "Banking Reform"; "The Bank Charter Act and the Currency Laws," *Tait's Edinburgh Magazine*, March 1857, pp. 129–134; William Latham, "Modern Reforms in Paper Money," *Fortnightly Review*, March 1, 1866, pp. 210–222; R. H. Patterson, "The Currency and Its Reform," *ibid.*, December 1, 1866, pp. 837–856; R. H. Patterson, "The State and the Currency," *ibid.*, July 1, 1867, pp. 77–95.

[64] *Fortnightly Review*, August 15, 1866, p. 27.

[65] Statistical Society of London, *Journal*, XXIX, 247, 250 (June 1866).

[66] David Ross, "Banking Considered with Special Reference to a Strictly Limited Issue of Government Paper Money," Statistical and Social Inquiry Society of Ireland, *Journal*, IV, 332–344 (November 1866); R. H. I. Palgrave, "Notes on Banking," Statistical Society of London, *Journal*, XXXVI, 27–152 (March 1873); *Westminster Review*, N.S., vol. XLIV, October 1873, art. i, "The Mint and the Bank of England."

grounds—the *natural* system of free trade as against the *sovereign* right of government over the money supply—and it produced little economic analysis. Probably one reason why in the 1850's and 1860's the literature in support of free banking was more extensive and on the whole more dogmatic than that specifically opposing free banking was the three-cornered controversy involved. It was not simply free banking versus the existing position of the Bank of England. Along with the free banking sentiment there was a growing opinion, apparently more powerful politically than free banking, for having all note issues concentrated in the government or in a State Bank. Hence much of the argument after the middle 1850's against free banking was subsumed in the argument against any private issues. Some, like an anonymous writer in the *Westminster Review,* pressed to the hilt the logic of the idea that a great majority of the English of the day accepted in principle even though they may have shrunk from its application: if the right of issuing money was a royal prerogative then the profits of issuing money should go to the state. The *Westminster* put it:

> In breaking this monopoly of the Bank, we should be taking a great stride towards the attainment of that ideal system of currency which Sir Robert Peel must have had in his heart when he passed his Currency Laws—a system under which the State shall be the sole fountain of issue, under which no money shall circulate on credit, or, if it does, shall circulate on the credit of the State, all bank-notes as well as coins bearing the image and superscription of the head of the State, and under which all profits upon the issue of money shall form part of the Imperial revenue . . .
>
> The Power of Issue is, and ought to be, a sovereign right . . . The Power of issue now exercised by the Bank of England, and by the English, Irish, and Scotch banks is a relic of feudalism, of those rough and rude times when every prelate and noble set up a mint under the shadow of his palace or castle, coined money in their own names as grantees of the King, and appropriated the profit of their mints as they appropriated the rent of their estates.[67]

Critics of the monopoly position of the Bank of England, who at the same time opposed free banking, saw the solution in a State Bank. This view seems to have been common in London. The *Times,* as early as 1856, although supporting most of the act of 1844, editorialized that it would "like to know how, upon the principles of the act of 1844, the continuance of the privileges of the Bank of England can be defended, and why the Government, after paying the Bank amply for all that it does for it in its

[67] "The Mint and the Bank of England," pp. 303–304.

capacity of banker, should delegate to it the privilege of creating 14,000,000 l. sterling for no consideration at all" (December 26, 1856).

Samuel Jones Loyd, raised to the peerage in 1850 as Lord Overstone, although not feeling as strongly as the *Times,* had no objection to separating the Issue Department from the Bank and making it a State agency.[68] This he felt would make no substantive change as the Issue Department "is nothing more than a department of the State, worked mechanically and clerically by the clerks of the Bank of England; but it is essentially a department of the State." [69] Those who were opposed to the creation of a State Bank, such as T. W. Weguelin (Q. 78–82), George Warde Norman (Q. 2953–2956), and John Stuart Mill (Q. 2047–2056) in their testimony of 1857, and R. H. I. Palgrave in a letter in the *Economist,*[70] based their position largely on grounds of administrative convenience. There was no real attempt, in the quarter century after 1847, to make a theoretical case against the monopoly of note issue by the State, except as the supporters of free banking opposed equally State issue or monopoly by the Bank of England as contrary to free trade.

A contributed article in the *Economist* in 1875 supported state issue because this would relieve the Bank of England of any responsibility for supporting the money market in time of crisis.[71] Remarks of others who were opposed to the Bank of England acting as a lender of last resort are also consistent with the view that they lent a receptive ear to suggestions that the government take over the note issue on the ground that stripping the Bank of its note issue would be a visible symbol that the Bank was free to act like any other bank. The *Economist,* under Walter Bagehot's editorship since 1860, opposed State issue, not on the ground that it was economically unsound, but because where possible it was better not to disturb existing arrangements. The net result of all this argument over a change in the legal conditions of note issue was that the controversy

[68] Commons *Committee,* 1848, Q. 5282–5283; *Committee on Bank Acts,* 1857, Q. 3664–3671.

[69] *Committee on Bank Acts,* 1857, Q. 3649. Others who supported a State Bank were an anonymous writer in the *North British Review,* vol. XXXV, November 1861, art. ii, "What is Money?" p. 189; David Ross, "Banking Considered with Special Reference to a Strictly Limited Issue of Government Paper Money"; Robert Baxter, "Principles which regulate the Rate of Interest and the Currency Laws," Statistical Society of London, *Journal,* XXXIX, 289 (June 1876); contributed article signed "G." in the *Economist,* February 27, 1875, pp. 242–245; letter from Manchester signed "Country Bank," *ibid.,* November 24, 1866; memorial of the Bristol Chamber of Commerce on Banking and Currency, *ibid.,* October 20, 1866, pp. 1224–1225.

[70] April 17, 1875, pp. 454–456.

[71] February 27, 1875, pp. 242–245.

was fought to a standstill as it was absorbed in the larger controversy over the clarification of the unwritten responsibilities of the Bank of England.

The Bank of England and International Economic Stability

On one theoretical point the years from 1845 to 1875 were barren: the influence of Great Britain, and particularly the Bank of England, upon the purchasing power of gold and upon the functioning of the international economy. This conclusion is contrary to a widely held belief of economists—expressed more in oral tradition than in formal presentation—that the successful operation of the international economy before 1914 was due to the Bank of England's action as managing director, or as executive secretary, of the international gold standard, and to the City of London's role as an international lender of last resort. Reflecting this view have been repeated statements in the last four decades from economists, the press, and political leaders to the effect that the international economy did not function successfully after the First World War because England was no longer in a position to exercise leadership, and that the United States lacked the training or the vision to assume leadership. This is a plausible hypothesis. It may be true, but I fail to find any suggestion that the Bank of England or the people of England felt any such responsibility in the thirty years after 1845. The record supports the statement of Viner, in his review of Clapham's *Bank of England:* "This history of the Bank reveals little or nothing to confirm the belief that the Bank or any other English institution deliberately or otherwise 'managed' the gold standard." [72]

In the first place the situation was intellectually chaotic as regards responsibility of the Bank to the United Kingdom, or even to the City of London, and it would be asking too much to assume that with a babel of voices telling the Bank what it should do for Lombard Street it should have any clear vision of what it was supposed to do for the world. There was even less discussion of the international effects of British monetary policy than in the early years of the century. The questions and answers at the committee hearings of 1848, 1857, and 1858, pamphlet literature, discussion in the *Times,* the *Economist,* in other periodicals and before the societies, reveal no evidence that the Bank was trying to manage anything for foreigners. Furthermore, they gave no indication that the public felt that the Bank should be doing any such management. The public—

[72] *Economica,* N.S., vol. XII, 63 (May 1945).

even staunch supporters of the gold standard—was much more concerned about the ways in which the international role of England made trouble for England than it was about how England could make an international system function more smoothly.

The same general comment can be made about foreign lending. The idea that the successful functioning of the international economy was dependent upon England being the international lender of last resort may have been believed in the last years of the century, but I cannot find a trace of such an idea up to 1875. Insofar as there was any moral responsibility associated with English lending in those years, it seems rather to have been that England would contribute to world economic progress by refusing to lend to countries that followed such economic heresies as inconvertible paper currencies or unbalanced budgets. Probably British policy did contribute to world monetary stability and world economic development in the decades before 1875, but insofar as it did the result was a manifestation of the eighteenth century Smithian harmony of economic interests and not of the purposeful assumption of larger responsibilities about which economists talk in the mid-twentieth century. In the heyday of laissez faire, if the financial leaders of England had been told that they were the managers of the international gold standard and the international lender of last resort, they would have been as amazed as that character in Molière's *Le Bourgeois Gentilhomme* who learned that, without knowing it, he had been speaking prose all his life.

IX

THE VICTORY OF THE BAGEHOT PRINCIPLE

T HE YEARS 1845–1875 had brought no substantive change in British monetary and banking law. The theoretical controversies of the period had little positive influence, and generally ended in the common-sense conclusion that it was better not to change long-established institutions or to antagonize politically powerful local interests. The really significant development of those years, in which monetary and banking orthodoxy was consolidated, was the acceptance of a set of traditions governing the behavior of the Bank of England and its relations with the Government.

It is customary to speak of the evolution of the Bank of England as a central bank, to try to date the first appearance of the idea of the Bank as the lender of last resort, and to bestow a mantle of tradition on the practices of modern central banking. A recent article illustrates this: "The Role of the Bank of England as Lender of Last Resort in the Crises of the Eighteenth Century."[1] More than one economist has pointed to an event in the Bank's history before 1844 as showing recognition of some principle of central banking. Francis Baring, Henry Thornton, the Bullion Committee, and at times Thomas Attwood, had preached a doctrine of the Bank's responsibilities that sounds surprisingly like the ideas that have come to be known as the Bagehot principle. Undoubtedly what the Bank did before the 1840's provided arguments for those who, after 1844, urged that the Bank was more than just a big commercial bank, and gave to the new philosophy the respectability of the past.

Yet in tracing the emergence of a philosophy of central banking in the years from 1845 to 1875, what happened before 1840 is hardly more than a footnote. This philosophy did not have a continuous growth, but was for all practical purposes born anew out of the controversies that followed

---

[1] Michael C. Lovell, in *Explorations in Entrepreneurial History*, X, 8–21 (October 1957).

Peel's legislation. Any connection with earlier Bank policy had been shattered by the widespread criticism of the Bank's discretionary action in the decade before 1844, by the legislative provisions of the act of 1844, and by the high tide of free trade philosophy. The result in the years after 1844 was a chaotic situation as regards opinion on what the Bank was and how it was supposed to act. The Bank of England certainly was less a central bank in 1845 than it had been in 1825, and probably less than it had been in 1793. Free trade and the act of 1844 had created an intellectual vacuum that was not filled for over a quarter of a century. The problem had two main aspects: first, the relation of the Bank of England to other banks, and specifically its responsibility as a lender of last resort; and second, the relation between the Bank and the Government.

Relation of the Bank of England to Other Banks

The principal supporters of the act of 1844 had, in their insistence on the rigid regulation of note issues, either specifically or implicitly taken the view that the Bank, in its banking operations, should act just like any other bank. The logical corollary of this was that the Bank had no responsibility in time of crisis greater than the ordinary bank had to its customers and the community, that it had no need to keep a larger reserve in its Banking Department than any other bank, and that it should strive to maximize profits in the same way as other banks. The proposition that the Banking Department should act like an ordinary bank was, however, not self-defining. Every banker presumably had some sense of responsibility to his customers, and probably to the general business interests of the community. But there was the question whether this responsibility was thought of as enlightened self-interest consistent with the narrowest conception of the economic man, or whether this responsibility involved a professional relation between banker and customers and community that occasionally called for actions inconsistent with maximum long-run profits. If one also asked the question whether the customers of the Bank of England included those who did only occasional discounting, and whether the community that it served included the entire United Kingdom, the answer as to what the Bank was expected to do in a specific situation raised complicated and controversial issues. Did acting "just like any other bank" mean that it should act in exactly the same way as a bank in a provincial town, or that it should apply the same philosophy of action, with the concrete manifestation of that philosophy being different because of the size, the location, and the type of business carried on by the Bank of England?

Moreover, it was not possible to divorce the question of how the Bank should act in time of crisis from its action in time of prosperity or from its relation to its stockholders. No matter what view the Bank might hold of its responsibility to lend in time of crisis, its ability to do so in a specific situation—assuming always its overriding responsibility to maintain the gold standard—was tied up with the size of its reserve. The action it could take in time of crisis would be one thing if reserves were 80 per cent, and another if they were only 20 per cent. In turn, the non-earning assets that the Bank held in good times were related to the ideas of the directors about how far the Bank should go in passing up profits to discharge a nebulous public responsibility. And to push the matter to its legal extreme, the directors could not maintain a policy in the face of an organized opposition of a stockholders' majority; and going back one step further the Government could hardly be expected to respect for long the "independence" of a Bank of England that defied Government policy.

Opinion after the Crisis of 1847

The crisis of 1847, although it resulted in widespread criticism of the idea that the Banking Department should act like any other bank, did not settle this controversy. As a result of dissension within the Bank Court as to what its responsibilities were, and the coloring of the whole issue by the dominant free trade philosophy, the problem of the Bank's responsibility was as controversial, and if anything more confused, in 1870 than it had been in 1847. This confusion was accentuated by the fact that sometimes the argument for "free banking" was part of a discussion of the whole position of the Bank of England. Furthermore, for many years the question of the need for the Banking Department to keep a larger reserve was often tied up, though in an ill-defined way, with the question of larger reserves for all banks.

The crisis of 1847 had become acute before the Bank, at the same time its reserves were falling, raised its discount rate and refused accommodation to many at any price. But much of the criticism of the Bank Act, both before and after the Government authorized its suspension, was not that the Bank had been prevented from being a lender of last resort. It was that the act had encouraged the Bank to expand credit in 1845 and 1846 in a way that no prudent bank should have done, so that when the crisis came the rigid requirements of the Bank Act meant that the Bank could not even function as an ordinary bank would in such a situation. This was the theme of James Wilson's articles between January 19 and May 29, 1847, and this continued to be the *Economist's* theory of Bank of England policy until Walter Bagehot's editorship.

Charles Turner, a Liverpool merchant, in testimony before the Commons Committee of 1848, had expressed a theory of a lender of last resort that included the essence of what Bagehot was to say—a high interest rate is not serious in time of crisis, but it is important to have assurance that credit is available at some rate (Q. 664). J. Horsley Palmer took essentially the same position in these hearings (Q. 2026-2027). In testimony before the Lords Committee of 1848, Palmer said that he was against the idea that the Bank should be managed as any other bank (Q. 881). But Palmer was a rebel within the Bank, and the official view of the Bank's management in 1848 was quite different.

When James Morris and Henry James Prescott, the governor and deputy governor, appeared before the Commons Commitee of 1848, the question was put: "With regard to the banking department, in what condition did the Act place you?"—and Prescott replied: "It placed the Bank of England in the condition of any other bank, except that we were carrying on business upon a much larger scale, and we had also the Government deposits to deal with" (Q. 2653).[2] Even more specific was the reply of Morris to the questions of Sir William Clay:

3224. There was an apprehension abroad, and there is in the public mind an impression that they are entitled to look to the Bank of England for the exertion of some species of power, apart from and independent of their resources as mere bankers, and that in the last resort they are entitled to come to the Bank, and to say, "You must give us assistance?"—Yes, in 1847, persons expressed disappointment that they did not receive the assistance from the Bank which they seemed to consider that they were entitled to.

3225. Do not you think it very important that the public mind should be disabused of that error?—I think that the public must now be enlightened on the subject.

3226. Do not you think that the power of relieving the pressure by the issue of paper can never be resorted to, and that experience has shown that it has never been resorted to, without ultimately enhancing the danger which it sought to obviate?—As a general principle, I think it is so.

And to leave no doubt on the view of the Bank's management, Morris, after a series of questions about the Bank's reserve policy and the possi-

[2] The same idea was developed in more detail in Q. 2845-2856.

bility of a conflict between the Bank's desire for profits and the interests of the commercial community, said: "I consider that with the powers that have been given to the Bank of England, they are no more bound to support commercial credit than any other bankers are, except, that being a more powerful body, and having greater means, they are enabled to accomplish that object to a larger extent" (Q. 3348). William Cotton, who had been a director since 1822, and governor when the act of 1844 was passed, gave the opinion: "I think the Bank of England should be conducted upon the same principle as any other bank is conducted" (Q. 4141). George Warde Norman, before the Lords Committee of 1848, criticized the "general Expectation that at all Times and under all Circumstances Persons possessed of Securities which are usually considered valid and merchantable shall be able to obtain Loans upon them at what they consider a moderate Rate of Interest, and in the last resort the Bank of England is looked to as the Source of such Assistance" (Q. 2746).

In view of these opinions, the statement in the report of the Commons Committee, although possibly technically correct in view of the wide coverage of the term "any obligation," certainly misrepresents the attitude of the Bank's management: "An opinion appears to have been entertained by some persons, though not by the Governor and Deputy-Governor of the Bank of England, that the Bank is released by the Act of 1844 from any obligation, except that of consulting the pecuniary interests of its Proprietors" (p. iv). The situation was rather the reverse, with those outside the Bank calling for a broader concept of its public responsibilities.

Thomas Tooke, though critical of the act of 1844, attacked the policy followed by the Bank in 1846 and 1847 and urged the maintenance of larger reserves. He had little to say about the rationale of the lender of last resort or of the philosophic and economic problems of the relation of stockholders and the public. He was content to reiterate with single-mindedness that the Bank should not be expected to act like other banks and must keep a larger reserve. He said that "a great mistake was committed by the framers of the Act of 1844, in the assumption, that the Banking Department of the Bank of England admits of being conducted in the same way, and with only the same effects on the interests and convenience of the Public, as any other non-issuing Joint-Stock Bank." [3] His general philosophy in hundreds of answers to the committees and in writings before and after 1844 never got much beyond this statement to

[3] *On the Bank Charter Act of 1844* (London, 1856), p. 142.

the Commons Committee of 1848: "I conceive that, as a general principle, the facility of maintaining the general commercial credit of the country under circumstances occasionally requiring large foreign payments, depends upon the habitual maintenance by the Bank of a very large amount of treasure" (Q. 5376).

This was sound advice, but it required the broader vision of Bagehot to blend it with a larger philosophy of action. Tooke, the master of figures, the shrewd judge of a particular problem, and the trenchant critic of the Bank's behavior in a given situation, was hopelessly at sea in developing a principle of action. An ardent free trader, he was opposed to rules in any form, yet his criticism of what he considered bad judgment of the Bank, both before and after 1844, would appear to be abundant grist for the mill of one who wanted more restrictions on the Bank's freedom of action. Tooke, no matter how severely he might criticize the behavior of directors in a particular situation, seemed always to come up with the same conclusion: the Bank should not be subject to any restrictions, nor should the Government have any voice in its management; it should keep a larger reserve, its directors should use better judgment, they should be selected with more care, and there should be a greater continuity in management.[4]

One of the best statements of the case against the theory that the Bank should act as any other bank, and in favor of its recognizing a larger responsibility, came from the cautious Quaker spokesman Samuel Gurney, whose belief in laissez faire, and whose financial success under it, was tempered by a sense of group responsibility. In testimony before the Lords Committee of 1848 he said that he had originally approved of the act of 1844, but had changed his opinion in the light of experience. His statement, "The Principle, that in the Banking Department they are to do as they please, and need not have any other consideration than the Profit only, is quite wrong" (Q. 1269), was followed by this dialogue: "But you did not object to that Portion of it [act of 1844] which enables the Bank to pursue its own Interest as private Bankers?—I had no Objection then. I had not had the Experience which I have since had. I have changed my Opinion from the Experience of the last Two Years" (Q. 1274). Joseph Pease before the Commons Committee of 1848 laid his finger on the weakness, later taken up by Bagehot, of the Bank's unwillingness to give assurance that it would lend in time of crisis: "I am speaking with reference to the ambiguous position of the Bank

[4] The fullest statement of this position was in *Bank Charter Act of 1844*, pp. 91–144.

of England, it being connected in some way or other with the Government, it frequently appears to me to act as a private individual would act, and then at other times it appears to act as having certain national objects to sustain or difficulties to meet; so that a country tradesman, like myself, has no idea what the policy of the Bank is" (Q. 4613).

Between 1848 and 1857 the problem of the Bank's responsibility in time of crisis and the related issue of its reserves and the effect that larger reserves would have on profits were quiescent, and controversy was centered on the consequences of the new gold. The one extended discussion was in a pamphlet by T. H. Milner, *Some Remarks on the Bank of England* (London, 1849), which apparently had no contemporary influence, but which reads well today in its discussion of the relation between notes and deposits, the difference between monetary expansion in a closed system and in an open system, the policy of the Bank in the face of a drain, and the peculiar position of the Bank as a *de facto* lender of last resort. Milner pointed out that the Bank as it then operated was both a public bank and a private bank, and hence "must keep a reserve in much larger proportion to its liabilities than required by any other banker" (p. 22). In 1855 the *Economist* preached in its leading article of "the fundamental duty of every banker, and of the Bank of England like others, to retain sufficient reserves to meet all demands upon them,"[5] but consistent with Wilson's belief in free trade in general and free banking in particular, without any suggestion of any special obligation of the Bank of England as lender of last resort.

Opinion in the Hearings of 1857 and 1858

In the hearings of the Committee on Bank Acts of 1857, just on the eve of the world-wide crisis of that autumn, and in the hearings of the committee of the following year after the Bank Act had been suspended, the question of the Bank's role was again raised, but virtually anew, and with almost no continuity with the discussions of 1848. The background of the crisis of 1857 had differed from that of 1847. The Bank had not expanded credit as in 1845 and 1846. The pressure in 1857 had come more from foreign developments, and the Bank had acted more the way later generations said a central bank should act. The pressure had simply been so massive that the Bank could not meet it without the assurance of suspension of the act.

In these hearings the Bank of England management gave unqualified

[5] "The Bank Charter Act, 1844," October 20, 1855, p. 1145.

support to the act of 1844. When Thomas Matthias Weguelin and Sheffield Neave, the governor and deputy governor, opened the hearings in
1857, in response to the question whether they had any alteration to
suggest in the act of 1844, Weguelin replied: "No; I have none to suggest" (Q. 37). After the crisis, when Neave, now governor, and Bonamy
Dobree, deputy governor, were asked in the 1858 hearings whether they
would "recommend that any change should be made in the provisions
of that law [of 1844]," Neave answered: "No, I do not" (Q. 71). But
with this support of the act of 1844 went a conception of the Bank's public
responsibilities that was virtually a reversal of the Bank's view in 1848.
Weguelin said that the Bank endeavored to keep a minimum reserve of
a quarter to a third, and "in times of abundance of capital our reserve
was considerably larger than that proportion" (Q. 277). He made it
clear that other banks regarded their deposits with the Bank as their
reserves and that the Bank recognized this situation in its reserve policy
(Q. 243–269). He submitted a letter that he had sent to the Chancellor
of the Exchequer in November 1856, in which after expressing general
approval of the act of 1844, he said:

> But, on the other hand, the Act, and more especially the reasoning of its
> supporters, encourage a dangerous theory that the Bank of England in its
> banking department may, in all respects, act as would a private banker in the
> management of his deposits. It thus favours the competition with private
> money-lenders, which in periods of large deposits is apt to produce an unwar-
> ranted inflation of credit . . . no distinction is drawn between a drain for exports,
> which is the consequence of an inflation of credit, and a drain for the internal
> accommodation of the country, which may be caused by discredit, or which
> may merely represent natural oscillation of the currency.[6]

William Newmarch, although opposed to the act of 1844, explained the
development that had led the Bank to be the holder of the country's gold
reserves, and the need for the Bank to hold larger reserves (Q. 1364).
John Stuart Mill, critical of the earlier action of the Bank in acting "on
the principle which was laid down for them by the great authorities at
the time when the act of 1844 was passed, viz., that in the management
of their banking department they had nothing whatever to consider but
their interest as a bank," said that since 1847 the Bank had not acted on
that principle (Q. 2032). He expressed his own philosophy: "At such a
time [of crisis] the Bank can hardly lend too much; it can hardly make

[6] *Committee on Bank Acts*, 1857, pt. ii, app. i, p. i.

advances to too great an extent, as long as it is to solvent firms, because its advances only supply the place of the ordinary and wholesome amount of credit, which is then in deficiency" (Q. 2031). From D. B. Chapman came a statement of the need for the Bank to support the market at a time of crisis (Q. 5192–5196).

This was not the unanimous opinion. In the hearings of 1858 David Salomons, an alderman of London, member of Parliament, and director of the London and Westminster Bank, was asked: "And do you think that it is part of the functions of the Bank of England to discount a bill for anybody, merely because the party holding the bill wishes to convert it into cash?" He replied: "As I said before, the Bank of England will have great difficulty in getting rid of that inconvenient idea which there is in the mind of the public, that the Bank of England is something more than an ordinary joint-stock bank. I think it must depend very much upon circumstances whether you can or cannot refuse the discount of good bills which are offered to you" (Q. 1195).

Samuel Jones Loyd, now Lord Overstone, was, with his years, wealth, and title, increasingly dogmatic. He could see nothing wrong with the act of 1844. In the hearings of 1857 he branded as "wholly unreasonable and untenable" the suggestion of Newmarch that the Bank should never lower its rate below 4 per cent (Q. 3658), and then expounded in more detail his philosophy, with its overtones that public policy should not be subordinated to profit: "I must of course presume that the Bank is not a fool, and that the Bank if it could not lend its money by discounts, would seek to lend it through other means . . . If you try the supposition at all you must suppose that the Bank ceases to employ its capital, a supposition which, I think, is not worth while discussing, because it is pure gratuitous theory which has no practical reality" (Q. 3660).[7]

Even within the Bank opinion was not unanimous. J. G. Hubbard, who had been deputy governor in 1851–1853 and governor in 1853–1855, and remained a member of the Bank Court until 1889, in the 1857 hearings opposed Tooke's proposal that the Banking Department strive for a minimum reserve of £10 to £12 million (Q. 2349). The clearest evidence that the Bank was not of a single mind was the view of George Warde

[7] Overstone, in addition to his testimony of 1857, published eight letters in the *Times* in 1855–1857 in defense of the act of 1844 under the signature "Mercator," which were reprinted in 1857 in *Letters of Mercator;* in 1862 he carried on a correspondence with Henry Brookes, which was published in a pamphlet, *Lord Overstone on the Bank Act and the Currency* (London, 1862).

Norman, a member of the Court from 1821 to 1872: "The banking department of the Bank of England is exactly like any non-issuing bank, that of Coutts & Co., or Smith, Payne & Smith" (Q. 2964).[8]

Opinion in the Press and Pamphlets on the Bank's Responsibility

The hearings were accompanied by, and followed by, similar discussions on the Bank's responsibility and its reserve position. Even more than in the hearings those who opposed the Bank's assumption of a special responsibility were outspoken. The editor who wrote "Money Market and City Intelligence" in the *Times* of October 27, 1858, was sarcastic over the idea that the Bank had a responsibility greater than that of any other joint-stock bank:

Old traditions are still strong upon them [the public], and among the majority the Bank is to this hour the same establishment that regulated the currency with the assistance of Lord Liverpool, instead of that which was placed on a rational basis and told to attend to nothing but its own interests by Sir Robert Peel . . . The notification that the Bank have put their rate up or down—and the authority it seems to bestow, that every other moneyed institution in the country may act accordingly—has no more inherent value than the proclamation to all the monarchs of the earth that they take their supper after the Emperor of China, but it unquestionably exercises a great influence on certain imaginations . . . The grand step will be for people to divest themselves of the solemn idea created by the title "Bank of England." It means nothing more, as far as any exclusive powers or duties are concerned, than the title of any other joint-stock bank.

In addition to articles and letters in the *Economist,* a number of pamphlets in the late 1850's and 1860's discussed the reserve position of the Bank and the question of its relation to other banks. M. B. Sampson, in an anonymous pamphlet, *The Currency under the Act of 1844* (London, 1858), reprinting articles that had appeared in the *Times* in 1857, felt that the duty of the Bank of England "is simply to take care of themselves, to make as much profit as they honestly can, and nothing more" (p. 14). James Stirling, in *Practical Considerations on Banks and Bank Management* (London, 1865), said that the act of 1844 had "reformed the banking function [of the Bank of England] by putting it on the footing of an ordinary business" (p. 15). Robert Baxter, in *The Panic of 1866 with its Lessons on the Currency Act* (London, 1866), opposed the concentration of reserves in the Bank and was against the idea that the Bank should be expected to support the market in time of crisis (pp. 42–

[8] Substantially the same statement was made in Q. 3461.

46). J. B. Smith, who as president of the Manchester Chamber of Commerce had been a witness before the committee of 1840, in *Inquiry into the Causes of Money Panics* (London, 1866), urged all banks to keep larger reserves (pp. 10ff). John P. Gassiott, in *Money Panics and Their Remedy* (London, 1867), criticized the idea that other banks should expect the Bank of England to help them in time of crisis (pp. 29–30). N. A. Nicholson, in *One Reserve or Many?* (London, 1867), wanted "to detach the bankers of London and the joint-stock banks from the Bank of England, and thereby for them to look out for themselves, and keep proper cash reserves" (p. 19).

The Bank as a Lender of Last Resort

The question of the role of the Bank of England was, however, not simply whether the Bank should keep a larger reserve or lend more freely in time of crisis than an ordinary bank. It also involved the deeper and more controversial issue, already touched on in connection with the hearings of 1848, whether the Bank should be a lender of last resort in the sense that it would give assurance in advance that any holder of a particular type of assets could turn them into cash at a moment's notice at some price. There was both the issue of "rationing" by direct action versus "rationing" by a high rate, and the issue of supporting the market *ex post,* as compared with giving assurance *ex ante* that credit would be available at some price. Historically, in a given situation the Bank might have advanced £5 million, but the result—and the expectations for the future—would be quite different if this were rationed credit, given as an *ex gratia* act by the Bank in a crisis, than if it had been known in advance that credit would be available at a uniform rate to all who wished it. To support the market in time of crisis is not necessarily to act as a lender of last resort in the Bagehot sense, as the action of the Bank in 1793, 1825, 1836, and 1847 had shown.

To the Committee on Bank Acts of 1857 Weguelin explained the Bank's current view that it should keep a substantial reserve and support the market in time of crisis. He also brought out the difference of opinion within the Bank's management about whether in time of pressure a rise in the discount rate or "restraint which is placed upon the term of bills" was preferable, and indicated that he favored the latter method (Q. 311). This questioning followed:

326. Are you prepared to inform the Committee which opinion is the general opinion of the Court upon that subject, if there is a general opinion of the

Court upon the subject?—I must say that the opinion of the Court fluctuates very much. At times the opinion which I advocate is in the ascendant, at other times the opinion that a uniform rate of interest is the best has the preference.

327. You are not prepared to say that there is one permanent, prevailing sentiment in the Court upon this subject?—No, there is not.[9]

One of the most direct statements, before Bagehot, of the need for the Bank not simply to support the market in time of crisis, but to make clear in advance that it would lend to all at a price, came from the House of Gurney, that source of so much simply phrased common sense before its new management in the late 1850's started it on the path of speculation and disaster. Its managing director, D. B. Chapman, explained to the committee of 1857 his philosophy that no one should look to Bank credit for capital to carry on regular operations, but that everyone should feel that the Bank would turn sound bills into cash when a crisis broke:

> 5192. Then you think that the Bank of England should not stop discounting for the discount houses in Lombard-street, at particular times at least, without causing great injury to the commerical community?—I think it would create very great injury indeed . . . assuming that there is a drain upon the monetary system, and that the great money dealers are driven to convert their bills more quickly than they fall due, I think it would be a very great calamity for the Bank to hesitate for a single moment; I cannot conceive any greater.

> 5193. No matter what the reserve of the Bank of England was at the time?— Certainly.

Revival of Controversy in the 1860's

The rapid economic recovery after 1857 temporarily stilled controversy over money and banking among men of affairs. They had their own more immediate problems arising out of the Civil War in the United States, and were content to let the theoretical economists and the societies discuss whether the new gold had raised prices. The Political Economy Club had no discussion between 1856 and 1866 about banking reserves or the role of the Bank of England. The years 1859–1864 were a low-water mark, since the resumption of gold payments in 1821, for pamphlets on banking. But two events in 1858, although they had no immediate impact on policy and sparked no debate on theory, prepared the way for a historic banking controversy. Thomson Hankey, a member of Parliament and a director of the Bank from 1835 to 1893—except when rotated out before 1849—and governor in 1851–1853, in a speech attacked

---

[9] The only direct evidence on the position of other individual members was the statement of George Warde Norman (Q. 2569–2570) that he favored changing the rate of discount rather than restricting the terms of the bills that it would discount.

the idea of a central reserve and of a special responsibility of the Bank in time of crisis.[10] Walter Bagehot, son-in-law of John Wilson, joined the staff of the *Economist*. In 1860, following Wilson's death in India, he became editor of the *Economist*. Bagehot, despite his devotion to the principle of free trade, soon developed a view that went beyond what Wilson had preached. He supported Wilson's idea that the Bank should keep larger reserves, but he added to this the wider concept of the Bank's public responsibility in time of crisis.

The proposal of Sir John Lubbock in 1860 that the London bankers remove their deposits from the Bank of England [11] probably contributed to the sharper definition of the position of Bagehot. The concentration of banking reserves in the Bank of England and the widespread belief that, no matter what the Bank might say, it would support the market in time of crisis, had no legislative foundation. Like the British Constitution, this situation had just grown. There were two alternative approaches: to regard it as so out of line with free trade principles that it should be changed as basically unsound, or to accept it as an institutional fact and to develop a philosophy of the Bank of England's responsibility and action to fit the facts. The situation had developed because the British bankers, and particularly the London bankers, had found it convenient and profitable. It was within the power of the London banks to change this at any time by the simple action of withdrawing their deposits from the Bank of England, and even holding their till money in coin. A bank could take such action on the economic grounds that it preferred this as a permanent policy, but it was not likely that any individual bank would take a step which would almost certainly decrease its earning power. A bank could take such action, as the rich man's counterpart of the earlier bank runs inspired by Cobbett, Place, and O'Connor, to use the legal power of a demand creditor to exercise claims that the "code" said should not be exercised as a means of forcing the Bank of England to change its policies. For an individual bank to raise the threat of deposit withdrawal as a weapon to force the Bank to change its policy would probably have been futile. And what is more important, such a violation of the "code" would almost certainly have discredited the offending banker with the banking fraternity, even though it might have agreed with him in wishing to see a change in Bank policy. This idea that anyone who exercised

[10] The speech was not printed at the time, but formed the substance of Hankey's book *The Principles of Banking*, first published in 1867. It came out in a second edition in 1873, when Hankey's controversy with Bagehot was at its height.

[11] In his pamphlet *On the Clearing of the London Bankers* (London, 1860).

his full legal rights in his creditor relation with a bank would be a financial outcast is hinted at several times by witnesses and writers of the period, but the most specific statement was made by D. B. Chapman, in his testimony before the Committee on Bank Acts of 1857: "I remember an instance perfectly well of a man with whom we had deposited India bonds; he brought the India bonds in one of those panics and said, 'Sir, what is the use of such stuff as this; give me my money.' I gave him his money, and begged him never to come to the house again" (Q. 5303).

To exercise successfully a City of London version of Place's slogan, and say "To get the Bank go for deposits," it would have been necessary for the London bankers to present a united front. That would have meant civil war in the City, and even those who thought that rebellion would succeed might still question whether the fruits of victory would equal the costs of victory. Leaders of threatened revolts rarely advertise their intentions openly, and one might expect this to be particularly true with gentlemen of the City of London. Only a little appeared in print, but what did would indicate that at various times the problem had been raised in private discussions. Hubbard was questioned in 1857 as to what would have happened if the London bankers had withdrawn their deposits in 1847 (Q. 2798–2799). A contemporary account[12] suggested that when the delegation of City bankers and merchants waited on the Chancellor of the Exchequer on October 23, the possibility was raised of large withdrawals of deposits from the Bank if the act were not suspended. It is not clear whether this withdrawal was presented as an unavoidable necessity or as a threat to force action. In any case it would have been in the tradition of the time to have presented the case in such a way that any implied threat, even in the minds of those making it, would have been assimilated with an economic necessity which no one could control. Lubbock's proposal, however, was not on its face an attempt to force the Bank to change its policy, but a carrying to its extreme of free trade philosophy and a logical corollary of Hankey's proposal.

Hankey in his lecture of 1858[13] stated that the banking operations of the Bank of England should be considered in exactly the same light as those of any other bank. As long as keeping the larger part of the reserves of the London banks with the Bank of England was taken as an institutional fact, the proposition that the Bank of England and all other banks

---

[12] *Circular to Bankers,* no. 1049, November 29, 1847, p. 171.

[13] I have used the text as printed in the second edition of *The Principles of Banking,* pp. 43–73, which apparently is the same as that of the original lecture, except for a few remarks at the end.

should keep larger reserves than they had been keeping could be accepted as good practice, without getting into philosophic subtleties about the peculiar position of the Bank. Once the question was raised—and a thoroughly reasonable one it was within the framework of free trade philosophy—whether it might not be better to have each London bank hold its own reserve, the role of the Bank became a basic issue. Bagehot considered it, and Bagehot the student of banking institutions and the realist who respected the power of tradition triumphed over Bagehot the free trader. He opposed Lubbock's plan and brought in the idea of the Bank as a lender of last resort in a way that ran counter to much of John Wilson's thought as expressed earlier in the *Economist*.[14]

The following year, in a leading article, "The Duty of the Bank of England in Times of Quietude," Bagehot gave this judgment: "They have a national function. *They keep the sole bullion reserve* in the country." To reconcile this view with the philosophy of laissez faire, and possibly as an answer to those who feared what such a policy might do to the Bank's profits, he had said: "The ultimate interest of the proprietors of the Bank, we believe, will be best advanced by the most complete discharge of the Bank's duty to the nation." [15] In the eyes of Bagehot banking statesmanship and the profit motive were to be happily married, and his great service to the next half century of central banking was that he convinced his countrymen that this was an honorable union blessed by the laws of free trade. Bagehot continued to preach the same doctrine throughout the 1860's, although there was no further widespread discussion of the problem until after the Overend and Gurney panic of 1866 and the third authorization to suspend the Bank Act.

Meetings of Stockholders of Bank of England

Questions about the Bank's operations and particularly its responsibility to its stockholders as compared with its public responsibilities were occasionally raised at the meetings of the Bank's stockholders each March and September, when dividends were approved. These meetings, however, are a meager source of information on the Bank's operations or on its philosophy of public responsibility. They generally were sparsely attended and perfunctory affairs, sometimes lasting only five minutes and taken up entirely by the governor reading a standard statement as to the purpose of

[14] *Economist*, September 29, 1860, pp. 1062–1063. "Sir John Lubbock's Proposal to Remove the Deposits of the London Bankers from the Bank of England."
[15] *Economist*, September 14, 1861, p. 1009.

the meeting and announcing the dividend, followed by resolutions approving the dividend and thanking the officers for their excellent administration of the Bank's affairs. No diplomatic protocol surpassed the stylized routine that dominated the meetings. A casual stranger in attendance never would have suspected that he was in the presence of the ultimate legal authority of the world's greatest financial institution.

The most frequent question was why the Bank was not declaring more of its profits as dividends, or why it was sacrificing profits by keeping such a large reserve. At the meeting of September 17, 1846, Mr. Hammond urged larger dividends, and his comment "If that was not done, it must now appear as though the proprietors were working for the interests of posterity, not for themselves," was greeted by "Hear, hear." These queries continued, and as late as 1874 and 1875 a stockholder protested against the Bank's reserve policy that kept such a large proportion of its assets in non-earning form.

The Bank consistently resisted any attempt from stockholders to get information about its operations. The *Times* had said of the meeting on March 18, 1841, when stockholders asked more questions than usual, that it was "as much distinguished as any that have preceded it for the disposition to counteract any attempts to penetrate the mystery which enwraps the transactions of that institution," and much the same remark could have been made of a score of meetings. When in September 1847 it was necessary to elect new directors to replace those who had been declared insolvent, to an inquiry from a stockholder whether it was customary to have a discussion "respecting the merits of the gentlemen proposed," Governor Morris replied that "it was not customary for any discussion to be entered into." On September 16, 1852, a stockholder pressed for details about the Bank's operations, and Governor Hankey silenced him by saying that "he is asking one to deviate from a course which had been adopted from time immemorial by the directors of the Bank of England."

The Bank's Acceptance of Responsibility as Lender of Last Resort

Although Bagehot in the early 1860's continued to discuss in the pages of the *Economist* the issue of the Bank's responsibility, the historian of banking theory and policy who had available only the evidence up to 1865 could reasonably have drawn the conclusion that this was a virtually dead issue, temporarily kept alive by the idiosyncracy and enthusiasm of Bagehot. It was not until 1865 and 1866 that the Bank's responsibility to the whole economy again became a subject of general discussion, and then largely as a by-product of the proposals for a State Bank and free banking. Why these proposals gained such strength at this particular time is difficult to explain, beyond the general statement that they were in line with economic philosophy of the period. Similar proposals were being made on the Continent during this period,[16] but if the British went outside of their own borders to find arguments for free banking it was probably to the United States.[17]

From many quarters were coming suggestions from 1865 on that it would be better to have either free banking or a State Bank, and much as the supporters of these proposals might appear to have disagreed with one another, their proposals in effect involved a repudiation of the idea of a central gold reserve and a lender of last resort. The Bank had loaned freely in the crisis of 1866, but gave no assurance that it would do the same in another crisis. It made no official statement, but powerful voices within the Bank were saying that they thought the whole idea of the Bank of England's responsibility, which Launcelot Holland, the governor of the Bank, had suggested in the stockholders' meeting in September 1866, and which the *Economist* was preaching, was wrong.[18] George Warde Norman, a former governor of the Bank, wrote from the Bank to the *Economist* after the crisis of 1866: "That the Bank of England should keep the whole unused reserve of the country seems to me an arrangement at once impracticable, and unsound in principle."[19] Hankey said at about the same time:

The "Economist" newspaper has put forth what in my opinion is the most mischievous doctrine ever broached in the monetary or banking world in this country; viz. that it is the proper function of the Bank of England to keep money available at all times to supply the demands of bankers who have rendered their own assets unavailable. Until such a doctrine is repudiated by the banking interest, the difficulty of pursuing any sound principle of banking in London will be always very great. But I do not believe that such a doctrine as that bankers are justified in relying on the Bank of England to assist them in time of need is generally held by the bankers in London . . . The more the

[16] See Vera C. Smith, *The Rationale of Central Banking* (London, 1936), chs. 6–8, and L. F. M. Wolowski, *La Banque d'Angleterre et les banques d'Ecosse* (Paris, 1867), pp. 189–411.

[17] As one example, see "A Bank Director on Banking and the Currency," *Economist*, December 8, 1866, pp. 1418–1419.

[18] The *Economist*'s report of this meeting is reprinted in Walter Bagehot, *Lombard Street* (London, 1873); New York reprint of 1895, note D.

[19] December 22, 1866, p. 1488.

conduct of the affairs of the Bank is made to assimilate to the conduct of every other well managed bank in the United Kingdom, the better for the Bank, and the better for the community at large.[20]

The following year Hankey's book appeared, and for several years his ideas seem to have been an important focus of discussion and were the occasion for a powerful leading article in the *Economist* on "The Dangerous Opinions of a Bank Director." [21]

Increasingly in the *Economist* from 1866 on came the idea that although it was not "natural" to have a single reserve, it was wise for England to accept the situation that history had given it. In 1873 Bagehot put together in *Lombard Street* the essence of what he had been saying in the *Economist*. His position is best stated in his own classic words:

> Theory suggests, and experience proves, that in a panic the holders of the ultimate Bank reserve (whether one bank or many) should lend to all that bring good securities quickly, freely, and readily. By that policy they allay a panic; by every other policy they intensify it. The public have a right to know whether the Bank of England—the holders of our ultimate bank reserve—acknowledge this duty, and are ready to perform it. But this is now very uncertain . . . that it is simply in the position of a Bank keeping the Banking reserve of the country; that it must in time of panic do what all other similar banks must do; that in time of panic it must advance freely and vigorously to the public out of the reserve . . . The end is to stay the panic; and the advances should, if possible, stay the panic. And for this purpose there are two rules: First. That these loans should only be made at a very high rate of interest . . . Secondly. That at this rate these advances should be made on all good banking securities, and as largely as the public ask for them . . . The only safe plan for the Bank is the brave plan, to lend in a panic on every kind of current security, or every sort on which money is ordinarily and usually lent. This policy may not save the Bank; but if it do not, nothing will save it.[22]

Bagehot may not have said more than Francis Baring and Henry Thornton had said over sixty years before, but he said it in a way that carried conviction to a wider audience and to a new generation who no longer accepted all of the premises from which Thornton's and Baring's conclusions had sprung.

There was no formal acceptance of Bagehot's views by the Bank, and both in and out of the Bank there were those who did not like them. Suggestions that the London bankers withdraw their deposits from the Bank of England and hold their own reserves were revived shortly after the

---

[20] As quoted in *Lombard Street,* pp. 169–171.
[21] November 16, 1872, pp. 169–171.
[22] Pages 173, 196, 197, 199.

publication of *Lombard Street*,[23] and the proposals for a State Bank continued to be associated with the idea that it was not the business of the Bank of England to stand as a lender of last resort. Increasingly this was a minority view. From the middle 1870's the principle was no longer in doubt, although there might, as in 1890 or 1907, be a question as to how that principle was to be put into effect. The Bank of England as a lender of last resort was, like the gold standard and the freedom of deposit banking, accepted as the foundation of monetary and banking orthodoxy.

Division of Authority between Government and the Bank

Since 1797 another major problem had lurked in the background of every controversy over policy and action in time of crisis: the relation of the Government and the Bank of England, and the ultimate responsibility for action in time of crisis. In logic this was even more important than the other issues, for on what the Government might enforce would depend the end result of policy. But no legislation by Peel had given the answer, and no *Lombard Street* provided an articulate rationalization that the weight of opinion could accept. The problem could be forgotten in good times by looking the other way, but in time of crisis it could not be ignored. Palgrave, in a laudatory review of *Lombard Street*,[24] spoke of the service of Bagehot in pointing out "in the clearest manner that the Bank of England is far more than a great trading company, that it is a great public institution charged with public duties, and carrying on what are really, in many respects the functions of a public office, and not even of the greatest and most powerful private company." Such a statement helped to define the problem but did not answer it, any more than it had been answered in many Parliamentary investigations since 1797.

There had always been an anomaly in the Bank's position, and the basis of its relation to Government had from its founding been a problem for the student of the theory of sovereignty. Before the broadening of political representation and the dominance of free trade philosophy in the second quarter of the nineteenth century the situation had been relatively simple. The Bank held a monopoly from the Government, and though the Government and the Bank's management might disagree, it was an internal fight in which the public had an interest only as they might be concerned with a controversy between two major figures in the

---

[23] Discussions of this idea are in the *Economist*, December 5, 1874, pp. 1449–1450, December 12, 1874, pp. 1477–1479, December 19, 1874, pp. 1505–1506; *Bankers' Magazine*, January 1875, pp. 13–18, 85–93, and in a number of items in the daily press.

[24] "Banking," *Fortnightly Review*, January 1, 1874, pp. 92–108.

Cabinet. With the rising tide of democracy as symbolized by the Reform Act, and the growing strength of laissez faire, the older conception of the Bank as the monopolistic agent of an oligarchic government could no longer stand. It was increasingly clear that the Bank, and all other banks of issue, were not just performing an incident of lending, but were in effect taking over the royal prerogative of issuing money. Peel and the currency school thought that they had the answer in the act of 1844. The Issue Department was to be in effect an agency of the State, and the Banking Department was to be just a big joint-stock bank, plus a little something that nobody could quite define in words. The necessity for the Government to authorize the Bank to overstep the restrictions of the act of 1844 three times in a little over two decades showed that they were mistaken. Granting that the Bank of England was a public servant, what was its relation to that other public servant, the Cabinet? In time of crisis what voice should the Government have in the Bank's policy when the limits set in 1844 were in danger; who decided whether these limits were to be overstepped; and who decided what the Bank's policy should be if the limits were overstepped?

Peel and other supporters of the act of 1844, and officials of the Bank, had been concerned in 1844 over the possibility that heavy demands on the Bank would make it impossible to stay within the limits of the act. Norman had suggested a provision, rejected by Peel, that on the authority of three ministers the Bank could exceed the fiduciary issue set in the act. To this problem the answer of Peel had been: "Call Parliament together ... The Bank was absolved from all such obligations."[25] Peel had written to Cotton, the governor of the Bank, on June 4, 1844: "My confidence is unshaken, that we are taking all the precautions which legislation can prudently take against the recurrence of a monetary crisis. It *may* occur in spite of our precautions, and if it does, and *if it be necessary* to assume a grave responsibility for the purpose of meeting it, I dare say men will be found willing to assume such a responsibility."[26] This idea that England would have her men of destiny in the hour of crisis was broad enough to cover trouble of any origin. However, in the context of Peel's background and the controversy of the time, almost certainly the statement represented concern—apparently reflecting memories of the Restriction period—with a situation arising out of demands on the Bank from the Government, rather than the demands from private parties that brought on the crises of 1847, 1857, and 1866.

[25] Memorandum in the Bank's records, quoted by Clapham, *Bank of England,* II, 188.
[26] C. S. Parker, *Sir Robert Peel from His Private Papers* (London, 1899), III, 140.

In the spring of 1847, when the Bank and the Chancellor of the Exchequer were in communication, delegations from Liverpool waited on the Bank and on the Chancellor of the Exchequer. Shortly after that the Bank increased its credits. The story of these visits was brought out in the testimony of James Morris, governor of the Bank, before the Commons Committee of 1848:

3287. Before the deputations from Liverpool went to the Government upon the subject of accommodation, did they, or did they not, apply to the Bank of England?—Whilst I was Deputy-governor, there were one or two deputations which applied to the Bank, and I believe, those deputations went up to the Government afterwards, but it was the representations which the deputations made to us, which induced us to relax, and not any instruction or any representation from Government.

3288. The Government did not hint to you that it might be safer for commerce that the relaxation should be afforded?—No.

3289. In all the advances that you have afforded during the last year to the commercial public, did you afford them in consequence of your own independent discretion, or had you any instigation from Government?—Excepting the issuing of the letter, on the 25th of October, the whole of the action of the Bank was entirely independent of any representation from the Government.

Substantially the same account was given by William Cotton, a Bank director (Q. 4085–4088). William Brown, a member of the Liverpool delegation that had waited upon the Chancellor of the Exchequer in October 1847 just before the Government sent the letter to the Bank, made an observation to the Lords Committee of 1848 that suggests that the Government did not play so passive a role: "From the constant Communication which goes upon between the Bank and the Chancellor of the Exchequer, the Government must necessarily, without its being done by Act of Parliament, have great influence with the Bank . . . I do not mean to say that the Chancellor of the Exchequer could control them further than by Suggestions and Opinions. He is always deeply interested in preventing Panics" (Q. 2249).

The elusive nature of the relations of the Bank and the Government is shown in connection with the Government's letter of October 25, 1847, authorizing suspension of the Bank Act. For the record the Bank did not want to be in the position of asking the Government for the letter, and the Government did not want to be in the position of being asked by the Bank. Whatever the result, the whole proceeding was within the philosophic framework of laissez faire; not an individual decision, but the impersonal forces of the market, produced the letter. The Government was but an agency through which these impersonal forces made clear their strength. On the morning of October 23 a delegation of leaders in the City of London waited on the Prime Minister and the Chancellor of the Exchequer, and though no assurance was given to the delegation the Prime Minister and the Chancellor immediately got in touch with the Bank. After some discussion as to whether a minimum rate should be fixed in the letter, and the decision that it should not be, the Bank was assured that a letter would go out on Monday the 25th.[27]

When the smoke had cleared and the events were reviewed before the Commons Committee of 1848 the official position of the Bank was that it had not requested the letter, and that in fact the issuance of the letter probably had been unnecessary. This is shown in the answers of H. J. Prescott and Morris to the questions of Thomas Baring:

3158. And the fact of the gradual decrease of notes out with the public showed that the drain upon the Bank was stopped by the letter of relaxation? — ... (Mr. Prescott) It proved that the panic was over, but it is a question whether it would not have ceased without the letter.

3159. In what way could it have ceased without the letter?—It is in the nature of panic to exhaust itself.

3160. That is, when a good many houses have failed, there are not so many remaining that can fail?—That is one reason; but I may add that in a week or two there must have been a great increase of the circulation by the importation of bullion.

3161. At that time you communicated constantly with the Government?— (Mr. Morris) We were in constant communication with the Government.

3163. Were the other members of the committee of treasury who communicated with the Chancellor of the Exchequer of the same opinion as yourself as to the strict maintenance of the Act of 1844, without any relaxation?—My impression is that they were.

3165. At that time did you communicate with any party, either directly or indirectly, not connected with the Government out of the direction of the Bank?—Not officially.

3166. But were those parties, with whom you communicated, parties who like yourself thought it right to maintain the Act in its full operation?—If any individual came to me at that period, whether he was favourable to the Act or not, naturally the conversation turned upon what was likely to happen, and upon the subject of the letter, and I may have talked the subject over with parties of all opinions.

3177. Did you not consult any particular party?—No.

Each person must judge for himself just what gentlemen of integrity may have understood when they talked "not officially," but the situation is

[27] This account closely follows Clapham, II, 208–211, and also draws on the evidence of Samuel Gurney before the Commons Committee of 1848 (Q. 1594–1603).

suggestive of loan negotiations between old-time Chinese merchants and bankers: long discussions about the weather, health of the family, and general business conditions, so that both parties knew the view of the other without any specific reference to a loan. No matter what the outcome, face was saved on both sides.

The same procedure, where nothing specific was said, but both parties had a pretty clear understanding of what the other meant, was repeated a decade later. Before the Committee on Bank Acts of 1857 Newmarch, from outside the Bank, gave a simple "Yes" to the question, "You are aware that at present the executive Government is not in the habit of interfering with the Administration of the Bank of England?" (Q. 1386). When this was followed by the query, "Do you think it desirable that they should interfere more than they do at present in the habitual management of the Bank?" Newmarch replied: "Distinctly not" (Q. 1387). J. G. Hubbard, from within the Bank, gave substantially the same picture (Q. 2383).

The words "habitual" and "habit of interfering" cover a large area, and the statement of D. B. Chapman, the managing director of Overend, Gurney & Co., of what happened in time of pressure has a more realistic ring. From four members of the committee of 1857 came questions as to why the Gurneys had increased discounts in the uncertain situation of October 1856:

4915. Mr. Gladstone] Did your business undergo a material contraction?— I should say not. But I am bound to tell you, speaking as I ought to do, without reserve, that we certainly did carry on our business under the tacit understanding conveyed to us, that if any real press did come we should have relief. I say it without hesitation.

4916. Mr. Hankey] Relief from where?—From the Government; there is no doubt about it.

4917. In 1856?—Yes.

4918. Chairman] (Chancellor of the Exchequer, Edward Cardwell) How did this tacit assurance reach you? I do not ask you to violate any confidence?— It came to me, not from any Member of Parliament, or from any person in direct connexion with the Government; but still from a person of such standing that I could not misunderstand it, that it was desirable that we should go on with our business, and we did so.

4920. Mr. Weguelin] The understanding to which you have alluded was from no person connected with the Bank of England?—It was not.

After the issuing of the Government's letter on November 12, 1857, authorizing suspension of the Bank Act, the Bank management's story, as told to the Committee on the Bank Acts of 1858, of what conversations and understandings there had been before the issuance of the letter makes

Chapman's account sound plausible. After some discussion of just what had taken place between the Bank and the Government before the letter was issued, and when the Bank was easing credit in the face of falling reserves, Sheffield Neave, governor of the Bank, was asked by Thomas Baring: "But were the Government aware that you were proceeding in a course which you would not have proceeded in, unless you had been convinced that the Government would interfere?" He replied, "That I am unable to answer" (Q. 95). The series of questions and answers that followed, in which the Chancellor of the Exchequer referred to the Bank of England as the "bankers' bank"—probably the first use of this term—included much verbal fencing, and some irony from Thomas Baring that shows even in the formal record of the printed page:

186. Does it not strike you that it might be an improvement if, in times of pressure, the Chancellor of the Exchequer on the one side, and the Bank on the other, without delicacy or difficulty, had the power of discussing confidentially and frankly with each other the adoption of such a measure?—I do not think I am quite understood. I think you suppose that the question never passed in the minds of either of us.

187. I am not speaking of your minds, but I am speaking of your mouths?— The question of the advisability of sending a letter certainly was never discussed by us (I speak of the Chancellor of the Exchequer and ourselves) till a day or two before the actual issue of it.

188. Then it was not demanded on the part of the Bank, but it turned up in conversation?—No; the whole of this pressure came up so rapidly, as you see, that the necessity for the letter was not apparent till the day before it was issued.

189. A few days before it was issued, did you, on the part of the Bank, represent to the Chancellor of the Exchequer the necessity of issuing such a letter?—No; we did not take upon ourselves to urge upon him a measure for which we considered the Government entirely responsible; but we gave him every information from which he could make a correct judgment.

190. You went as near the wind as you could, I suppose?—No; I did not use that expression, "near the wind;" but we gave him every information which we possessed ourselves.

191. You did not give him your advice or opinion, but you gave him the facts?—We gave him all the facts.

192. What restrained you from giving your advice or opinion upon it?— There was nothing to restrain us; our communications were confidential."

After the hearings of 1858 the Bank and the Government, though they continued the fiction of official independence, were in close touch over the embarrassing threat that the Gurney firm, now in new hands, was planning a high-level Francis Place maneuver, to make a run on the Bank to force it to change its discount policy.[28] Much the same story as 1847 and 1857 was repeated in 1866, although the lack of a Parliamentary post-mortem does not give the full documentation that is available for the earlier crises. Delegations waited upon the Bank and the Government, the Bank and the Government were in close touch, but the Bank made no request for a suspension of the act. The Government sent its letter on May 11, 1866, but went beyond the two previous letters by setting a minimum rate of 10 per cent, by reserving "to themselves to recommend, if they should see fit, the imposition of a higher rate," and by providing that "after deduction by the Bank of whatever it may consider to be a fair charge for its risk, expense, and trouble, the profits of these advances will accrue to the public." [29] But the façade of the separation of Government policy, decided independently of the Bank, and of Bank action, made without any guidance from Government, remained unbroken. When a week after the issuance of the letter the Chancellor of the Exchequer was pressed as to just what the Bank was doing, his attitude was that the Government did not interfere in the details of the Bank's operations.[30] When questioned further he replied, "I am clearly of opinion that nothing could be more inconvenient than the assumption of responsibility by the Government in the conduct of the ordinary business of the Bank." [31]

Officially the Bank made no suggestions to the Government, and officially the Government did nothing beyond telling the Bank that it was free to break the law if it felt this necessary to carry out its public responsibilities. What went on in the clubs, at the country estates, at the meetings of old Etonians, Oxonians, and Cantabrigians, and possibly at the Political Economy Club, was another matter. The important thing was that somehow or other the Government and the Bank worked things out reasonably well.

In the hearings of 1848, 1857, and 1858, in addition to proposals that the restrictions in the act of 1844 on the Bank's note issues be repealed, sugges-

---

[28] The story is told in Clapham, II, 242–246, in large part from material in the Bank's records. The rumor that "the discount houses" were back of a concerted demand for redemption of Bank notes was discussed in the Commons on April 19, 1860 (3 *Hansard* CLVII, 2002–2004).

[29] The correspondence between the Bank and the Government is reprinted in Gregory, *Select Statutes, Documents & Reports,* II, 124–127; on pp. 127–186 are reprinted contemporary articles from the *Times* and the *Economist.* The issuance of the letter was discussed in Parliament on May 11, 1866 (3 *Hansard* CLXXXIII, 772–774), and a number of times between then and August 6, 1866. Clapham's account, II, 262–270, makes use of unpublished material in the Bank's records.

[30] 3 *Hansard* CLXXXIII, 1050–1053, May 17, 1866.

[31] 3 *Hansard* CLXXXIV, 717, July 5, 1866.

tions had been made that the Bank should be given a discretion to overstep the limits of the act, or that authority to permit this should be clearly vested in designated Government officials. Nothing came of these suggestions. Proposed legislation in 1873[32] rekindled discussions, both in and out of Parliament, as to whether, in the measured words of William Fowler, "it might be a fair subject for inquiry whether some plan could not be invented by means of which the necessary relaxation, for it must come, could be given by and not against law."[33] But the exchange rate with India, as the price of silver fell, and the financial collapse in the United States in 1873, were much more immediate topics. The Bank, although officially silent, was taking to heart the advice of Bagehot, and the ever increasing importance of deposit banking made it less likely that the special note issue restrictions, no matter what theory might say as to their absurdity, would present any problem.

Institutional Practices Become Economic Orthodoxy

Until August 1914 there were no further suspensions of the Bank Act. Delegations of merchants and bankers continued to bring their troubles to Threadneedle Street and to Downing Street. The Bank and the Government discussed problems informally but officially each stayed within its sphere. Increasingly, with no new letters of indemnity, the idea of the complete separation of Bank and Government took on added prestige. The whole situation fitted in nicely with the idea that government was one thing and private business another, and that the less the two had to do with each other the better. Besides, it seemed to work, and the British liked it that way.

The main features of the system were clear. That the gold standard was inviolate was a decision of Government. The task of maintaining the gold standard was entrusted to the Bank of England, and as long as it carried out this mission the Government left to it the operating details. No matter what the theorists might say about bank deposits being money, legislation treated their creation as being something quite different into which the State had no right to pry, but the Government's right to control note issue was paramount. The lessons of experience, the absorption of weaker banks, and the strengthening forces of tradition on the behavior

---

[32] See above, pp. 220–221.

[33] 3 Hansard CCXV, 140, March 25, 1873. The subject was discussed in the *Economist*, June 21, 1873, pp. 741–742; by R. H. I. Palgrave in the *Fortnightly Review*, January 1, 1874, pp. 98–101; in the *Bankers' Magazine*, July 1873, pp. 590–592; and in a number of items in the *Times*.

of the joint-stock banks achieved a stability greater than laws had given in other countries. What emerged was the "monetary and banking orthodoxy" that by 1914 had in varying degrees left its impact on almost every country of the world. Yet the British, at the time that they adopted these policies that later generations called "sound economics," did so for reasons that went beyond economics in the narrower sense. The developments that made gold rather than silver emerge as the legal standard in the first part of the nineteenth century involved more than economic analysis, and political crosscurrents played an important role in shaping the resumption legislation of 1819. For at least a decade after 1821 the leading defense of the resumption of that year at the old par was not that it was the best economic decision, but that having been made it should not be changed. The idea that notes should be subject to restrictions that did not apply to deposits was the product of the "lessons of history" and of political expediency rather than of pure theory. Bagehot's acceptance of the single reserve system and his development of the idea that the Bank of England must be prepared to act as a lender of last resort were based on the idea that although this was all contrary to the teachings of political economy it was the best system under the circumstances. The story provides abundant material for philosophers and political scientists to work on after the economists have left off.

BIBLIOGRAPHICAL NOTES

CONTEMPORARY BOOKS AND PAMPHLETS

Research for this study covered every book and pamphlet on the monetary and banking situation in Britain and Ireland published between 1776 and 1875 and available in the Goldsmiths' Library of the University of London, the Kress Library at Harvard University, the Henry R. Wagner Collection of Yale University, and the Seligman Collection at Columbia University. These total over 1300 items, in addition to the standard works of Adam Smith, Malthus, Ricardo, the Mills, Nassau Senior, and Tooke and Newmarch's invaluable *History of Prices.*

These contemporary publications are cited in the text only when a discussion or interpretation is based primarily upon particular items. Many of my conclusions, such as the role of the executions for forgery in hastening the decision of 1819 to resume specie payments, provincial opposition to the gold standard and to the Bank of England, and Scottish opposition to Parliamentary interference with Scottish banking, are sometimes supported by citation and quotation, but frequently are based on many statements or attitudes, often individually not important but in the aggregate indicative of a widely held view.

PARLIAMENTARY DEBATES

Up to 1803 all citations and quotations are based on William Cobbett's *Parliamentary History of England from the Earliest Times to the Year 1803,* 36 vols. (London, 1806–1820), except for a few cases where it failed to report, or reported inadequately, a debate, and in these cases I have cited the *Parliamentary Register.* Beginning in 1803 all references are to T. C. Hansard, *Parliamentary Debates.* The First Series of Hansard covered 1803–1820, a New Series 1820–1829, and a Third Series from 1830 on. These are cited as 1 *Hansard,* 2 *Hansard,* and 3 *Hansard.*

REPORTS OF PARLIAMENTARY COMMITTEES

Unless otherwise indicated all reports are of Commons committees. The Lords reports are in separate Lords printings, but the listing below is of the Commons editions of these reports, generally more readily available. The titles of some of the reports refer to the Minutes of Evidence and Appendices, but other reports make no such reference in the title. To simplify matters I have omitted such references.

1793 *Report from the Select Committee Appointed to take into Consideration the Present State of Commercial Credit.* Reprinted in P.P. 1826, (23) III.

1797 *Reports from the Committee of Secrecy on the Outstanding Demands of the Bank of England.* Printed as a separate volume in 1797; in *Reports from Committees of the House of Commons,* vol. XI: *Miscellaneous Subjects,* pp. 119–231, and in P.P. 1826, (26) III. All citations are to the separate printing.

1797   *Report of the Lords' Committee of Secrecy.* Printed as a separate volume in 1797; in the *Journals of the House of Lords;* and in P.P. 1810, (17) III. All citations are to the separate printing.

1800   *Reports from the Select Committee Appointed to Consider the present high Price of Provisions.* P.P. 1801, (174) II.

1804   *Report from the Select Committee on the Circulating Paper, the Specie and Current Coin of Ireland.* P.P. 1803–04, (86) IV.

1810   *Report from the Select Committee on the High Price of Gold Bullion.* P.P. 1810, (349) III.

1811   *Report from the Select Committee on the State of Commercial Credit.* P.P. 1810–11, (52) II.

1819   *Reports from the Secret Committee on the Expediency of the Bank Resuming Cash Payments.* P.P. 1819, (202, 282) III.

1819   *Reports by the Lords Committees Appointed a Secret Committee to enquire into the State of the Bank of England, with respect to the Expediency of the Resumption of Cash Payments.* P.P. 1819, (291) III.

1820   *Report from the Select Committee on Petitions complaining of Agricultural Distress.* P.P. 1820, (255) II.

1821   *Report from the Select Committee on the Petitions complaining of the depressed state of the Agriculture of the United Kingdom.* P.P. 1821, (668) IX.

1822   *Report from the Select Committee on the Several Petitions complaining of the depressed state of Agriculture of the United Kingdom.* P.P. 1821, (165) V.

1825   *Reports from the Select Committee on the State of Ireland.* P.P. 1825, (129) VIII.

1826   *Report from the Select Committee on the Circulation of Promissory Notes under the Value of £5 in Scotland and Ireland.* P.P. 1826–27, (402) III.

1826   *Report from the Lords' Committee on the Circulation of Promissory Notes under the Value of £5 in Scotland and Ireland.* P.P. 1826–27, (245) VI.

1832   *Report from the Committee of Secrecy on the expediency of renewing the Charter of the Bank of England, and on the system on which Banks of Issue in England and Wales are conducted.* P.P. 1831–32, (722) VI.

1833   *Report from the Select Committee on the present State of Agriculture.* P.P. 1833, (612) V.

1833   *Report from the Select Committee on the present state of Manufactures, Commerce and Shipping in the United Kingdom.* P.P. 1836, (690) VI.

1836   *First Report from the Select Committee appointed to inquire into the State of Agriculture,* P.P. 1836, (79) VIII, pt. i; *Second Report,* P.P. 1836, (189) VIII, pt. i; *Third Report,* P.P. 1836, (465) VIII, pt. ii.

1836   *Report from the Select Committee of the House of Lords appointed to Inquire into the State of Agriculture in England and Wales.* P.P. 1837, (464) V.

1836   *Report from the Secret Committee on Joint Stock Banks.* P.P. 1836, (591) IX.

1837   *Report from the Secret Committee on Joint Stock Banks.* P.P. 1827, (531) XIV.

1837   *Report from the Select Committee on the Royal Mint.* P.P. 1837, (465) XVI.

1838   *Report from the Secret Committee on Joint Stock Banks.* P.P. 1837–38, (626) VII.

1840   *Report from the Select Committee on Banks of Issue.* P.P. 1840, (602) IV.

1841   *First and Second Reports from the Select Committee on Banks of Issue.* P.P. 1841, (366, 410) V.

1848   *First Report from the Secret Committee on Commercial Distress,* P.P. 1847–48,

(395) VIII; *Second Report,* P.P. 1847–48, (584) VIII; *Appendix,* P.P. 1847–48, (395, 584) VIII.

1848 *Report from the Secret Committee of the House of Lords, Appointed to Inquire into the Causes of the Commercial Distress.* P.P. 1847–48, (565) VIII, pt. iii.

1853 *Report from the Select Committee on Decimal Coinage.* P.P. 1852–53, (851) XXII.

1857 *Report from the Select Committee on Bank Acts,* pts. i and ii. P.P. 1857, (220) X.

1858 *Report from the Select Committee on the Bank Acts.* P.P. 1857–58, (381) V.

1858 *Report from the Select Committee on Savings Banks.* P.P. 1857–58, (441) XVI.

1875 *Report from the Select Committee on Banks of Issue.* P.P. 1875, (351) IX.

OTHER GOVERNMENT REPORTS

1813 *Report from the Commissioners . . . for the Issue of Exchequer Bills,* P.P. 1813–14, (53) III.

1816 *Report of the Lords of the Committee of Council, appointed to take into Consideration the State of the Coins of the Kingdom.* P.P. 1816, (411) VI.

1830 *Minutes of Evidence, taken in 1828, before the Committee for Coin, at the Board of Trade.* P.P. 1830, (31) XVII. Reprinted in P.P. 1848, (718) XXXIX.

1857 *Preliminary Report of the Royal Decimal Coinage Commission.* P.P. 1857, [2212] XIX.

1857 *Questions Communicated by Lord Overstone to the Decimal Coinage Commissioners with Answers.* P.P. 1857, [2213] XIX.

1868 *Report of the Royal Commission on International Coinage.* P.P. 1867–68, (4073) XXVII.

BOOKS DEALING WITH THE PERIOD 1797–1875

Monetary and banking developments in Britain between 1797 and 1875 have been covered in the last forty years in a large volume of literature. My approach has been in terms of what people said during the years up to 1875, rather than what others later said about the ideas and developments of those years, but my own treatment has inevitably been influenced by the marshaling of facts and the interpretations in this more recent literature. A number of these books have been cited and quoted, but some are nowhere mentioned in the text. Among the more important of these books are:

Acres, W. Marston. *The Bank of England from Within, 1694–1900.* 2 vols. London: Oxford University Press, 1931.

Angell, James W. *The Theory of International Prices.* Cambridge, Mass.: Harvard University Press, 1926.

Clapham, Sir John. *The Bank of England: A History.* 2 vols. Cambridge: The University Press, 1945.

Craig, Sir John. *The Mint: A History of the London Mint from A.D. 287 to 1948.* Cambridge: The University Press, 1953.

Cramp, A. B. *Opinion on Bank Rate, 1822–1860.* London: London School of Economics and Political Science, 1961.

Feavearyear, A. E. *The Pound Sterling: A History of English Money.* 2d ed. London: Oxford University Press, 1963.

Gayer, Arthur D., W. W. Rostow, and Anna Jacobson Schwartz. *The Growth and Fluctuation of the British Economy, 1790–1850.* 2 vols. Oxford: Clarendon Press, 1953. "Microfilm Appendix," Ann Arbor: University Microfilms, 1953.

Gregory, T. E. *An Introduction to Tooke and Newmarch's* A History of Prices. New York: Adelphi, 1928. Reprinted by the London School of Economics and Political Science, Series of Reprints of Scarce Works on Political Economy, No. 16. London, 1962.

—— ed. *Select Statutes, Documents & Reports Relating to British Banking, 1832–1928.* 2 vols. London: Oxford University Press, 1929.

Hawtrey, Sir Ralph. *Currency and Credit.* 3d ed. London: Longmans, Green, 1928.

Higgs, Henry, ed. *Political Economy Club.* London: Macmillan, 1921.

King, W. T. C. *History of the London Discount Market.* London: Routledge, 1936.

Mackenzie, A. D. *The Bank of England Note: A History of Its Printing.* Cambridge: The University Press, 1953.

Matthews, R. C. O. *A Study in Trade-Cycle History: Economic Fluctuations in Great Britain, 1833–1842.* Cambridge: The University Press, 1954.

Morgan, E. Victor. *The Theory and Practice of Central Banking, 1797–1913.* Cambridge: The University Press, 1943.

Pressnell, L. S. *Country Banking in the Industrial Revolution.* Oxford: Clarendon Press, 1956.

Robbins, Lionel. *Robert Torrens and the Evolution of Classical Economics.* London: Macmillan, 1958.

Thomas, S. Evelyn. *The Rise and Growth of Joint Stock Banking,* vol. I. London: Pitman, 1934.

Thornton, Henry. *An Enquiry into the Nature and Effects of the Paper Credit of Great Britain* (1802); ed. F. A. Hayek, London: George Allen and Unwin, 1939.

Viner, Jacob. *Studies in the Theory of International Trade.* New York: Harper, 1937.

Wood, Elmer. *English Theories of Central Banking Control, 1819–1858.* Cambridge, Mass.: Harvard University Press, 1939.

PERIODICALS

REVIEWS

Blackwood's Edinburgh Magazine, 1817–1876
British and Foreign Review, 1835–1844
British Quarterly Review, 1844–1876
Contemporary Review, 1866–1876
Edinburgh Review, 1802–1876
Foreign and Colonial Quarterly Review (title varies), 1843–1847
Foreign Quarterly Review, 1827–1845
Fortnightly Review, 1865–1876
North British Review, 1844–1871
Quarterly Review, 1809–1876
Saturday Review of Politics, Literature, Science, and Art, 1855–1875
Westminster Review, 1824–1876

GENERAL

Athenaeum, 1847–1858
Belfast Monthly Magazine, 1808–1814
Dublin University Magazine, 1832–1876

Fraser's Magazine, 1830–1875
Illustrated London Times, 1854–1856
Meliora, 1859–1866
Punch, 1841–1876
Spectator, 1828–1872
Tait's Edinburgh Magazine, 1832–1860

PREDOMINANTLY ECONOMIC

Bankers' Magazine, 1844–1876
Circular to Bankers (title varies), 1828–1860
Economist, 1843–1876
Farmer's Magazine, 1806–1825; New Series, 1838–1857
Journal of Industry, 1850–1851
The League (organ of the Anti-Corn Law League), 1843–1846
Manchester Magazine, 1838
The Money Bag, 1858
The Struggle: devoted to Free Trade and the Repeal of the Corn Laws, 1844–1846

PRIMARILY CONCERNED WITH POLITICAL AND ECONOMIC REFORM

Statements about the attitude of political radicals and labor groups toward monetary and banking problems have drawn heavily on material in these periodicals.

Black Dwarf, 1817–1824
Bristol Job Nott, or Labouring Man's Friend, 1831–1833
Cobbett's Political Register (title varies), 1802–1835
The Crisis, 1832–1833
Examiner, 1809–1833; 1844–1847
Friend of The People, 1850–1851
Gauntlet, 1833–1844
The Gorgan, 1818–1819
Labourer, 1847–1848
Newgate Monthly Magazine, 1824–1826

Penny Paper for the People, 1830–1831
Poor Man's Guardian, 1831–1835
Potters' Examiner and Workman's Advocate, 1845
Red Republican, 1850
Sherwin's Political Register, 1817–1819
The Union: A Monthly Journal of Moral, Social, and Educational Reform, 1842
White Dwarf (a conservative organ, in answer to the *Black Dwarf*), 1817–1818
Working Bee, 1839–1840

NEWSPAPERS

LONDON

British Freeholder, 1821
British Press, 1809–1810
Courier, 1809–1811
Englishman, 1820
General Evening Post, 1809–1810
Independent Observer, 1821
Morning Advertiser, 1809–1810
Morning Chronicle, 1807–1833
Morning Herald, 1809–1810, 1820–1821
Morning Post, 1809–1811, 1820–1821, 1825
Observer, 1820
Pilot, 1809–1811
Star, 1809–1811
Statesman, 1809–1810
Sun, 1809–1811, 1820
Times, 1790–1875

OUTSIDE OF LONDON

Aris's Birmingham Gazette, 1808–1843
Birmingham Advertiser, 1835–1837
Birmingham Journal, 1830–1842
Derby Mercury, 1830
Dublin Evening Post, 1796–1797
Hibernian Chronicle (Cork), 1796–1797
Leeds Intelligencer, 1829–1830
Liverpool Album, 1830
Liverpool Times, 1830
Manchester Guardian, 1830
Newcastle Chronicle, 1796–1797
Newcastle Courant, 1796–1797
Nottingham Journal and General Advertiser, 1830
Saunders News Letter (Dublin), 1797, 1803–1804

JOURNALS AND TRANSACTIONS OF SOCIETIES

British Association for the Advancement of Science. *Transactions*, 1831–1876; *Proceedings*, 1843–1876
Cambridge Philosophical Society. *Transactions*, 1819–1876
Manchester Statistical Society. *Transactions*, 1854/55–1875/76
Statistical and Social Inquiry Society of Ireland (name varies). *Transactions, Proceedings*, and *Journal*, 1847–1875.
Statistical Society of London (later Royal Statistical Society). *Journal*, 1839–1875.

MANUSCRIPTS

Lord Auckland Papers (principally on Irish monetary conditions, 1796–1801). John Rylands Library, Manchester
E. D. Davenport Papers (principally letters from Matthias Attwood, Thomas

Attwood, John Rooke, and James Taylor). John Rylands Library, Manchester

Henry Dundas Papers (principally on monetary situation in 1796 and 1797). Kress Library, Harvard University

John Foster Papers (principally on Irish monetary situation, 1808–1810). Public Record Office of Northern Ireland, Belfast

William Gladstone Papers. British Museum

Sir James Graham Papers. Microfilm at Newberry Library, Chicago, of originals in possession of Sir Fergus Graham

Hudson Gurney Papers. In possession of Major Quintin E. Gurney, Bawdeswell Hall, Norfolk

Earl of Hardwick Papers (principally on Irish monetary situation in 1804). British Museum

John Charles Herries Papers. In possession of Lt. Col. A. H. Spottiswoode, on deposit at National Register of Archives

Francis Horner Papers. In possession of Lady Eleanor Langman, on deposit at London School of Economics

William Huskisson Papers. British Museum

Liverpool Parliamentary Office Records (1810–1836). Liverpool Reference Library

Records of Manchester Chamber of Commerce. Manchester Chamber of Commerce

Sir Henry Parnell Papers (principally on banking situation in 1820's). In possession of Lord Congleton

Sir Robert Peel Papers. British Museum

Earl of Pelham Papers (principally on Irish monetary situation in 1797). British Museum

James Pennington Letters. University of Chicago Library

Spencer Perceval Papers. In possession of Mr. David Holland; in possession of Mr. Dudley Perceval, on deposit at National Register of Archives

Henry Thornton Papers. In possession of Mr. E. M. Forster, King's College, Cambridge

Nicholas Vansittart (Lord Bexley) Papers. British Museum

Samuel Whitbread Papers. In possession of Major Simon Whitbread, Southill, Bedford

INDEX

DATE DUE

DEC 5 1969			
FEB 7 1974			